Volumes 2 and 3 of the
Plain Language A Course in Miracles:

2

Practicing *A Course in Miracles*

A translation of the Workbook in plain language, with mentor's notes

****

3

The Way of *A Course in Miracles*

A translation of the Manual for Teachers in plain language, with mentor's notes

Also by Liz Cronkhite:

The Message of *A Course in Miracles*: A translation of the Text in plain language

The ACIM Mentor Articles: Answers for Students of *A Course in Miracles*

Preface

A Course in Miracles is comprised of three volumes: Text, Workbook, and Manual for Teachers. The Text lays out the theoretical concepts of the *Course*, the Workbook teaches you how to apply the *Course*, and the Manual for Teachers sets forth your path as a student of the *Course*. All three volumes are important, but while the Text can stand alone, both the Workbook and the Manual for Teachers are dependent on the Text for context. So, when I completed *The Message of a Course in Miracles: A Translation of the Text in plain language*, I realized that the translations of the Workbook and Manual for Teachers should be combined in one book as a companion to *MACIM*. This is that combined volume.

The 'teachers' referred to in the Manual for Teachers are 'teachers of God', a term that the *Course* uses for anyone who has had a conscious experience of God. As the purpose of the Workbook is to open you to experience God directly through the miracle and/or Revelation, 'teachers of God' refers to students of the *Course* who have completed the Workbook.

A mentor is one who offers guidance through their greater experience to others in a given area of endeavor. I have been a student of the *Course* since 1984, and I offer myself as a mentor to other teachers of God. As such, I have included in these volumes mentoring notes for both *PACIM* and *WACIM*.

Peace to you as you use this book to further your understanding and acceptance of your Oneness with God.

Liz Cronkhite
Las Vegas, 2010

First published by O-Books, 2011
O-Books is an imprint of John Hunt Publishing Ltd., Laurel House, Station Approach,
Alresford, Hants, SO24 9JH, UK
office1@o-books.net
www.o-books.com

For distributor details and how to order please visit the 'Ordering' section on our website.

ISBN: 978 1 84694 403 1

A CIP catalogue record for this book is available from the British Library.

Design: Stuart Davies

Printed in the UK by CPI Antony Rowe
Printed in the USA by Offset Paperback Mfrs, Inc

2

Practicing *A Course in Miracles*

A translation of the Workbook in plain language, with mentor's notes

****

3

The Way of *A Course in Miracles*

A translation of the Manual for Teachers in plain language, with mentor's notes

Winchester, UK
Washington, USA

CONTENTS

Part Two

Translator's Introduction

You are One with God.

How does this become more than simply a nice idea when your mind is so filled with a world that is the opposite of God in every way? In your perception that you are separate from God, your mind is undisciplined, and it thinks in a completely unnatural way. You have to make a conscious effort to retrain it so that the idea that you are One with God shifts from being merely an intellectual concept to your actual living awareness. *Practicing A Course in Miracles* trains your mind in the direction it needs to go to return you to your natural state of Limitless Love, Peace, and Joy in God.

PACIM is a translation of the Workbook of *A Course in Miracles* into plain, everyday language. It is a companion to *The Message of* A Course in Miracles*: A translation of the Text in plain language.* But *PACIM* is not just the Workbook with a language and style that are consistent with the translation of the Text. Like *MACIM*, it is an interpretation of the Workbook through the central message of the *Course*, and the translator's own experiences of Oneness with God. This brings the central message of the *Course* into sharper focus sooner, and you will find yourself absorbing its ideas faster and deeper than you would with the original. Mentoring notes have been added to clarify some of the lessons even further.

Where the Text lays out the theoretical foundation of the *Course*, this Workbook offers you the means to the experiences that are truly transformative. Its one year of lessons consist of a simple daily thought each day, the practice of which undoes the thought system of the personal mind, lines up your conscious thoughts with God, and teaches you how to open your mind to God.

You are asked to do these exercises in the midst of your ordinary life in your perception that you are in a world, because it is in your encounters with the world that you bump into the thoughts that bind you to it as your reality. In itself, the world is neutral, so you can make another choice in how to perceive it, and this is what these lessons give you. This new Perception, which comes from the Christ Mind within you, acts as a bridge by reflecting God's Love, and It therefore reminds you that you are One with God. When you have forgiven, or released, all of the perceptions that seem to 'prove' that you are separate from God, the world will fall away from your mind, and you will *be* God again.

You only have to work through the lessons once. At the end, the lessons prepare you to turn to the Holy Spirit for continuing mind training. This Workbook is geared toward new students who are still very identified with a personal self, and doing the lessons again and again can hold you back in that mind-set. But many students who have completed the year of lessons find it helpful to study the Workbook as they would the Text, as it is full of practical ideas that elaborate on what is in the Text.

This Workbook is based on the first edition Workbook of *A Course in Miracles*, which is in the public domain. Its paragraphs have been numbered for easy comparison with later editions.

Introduction

1. The Text of A Course in Miracles provides a theoretical foundation for its goal, which is to help you to remember your Oneness with God. But it is the exercises in this Workbook that will make this goal possible for you because, untrained, your mind cannot accomplish it. The purpose of this Workbook, then, is to train your mind to think in line with the concepts in the Text.

2. Your training period is one year, and the lessons are numbered from 1 to 365. You have one lesson per day and you should not do more than one lesson per day. The exercises are very simple. They do not require a lot of time, it does not matter where you do them, and you do not need to prepare for them.

3. The Workbook is divided into two sections: The first deals with your perception of separation from God, and the second deals with your acquiring Real Perception, which is a way of perceiving that reflects your awareness of your Oneness with God. Each day's exercises are planned around one central idea (with the exception of review periods, which have several ideas for the day). The idea is stated first, and then is followed by a description of the specific procedures by which you are to apply the idea.

4. The purpose of this Workbook is to train your mind in a systematic way to a different perception of everything and everyone in the world that you perceive. The exercises are planned so that you can generalize the lesson by seeing it as equally applicable to everything and everyone.

5. Your Real Perception is different from the personal mind's perception in that, when you attain It in connection with any person or situation, then it automatically transfers to everyone and everything. And if you hold one person or thing apart from your Real Perception, then you cannot attain It, and therefore It cannot transfer.

6. So the only general rules for you to follow throughout your

practice of the lessons are: First, that you practice the exercises as specifically as indicated. This will help you to generalize the ideas in the lesson to every situation in which you find yourself, and to everyone and everything involved in it. And second, that you do not decide for yourself that there are some people, things, or situations to which you cannot apply the ideas. This will interfere with your transfer of the lesson. The very nature of Real Perception is that It is limitless. It is the opposite of the way that you now perceive.

7. The aim of the exercises is to increase your ability to extend the ideas in the lesson to include everything. This does not require effort on your part because the exercises themselves are inherently transferable to everything.

8. You will find some of the ideas in this Workbook hard to believe, or quite startling. This does not matter. You are asked only to apply the ideas as you are directed. You are not asked to judge them; you are asked only to use them. Using them will make them meaningful to you, and will show you that they are true.

9. Only remember this: You do not need to believe the ideas in this Workbook, you do not need to accept them, and you do not even have to welcome them. You might even actively resist some of them. None of this matters, nor will any of this decrease their effectiveness. But do not allow yourself to make exceptions in applying them and, whatever your reactions to them, *use them*. This is all that is required of you.

Part One

Lesson 1

'Nothing that I see in this room (on this street, from this window, in this place, etc.) has a meaning of its own.'

1. Repeat to yourself the idea above, then look slowly around you and apply this idea very specifically to whatever you see. For example:

'This table does not have a meaning of its own.'
'This chair does not have a meaning of its own.'
'This hand does not have a meaning of its own.'
'This foot does not have a meaning of its own.'
'This pen does not have a meaning of its own.'

2. Then look away from your immediate area, and apply the idea to a wider range of objects. For example:

'That door does not have a meaning of its own.'
'That body does not have a meaning of its own.'
'That lamp does not have a meaning of its own.'
'That sign does not have a meaning of its own.'
'That shadow does not have a meaning of its own.'

3. Notice that these statements are not arranged in any order, and that they are applied to a wide variety of things; this is the purpose of this exercise. Apply it to anything that you see at random, but do not apply it to everything that you see. These exercises should not become a ritual. Only be sure to not deliberately exclude anything you see. As far as applying this lesson is concerned, one thing is like another.

4. Apply this lesson once in the morning and once in the evening. You should do it for a minute or so, unless this makes you feel

rushed. Apply it with a comfortable sense of leisure.

Mentor's Notes

This lesson teaches you that the physical world that you perceive is neutral; it has no meaning of its own.

Lesson 2

'I have given everything that I see in this room (on this street, from this window, in this place, etc.) all the meaning that it has for me.'

1. Do the same with this idea as you did with the first idea: Repeat the lesson, then apply it specifically to those things near you; whatever your eyes rest on. Then move your gaze outward. Turn your head to either side, and, if possible, turn around and apply the idea to what is behind you. Be sure to randomly choose to what you will apply the idea, do not concentrate on anything in particular, and do not attempt to include everything in an area. Otherwise you will feel strain.

2. Simply glance easily and quickly around you, and try to avoid selecting things by size, brightness, color, material, or importance to you. Take each item simply as you see it. Apply the idea with equal ease to a body or a button, a fly or a floor, an arm or an apple. The only criterion for choosing an item is that you happen to look at it. Make sure you do not choose anything in particular at which to look, and that you do not deliberately exclude anything at which to look.

3. Apply this lesson once in the morning, and once in the evening. You should do it for a minute or so, unless this makes you feel rushed. Apply it with a comfortable sense of leisure.

Mentor's Notes

This lesson follows easily from the first. The physical world has no meaning of its own, so all the meaning it has for you is projected onto it from your own mind.

Lesson 3

'I do not understand anything that I see in this room (on this street, from this window, in this place).'

1. Apply this idea as you did the previous two: repeat the idea, then apply it specifically. Make sure that you do not make a distinction of any kind in the things upon which you choose to look. Whatever you see is appropriate for your application of this idea, so do not question its suitability. These are not exercises in judgment. Some of the things that you look upon may have emotionally charged meaning for you. Lay your feelings aside, and merely use those things as you would anything else.

2. The point of these exercises is to help you clear your mind of all past associations when you look upon something, so that you can see that they are neutral, and realize how little you understand them. It is essential that you keep your mind open and without judgment when you select items for applying today's idea. For this purpose, one thing is as equally suitable and useful as another.

3. This lesson should be applied once in the morning and once in the evening. You should do it for a minute or so, unless this makes you feel rushed. Apply it with a comfortable sense of leisure.

Mentor's Notes

When you project meaning onto something, you cannot see that it has no meaning in itself. Therefore, you do not understand what it is.

Lesson 4

'These thoughts that I think with a personal mind are without meaning, just like the things that I see in this room (on this street, from this window in this place, etc.).'

1. Today's exercise does not begin with the idea above. Instead, for about a minute, note the thoughts that are crossing your mind, then apply the thought above to them. If you are already aware of unhappy thoughts, use them for this idea, but do not select only the thoughts that you judge as 'bad'. You will find that, if you train yourself to look at your thoughts, each represents such a mixture within itself, that you cannot call them either 'good' or 'bad'. That is why they are without meaning.

2. Be specific in selecting thoughts for today's idea. Do not be afraid to use thoughts that you judge as 'good' as well as those that you judge as 'bad'. None of them represent your Real Thoughts, Which are covered by them. The thoughts that you judge as 'good' are only shadows of What lies beyond them, and shadows make using your Real Perception difficult. The thoughts that you judge as 'bad' are ones that block your Real Perception, and make it impossible for you to see Truth. You do not want either.

3. This is an important exercise, and it will be repeated in other lessons in different forms. The aim is to train you in the first steps toward separating in your mind what has no meaning from What has Meaning. This lesson is the first attempt in the long-range purpose of your learning, which is to see what has no meaning as not really a part of you, and What has Meaning as part of you. It is also the beginning of training your mind to recognize what is the same, despite *seeming* differences, from what *is* different.

4. In using your thoughts for applying today's lesson, identify each thought by a central figure or event. For example:

> 'This thought about ______ is without meaning, just like the things that I see in this room (on this street, etc.).'

5. You can also use this idea for a particular thought that you find painful. Though this practice is useful, it is not a substitute for applying the lesson at random. Do not examine your mind for more than a minute or so. You are too inexperienced at this stage to avoid a tendency to become pointlessly preoccupied.

6. Also, you may find suspending judgment with regard to your thoughts difficult. Do these exercises three or four times today. You will return to them later.

Mentor's Notes

This lesson is the beginning of your learning that what seems like your private thoughts and what you perceive in a world that seems outside of you are really the same, because it is your mind that thinks and perceives them. It also begins to teach you that, despite the appearance of differences among the forms of your thoughts, they are all the same, because their content is the same. Neither the physical world nor personal thoughts come from God, so they are both without meaning.

Lesson 5

'I am never upset for the reason that I think I am.'

1. You can use this idea with any person, thing, or situation that you think is causing you pain. Apply it specifically to whatever you think is the subject of your upset, using whatever term accurately describes the form of upset that you feel. For example: fear, worry, depression, anxiety, anger, hatred, jealousy, etc. You perceive all of these forms of upset as different from each other, which is not a fact, but until you learn that content, not form, is what matters, any form is appropriate for today's idea. Applying the same idea to each form of upset separately is the first step in your ultimately recognizing that they are all the same.

2. Use today's idea for both the specific form and the perceived subject of upset when it occurs. For example:

'I am not angry at ______ for the reason that I think I am.'
'I am not afraid of ______ for the reason that I think I am.'

3. This practice should not be a substitute, however, for the practice periods in which you search your mind for perceived 'sources' of upset in which you believe, or for forms of upset, which you think are their results.

4. In these practice exercises, more than when you find yourself spontaneously upset, you may find it hard to choose upsets randomly, and you may give more weight to some upsets than to others. In this case, you may find it helpful to precede your practice period with:

'There are no small upsets, because all upsets equally disturb my peace of mind.'

5. Then examine your mind for whatever is disturbing you, no matter how much, or how little, it seems to be doing so.

6. You may also find yourself less willing to apply today's idea to some sources of upset than to others. If this occurs, think:

> 'I cannot hold onto this form of upset and let the others go, because then I will still be upset. This is why all upsets are the same, and I must let go of all of them.'

7. Then search your mind for no more than a minute or so. Try to identify a number of different forms of upset, regardless of how important some seem to you. Remember to identify both the source that you perceive for the upset, and the specific feeling that you experience. More examples:

> 'I am not worried about ______ for the reason that I think I am.'
> 'I am not depressed about ______ for the reason that I think I am.'

Practice today's idea three or four times during the day.

Mentor's Notes

This lesson opens your mind to the idea that there is more going on in your mind than what appears on the surface. You are upset, and you think you know why, but you are mistaken. The next lesson explains *why* you are never upset for the reason that you think.

This lesson also reinforces the idea that perceived differences in form are meaningless, because the content of upset is always that your peace of mind is disturbed.

Lesson 6

'What is upsetting me is not really here.'

1. Again, in these exercises, name both the form of your upset (anger, fear, worry, depression, etc.) and the subject of the upset very specifically. For example:

'I am angry at ______, because I see something in them that is not here.'

'I am worried about ______, because I see something in it that is not here.'

2. You can apply today's idea to anything that seems to upset you throughout the day. However, precede your three or four practice periods with a minute or so of mind searching. Remember to apply it to each upsetting thought you uncover.

3. Again, if you resist applying today's idea to certain upsetting thoughts, remind yourself:

'There are no small upsets, because all upsets disturb my peace of mind equally.'

And:

'I cannot hold onto this form of upset and let the others go, because then I will still be upset. This is why all upsets are the same, and I must let go of each of them.'

Mentor's Notes

This lesson opens your mind to the idea that you are projecting something onto the neutral world, and it is what you are projecting that is really upsetting you. The next lesson explains what you are really seeing.

Lesson 7

'I perceive only a personal past.'

1. You might find this idea difficult to believe at first, but it is the rationale for the preceding lessons:

2. It is because you perceive only a personal past that the meaning you see in anything is not its own.

It is because you perceive only a personal past that everything you see has only the meaning that you have given to it.

It is because you perceive only a personal past that you do not understand anything that you see.

It is because you perceive only a personal past that your thoughts are without meaning, and why they are like the things that you see.

It is because you perceive only a personal past that you are never upset for the reason that you think you are.

It is because you perceive only a personal past that you are upset at something that is not here.

3. It is very difficult for you to change your beliefs about time, because everything that you believe now is rooted in time. But you need new beliefs about time, *because* your current belief system depends on time. This first lesson about time is not really as strange as it may sound to you at first.

4. For example, look at a cup. Do you really see the cup, or your personal past experiences with this cup? Being thirsty, drinking from it, feeling the rim of it against your lips, having breakfast with it, etc.? You even know whether the particular materials out of which the cup is made will break if you drop it, because of what you learned in a personal past. You have no idea what that cup is, except for what you learned in a personal past, so you do not really see it.

5. Look around you. This is equally true for everything that you see. Acknowledge this by applying today's idea randomly to whatever catches your eye. For example:

'I perceive only a personal past in this pencil.'

'I perceive only a personal past in this shoe.'
'I perceive only a personal past in this hand.'
'I perceive only a personal past in that body.'
'I perceive only a personal past in that face.'

6. Do not linger on any one thing in particular, or deliberately omit anything. Glance briefly at each object, then move on to the next object. Practice this three or four times today, each time for a minute or so.

Mentor's Notes

You believe that you are a personal self in a body in a world, and you have a story for that 'self', which is its past. You look at everything in the world that you perceive through the lens of this story. This is not 'wrong' or 'bad', it's simply a fact that this is how you think when you identify with a personal self. This is your first lesson in recognizing how you really think with a personal mind, which is necessary so that, in time, you will learn to sort out the personal mind's thoughts from the thoughts of your Christ Mind, Which is your Real Mind. Only then will you be able to make a choice between them.

Lesson 8

'My mind is preoccupied with thoughts from a personal past.'

1. This idea is the reason why you can see only a personal past. When you identify with a personal self, you do not really see anything; you see only your own thoughts projected outward. The personal mind's preoccupation with the past is the misconception about time from which your perception suffers. With a personal mind you cannot grasp the present, which is the only time that there is. Therefore, you cannot understand time, or, really, anything at all.

2. The one wholly true thought that you can hold about the past is that it is not here. When you think about it at all, then, you are thinking about an illusion. Your mind is actually blank when you think about the past, because you are not really thinking about anything.

3. The purpose for today's exercises is for you to begin to train your mind to recognize when it is not really thinking at all. While you are preoccupied with illusory ideas, the Truth is blocked from your mind. Recognizing that your mind is really blank, rather than believing that it is filled with real ideas, is the first step in opening your mind to your Real Perception.

4. You should do today's exercises with your eyes closed. This is because what you seem to see with the body's eyes is really an idea pictured in your mind, and it is easier for you to recognize with your eyes closed that, no matter how vividly you picture a thought, nothing is really there. For the usual minute or so, and with as little investment as possible, search your mind, merely noting the thoughts that you find there. Name each thought by the central object or theme it contains, then pass on to the next thought. Say to yourself:

'I seem to be thinking about_______.'

Then name each of your thoughts specifically:

'I seem to be thinking about (name of a person), about (name of an object), about (name of an emotion), etc.'

Conclude the end of your mind searching with:

'But my mind is preoccupied with thoughts from a personal past.'

5. Do this four or five times during the day, unless you find you get irritated. If you find it too uncomfortable, three or four times are enough. You might find it helpful, however, to include your irritation, or any other emotion that today's idea may induce in you, in the exercise.

Mentor's Notes

In this course, *perception* refers to both *what* you perceive and *how* you perceive it. The previous lessons dealt with *how* you perceive, emphasizing that through the personal mind you perceive a personal past that you project onto the present. In paragraph 4 above, the concept that *what* you perceive is also in your mind is introduced. The *what* that you perceive (the physical world) is neutral, because it has no meaning of its own; *how* you perceive it is what gives it the meaning that it has for you. This course's emphasis is on *how* you perceive, because your perceptions reflect whether you are perceiving from a personal mind or from your Christ Mind.

Inevitably, the question that arises here is: How is that, if the world that I perceive is in my mind, that I and another see the same world? The answer is that only one mind mistakenly perceives itself as separate from God. It continues to fragment and separate itself by seeming to split into many seemingly individual minds, each with its own separate past, or story, for itself. Though individual minds take billions of different forms, their content is all the same, as each is a miniature of the split in the one mind of which they are a part. So the reason that you and other personal selves can agree on *what* you perceive is that you are all part of the one mind that made the world. But no two personal selves wholly agree on *how* to perceive anything, because of their seemingly individual pasts, which gives them a unique point of view on the world. For example, you and another might both agree that the sky is blue, but you will probably argue about exactly what shade of blue it is! Diverse forms are the great deception of your perception of separation from God. In content, each mind is exactly the same, so your mind is really *the* mind that perceives separation from God. That is why remembering your Oneness with God is an inward journey, and you only have to accept correction of the perception of separation from God *for yourself*. When you accept correction for yourself, you do it for your entire mind, which is the one mind that seems split between God and not-God.

Lesson 9

'I perceive nothing as I could perceive it *now*.'

1. This idea obviously follows from the last two. While you may be able to accept it intellectually, it may not really mean anything to you yet. However, your understanding is not necessary at this point. In fact, your recognizing that you *do not* understand is necessary for undoing your false ideas. These exercises are about practice, not understanding, because you do not need to practice what you already understand. It makes no sense to aim at understanding if you already have it.

2. It is probably difficult, in your identification with a personal self, for you to believe that what you seem to see is not here. You might find this idea disturbing, and resist it in many forms. Yet that does not rule out your applying it. Applying them is all that you are required to do for any of these exercises. Each small step will clear a little of the darkness from your mind, and understanding will eventually come to lighten it.

3. Three or four practice periods are enough for these exercises today. Look around, and apply today's idea to whatever you see, at random, and without excluding anything deliberately. For example:

'I do not perceive this computer as I could perceive it *now*.'
'I do not perceive this telephone as I could perceive it *now*.'
'I do not perceive this arm as I could perceive it *now*.'

4. Begin with things that are near you and then extend the idea outward:

'I do not perceive that coat rack as I could perceive it *now*.'
'I do not perceive that door as I could perceive it *now*.'
'I do not perceive that face as I could perceive it *now*.'

5. Remember, do not try to include everything, and do not delib-

erately exclude anything. Be sure that you are honest with yourself when you are making this distinction, because you may be tempted to obscure it.

Mentor's Notes

It follows that if the personal mind only sees its past, and that what it shows you is 'proof' of your separation from God, then your Real Perception will show you evidence of your Oneness with God *now*. Your Real Perception looks on all things with Love, because it comes from the Love within you.

Do not allow the personal mind to distract you by obsessing on how much you are including, or what you may be excluding, from these exercises. If you do, laugh it off and continue with your exercise. You are not asked to be perfect, and this is not a test. You are asked to do your best *for your own sake.* Guilt in connection with these exercises is inappropriate.

Lesson 10

'My personal thoughts have no meaning.'

1. This idea is to be applied to all the thoughts to which you become aware during your practice periods. The reason that you can apply this idea to all of them is that they are not your Real Thoughts. This distinction has been made in this Workbook before, and it will be made again. You do not yet have a basis of comparison between the thoughts of the personal mind and your Real Thoughts. When you do, you will know that the personal mind's thoughts that you once believed were your own were not about anything real.

2. This is the second lesson with this type of idea. The form today is only slightly different from Lesson 4, which began with 'These thoughts...' instead of, 'My personal thoughts...', and today's idea will be linked with the things that you see around you. This lesson emphasizes the lack of reality of what you think with a personal mind.

3. This correction process began with the idea that the personal thoughts of which you are aware are meaningless, and are not a part of you in Truth. Then, their past rather than their present status was emphasized. Now you will be emphasizing that the presence of these 'thoughts' means that you are not really thinking at all. This is another way of reinforcing the earlier idea that your mind is really blank when you think with a personal mind. When you recognize this, you will recognize that the personal mind is really nothing. This is required for you to accept your Real Perception.

4. For these exercises, close your eyes, and begin them by repeating today's idea slowly to yourself. Then add:

'This idea will help to release me from all that I now believe.'

Search your mind for all of the thoughts that are available to you, without selection or judgment. Try to avoid labeling them in any way (good, bad, right, wrong, meaningful, meaningless, etc.) In fact, if you find it helpful, visualize your thoughts as an oddly assorted procession passing by you, which has no personal meaning for you. As each thought crosses your mind, say:

'My personal thoughts about ______ have no meaning.'

5. This thought can obviously serve you for any thought that distresses you at any time today, in addition to the five practice periods that you put aside for it. Your practice periods should be about a minute or so, and no longer. Reduce them to half a minute if you experience discomfort. Remember, repeat today's idea slowly before applying it specifically, and then add:

'This idea will help to release me from all that I now believe.'

Lesson 11

'Personal thoughts without meaning are showing me a world without meaning.'

1. This is the first idea related to a major phase of your correction process: The reversal of the way that you think about the world. You think that the world determines what you perceive; today's idea introduces you to the concept that your thoughts determine the world that you see. Be glad to practice this idea, because your release from the pain of the personal mind is made certain in it. The key to true forgiveness lies in today's idea.

2. Today's practice periods will be a little different from the previous lessons. Begin with your eyes closed, and repeat today's idea slowly to yourself. Then, open your eyes and look around: near and far, up and down; anywhere. During a minute or so of doing this, repeat today's idea. Do it slowly and calmly, without rushing or urgency or effort.

3. For maximum benefit, your eyes should move from one thing to another fairly quickly, since they should not linger on anything in particular. Repeat the words leisurely. Your introduction to this idea in particular should be practiced as casually as possible, because it contains the foundation for the peace, relaxation, and freedom from worry that you are trying to achieve. When you are finished with this exercise, close your eyes, and repeat the idea slowly to yourself once more.

4. Three practice periods are enough for today. However, if you are comfortable and you feel inclined to do more, you may do as many as five. Do not do more than five.

Mentor's Notes

Both the world and personal thoughts are without meaning, because they do not come from God. But where the world is neutral and can be perceived through either a personal mind or your Christ Mind, personal thoughts are not neutral, because they result only in personal perception. Personal perception cannot see any real meaning, since it is not from God.

Lesson 12

'I am upset because I perceive a world without meaning.'

1. Today's idea is important, because it contains a correction for a major perceptual distortion of your mind. You think that what upsets you is a frightening world or a sad world or a violent world or an insane world. But all of these are attributes that you project onto the world. The world has no meaning in itself.

2. Do today's exercises with your eyes open. Look slowly around you. Let your eyes shift from one thing to another at a consistent pace. What you look at does not matter, and you teach yourself this as you let your glance rest on each thing with equal attention and equal time. This is the first step in your learning to give everything that you see in the world equal value.

3. As you look around, say to yourself:

'I think I see a fearful world, a dangerous world, a hostile world, a sad world, a wicked world, a crazy world, etc.'

Use whatever descriptive terms occur to you. If terms which seem positive occur to you, use them as well. For example, you may think 'a good world' or 'a satisfying world.' These 'nice' adjectives belong in this exercise, too, because the world is without meaning of its own, and a 'positive' perception of the world is just as much a projection from you as a negative perception. All of the terms that cross your mind are suitable for today's exercises.

4. Be sure that you do not change your pace as you switch from 'positive' to 'negative' terms, because there is no difference between them. At the end of the practice period add:

'But I am upset because I perceive a world without meaning.'

5. What has no meaning is neither good nor bad, so the world should not upset you. If you can accept that the world has no

meaning, and let the Holy Spirit write the Truth on it for you, it will make you indescribably happy. But in the absence of the Holy Spirit in your awareness, you are impelled to project from a personal mind, and it is these projections that you have been seeing. And what the personal mind projects is empty of any real meaning. Yet, beneath this perception is your Real Perception, Which reflects God's Love. The fact that you are seeing a world without meaning might upset you now, but when you have removed the personal mind's projections, you will see with your Real Perception. That is the ultimate purpose for these exercises.

6. Practice three or four times today, for no more than a minute each. You might find even this too long, so stop the exercise whenever you experience a sense of strain.

Mentor's Notes

God's Mind is One; duality is a concept of the personal mind. Judgments like 'good/bad', 'right/wrong', 'meaningful/meaningless' are used by the personal mind to make the world seem to have a meaning of its own; to make it real to you. The Holy Spirit looks at the world and sees what is useful to help you remember your Oneness with God, and It disregards the rest. What is useful can be said to be 'good', 'right', or 'meaningful'. As long as you think in dualistic terms, the Holy Spirit will use them for Truth.

Paragraph 5 in this lesson introduces you to the purpose for these early lessons, which are teaching you to recognize the way that the personal mind thinks, but are not yet giving you anything to replace it. Those lessons which lead you to your True Perception come later.

Lesson 13

'A world without meaning makes me fearful.'

1. Today's idea is another form of the preceding one, but it specifically mentions the emotion a world without meaning arouses in you. (A world without meaning is actually impossible, because nothing without meaning exists. But you can perceive something that does not exist, and therefore that has no meaning. In fact, this is what you do.)

2. In your identification with a personal self, recognizing that the world has no meaning in itself causes you intense anxiety, because it seems to set 'you' and God against each other to determine which meaning is going to be written on the world. The personal mind has rushed in first to establish its own ideas, because it is afraid that the world will be used by the Holy Spirit to demonstrate the personal mind's powerlessness and unreality. It is correct in this.

3. Therefore, it is essential that you learn to recognize that the world has no meaning in itself, and to accept this without fear. If you are afraid, you will project your fear onto the world, and you will perceive in the world attributes that it does not possess, and crowd it with images that do not exist. To the personal mind, illusions are safety devices, and they are the same to you when you identify with a personal self.

4. Practice today's exercises three or four times for no more than a minute each time. With your eyes closed, repeat today's idea to yourself. Then, open your eyes, look around you slowly, and say:

'I am looking at a world without meaning.'

Repeat this statement to yourself as you look around. Then, close your eyes and finish with:

'A world without meaning makes me fearful, because I think I am competing with God.'

5. You may find yourself resisting this last statement in one form or another, but acknowledge to yourself that you are really afraid of this statement because you think that God might punish you for competing with It. You are not expected to believe this last statement at this point, and you may dismiss it as preposterous. Note carefully, however, any signs of conscious or unconscious fear which it may arouse in you.

6. This is the first lesson to state a cause and effect relationship that you are inexperienced in recognizing. Do not dwell on the last statement, and try not to think about it outside of the practice periods.

Lesson 14

'God did not create a world without meaning.'

1. Today's idea is, of course, the reason why a world without meaning is not possible. What God did not create does not exist, and Everything that God created exists as God created It. The world that you perceive has nothing to do with Reality. You made it, but it does not exist in Reality.

2. For this exercise, keep your eyes closed the whole time. Keep the time you search your mind short; a minute at the most. Three practice periods today are enough, unless you feel comfortable doing them. If this is so, it is because you really understand what they are for.

3. Today's idea is another step in learning to let go of what you have projected onto the world from the personal mind, so that your Real Perception can be extended to it instead. You might experience the early steps in this exchange as difficult and painful. You might even find some of them frightening. But you will not be left in fear; you will go beyond fear to your Goal, Which is Perfect Safety and Perfect Peace.

4. With your eyes closed, think of all of the horrors of the world that cross your mind. Name each one as it occurs to you, then deny its reality. Say:

> 'God did not create this (war, plane crash, hurricane, etc.), so it is not real.'

5. Also, include anything that you are afraid might happen to you or another. In each case, name the 'disaster' specifically; do not use general terms. For example, say 'God did not create cancer' instead of 'God did not create illness.'

6. You will be looking at your personal collection of horrors. They are part of the world that you see. Some of them are illusions you seem to share with others, some are part of your personal hell. It

does not matter. What God did not create can only be in your mind apart from God, so it has no meaning. In recognition of this, finish today's practice periods by repeating today's idea:

'God did not create a world without meaning.'

7. Of course, apply this idea to anything that disturbs you during the day apart from your practice periods. Be very specific in your application. For example:

'God did not create a world without meaning. God did not create (the situation that disturbs you), so it is not real.'

Mentor's Notes

This lesson is very important, because with it you make an important distinction between What God created and what God did not create. This is the beginning of your sorting out Truth from illusion, which will often turn your current beliefs on their head. The personal mind teaches you that God made the world, but the world has no meaning, so it cannot come from God.

Lesson 15

'I have made the images that I see with my own thoughts.'

1. It is because the thoughts that you think with a mind that seems separate from God appear as images to you that you do not recognize that they are nothing. You think that you think them, so you think that you see them. This is how 'seeing' is made in the split mind, and it is the function that it gives to bodies' eyes. Image-making is not your Real Perception. It takes the place of your Real Perception, and replaces It with illusions.

2. This introduction to your process of image-making will probably not mean much to you at this stage. You will begin to understand it when you see little edges of light around familiar objects. That will be the beginning of Real Perception for you. When it occurs, Real Perception will come to you quickly.

3. As you go along, you may have many episodes of 'light'. They may take different forms, some of which you may not expect, but don't be afraid of them, because they are the signs that you are opening your mind to Truth at last. They will not stay, because they only symbolize your Real Perception, and they do not come from God. These exercises will not reveal God to you, but they will prepare you to return to full awareness of God again.

4. For today's practice, repeat today's lesson to yourself, then apply it to whatever you see around you. Use the name of what you see, and, keeping your eyes on it, say:

'That ______ is an image that I have made.'

It is not necessary for you to include a large number of specific subjects for today's idea. It is necessary, however, for you to continue to look at the subject while you repeat the idea to yourself. Repeat the idea slowly each time.

5. Although you will not be able to apply today's idea to many things during each one-minute practice period, try to make your

selection of subjects as random as possible. If you feel uncomfortable, less than a minute will be enough. Three practice periods will be enough, unless you feel completely comfortable. Even then, do only four. You can also apply today's idea as you need to throughout the day.

Mentor's Notes

In paragraph 1, your 'split mind' refers to the one mind that makes the world through images that seemingly separate personal minds then perceive, or interpret. As a personal self, you seem to be within a world that is not of your making, but all that you perceive is your entire mind, because you are actually the one mind in which it exists. You cannot understand this in your identification with a personal self, because identifying with a personal self is how you deny that all that you perceive is your entire mind. But you *will* understand this as you claim your Real Perception, and you watch what you perceive change as you change your mind.

Lesson 16

'I have no neutral thoughts.'

1. Today's idea is the first step in dispelling your belief that your thoughts have no effect. Everything that you see is the result of your thoughts, and there is no exception to this fact. Thoughts are not big or little or powerful or weak; they are merely True or false. Those that are True extend Themselves Eternally and Infinitely; those that are false make limited, false images.

2. No thought contradicts the Power of your mind more than the concept that you have 'idle thoughts'. A mind that makes a whole world can hardly be called idle! Every thought that you have either extends Truth or multiplies illusions in your mind. You can multiply illusions, but you can never make them Real.

3. Besides recognizing that your thoughts are never idle, your salvation also requires that you recognize that every thought that you have brings you conflict or Peace; fear or Love. A thought cannot result in a neutral result, because your thoughts cannot be neutral. You might be tempted to dismiss fearful thoughts as unimportant, trivial, or not worth bothering with, but you must recognize that they are all equally destructive to your Peace, and are all equally unreal. You will practice this idea in many forms before you really understand it.

4. For today's practice, search your mind for a minute or so with your eyes closed. Be sure to not overlook any 'little' thought. This might be quite difficult, until you get used to practicing it. You will find it is hard for you to avoid making artificial distinctions between your thoughts. Every thought that occurs to you, no matter its seeming qualities, is suitable for applying today's idea.

5. In the practice periods, first repeat today's idea to yourself. Then, as other thoughts cross your mind, hold them in your awareness while you tell yourself:

'This thought about ______ is not a neutral thought.'

As usual, use today's idea whenever you are aware of a thought that makes you uneasy. Say:

'This thought about ______ is not a neutral thought because I have no neutral thoughts.'

6. If you can do them without effort, do four or five practice periods. If you are experiencing strain, however, three periods will be enough. Reduce the length of a practice period if you are experiencing discomfort.

Mentor's Notes

You might find it impossible to believe the idea that your thoughts make the whole world that you perceive, but that's because you are used to thinking of your mind as limited to a personal mind. But your mind is, in fact, everywhere. This will be emphasized in coming lessons.

Lesson 17

'I cannot perceive neutral things.'

1. This is another step in your identifying cause and effect in your perception that you are in a world. You see no neutral things, because your thoughts are not neutral. A thought always precedes your perception, despite the appearance that it happens the other way around. This is not what the personal mind teaches you, but you must learn that it *is* the way that you think. If this were not so, your perception would have no cause, and it would be Reality. But this cannot be so, since perception is not consistent.

2. For today' practice, with your eyes open, say to yourself:

'I cannot perceive neutral things, because I have no neutral thoughts.'

Then look around you, and look at each thing long enough to say:

'I do not perceive a neutral ______, because my thoughts about ______s are not neutral.'

For example, you might say:

'I do not perceive a neutral wall, because my thoughts about walls are not neutral.'
'I do not perceive a neutral body, because my thoughts about bodies are not neutral.'

3. Do not make a distinction between what you believe to be living or inanimate, pleasant or unpleasant. No matter what you may believe, you do not perceive anything that is really Living or really Joyous. This is because you are not yet aware of your True and Happy Thoughts.

4. Three or four practice periods are recommended for today. Do not do less than three, even if you experience resistance. However, if you do experience resistance, you may reduce the length of the practice period to less than a minute.

Lesson 18

'I am not alone in experiencing the effects of my perception.'

1. Today's idea again reinforces your awareness that the thoughts which give rise to what you see are never neutral or unimportant. It also emphasizes that the personal mind is not the limit of your mind, which will be given emphasis later on.

2. Today's idea does not refer to *what* you see as much as to *how* you see it. Do three or four practice periods as follows:

3. Look around you, and select subjects for today's idea as randomly as possible. Keep your eyes on each long enough to say to yourself:

'I am not alone in experiencing the effects of how I see ______.'

Finish the practice period with today's more general statement:

'I am not alone in experiencing the effects of my perception.'

4. A minute or less is enough for each practice period.

Mentor's Notes

The concept of 'aloneness' really only has meaning in your identification with an isolated personal self. In Truth, your Mind is One, and 'aloneness' is a meaningless concept, because there is no 'other' mind. But in your perception of separation from God, there seems to be 'you' in a world that seems outside of you. This lesson points out that your mind is not limited to an isolated personal self. How you perceive affects not just what seems like 'your' individual mind, but also the whole world, because it is all in your mind.

Lesson 19

'I am not alone in experiencing the effects of my thoughts.'

1. You will notice in this Workbook that sometimes ideas related to your thoughts precede ideas related to your perception, and that sometimes this is reversed. This is because the order does not matter. Your thoughts and the perception which are their results are simultaneous, because cause and effect are never separate.

2. Today's lesson again emphasizes that your mind is not limited to an isolated personal mind. You probably won't welcome this idea at first, because you may think it carries an enormous responsibility. You also may regard it as an attack on your privacy. But it is a fact that you have no private thoughts. Despite your initial resistance, you will eventually understand that this must be true if it is possible for you to be saved from your belief that you are limited to a personal self. And your salvation from this *must* be possible, because it is the Will of God that you are Limitless.

3. Today's exercises should be done for a minute or so, with your eyes closed. First, repeat today's idea, then, observe the thoughts which are crossing your mind. Name each thought in terms of the central person or theme it contains, and hold it in your mind. As you do so, say to yourself:

'I am not alone in experiencing the effects of this thought about ______.'

4. The requirement that you be random in selecting subjects for applying each lesson will no longer be repeated each day, though you will be reminded occasionally. Do not forget, however, that randomly choosing subjects remains essential for each lesson. Lack of order in choosing subjects will ultimately make lack of order in miracles meaningful to you.

5. Do three or four practice periods today, shortening their duration if they become uncomfortable. Also, apply today's idea as

you need throughout the day.

Mentor's Notes

'Your thoughts are not private' is referring to content, not to form. For example, it does not mean that everyone in the world knows what you are thinking about your Aunt Mary, but that the *effects* of your thoughts about your Aunt Mary are not limited to you as a personal self; they affect your entire mind, which means the part of your mind where you perceive a world, as well as what you think of as 'you'. As it says in Lesson 16, your thoughts either extend Truth or perpetuate illusions in your mind.

Lesson 20

'I am determined to perceive differently.'

1. So far, your practice periods have been quite casual. You have not been directed when to do them, little effort has been asked of you, and you have not even been asked for your active cooperation and interest. This has been intentional and carefully planned; the crucial importance of reversing your current thinking has not been neglected. The salvation of your entire mind depends on these lessons. The lessons have been casual so far because you will not see truly if you feel you are being coerced, or if you give in to resentment and resistance.

2. This is the first lesson to introduce structure; do not misunderstand it as an attempt to force you or to put pressure on you. You want salvation; you want to be Happy and at Peace. You do not have this now because your mind is undisciplined, and you cannot distinguish between Joy and sorrow, Real Pleasure and pain, or Love and fear. Now you are learning to tell them apart and, when you do, your reward will be great indeed!

3. Your decision to perceive differently is all that is required for you to gain your Real Perception. What you want is yours. Do not make the mistake of thinking the little effort required from you means the Goal has little worth. Saving your entire mind is not a trivial purpose. You must heal your mind to heal the world, because they are one and the same. In Truth, your Mind is One with God, and this Oneness is your resurrection and your Life. The Will of your Mind in God is done, because all of the Power of Heaven is in It, and It has all power over the part of your mind where you perceive a world. In your determination to perceive differently, your Real Perception is given to you.

4. With today's exercises, you are reminding yourself throughout the day that you want a different perception. This implies that you do not like how you perceive now, so as you repeat today's idea, you are stating that you are determined to change your experience for a

better one, and one that you really want.

5. At least twice an hour, preferably every half-hour, repeat today's idea slowly and positively. Do not be upset if you forget to do this, but make a real effort to remember. Also, use the lesson for any situation, person, or thing which upsets you. You can perceive them differently, and you will. What you desire, you will see. This is how the law of cause and effect works in your mind where you perceive a world.

Mentor's Notes

You do not have to decide for yourself how 'differently' will look. Just open your mind to the awareness that you have a choice in how you perceive.

Lesson 21

'I am determined to perceive truly.'

1. Today's idea is a continuation and extension of yesterday's idea. This time, however, your practice will include specific mind-searching. Practice five times today, for a full minute each time. Also, apply the idea to appropriate situations as they happen.

2. Begin the practice period by repeating today's idea to yourself. Then close your eyes, and carefully search your mind for any situation, past, present, or which you anticipate, that arouses anger in you. Anger can take the form of anything from mild irritation to full-out rage. The degree of your emotion does not matter. In time, you will become aware that a slight twinge of annoyance is just the tip of an intense rage in your mind.

3. So, try not to let any 'little' thoughts of anger escape your practice. Remember, you do not really recognize what causes your anger, and anything that you believe does cause your anger really means nothing. You may be tempted to dwell more on some situations or persons than on others in the false belief that they are more 'obvious'. This is only an example of your belief that some forms of attack are more justified than others.

4. As you search your mind for all of the forms that attack thoughts take, hold each one in your mind as you tell yourself:

'I am determined to perceive ______ (name of person) truly.'
'I am determined to perceive ______ (situation) truly.'

5. Be as specific as possible. You may, for example, use a specific attribute of a person which you believe is the limited cause of your anger. If your perception is distorted by this, say:

'I am determined to perceive _______ (attribute) in ______ (person) truly.'

Mentor's Notes

Do not concern yourself with what 'truly' means yet. That will come in time. For now, simply focus on being *willing* to perceive truly.

If you feel guilty for your anger, apply today's idea to it. Your guilt is not justified, because anger is only a mistake, and these lessons are the correction for it.

Lesson 22

'What I perceive with a personal mind is a form of attack on myself.'

1. Today's idea describes the way that you must perceive the world when you identify with a personal self. Your belief that you are a personal self is an 'attack' on yourself, because it is not true. Unable to accept attack in your own mind, you project it onto the world. Now the world seems to be attacking you, and you feel that you must attack back to protect yourself. This vicious cycle of attack/counter-attack will fill your mind until you change your mind. Until then, Peace of mind will be impossible for you.

2. This perception of the world is the savage fantasy from which you want to escape. Isn't it joyous news to learn that it is not real, and that you can escape from it? You made everything that you hate, and want to attack and kill. Everything that you fear does not exist.

3. At least five times today, look at the world around you for a minute. As your eyes move from one object to another, or from one body to another, say to yourself:

'What I see is perishable and will not last, so it is not real. I am perceiving a form of attack on myself.'

At the end of each practice period, ask yourself:

'Is this what I really want to perceive?'

The answer is obviously, 'no'!

Mentor's Notes

This lesson's emphasis is on *what* you perceive.

It is not an attack on yourself to simply perceive the world. It is perceiving it as your *reality*, which you do in your identification with a personal self, that makes it an attack on yourself. The perishable and temporary are not worthy of you, who are Eternal.

Lesson 23

'I can escape from the world that the personal mind shows me by giving up attack thoughts.'

1. Today's idea contains the *only* way out of fear for you. Every thought that you have makes up some segment of the world that you see. So you must change your thoughts to change your perception of the world.

2. Since the cause of the world that you perceive is the attack thoughts of the personal mind, you must learn that it is these thoughts that you do not want. There is no point in lamenting the world or in trying to change it, because the world cannot change; it is only an effect of your mind. Change a cause and its effect will automatically change. So change your thoughts about the world, and it will change for you.

3. The world that you perceive through the personal mind is an attack on yourself, and everything in it is a symbol of attack. Your perception of an 'external reality' is a pictorial representation of your own attack thoughts. This is not really *seeing* but *fantasizing*, and its result is more correctly called an *hallucination*.

4. You do not see that you are the image-maker of the world that you perceive. You do not have to be saved from the world as you perceive it now, but from your identification with a personal self. This is what your salvation is, because the world that you now perceive will be gone when its cause is gone. Your Real Perception already has a replacement for everything that you think you perceive now. The images that your split mind makes can be lit with Loveliness. It can transform them with Love, even though they were made for attack, because you will not be making them with a personal mind, but with your Christ Mind.

5. Today's idea introduces you to the idea that you are not trapped in the world of attack that you now see, because it can be changed. This change requires, first, that you recognize that its cause is your own thinking; second, that you let it go; third, that you let it

be replaced. The first two steps require your cooperation, but replacing the world you now see does not. The images that you have made have already been replaced, because the idea that you can be separate from God was undone the moment that the thought occurred. When you take the first two steps, you will automatically see that this is so.

6. Apply today's idea throughout the day as you need it. For your five practice periods, look around you, and repeat today's idea slowly. Then, close your eyes, and spend about a minute searching your mind for its many attack thoughts. As each one crosses your mind, say to yourself:

> 'I can escape from the world that I now perceive by giving up attack thoughts about ______.'

Hold each attack thought in mind as you say this, then dismiss the thought and go onto the next one.

7. In the practice periods, be sure to include both your own attacking thoughts, and your thoughts of being attacked by others. Their effect on you is exactly the same, because they are exactly the same: They are both occurring in your mind. You might not recognize this yet, and you are asked only to treat them as the same in your practice periods for now. You are still at the stage of identifying the cause of the world that you now perceive. When you finally learn that attack that seems to come from you and attack that seems to come from others is the same, you will be ready to let go of their cause.

Mentor's Notes

This lesson's emphasis is on *how* you perceive.

Though the world was made by your split mind to make separation from God seem real, it is neutral in itself. You can continue to perceive it through the personal mind, which will project attack onto it, keeping you in a cycle of attack/counter-attack;

or, you can let go of that perception, and let your Christ Mind extend God's Love to the world, your Perception of Which will prepare you to return to full awareness that you *are* God's Love. The Perception of your Christ Mind is here waiting for you, because you have not really left God; you only think that you have.

Lesson 24

'I do not yet perceive what is truly good for me.'

1. Because you identify with a personal self, you do not know the outcome that would make you truly happy in any situation. So you have no guide to appropriate action, and no way of judging the results of your actions. What you do is determined by your perception of a situation, and your perceptions have been wrong. It is inevitable, then, that you do not know what is truly good for you. Yet, you must make what is truly good for you your only goal in any situation; otherwise you will be confused about what is truly good for you.

2. If you accept that you do not recognize what is truly good for you, then you can be taught what it is. But while you think that you know what is truly good for you, your mind is closed, and you cannot learn. Today's idea is a step toward opening your mind so that you can learn what is truly good for you.

3. Today's exercises require you to be much more honest with yourself than you are used to being. Search your mind for two minutes in each of today's five practice periods.

Only a few subjects, honestly and carefully looked at, will be more helpful to you than a passing look at many subjects.

4. Begin each practice period by repeating today's idea, then search your mind, with your eyes closed, for unresolved situations with which you are now concerned. Pay attention to the outcome that you want for each of them. You will quickly realize that you have many goals in mind for each of them, and that these goals are on many levels and often conflict.

5. Name each situation that occurs to you, and then look carefully at each of the goals that you want to be met with each one. Say to yourself something like:

'With regard to ______ (the situation), I want ______ and ______ and ______ etc.'

Try to cover as many different types of goals that you have honestly found for each one, even if some of the goals do not appear to be directly related to the situation.

6. If you do this exercise correctly, you will quickly see that you are making a large number of demands of each situation, many of which do not have anything to do with the situations. You will also recognize that many of your goals contradict each other, that you have no unified outcome in mind, and that you will inevitably experience disappointment in connection with some of your goals.

7. After covering the list of as many hoped-for goals for each situation that crosses your mind, say to yourself:

'I do not yet know what is truly good for me.'

Then, go on to the next one.

Mentor's Notes

Here's an example of an unresolved situation with many goals, some of which are not directly related to the situation. Let's say you are awaiting the results of a job interview:

'With regard to the job (be specific) interview, I want to get the job (money, position), I want to have failed the interview (too much responsibility, too long a commute), I want the interviewer's approval, I want to travel (hoping money facilitates this), I want Dad's approval, I want to stay where I am, etc.'

Lesson 25

'I do not know yet what anything in the world is for.'

1. Purpose is meaning. Today's idea explains why nothing that you see with the personal mind means anything, because, with the personal mind, you don't know what anything is for. It should be that everything in the world is for your own good, that that is its purpose, and that it is in recognizing this that your goals become unified, and that everything in the world becomes truly meaningful to you.

2. Right now, you perceive the world, and everything in it, as meaningful in the personal mind's terms. These goals have nothing to do with what is truly good for you, because the personal self is not you. Your false identification with it makes you incapable of understanding what anything is really for, so you misuse everything. When you understand this, you will stop reinforcing the personal mind's goals for the world, and you will withdraw them.

3. You are not a personal self, so personal goals are really concerned with nothing. In cherishing them, you have no real goals at all, so you don't know what anything is for.

4. At a superficial level, the personal mind does recognize purpose, but you can't understand true purpose at a superficial level. For example, at a superficial level you do understand that a telephone is for contacting someone who is not physically present. What you cannot understand with the personal mind, though, is your true purpose in contacting someone. And it is whether or not you meet your true purpose that makes your contact with them meaningful or not.

5. It is essential for your learning that you give up the personal goals that you have given to everything. The only way to accomplish this is to recognize that personal goals are meaningless, rather than that they are 'good' or 'bad'. Today's idea is a step in that direction.

6. Today's lesson requires six practice periods of two minutes each. Begin each lesson by saying today's idea to yourself. Then,

look around you, and let your eyes rest on whatever catches your attention, near or far, 'important' or 'unimportant', human or not human. As you look at each subject say:

'I do not know what this ______ (be specific) is for.'

Say this slowly, keeping your eyes on the subject until you have completed this statement. Then move on to the next subject.

Lesson 26

'My attack thoughts are attacking my Invulnerability.'

1. It is obvious that if you can be attacked you are not Invulnerable. In your identification with a personal self, you believe that attack is real, because you believe that you have really attacked yourself. What has effects *through* you must also have effects *on* you. This is a Law of Mind that will ultimately save you from your limiting identification with a personal self, but now you are misusing it in your identification with a personal self. Therefore, you must learn how to use it for your own true good, instead of against yourself.

2. Because you project your attack thoughts, you fear attack. And since you fear attack, you do not believe that you are Invulnerable, Which is an Attribute of God. Attack thoughts, then, make you vulnerable in your own mind, which is where the attack thoughts are. You cannot hold both attack thoughts and your own Invulnerability together in your mind, because they contradict each other.

3. Today's idea introduces you to the awareness that you always attack yourself first. Attack thoughts in your mind, even directed toward others, always entail you believing that you are vulnerable, and their purpose is to weaken you in your own estimation. And if you believe that you are vulnerable, you are attacking yourself, because in Truth you are Invulnerable. In your belief that you are vulnerable, you no longer believe in yourself, and a false image of yourself comes to take the place of What you are.

4. Your practice of today's idea will help you understand that your feeling that you are vulnerable or Invulnerable is the result of your own thoughts. Only your own thoughts can attack you, only your own thoughts can make you feel vulnerable, and only your own thoughts can prove to you that this is not so.

5. Practice six times today for two minutes each time. If you are too uncomfortable, you may reduce the length of a practice period

to a minute, but no less.

6. Begin each practice period by repeating today's idea. Then, close your eyes, and review any unresolved situations whose outcome is concerning you. Concern may take the form of depression, worry, anger, a sense of imposition, fear, foreboding, or preoccupation. Any unsettled situation that occurs to you again and again throughout the day is suitable for today's lesson. You will not be able to use many situations for each practice period, because you will be spending a longer time than usual with each idea. Apply today's idea as follows:

First, name the situation: 'I am concerned about ______.'

Then, go over every possible negative outcome that has occurred to you in connection with the situation about which you are concerned. Refer to each outcome specifically:

'I am afraid ______ will happen.'

7. If you are doing this exercise properly, you will have five or six distressing possible outcomes from each situation that you use. You may even have more. It is better for you to cover a few situations thoroughly, than to cover many situations briefly. As your list of anticipated outcomes for each situation continues, you will probably find that the outcomes become less and less acceptable to you, but try to keep them all alike to you to whatever extent that you can.

8. After you have named each outcome of which you are afraid, tell yourself:

'That thought is an attack on myself.'

Conclude each practice period by repeating today's idea to yourself again.

Mentor's Notes

'What has effects through you must also have effects on you.' This sentence from paragraph 1 brings forward the idea introduced in the Text that ideas do not leave their source. Your thoughts do not leave your mind, which is where they have an effect. If you believe attack is possible, you will experience it, because it is an idea in your mind.

The personal mind teaches that attack is strength, but it is obvious that you attack only when you perceive yourself as vulnerable. The only possible motive for attack is self-defense, whether to pre-empt an attack or to fight off an attack. That is why attack thoughts reinforce your sense of vulnerability.

You might find it hard to accept that you are Invulnerable when the world that you perceive seems to present you with so much evidence that you are vulnerable. But remember that the witnesses that the world presents to you, you have put there to see.

Lesson 27

'Above all else, I want to perceive differently.'

1. Today's lesson expresses something stronger than the determination that you expressed in lesson 20, because it prioritizes your desires. You may hesitate to use this idea because you are not yet sure that you really mean it, but this does not matter. The purpose of today's idea is to bring closer the time when you really mean it.

2. You may be tempted to believe that you are being asked to sacrifice when you say that you want to perceive differently more than you want anything else. If the strength of today's statement makes you uncomfortable, say to yourself:

'My Real Perception has no cost.'

And if your fear persists, say to yourself:

'My Real Perception can only bless me.'

3. Today's idea needs many repetitions to be of maximum benefit to you. Use it every half-hour at minimum; try for every 15 or 20 minutes. When you start your day, set a definite time interval between each statement of today's idea, and try to stick to it throughout the day. This is only one short sentence, which you can say to yourself even when you are speaking with others or occupied with a task.

4. You will remember to do today's idea to the extent that you want it to be true. You might forget to use it quite often, but do not be disturbed by this. Just start up your statement schedule again when you do remember. If only once during the day you feel you sincerely mean today's idea, you will save yourself many years of effort.

Lesson 28

'Above all else, I want to perceive truly.'

1. Today's lesson gives specific application to yesterday's idea. In today's practice periods, you will be making a series of definite commitments. Whether or not you keep these commitments is not a concern. If you are willing to make them now, you have started on your way to keeping them. You are still at the very beginning of your journey.

2. You may wonder why it is important to say, 'Above all else, I want to perceive truly.' Separating this statement out, and asking about its meaning, is characteristic of the way that the personal mind thinks. It perceives everything as separate, and tries to give each thing a meaning in itself. But perceiving this way is not perceiving anything real at all. Your Real Perception does not work this way. When you see one thing Truly, you will see all things Truly, because the Truth that you see in one thing is the Truth that you see in all things.

3. When you apply today's lesson to, for example, a table, you are acknowledging that you are not perceiving it Truly now, and you are making a commitment to withdraw your current ideas about the table. You are opening your mind to what the table Truly *is* and what it is Truly *for* from the perspective of your Christ Mind. You are no longer defining it in terms of the personal self's past, and you are no longer telling yourself what the table is, but you are asking your Christ Mind to tell you what the table is. You are not binding the table's meaning to your past experience with tables, and you are not limiting its purpose to the personal mind's 'story' for it.

4. When you have already defined something, your mind is closed, and you will not question your definition of it. The purpose of today's exercises is for you to open your mind by asking questions to receive answers. By saying today's lesson, you are committing yourself to your Real Perception. This is not an exclusive commitment to the specific subjects you use, because it applies to

everything else, no more and no less.

5. But, in fact, you can attain your Real Perception by applying today's idea to just a table, for example, if you withdraw the personal mind's ideas from it, and open your mind. It has Something to show you; Something Beautiful and Clean and full of Happiness and hope; Something of Infinite Value. Hidden under the personal mind's ideas about its purpose is the true purpose that it shares with everything.

6. In using a table, or anything else, as a subject for today's idea, you are really asking to see your Christ Mind's purpose for everything in the world that you perceive. You will make this same request of each subject that you choose today. You are making a commitment to let each subject's real purpose be revealed to you, rather than placing the personal mind's judgment on it.

7. Today, do six two-minute practice periods. First, state today's idea, then, apply it to whatever you see around you. Choose subjects randomly, and apply today's idea to each subject equally, in acknowledgment that each is of equal value in its contribution to you attaining your Real Perception.

8. As usual, name the subject at which you are looking, and, holding it in your gaze, say to yourself:

'Above all else, I want to see ______ truly.'

Say this as slowly and thoughtfully as you can for each subject. There is no hurry.

Mentor's Notes

God did not make the world, but remember that the world has no meaning in itself and is open to different perceptions, or interpretations. It can be used for the personal mind's purpose of keeping you in a perception of separation from God, or for your Christ Mind's purpose of leading you back to an awareness of your Oneness with God. This is equally true for everything in the world.

In the personal mind's perception of separation, everything has a different meaning and purpose in itself. Everything is a goal and an end in itself. In your Christ Mind's perception, everything has the single purpose of helping you to remember your Oneness with God. Everything is a means to help you reach your Goal, rather than an end in itself.

Lesson 29

'I can perceive God in everything.'

1. Today's idea explains why you can see one purpose in everything that you perceive. It explains why you do not have to perceive everything as separate from everything else, and why the way that you perceive things now means nothing. In fact, it explains every idea in this Workbook so far, and all the ones that follow. Today's idea is the whole basis for your Real Perception.

2. You might find it difficult to understand today's idea at this point. You may find it silly, irreverent, senseless, funny, and even objectionable. Of course, God is not really *in* a table, for example. But remember, yesterday's lesson emphasized that everything you perceive can share a single purpose with your Christ Mind. What shares Christ's purpose shares God's Purpose, because They are One.

3. Today, begin to perceive all things with love, appreciation, and open-mindedness. You do not see a real purpose in anything now. Do you want to? The Holy purpose for everything stands beyond the range of the personal mind. When your Real Perception shows you the Holiness that can make the world Lovely, you will understand today's lesson perfectly, and you will not understand how you ever found it difficult.

4. Today's six, two-minute practice periods should follow a pattern that is familiar to you by now: Repeat today's idea, then apply it to randomly chosen subjects around you, naming each subject specifically. Avoid self-directed selection, which you may be particularly tempted to use today, because of its alien nature. Remember, any order that you impose on your selection is equally alien to Reality, Where Everything is the Same.

5. Your list of random subjects would be like this:

'I can perceive God in this coat hanger.'
'I can perceive God in this magazine.'
'I can perceive God in this finger.'

'I can perceive God in this lamp.'
'I can perceive God in that body.'
'I can perceive God in that door.'
'I can perceive God in that trash can.'

In addition to the practice periods, repeat today's idea at least once an hour, looking slowly around you as you say the words unhurriedly to yourself. At least once or twice, you should experience a sense of restfulness as you do this.

Mentor's Notes

The next lesson explains *how* it is that you can perceive God in everything.

Lesson 30

'I can perceive God in everything, because God is in my mind.'

1. Today's idea is the foundation of your Real Perception. The world will open for you, and you will see it as you have never done before. And the way that you have been seeing with the personal mind will be gone.

2. Today, you are going to use 'extension' instead of 'projection'. Projection is perceiving what is in your mind as outside of you, because you do not like it. Today, you will perceive What is in your mind, because you *do* want to recognize It is there. You will join with What you perceive, rather than keep it apart from you. This is the fundamental difference between your Real Perception and the way that the personal mind perceives.

3. Apply today's idea as often as possible throughout the day. Whenever you have a moment, repeat today's idea to yourself slowly as you look around you. Realize that today's idea applies to everything that you do see now, and to everything you that could see if it was within your sight.

4. Real Perception is not limited to concepts like 'near' and 'far'. To help you get used to this idea, apply the lesson to things beyond your present range of vision as well.

5. Real Perception is not only *not* limited by space and time, but it does not rely on the body's eyes at all. Your Mind is its only Source. To help you get used to this idea, devote several practice periods to applying today's idea, with your eyes closed, to whatever subjects come to mind, looking within rather than outside yourself. Today's idea applies equally to both.

Mentor's Notes

The first lessons taught you that the world has no meaning in itself, and that you can choose how to perceive it. They then asked you to open your mind, and to let go of how you have perceived it. With these last two lessons, you begin to fill in your open mind with

What is really there.

The Law of Mind is that It extends Itself. In other words, Mind can only know Itself. At the level of perception, this Law is expressed as either *extension* or *projection*. They are the same mechanism of the mind, but *projection* is *extension with denial*. As the earlier lessons showed you, for example, if attack is in your mind, you will perceive it in the world, because you do not want to acknowledge that it is in your mind. You *are* perceiving what is in your mind, but denying that this is what is happening.

You have been used to denying that your perception of the world comes from your own mind, and you have believed that the world teaches you what it is and, therefore, what you are. Now, you begin to teach yourself What you are by extending It to the world to perceive It and increase It in your awareness.

In paragraph 5 above, it says that your Real Perception does not rely on the body's eyes at all, and that your Mind is Its Source. Actually, the personal mind does not really see with a body either, but sees images projected from your split mind. The difference is that when you experience your Real Perception, you are aware that everything is in your mind, and form recedes as the True Content of your mind takes precedence. The personal mind, however, denies that form is an image in your mind, and denies that it provides its own meaning to everything.

Lesson 31

'I am not a victim of the world that I perceive.'

1. Today's idea is your declaration of release from victimhood. The idea should be applied to both the world that you perceive outside of you, and to the world that you perceive when you close your eyes. You are also being introduced to a form of practice today that you will use more and more, with changes that will be indicated. Generally, apply the idea in a sustained way during the required practice periods, then frequently throughout the day.

2. For today's exercises, do two 3-5 minute practice periods, one in the morning and one at night. During that time, look slowly around you while you repeat the idea two or three times. Then close your eyes, and apply it to the world that passes through your mind. You will escape from both together, because your inner world is the cause of the outer world that you perceive.

3. As you observe your inner world, let whatever thoughts happen to cross your mind come up, consider each for a moment, then let the next thought come up. Do not establish any order (good/bad, big/little, important/unimportant, etc.) among them. Let them stream by as you watch them calmly and with detachment. As you do this, repeat today's idea to yourself, as often as you want, but with no sense of hurry.

4. Throughout the day, repeat today's idea as often as possible. Remind yourself that you are declaring your own independence from victimhood. In your freedom lies the freedom of your mind where you perceive a world.

5. Today's idea is also particularly useful as a response any time that you are tempted to feel sorry for yourself, put upon, or see yourself as a victim. It is a declaration that you will not yield to it, or limit yourself to the personal mind's idea of you.

Lesson 32

'I have invented the world that I perceive.'

1. Today, you continue with the theme of cause and effect. You cannot be the victim of the world that you perceive, because you invented it. You can give it up as easily as you made it up. You perceive it or don't perceive it, as you desire. While you want the world, you will perceive it; when you no longer want it, you will no longer perceive it.

2. Today's idea applies to both your inner and outer worlds, which are the same. But, since you perceive them as different, the practice periods will consist of two phases: one involving the world that you perceive outside of you, and the other the world that you perceive in your mind. For today's exercises, try to introduce the idea that both are in your imagination.

3. Begin your morning and evening practice periods by repeating today's idea two or three times as you look around you at the world that seems outside of you. Then, close your eyes and look around your inner world. Try to treat them as both equally possible of being caused by your imagination. Repeat today's idea slowly, as often as you want, and watch the images your imagination presents to your awareness.

4. Spend three to five minutes for the practice periods. Do no less than three minutes, but you may do more than five minutes, if you find the exercise restful. To help this, choose a time when you are less likely to be distracted, and when you feel ready for the lesson.

5. Use today's idea throughout the day, as often as possible. These shorter applications consist of repeating today's idea to yourself slowly as you observe either your inner or your outer world. It does not matter which you choose, since they are the same.

6. Also, apply today's idea to any situation which distresses you. Say to yourself:

'I have invented this situation, which I perceive.'

Mentor's Notes

Today's lesson refers to both the *how* and *what* of perception. *How* you perceive the world will change when you want it to; the world itself will disappear when you no longer want it at all. As you change *how* you perceive the world through your Real Perception, it will have less and less value for you, until you finally let it go altogether. This will happen when you have completely learned through it that you are One with God.

Lesson 33

'There is another way to perceive the world.'

1. With today's idea, you can shift your perception of both your inner and your outer worlds. Devote a full five minutes to each practice period, morning and evening. In these practice periods, repeat today's idea as often as you find comfortable, making sure to remain unhurried. Alternate between observing your outer and your inner perceptions, but without abruptly shifting between them.

2. Simply glance around the world that you perceive as outside of you, then close your eyes, and observe your inner thoughts equally casually. Try to remain detached from both, and maintain this detachment as you repeat the idea throughout the day.

3. Your shorter exercise periods should be as frequent as possible. Also, when any situation arises which tempts you to become disturbed, say:

'There is another way to perceive this.'

4. Remember to apply today's idea the moment that you are aware of distress. It may be necessary to take a minute or so to sit quietly and repeat the idea to yourself several times. Closing your eyes for this will probably be helpful.

Lesson 34

'I can perceive Peace instead of this.'

1. Today's idea describes the other way of seeing, which you acknowledged yesterday. Peace of mind is clearly an internal state. It begins with your own thoughts, and extends outward in your perception. From your Peaceful mind will come a Peaceful perception of the world.

2. Do three practice periods for today's exercises: one in the morning, one in the evening, and one any time in-between, when you feel most ready for it. Do the exercises with your eyes closed, because today's idea should be applied to your inner world.

3. Spend five minutes searching your mind in the practice periods. Search for fearful thoughts, anxiety-provoking situations, 'offending' personalities or events, and any other form of un-loving thoughts. Note them all casually, repeating today's idea slowly as you watch each thought arise, and as you let it go to be replaced by the next thought.

4. If you run out of subjects, then continue to repeat today's idea to yourself in an unhurried manner, without applying it to anything specific. Be sure, however, that you do not exclude any subjects which come to mind.

5. You should also have many shorter applications of today's idea whenever you feel your Peace of mind threatened in any way. The purpose in this is to prevent you from feeling tempted to give into un-Peaceful thoughts throughout the day. When a specific form of un-Loving thought arises, say to yourself:

'I can see Peace in this situation, instead of what I am seeing now.'

6. If your lack of Peace takes a more generalized form, such as depression, anxiety, anger, or worry, then use today's idea in its original form. If you find that saying today's idea once is not enough to help you change your mind in a specific context, try to devote

several minutes to repeating today's idea slowly, until you feel a sense of relief. Tell yourself specifically:

> 'I can replace my feelings of (depression, anxiety, anger, worry, etc.) or thoughts about (a situation, person, event, etc.) with Peace.'

Mentor's Notes

Don't worry about what Peace looks or feels like. Today, you are simply opening your mind to the awareness that you can experience Peace instead of anything else. You do not have to make this happen. When you are open to Peace, It will enter your awareness of Itself.

Lesson 35

'My mind is part of God's Mind. I am very Holy.'

1. Today's idea does not describe the way that you see yourself in your identification with a personal self. But it does describe what your True Perception will show you. Because you believe that you are in a world, it is difficult for you to believe that you are Holy. In fact, the reason that you believe that you are in a world is because you do not believe that you are Holy.

2. You will believe that you are a part of the environment in which you perceive yourself. This is because you perceive the environment that you want. You want a world to protect the image of yourself that you made, and this image is a part of the world that you made. What you see while you believe that you are in a world, you see through the eyes of the image of yourself that you made to be in the world. This is not your Real Perception; an image does not really see.

3. Today's idea presents you with a very different perception of yourself from the perception of the personal mind. By first establishing your Source, it establishes your True Identity. You will apply today's idea differently today, because its emphasis is on you as the perceiver, rather than on what and how you perceive.

4. Today, you have three 5-minute practice periods. Begin by repeating today's idea to yourself, then close your eyes and search your mind for the various kinds of descriptive terms that you use for yourself. Include all personal-self attributes that you ascribe to yourself, positive and negative, desirable and undesirable, puffed-up or insecure. All of them are equally unreal, because they do not come from your Real Perception.

5. In the early part of your mind-searching exercises, you may emphasize what you consider your 'negative' attributes. Later, you will probably use more self-inflating terms for yourself. Recognize that the direction of your fantasies about yourself does not matter. Illusions have no meaning in Reality; all illusions are equally untrue.

6. A list for today's idea may be like:

'I see myself as imposed on.'
'I see myself as depressed.'
'I see myself as failing.'
'I see myself as endangered.'
'I see myself as helpless.'
'I see myself as victorious.'
'I see myself as losing out.
'I see myself as charitable.'
'I see myself as virtuous.'

7. Do not think of these terms in an abstract way; let them come to you as various situations in which you see yourself cross your mind. Pick any specific situation that occurs to you, identify the descriptive term or terms that you feel are appropriate to describe you in the situation, and use it with today's idea. After you have named each attribute add:

'But my mind is part of God's Mind. I am very Holy.'

8. In these longer exercises, you may have intervals when you run out of specific attributes. Do not 'dig out' any specific attributes, and also do not omit any specific attributes. Simply relax, and repeat today's idea until something occurs to you. Do not use force or discrimination in your mind searching.

9. As often as possible during the day, pick up any specific attribute or attributes that you are ascribing to yourself at the time, and apply today's idea to them in the form stated just above for each of them. If nothing in particular occurs to you, just repeat today's idea to yourself with your eyes closed.

Mentor's Notes

The first paragraph turns upside down the way that the personal mind thinks: It teaches you that, because you perceive yourself in a world (separate from God), you are not Holy (One with God). But, in fact, you first believe that you are not Holy, *then* you perceive yourself in a world, which seems to 'prove' this. This reverses cause and effect, so that you understand that the world is not the *cause* of your sense of separation from God, but is the *result* of your belief that you can be separate from God.

It is very important that you realize that, however you believe yourself to be as a 'person', it does not matter at all to God, because God does not know you as a 'person', but as One with God. For you to remember that you are One with God, you do not have to become a certain type of person, but rather you must let go of your identification with a personal self altogether. The attributes, attitudes, and behaviors that you ascribe to yourself as a personal self are never 'good' or 'bad' or 'right' or 'wrong'; they are always only meaningless, because they are never really you.

Lesson 36

'My Holiness envelops everything that I perceive.'

1. Today's idea extends yesterday's idea from you, the perceiver, to the world that you perceive. You are Holy, because your mind is part of God's Mind. Because you are Holy, your Real Perception must be Holy as well. Since your mind is part of God's Mind, you must be Innocent, or a part of God's Mind would be guilty. To be Innocent, you must be wholly without guilt, because you cannot be a little guilty and still be Innocent. Your Real Perception is related to God's Holiness in your mind, not to the personal self, and therefore not to the body.

2. Today, you have four 3-5 minute practice periods. Try to distribute them evenly throughout your day, and make many shorter applications throughout the day to maintain your freedom from un-Loving thoughts. Your longer practice periods should take this form:

3. First, close your eyes, and repeat today's idea several times slowly. Then, open your eyes, and look slowly around you, applying today's idea specifically to whatever you see. Do this casually. For example, say:

'My holiness envelops that rug.'
'My holiness envelops that wall.'
'My holiness envelops these fingers.'
'My holiness envelops that chair.'
'My holiness envelops that body.'
'My holiness envelops this pen.'

Close your eyes several times during the practice period, and repeat today's idea to yourself. Then, open your eyes and continue with specific subjects.

4. For your shorter practice periods, close your eyes and repeat today's idea. Look around you and repeat it again, then conclude

with one more repetition with your eyes closed. Be sure to always apply today's idea slowly and effortlessly.

Mentor's Notes

This lesson introduces the idea that for you to identify with a personal self is for you to identify with guilt. In Truth, you are not a personal self in a body in a world, but you are One with God and Wholly Innocent. Any guilt you may feel in association with doing these lessons does not come from God, but from your identification with a personal self.

Lesson 37

'My Holiness blesses the world that I perceive.'

1. This idea contains a glimmer of your function in your perception that you are in a world, as given by your Christ Mind. Your purpose is to see the world through your Holiness, so that you and your mind where you perceive a world are blessed together. There is no loss in this; only gain to your entire mind. This lesson signifies the end of your sacrifice to the personal self, because it offers you your Limitless Mind.

2. There is no other way that the idea of sacrifice can be removed from your mind's thinking. Any other way of perceiving inevitably demands that you ask someone or something in the world to sacrifice to make you whole, and as a result, you suffer without understanding that it is because you are limiting yourself to a personal self. But your Wholeness is restored to you through your Real Perception, and It blesses your perception of the world, because you ask nothing of the world. When you see yourself as Whole, you will make no demands of the world as though it is something separate from your mind.

3. Your Holiness saves your perception of the world, because you can extend your Holiness to it. You do not do this by preaching or telling the world anything, but merely by quietly recognizing that, in your Holiness, everything in your mind is blessed with you.

4. Today's four exercises are 3-5 minutes. Begin by repeating today's idea, then spend a minute or so looking around you as you apply today's idea to what you see, in this way:

'My Holiness blesses this chair.'
'My Holiness blesses that window.'
'My Holiness blesses this body.'

Then close your eyes, and apply today's idea to any person who crosses your mind, using their name:

'My Holiness blesses you, (name).'

5. You may practice today's lesson by alternating, in whatever way you choose, between applying it to what you see with your eyes open, and to those individuals that you picture with your eyes closed. Finish the exercise with a repetition of today's idea with your eyes closed, then open your eyes and say it again.

6. Throughout the day, repeat today's idea as often as you can. Say it silently to anyone you meet, using their specific name. It is particularly essential to do this if you have a negative reaction to someone. Offer them the blessing of your own Holiness immediately, so that you learn to keep your Holiness in your awareness.

Mentor's Notes

God did not make the world, so it has no inherent purpose from God. But, because the world is neutral, your Christ Mind has given it the purpose of reminding you that you are One with God.

Your mind and what it perceives are not separate, as the personal mind would have you believe. As you perceive the world, you perceive yourself. You can project the personal mind's illusion of separation onto the world and remain in a perception of separation from God and from the rest of your mind, which you perceive as a world outside of you, or you can extend your Holiness to the world to remember that you are Holy.

Lesson 38

'My Holiness can undo any discord that I perceive.'

1. Your Holiness reverses all the 'laws' of the world in your mind. It is beyond every restriction of time, space, distance, or limits of any kind. Your Holiness is totally unlimited in Power, because it establishes your Oneness with God.

2. Through your Holiness, the Power of God is made manifest to you. Through your Holiness, the Power of God is made available to you. The Power of God can undo discord in any form that you perceive. Your Holiness, then, can remove all pain, end all sorrow, and solve all problems. It can do so in connection with yourself, and anyone that you perceive. Its Power can help anyone that you perceive without exception, because Its Power can save anyone that you perceive without exception. Your mind is one.

3. You are God's Whole Creation, and you are Holy. In today's exercises, you will apply the Power of your Holiness to all problems, difficulties, and sufferings in any form that you happen to perceive. You will make no distinction between yourself and others, because there is no distinction between you and what is in your mind.

4. In your four 5-minute practice periods, repeat today's idea, close your eyes, then search your mind for any loss or unhappiness that you perceive. Make no distinction between a situation that you perceive as difficult for you, and one that you perceive as difficult for another. Identify the situation specifically, and also apply the name of the person concerned when appropriate. Use this form for today's practice:

> 'My Holiness can undo the discord I perceive in the situation involving ______, in which I perceive myself.'
> 'My Holiness can undo the discord I perceive in the situation involving ______ (situation), in which I perceive ______ (person).

5. You might want to occasionally vary this procedure by adding

some relevant thoughts of your own. You might include such thoughts as:

> 'My Holiness can undo any unhappy situation, because the Power of God lies in It.'

Introduce whatever variations work for you, but keep the exercises focused on the theme, 'My Holiness can undo any discord that I perceive.' Today's lesson begins to instill in you a sense that you have power over everything that you perceive, because of What you are.

6. In frequent, shorter applications, apply today's idea in its original form, unless a specific problem comes to mind that involves you or another. Then, use the more specific form of today's idea.

Mentor's Notes

Today's lesson applies to both *how* and *what* you perceive. When you really get today's lesson, sometimes *how* you perceive a situation changes, because you come to recognize that there is really no discord there; sometimes *what* appears in the world as discord seems to dissolve in the world. Whether it is one or the other is not important, nor is it your concern which it should be. When you change your mind, your perception automatically changes in the way that is most appropriate for the situation. If you insist on how the change should manifest, you are defining yourself by the perceived discord, rather than by its Solution.

Lesson 39

'My Holiness is my salvation from hell.'

1. If guilt is hell, what is its opposite? Just as in the Text for this course, the ideas in these exercises are very simple, clear, and obvious. It is not concerned with intellectual feats or logical toys. It deals only in the very plain, which you have overlooked in the clouds of complexity with which you think with a personal mind.

2. If guilt is hell, what is its opposite? Surely, answering this is not difficult. If you hesitate to answer, it is not because the question has more than one answer. But do you believe that guilt is hell? If you did, you would see how direct and simple the Text is, and you would not need this Workbook at all. You don't need practice to gain what is already yours.

3. Lesson 37 already stated that your Holiness saves your perception of the world, but what about your own salvation? You cannot extend in your perception what you do not have. To save your perception of the world, you must already have within you What you extend to it. Today's exercises apply to you in the recognition that your salvation from hell is crucial to save your entire mind from hell. As you apply the exercises to yourself, your perception of the world will benefit.

4. Your Holiness is the answer to every question that you have ever asked, that you are asking now, and that you will ask in the future. Your Holiness means the end of your guilt, so it means the end of hell for you. Your Holiness saves your mind where you perceive a world, so it is your salvation as well. You cannot be excluded from the Holiness that you extend in your perception. God does not know un-Holiness, so God must know you.

5. Do four 5-minute practice periods today. Longer and more frequent practice periods are encouraged. You may exceed both the amount and the length of the suggested practice sessions.

6. Begin the practice periods as usual, repeating today's idea to yourself. Then, with your eyes closed, search out un-Loving

thoughts in your mind in whatever form they appear: uneasiness, anger, depression, fear, worry, attack, insecurity, etc. Whatever form they take, they are un-Loving, therefore frightening, so it is from them that you need to be saved.

7. Specific situations or personalities which you associate with un-Loving thoughts of any kind are suitable subjects for today's exercises. It is important for your salvation that you see them differently. It is your blessing on them that will save you from hell, and bring you your Real Perception.

8. Slowly, and without conscious selection or emphasis on any thought in particular, search your mind for every thought that stands between you and your salvation from hell. Apply today's idea to each of them in this way:

> 'My un-Loving thoughts about ______ are keeping me in hell. But my Holiness is my salvation.'

9. You may find these practice periods easier if you break them up with several short intervals, during which you simply repeat today's idea to yourself a few times slowly. You may also find it helpful to include a few short intervals when you relax, and do not think of anything at all. Sustained concentration can be very hard for you at first; it will become much easier as your mind becomes more disciplined and less distractible.

10. Feel free to introduce variety into the exercise periods in any form that you like, but do not change today's idea as you vary your method of applying it. However you state it, you want to mean that your Holiness is your salvation. End each practice period by repeating today's idea in its original form, adding:

> 'If guilt is hell, what is its opposite?'

11. Three or four times an hour, if possible, ask yourself this question, and repeat today's idea. When you are tempted into hellish

thoughts, say to yourself:

'My Holiness is my salvation from this.'

Mentor's Notes

Depending on your own personal story, you may judge that the idea that the world that you perceive with a personal mind is hell as accurate, ridiculous, or something in between. You also might find it frightening or offensive. But the state of identifying with a personal self *is* guilt, because it is your belief that you attacked God. The evidence that you believe that you are guilty is there in your un-Loving thoughts and perceptions. But remember, the idea that you are guilty is only in your mind; it does not come from God.

Of course guilt is hell, and of course it's opposite is your Innocence or Holiness. Both are in your mind, but only your Holiness is Truth, and only your awareness of your Holiness can save you from the hell of guilt.

Lesson 40

'I am blessed in my Oneness with God.'

1. Today you will begin to assert the happy things to which you are entitled, because you are One with God. Instead of long practice periods, you will have frequent short ones. Once every ten minutes is recommended, and you should try to stick to this schedule. If you forget, simply do the exercise again. If you have long interruptions where your attention must be elsewhere, simply do the exercise again as soon as you can. Whenever you remember to do so, do the exercise.

2. You don't need to close your eyes for today's exercises, but you may find it helpful to do so. However, you will probably find yourself in situations where closing your eyes is not reasonable. Do not miss a practice period because of this. If you sincerely want to, you can do today's exercises under any circumstances.

3. Today's exercises take little time or effort. Repeat today's idea, then add several attributes which you associate with your Oneness with God. For example, you might say:

> 'I am blessed in my Oneness with God. I am Happy, Peaceful, Loving, and Whole.'
>
> Or:
>
> 'I am blessed in my Oneness with God. I am Calm, Quiet, and Confident.'

If you only have a very brief moment available, simply tell yourself that you are blessed in your Oneness with God.

Lesson 41

'God is with me, wherever I perceive myself.'

1. Today's idea will eventually completely overcome any loneliness or sense of abandonment you feel because of your identification with a limited personal self. Depression, anxiety, worry, helplessness, misery, suffering, and an intense fear of loss are all the inevitable result of your belief that you are separate from God.

2. Your split mind has invented many 'cures' for what it calls these 'ills of the world'. But one thing it does not want you to do is to question the reality of the world that it teaches you is their cause. Yet these 'ills' cannot be 'cured' by the world, because the world is not their real cause. Today's idea has the power to end all this foolishness in your mind forever. And it *is* all foolish, despite the serious and tragic forms these 'ills' may take.

3. Deep within you is Everything that is Perfect and ready to radiate outward in your perception. It will cure all of your sorrow, pain, fear, and loss, because it will heal your mind, which thinks these things are real, and which has suffered because of its allegiance to them.

4. You are never deprived of your Perfect Holiness, because It is with you, wherever you perceive yourself; you can never really suffer, because the Source of Joy is with you, wherever you perceive yourself; you are never limited to a personal self, because the Source of Limitlessness is with you, wherever you perceive yourself. Nothing can destroy your Peace of mind, because God is with you wherever you perceive yourself.

5. You probably don't believe this yet, because the Truth is hidden deep within you, under heavy, insane, dense, and obscuring thoughts that permeate all that you perceive. Today, you make your first real attempt to go past these dark thoughts to the Truth beyond them.

6. Today, you have only one long practice period. In the morning, as soon as possible after you wake up, sit quietly for three to five

minutes with your eyes closed. Repeat today's idea slowly, then do not make an effort to think about anything. Turn inward, past all idle thoughts of the world. Enter very deeply into your own mind, and let go of all thoughts that distract you.

7. If it helps you to quiet your mind, you may occasionally repeat today's idea slowly to yourself. But, most importantly, sink down and inward in your mind, away from the world and all thoughts of the world. You are attempting to reach past appearances to approach Reality.

8. It is very easy for you to reach God, because it is the most natural thing for you, as you are One with God. Your mind will open to God if you simply believe that it is possible. This exercise can bring startling results for you, even this first time. It can never fail completely, and instant success *is* possible. In later lessons, you will be given more details for this type of exercise.

9. Often throughout the day, repeat today's idea slowly to yourself, preferably with your eyes closed. Think of what you are saying, and contemplate what the words mean. Concentrate on the Holiness that they imply about you, on the Constant Companionship that is always with you, and on the Complete Protection which surrounds you.

10.You can indeed laugh at fearful thoughts, when you remember that God is with you, wherever you perceive yourself.

Mentor's Notes

Whenever you simply open your mind to God as this lesson teaches, you are truly praying. You may not feel immediate results, but you will find your overall experience transforming toward Peace, even when you are not meditating. This simple communing with God is the most important, and the mort transformative, type of practice that you can do.

Lesson 42

'God is my Strength. Real Perception is God's Gift to me.'

1. Today's idea combines two powerful thoughts, both very important to you. It also describes a cause-and-effect relationship that explains why you cannot fail to achieve your goal of remembering your Oneness with God. You *will* gain your Real Perception, because it is the Will of God that you do so. It is God's Strength, not the personal mind, Which gives you Power. And Real Perception is God's Gift to you; it does not come from the personal mind.

2. God is indeed your Strength, and What God Gives is wholly given to you. This means that you can receive It anytime and in any situation in which you perceive yourself. From your Christ Mind's perspective, your passage through time and space is not random: Every moment and every place is the right time and the right place for you to open yourself to your Real Perception. It is the Strength of God that God is Everywhere, Always, and it is the same for God's Gifts.

3. Today, you have two 3-5 minute practice periods, one as soon as possible after you wake up, and one as close as possible to when you go to sleep again. However, it is more important that you do the practice when you can sit quietly by yourself and when you feel ready, than that you be too concerned with the actual time you do the practice.

4. Begin today's exercise by repeating today's idea slowly to yourself, with your eyes open and looking around you. Then, close your eyes and repeat the idea even slower. Sit quietly, and let go of all thoughts, except those that occur to you in relation to today's idea. For example, you may think:

> 'Real Perception must be possible, because God gives It to me.'
>
> Or:
>
> 'The Gifts that God gives to me *are* mine, *because* They come from God.'

5. Any thought that occurs to you that is related to today's idea is suitable for the exercises. In fact, you might be surprised at the amount of thoughts that you have that reveal your understanding of this course. Let these thoughts simply come to you, but don't let your mind wander or let irrelevant thoughts intrude. You also may reach a point where no thoughts come to your mind. If distractions occur or nothing comes to mind, open your eyes, and repeat today's idea again while you look slowly around you. Then, close your eyes, and repeat today's idea once more as you continue to look for related thoughts.

6. Active searching for relevant thoughts is not appropriate for today's exercises. Just step back, and let the thoughts come. If you find this difficult, then spend the practice period alternating between slow repetitions of today's idea with your eyes open, then with your eyes closed. This is better than straining to find suitable thoughts.

7. There is no limit to the number of short practice periods that will be of benefit to you today. Today's idea is the first in bringing thoughts together to teach you that you are studying a unified thought system in which nothing you need is lacking, and nothing contradictory or irrelevant is included.

8. The more often you repeat today's idea, the more often you will be reminding yourself that the Goal of this course is important to you, and that you have not forgotten It.

Mentor's Notes

Real Perception is God's correction for your error of perceiving yourself as separate from God. It is God's Gift to you and, like God, It is always with you. You do not perceive God with your Real Perception, but you perceive *Lovingly*, like God would if God perceived. God is beyond perception, which is open to interpretation, because God is Knowledge, Which simply *is*. This is explained further in the next lesson.

You may experience your Real Perception as a Perception of Something beyond the world, or as a transformed perception of the world.

Lesson 43

'God is my Source. My perception has no Reality apart from God.'

1. *Perception* is not an attribute of God, because God is *Knowledge*. But the Holy Spirit in your mind is One with God, and It is the Mediator between your *Knowledge of God* and *perception*, which your split mind made. Without this Link, perception would replace Knowledge in your mind, which is impossible. But with this Link, your perception will become so purified that it will lead you back to Knowledge of God. From the Holy Spirit's perspective, that is perception's only real function.

2. You do not *perceive* in God, so perception does not really exist. Yet, perception has a mighty function in your salvation from what has not really happened. Perception was made by your split mind for an unholy purpose, but with the Holy Spirit it becomes the means of restoring your Holiness to your awareness. Perception has no meaning of its own, but the Holy Spirit gives it a meaning close to God's. Your healed perception will be the means by which you forgive the 'evidence' of your separation from God in all that you perceive, and therefore forgive yourself.

3. You cannot be apart from God, so you cannot really perceive apart from God. Whatever you do, you do in God, because you think with God's Mind. Your perception is real to the extent that it shares the Holy Spirit's purpose, so with your Real Perception you do not perceive apart from God.

4. Do three 5-minute practice periods today, one as early and one as late in the day as possible, and one that you undertake at a time when it is convenient, and you are ready. Begin these practice periods by repeating today's idea with your eyes open. Then, look around you, and apply it specifically to what you see. Four or five subjects for this phase of the exercise are enough. For example, you may say:

'God is my Source. I cannot really perceive that desk apart from God.'

5. Although this phase should be short, make sure you select subjects randomly, and do not deliberately include or exclude anything. For the longer phase, close your eyes, repeat today's idea, then let whatever relevant thought occurs to you add to the idea in your own individual way. Thoughts such as:

'I perceive through the eyes of forgiveness.'
'I perceive the world as blessed.'
'The world can show me my True Self.'
'I perceive my own Thoughts, Which are like God's.'

Any thought that relates to today's idea is appropriate. These thoughts do not have to obviously state today's idea, but they should not oppose it, either.

6. If you find your mind wandering, if you begin to be aware of thoughts that are out of accord with today's idea, or if you seem to be unable to think of anything, open your eyes, repeat the first phase of today's exercise, then attempt the second phase again. Do no allow yourself to become preoccupied with irrelevant thoughts for any length of time. Return to the first phase of today's exercise as often as necessary to prevent this.

7. Your shorter applications of today's ideas may vary in form according to the situations in which you find yourself. For example, when you are with someone, try to remember to say to them in your mind:

'God is my Source. I really cannot perceive you apart from God.'

Apply this as equally to strangers as to those you think of as close to you. Try not to make these types of distinctions today.

8. Apply today's idea to various situations throughout the day,

particularly to those which seem to distress you in any way. For this purpose, apply the idea in this form:

'God is my Source. I cannot really perceive this apart from God.'

9. If no particular subject presents itself, simply repeat today's idea in its original form throughout the day. Try not to let any long periods of time pass without remembering today's idea and therefore your function.

Mentor's Notes

As was stated in an earlier lesson, when you think apart from God, your mind is really blank. So, when you perceive apart from God, nothing is really happening. The only 'reality' perception can be said to have is when it comes from the Holy Spirit in your mind and reflects God's Love.

If you have not yet experienced your Real Perception, do not be concerned with how the world looks with It. For now, it is enough that you recognize that the way that you perceive things with a personal mind is not the only way for you to perceive, and that it does not reflect Reality.

Lesson 44

'God is the Light of my Real Perception.'

1. Today you continue with yesterday's idea, with another dimension added to it. You cannot use your Real Perception with a mind that is darkened by your denial of God. And the personal mind cannot make the Light in Which you perceive with your Real Perception. This Light comes from God and is an Aspect of your mind in Oneness with God. You can deny God and think that you perceive something in the darkness, but God's Light reflects Reality, Which you share with God. Reality and darkness cancel out each other in your mind, but Reality and Light go together in your mind, because both are from God.

2. In order for you to perceive with your Real Perception, you must recognize that the Light from Which your Real Perception comes to you is within you. Your Real Perception does not look outside of you, and the Light that is the Source of your Real Perception is not outside of you. This Light is with you always, making your Real Perception possible in every circumstance.

3. Today, you are going to attempt to reach the Light within you. For this purpose, you will use a form of exercise which you used before and will use more and more. It is particularly difficult for your untrained mind, but this form of exercise is a major goal of your mind training. You need this training, so that you can use your Real Perception.

4. Today, do at least three practice periods of three to five minutes each. Take longer if you find time slipping past with no sense of strain. The form of today's exercise is the most easy and natural one for a trained mind; it is a most difficult and unnatural exercise for an untrained mind.

5. Your mind is no longer wholly untrained, and you are quite ready to learn today's form of exercise. Still, you may find that you are very resistant, because, with this form of practice, you leave behind everything that you now believe and the whole world that

you made up. Properly speaking, this is your release from hell. But the personal mind will tell you that you are losing your identity and descending into hell.

6. If you can detach from the personal mind even a little, you will have no problem recognizing that its opposition and its fears are meaningless. You might find it helpful to remind yourself throughout the exercise that to reach the Light is to escape from the dark, whatever the personal mind may say to the contrary. God is the Light of your Real Perception. You are attempting to reach God.

7. Begin your practice periods by repeating today's idea with your eyes open. Then, slowly close your eyes, repeating today's idea several times. Sink into your mind, past every type of distraction. Your mind will not stop doing this, unless you stop it yourself, because your mind is merely taking its natural course. Try to observe your passing thoughts without attachment, and let them go by.

8. No one particular approach is necessary for this type of exercise, but what you need is a sense of the importance of what you are doing, of its immeasurable value to you, and an awareness that you are attempting something very Holy. Your salvation from hell is the happiest goal that you can accomplish. It is the only goal that has any real meaning for you, because it is the only one that has any real value for you.

9. If you are resistant in any form, pause long enough to repeat today's idea, keeping your eyes closed, unless you are afraid. If this is so, you will probably find it more reassuring to briefly keep your eyes open. Try to return to the exercise with your eyes closed as soon as possible.

10. If you are doing the exercises correctly, you will feel yourself relax, and you will even sense that you are approaching, if not actually entering, the Light. Try to visualize light, formless and limitless, as you let go of all thoughts about the world. Remember, these thoughts cannot hold you to the world, unless you give them the power to do so.

11. Repeat today's idea often throughout the day, with your eyes opened or closed; whichever seems best for you at the time. Above all, be determined to remember today's idea.

Mentor's Notes

'Light' is used throughout spiritual teachings as an apt description of the experience of God, because the experience of God is one of your mind being filled with a Light Which extends Infinitely. This is why one who has come to full God-consciousness is called 'en-*light*-en-ed'.

'Light versus darkness' is also an apt metaphor for being aware of God versus denying God, because light and darkness are mutually exclusive, just as being aware of God and denying God are mutually exclusive. When light comes, darkness is banished; when God dawns on your mind again, your denial of God disappears.

'Light' also works in the sense of 'weight'. The limited experience of the personal mind is binding and 'heavy', relative to the Free and Limitless experience of God. The Joy of God is a feeling of 'light-heartedness' and of being 'uplifted', as though a weight is lifted, and you are 'lighter' and can float free of limitations.

In paragraph 8, it says that no one particular approach is necessary for this form of practice. This means that you may use another technique to quiet your mind. For example, instead of slipping down deeper into your mind, you may picture yourself rising up past the personal mind's thoughts. Or you may simply sit still and watch your thoughts go past as your mind gets quieter and quieter. Use whatever technique works for you to still and quiet your mind, so that you can commune in Peace with God.

Lesson 45

'God is the Mind with Which I really think.'

1. Today's idea holds the key to your Real Thoughts. Your Real Thoughts are nothing that you think you think now with a personal mind, just as what you think you perceive with a personal mind is not related to your Real Perception at all. There is no relationship between What is Real and what you are used to thinking is real. Nothing that you now think are your real thoughts resembles your Real Thoughts in any way. Nothing that you think you perceive bears any resemblance to What your Real Perception will show you.

2. You can only really think with the Mind of God, so God's Thoughts are your Thoughts. They are the same Thoughts, because they are thought with the same Mind. The Thoughts that you think with God never leave your mind, because they cannot leave their Source. You and your Thoughts are in the Mind of God, and your Real Thoughts are still in your mind, as God is.

3. Where are your Real Thoughts, then? Today you will attempt to reach Them in your mind, where They are. They must still be there, because They cannot leave their Source. The Thoughts that you think with the Mind of God are Eternal, being One with God.

4. Your three 5-minute practice periods will take the same form as yesterday's exercises. You will leave the unreal for the Real; you will deny the world in favor of the Truth. You will not let the world hold you back; you will not let the personal mind tell you that what God wants you to do is impossible. Instead, you will recognize that *only* what God wants you to do *is* possible.

5. You will also recognize that only what God wants you to do is what you want to do. You cannot fail in what God wants you to do, and you have every reason to be confident that you will succeed today, because it is the Will of God that you do so.

6. Begin today's exercises by repeating today's idea to yourself with your eyes closed. Then, spend a short period thinking a few relevant thoughts of your own, keeping today's idea in your mind.

After you have added some four or five thoughts of your own, repeat today's idea again, and gently tell yourself:

'My Real Thoughts are in my mind. I want to find Them.'

Then try to go past all the unreal thoughts of the personal mind, which cover the Truth in your mind, to reach the Eternal.

7. Under all the senseless thoughts and mad ideas with which you have cluttered your mind, are the Thoughts that you have always thought with God. They are in your mind now, completely unchanged. They will always be in your mind, exactly as They have always been. Everything you think apart from Them will change, but Their Foundation is Changeless.

8. It is this Foundation toward Which today's exercises are directed. Here, your mind is joined with God's Mind; Here, your thoughts are One with God's Thoughts. For this kind of practice, only one attitude is necessary: Approach it as you would an altar dedicated in Heaven to God and to your Oneness with God. This is the Place that you are trying to reach. You probably do not yet realize how far you are trying to go. But, even with the little understanding that you have already gained, you should be able to remind yourself that this is not an idle game, but an exercise in Holiness, and an attempt to reach Heaven.

9. In today's shorter exercise periods, try to remember how important it is to you to understand the Holiness of your mind, which thinks with God. Take a minute or two, as you repeat today's idea throughout the day, to appreciate your mind's Holiness. Stand aside, if only for a moment, from all thoughts that are unworthy of God, with Which you are One. And thank God for the Thoughts that you think with God.

Lesson 46

'God is the Love in Which I forgive.'

1. God does not forgive you, because God has never condemned you, and there must be condemnation for forgiveness to be necessary. You greatly need to forgive, or to let go of, the world, because it is an illusion to which you have condemned yourself. By forgiving the world, you release yourself from illusions. When you withhold forgiveness, you bind yourself to illusions. You can condemn only yourself, so you can forgive only yourself.

2. Though God does not forgive, It is God's Love that is the basis of your forgiving yourself. Fear condemns and Love forgives. Your forgiving, then, undoes what you made with fear, returning your mind to an awareness of God. Your forgiving can truly be called your salvation from hell. It is the means by which illusions disappear from your mind.

3. Today, do at least three 5-minute practice periods, with as many shorter ones as possible. Begin the longer practice periods, as usual, by repeating today's idea. Close your eyes as you do so, and search your mind for a minute or two for those people who you have not yet released from the personal mind's projections. It does not matter 'how much' you have not forgiven them. Forgiveness is total, or it is not forgiveness at all.

4. If you are doing these exercises well, you will have no difficulty in finding many people who you have not forgiven your projections onto them. It is a safe rule that anyone that you do not like is a suitable subject for today. Mention each one by name:

'God is the Love in Which I forgive you, (name).'

5. The purpose of this first phase in today's practice periods is to put you in a position to forgive yourself. After you have applied today's idea to all of those who come to mind, tell yourself:

'God is the Love in Which I forgive myself.'

Then spend the remainder of the practice period adding related ideas, such as:

'God is the Love with Which I love myself.'
'God is the Love with Which I am blessed.'

6. You may vary considerably the form of the ideas that you use, but do not lose sight of today's central idea. For example, you might say:

'I cannot be guilty, because I am One with God.'
'I live in a state of forgiveness, because I have done nothing wrong.'
'My mind is loved by God, so fear is impossible.'
'I have no need to attack anyone, because Love does not condemn me.'

Be sure to end the practice period by stating today's idea in its original form.

7. In your shorter practice periods, you may use either today's idea in its original form, or a related form. But, be sure to make specific applications as they are needed. They will be needed any time during the day when you become aware of any negative reaction to anyone, present or not. In this event, in your mind tell them:

'God is the Love in Which I forgive you.'

Mentor's Notes

Remember, true forgiveness is not the forgiveness that you have learned through the personal mind. True forgiveness recognizes that *only God is Real,* so you can let go of anything that is not-God. God is the Love in Which you forgive, because you recognize that God's Love is What is Real, not the 'story' that you have for someone in the world or for what they did to you.

Lesson 47

'God is the Strength in Which I trust.'

1. If you are trusting in the personal self with which you are used to identifying, then you have every reason to be apprehensive, anxious, and fearful. What can it predict or control? What is there in it that you can count on? Does it have the ability to be aware of all facets of a problem, and to resolve them in such a way that only good can come of it? What does it have that gives you the recognition of the right solution, and the guarantee that it will be accomplished?

2. With the personal mind, you can do none of these things. If you believe that you can, then you are putting your trust where it is unjustified, and you are justifying your fear, anxiety, depression, anger, and sorrow. You cannot put your faith in weakness and feel safe, but if you put your faith in your Real Strength, you will not feel weak.

3. God is your Safety in every circumstance. The Holy Spirit within you speaks for God in every situation, and in all aspects of every situation, telling you exactly what to do to feel God's Strength and Protection. There are no exceptions to this, because God does not make exceptions, and the Holy Spirit thinks as God does.

4. Today, you will reach past the personal self's weakness to the Source of your Real Strength. Do at least four 5-minute practice periods; more and longer practice periods are encouraged. Close your eyes, and begin, as usual, by repeating today's idea. Then spend a minute or two searching your mind for situations in your life in the world that you have invested with fear. Dismiss each one by telling yourself:

'God is the Strength in Which I trust.'

5. Now, slip past all concerns related to your own sense of inadequacy. Obviously, your being concerned about a situation means that you feel inadequate to handle it. And trusting the limited personal

self, which you have been trusting, will not give you confidence. But the Strength of God within you is successful in all things.

6. Your recognizing the personal self's limitations is a necessary step for you to correct your frightening perceptions, but this does not give you the confidence you need, and to which you are entitled. You must also become aware that confidence in your Real Strength is fully justified in every respect and in every situation.

7. In the second part of your practice periods, reach down to a Place in your mind of Real Safety. You will know that you have reached It when you experience deep Peace, even if only briefly. Let go of all the trivial thoughts that churn and bubble on the surface of your mind, and reach below them to your Oneness with God. There is a Place in you Where there is Perfect Peace, there is a Place in you Where nothing is impossible, there is a Place in you Where the Strength of God abides.

8. Repeat today's idea often throughout the day. Use it as your answer to any disturbance. Remember that Peace is rightfully yours when you invest your Trust in the Strength of God.

Lesson 48

'There is nothing for me to fear.'

1. Today's idea states a simple fact. It is not a fact to you when you identify with a personal self, because illusions are not facts, therefore they inspire fear. But in Truth, there is nothing for you to fear. This is easy for you to recognize, unless you want illusions to be true.

2. Today's practice periods will be very short, very simple, and very frequent. Merely repeat today's idea as often as possible. You can use it with your eyes open anytime and in any situation, but take a minute whenever possible to close your eyes, and repeat today's ideas slowly to yourself several times. It is particularly important that you use this idea immediately if anything disturbs your Peace of mind.

3. Any experience of fear means that you are trusting in the personal self. Your awareness that there is nothing for you to fear means that, somewhere in your mind, you have remembered God, and you have let God's Strength take the place of the personal self's weakness. The instant that you are willing to do this, indeed, there is nothing for you to fear.

Lesson 49

'The Holy Spirit speaks to me all through the day.'

1. It is quite possible for you to listen to the Holy Spirit throughout the day without interrupting your regular activities. This Part of your mind Where Truth abides is in Constant Communication with God, whether you are aware of this or not. The other part of your mind thinks that it is in a world, and it obeys the personal mind's 'laws'. This part is constantly distracted, disorganized, and uncertain.

2. The Holy Spirit in your mind is calm, always at rest, and wholly certain. This is the only Real part of your mind. The other part is a wild illusion, frantic and distraught, and without reality of any kind. Today, try not to listen to it. Try to identify with the Part of your mind Where Stillness and Peace reign forever. Try to hear the Holy Spirit Lovingly remind you that God has not forgotten you, who are One with God.

3. Today, do at least four 5-minute practice periods; do more if possible. You are going to listen for the Holy Spirit reminding you of God and of your True Self in God. You will approach this Happiest and Holiest of Thoughts with confidence, knowing that you are joining your will with God's Will. God wants you to hear the Holy Spirit, because God gave you Holy Spirit, so that you can hear It.

4. Listen in deep silence. Be very still, and open your mind. Go past all the raucous shrieks and sick thoughts that cover your Real Thoughts and obscure your Eternal Link to God. Sink deep into the Peace that waits for you beyond the frantic, riotous thoughts and sights and sounds of the insane world. You do not live there; you are trying to reach your Real Home; you are trying to reach the Place Where you are truly welcome; you are trying to reach God.

5. Remember to repeat today's idea very frequently today. Do so with your eyes open when necessary, but closed when possible. Be sure to sit quietly and repeat today's idea whenever you can, closing your eyes on the world, and inviting the Holy Spirit to speak to you.

Lesson 50

'I am sustained by the Love of God.'

1. Here is your answer to every problem that you could ever confront, today, tomorrow, and throughout time. In your perception that you are in a world, you believe that you are sustained by anything *but* God. You put your faith in trivial and insane symbols: pills, money, 'protective' clothing, prestige, being liked, knowing the 'right' people, and an endless list of forms of nothingness that you endow with magical powers to make you feel safe and whole.

2. All of these things are replacements for God's Love, which you cherish as ways to perpetuate your identification with a body. They are songs of praise to the personal self. Do not put your faith in the worthless, because it will not sustain you.

3. Only the Love of God protects you in every situation. It lifts you out of every trial, and raises you above all the dangers that you perceive in the world, and into Perfect Peace and Safety. It transports you into a State of Mind Which nothing can threaten, nothing can disturb, and Where nothing can intrude upon the Eternal Calm of your Oneness with God.

4. Do not put your faith in illusions; they will fail you. Put all of your faith in the Love of God within you; It is Eternal, Changeless, and Forever Unfailing. This is the answer to whatever confronts you today. Through the Love of God within you, you can resolve all seeming difficulties, without effort and in confidence. Tell yourself this often today; it is your declaration of release from your belief in idols. It is your acknowledgement of the Truth in you.

5. Twice today, for ten minutes, morning and evening, let today's idea sink deep into your consciousness. Repeat it, think about it, let related thoughts come to help you recognize its Truth and allow Peace to flow over you like a blanket of protection and confidence. Do not let idle and foolish thoughts enter your Holy mind, which is One with God. In today's idea is Heaven, Where you rest with God Forever.

Review 1

1. Beginning today, you will have a series of review periods. Each of them will cover five of the ideas that you have already covered, starting with the first and ending with the fiftieth. There are a few short comments after each idea, which you should consider in your reviews. In the practice periods, do the exercises as follows:

2. Begin the day by reading the five ideas for that day, along with the comments that follow each idea. For the rest of the day, it is not necessary for you to follow any particular order in considering them, though you should practice each at least once during the day. Devote two or more minutes to each practice period, thinking about the selected idea and the comments relating to it. Do this as often as possible throughout the day. If any of the five appeals to you more than the others, concentrate on that one most often. At the end of the day, be sure to review them all once more.

3. You do not have to cover the comments that follow each idea, either literally or thoroughly, during the practice periods. Try to emphasize the central point instead, and think about it as part of your review of the idea to which it relates. After you have read the idea and related comments, close your eyes to consider the idea. You should do these exercises alone, in a quiet place if possible.

4. Being alone and in quiet is emphasized for your practice periods at this stage of your learning. However, it will be necessary that you learn to require no special setting in which to apply what you are learning. You need what you are learning most in situations that appear to be upsetting to you, rather than in those that already seem to be calm and quiet. The purpose of your learning is to teach you to bring the Quiet with you, to heal your perceptions of distress and turmoil. You cannot do this by avoiding them and isolating yourself.

5. You will learn that Peace is part of you, and that It only requires your presence to embrace any situation that you perceive. You will learn that there is no limit to where you are, so your Peace

is everywhere with you.

6. For review purposes, some of the ideas are not in their original form. Use them as they are given here. It is not necessary for you to return to the original statements, or to applying them as was originally suggested. These reviews emphasize the relationship among the first fifty ideas that you have covered, and the cohesiveness of the thought system to which they are leading you.

Lesson 51

Today's review covers the following ideas:

1. (1) 'Nothing that I see has a meaning of its own.'

Nothing that I see has a meaning of its own, because there is really nothing there. I must recognize this, so that I can learn to see with my Real Perception. What I think I see with the personal mind is taking the place of my Real Perception. I must let it go by recognizing that it has no meaning, so that my Real Perception can take its place.

2. (2) 'I have given what I see all the meaning that it has for me.'

With the personal mind, I judge everything that I see, and it is only my own judgment that I see. This is not my Real Perception, but an illusion, because these judgments are made apart from my Reality. I am willing to recognize the lack of validity in these judgments, because I want my Real Perception. The personal mind's judgments hurt me, and I do not want to perceive with them.

3. (3) 'I do not understand anything that I see with a personal mind.'

I cannot understand what I see with a personal mind, because its judgment is faulty. What I see with it is a projection of its erroneous thinking, so I do not understand what I see with it, because it is not understandable. There is no sense in my trying to understand it, but there is every reason for me to let it go to make room for What I can understand and love. I can exchange what I see with a personal mind by simply being willing to do so. This is a better choice.

4. (4) 'These thoughts that I think with a personal mind do not mean anything.'

These thoughts of the personal mind of which I am aware do not mean anything, because I think them without God. They are not 'my' thoughts at all, because my Real Thoughts are Thoughts that I think with God. I am not aware of my Real Thoughts, because I have made these other thoughts to take Their place. I am willing to recognize that the thoughts that I think with a personal mind do not mean anything, and to let them go. I choose to have them be replaced by What *they* were intended to replace. Personal thoughts are meaningless, but my Oneness with God lies in the Thoughts that I think with God.

5. (5) 'I am never upset for the reason that I think I am.'

I am never upset for the reason that I think, because I am constantly trying to make real the thoughts that I think with a personal mind. In my identification with a personal self, I make all things my enemy, so that my anger and attacks are justified. I have not realized how much I have misused everything that I perceive by assigning this role to it. I have done this to defend a thought system that hurts me, and that I no longer want. I am willing to let it go.

Lesson 52

Today's review covers the following ideas:

1. (6) 'What is upsetting me is not really here.'

Reality is never frightening; it is impossible for It to upset me. Reality brings me only Perfect Peace. When I am upset, it is always because I have replaced Reality with illusions that I have made. Illusions upset me, because I think that they are real, therefore I regard Reality as an illusion. But my Oneness with God is not affected in any way by this confusion of mine. I am always upset by nothing.

2. (7) 'I perceive only a personal past.'

As I look around, I condemn the world that I perceive, and I think that it is real. I hold a personal past against everyone and everything and make them my enemies. When I have forgiven myself by remembering Who I really am, I will bless everyone and everything that I perceive. I will not perceive a past, therefore I will not perceive enemies. I will look with Love on all that I failed to perceive Truly before.

3. (8) 'My mind is preoccupied with thoughts from a personal past.'

I perceive only the personal mind's thoughts, and the personal mind is preoccupied with its past, so I do not perceive anything as I could see it *now*. I realize that I look on a personal past to prevent Present Love from dawning on my mind. I understand that I am trying to use time against God. I am willing to learn to let go of the past, because I realize that in doing so I give up nothing.

4. (9) 'I perceive nothing as I could perceive it now.'

Since I see nothing as I could see it *now*, then I see nothing. I can only Perceive Truly what is *now*. My choice is not whether to see a personal past or the present, but merely whether to Perceive Truly or not. What I have chosen to perceive has cost me my Real Perception; now I choose again, so I can use my Real Perception.

5. (10) 'My personal thoughts have no meaning.'

Really, I have no private thoughts, but it is only of private thoughts that I seem to be aware. These thoughts mean nothing, because they do not really exist. My mind is One with God, and I want to join with God's Thoughts, rather than obscure What is really mine with pitiful and meaningless private thoughts.

Lesson 53

Today's review covers the following ideas:

1. (11) 'Personal thoughts without meaning are showing me a world without meaning.'

Since the personal thoughts of which I am aware do not mean anything, the world that they show me has no meaning. What makes the world is insane, so the world it makes is insane. Reality is not insane, and I have Real Thoughts to replace insane ones. I can use my Real Perception, if I use my Real Thoughts as a guide for perceiving.

2. (12) 'I am upset because I perceive a world without meaning.'

Insane thoughts upset me. With them I perceive a world in which there is no order anywhere. Only chaos rules a world that represents my chaotic thinking. I cannot live in Peace while perceiving such a world. I am grateful that the world is not real, and that I do not have to perceive it at all, unless I choose to value it. I do not choose to value what is totally insane and without meaning.

3. (13) 'A world without meaning makes me fearful.'

A totally insane world makes me fearful, because it is undependable, and I cannot trust it. Nothing in madness is dependable; it offers no safety or hope. But that world is not real. I have given it the illusion of reality, and I have suffered by believing in it. Now, I choose to withdraw my belief and place my trust in Reality. In choosing this, I will escape from all of the effects of the world of fear, because I will be acknowledging that it is not real.

4. (14) 'God did not create a world without meaning.'

A meaningless world does not exist, because God did not create it. God is the Source of all Meaning, and Everything that is Real is in God's Mind. It is in my mind, too, because God created It with me. Why should I continue to suffer from the effects of my own insane thoughts when the Perfection of Creation is my Home? Let me remember the power of my choosing, and recognize Where I really abide.

5. (15) 'I have made the images that I see with my own thoughts.'

Whatever I see reflects my thoughts. My thoughts tell me where I am and what I am. Because I see a world in which there is suffering and loss and death, I recognize that I am seeing only the representation of insane thoughts, and I am not allowing my Real Thoughts to cast Their Beneficent Light on my perception. But God's Way is sure. The images that I have made cannot prevail against God, because it is not my will that they do so. My will is God's Will; I place no other gods before God.

Lesson 54

Today's review covers the following ideas:

1. (16) 'I have no neutral thoughts.'

Neutral thoughts are impossible for me, because all of my thoughts have power. They either make a false world, or they lead me to my Real Perception, but they cannot be without effects. As the world that I perceive arises from my erroneous belief that I am separate from God, so my Real Perception will rise as I let this error be corrected. My thoughts cannot be both true and false; they must be one or the other. What I perceive shows me which they are.

2. (17) 'I cannot perceive neutral things.'

What I perceive witnesses to what I think. Life is thought, and if I did not think, I would not exist. What I perceive represents my state of mind. I know that I can change my state of mind, so I can change my perception as well.

3. (18) 'I am not alone in experiencing the effects of my perception.'

My thoughts are not isolated to a personal mind, and the world that I perceive is not separate from me. The mad idea of separation from God had to be projected away from my split mind, and it formed the world that I perceive. Yet, because I cannot really be separate from God, that world is based on nothing. I can also call upon my Real Thoughts, Which will extend to be all that I perceive. As my thoughts of separation show me a world that is separate from me, so my Real Thoughts show me that the world is not separate from me.

4. (19) 'I am not alone in experiencing the effects of my thoughts.'

I am never limited to a personal self. Everything that I think or say or do affects the world that is in my mind. I cannot think or speak or act without affecting the part of my mind where I perceive a world, because my mind is One, being of God. It is in my power to change my entire mind, because my Power comes from God.

5. (20) 'I am determined to perceive differently.'

In recognition that my thoughts determine what and how I perceive, I am determined to perceive differently. I will look on witnesses that show me that my thinking has changed. I will behold proof that the change that has been done through me has enabled Love to replace fear, laughter to replace tears, and Abundance to replace loss. I will use my Real Perception, and let It teach me that my will and God's Will are One.

Lesson 55

Today's review covers the following ideas:

1. (21) 'I am determined to perceive truly.'

What I perceive with a personal mind are disease, disaster, and death. This cannot be what God created. The fact that I perceive them is proof that I do not understand God, and therefore I do not understand myself. Perceiving them, I do not know What I am, so I am determined to perceive witnesses to the Truth in me, rather than those that show me an illusion of myself.

2. (22) 'What I perceive with a personal mind is a form of attack on myself.'

The world that I perceive does not represent my Loving Thoughts. It is a picture of attack on everything by everything, and it certainly does not reflect God's Love or mine. It is my attack thoughts that give rise to this picture. My Loving Thoughts will save me from this perception, and give me the Peace that God wants me to have.

3. (23) 'I can escape from the world that the personal mind shows me by giving up attack thoughts.'

Only this is my salvation. Without attack thoughts, I will not perceive that a world of attack is real. As my forgiving allows Love to return to my awareness, I will see Peace and Safety and Joy. And it is These that I choose to perceive, in place of what I perceive now.

4. (24) 'I do not yet perceive what is truly good for me.'

With a personal mind, I cannot perceive what is truly good for me, since I do not know What I am. What the personal mind thinks is best for me only binds me to illusions. I am willing to follow the Holy Spirit, the Guide that God has given to me, to find out what is truly good for me, because I cannot perceive this with a personal mind.

5. (25) 'I do not yet know what anything in the world is for.'

For the personal mind, the purpose of everything is to prove to me that its illusions about me are real. When I identify with a personal self, I use everyone and everything for this purpose, and this purpose is what I think the world is for. This purpose that the personal mind gives to the world has led me to a frightening picture of the world. I am willing to open my mind to the Holy Spirit's purpose for the world by withdrawing the one that the personal mind has given to it.

Lesson 56

Today's review covers the following ideas:

1. (26) 'My attack thoughts are attacking my Invulnerability.'

I cannot know What I am when I see myself under constant attack. Pain, illness, loss, age, and death seem to threaten me, and all my hopes, wishes, and plans appear to be at the mercy of a world that I cannot control. But Perfect Security and Complete Fulfillment are mine in my Oneness with God. I have tried to give Them away in exchange for the world that I perceive, but God keeps What is mine safe for me. My own Real Thoughts will teach me What They are.

2. (27) 'Above all else, I want to perceive differently.'

What I perceive reflects what I believe I am. Recognizing this, I realize that perceiving differently is my greatest need. The world that I perceive attests to the fearful self-image that I have made. But I want to remember What I am, so it is essential that I let go of this image of myself. As it is replaced by Truth, my Real Perception will come to me, and I will perceive myself and all that I look upon with charity and Love.

3. (28) 'Above all else, I want to perceive truly.'

The world that I perceive holds my fearful self-image in my mind, and guarantees its continuance. While I see the world, Truth cannot come into my awareness. I will look past this world and perceive What reflects God's Love.

4. (29) 'I can perceive God in everything.'

Because everything that I perceive is in my mind, the Truth

remains unchanged behind every image that I have made. Behind every veil that I have drawn across my awareness of Love, Love's Light still shines. Beyond all the insane wishes of the personal mind is my will, which is One with God's Will. God is in my mind, so God is everywhere and in everything that I perceive. Since I am One with God, I will look past all appearances, and recognize the Truth beyond them.

5. (30) 'I can perceive God in everything, because God is in my mind.'

Behind all the insane thoughts of separation from God and attack in my mind is my Knowledge that All is One forever. I have not lost my Knowledge of What I am just because I seem to have forgotten It. It has been kept for me in the Mind of God, with Which I am One.

Lesson 57

Today's review covers the following ideas:

1. (31) 'I am not a victim of the world that I perceive.'

I cannot be a victim of a world that can be completely undone by my choice. I am not bound to the world, and I can let it go simply by desiring to do so. Only my wish to stay in the world holds me to the world. I want to give up this insane wish and walk into an awareness of God again.

2. (32) 'I have invented the world that I perceive.'

I made up the world that seems to limit me. All I need to do is recognize this, and I am free. I have deluded myself into believing that I can limit What is Limitless in God. I was bitterly mistaken in this belief, which I no longer want. What is One with God must be Limitless. I am One with God, not with that to which I have tried to limit myself.

3. (33) 'There is another way to perceive the world.'

Since the Holy Spirit's purpose for the world is not the one that the personal mind ascribes to it, there must be another way to perceive it from that the way that I have been perceiving it. With a personal mind, I perceive everything upside down, and my thoughts are the opposite of Truth. The personal mind sees the world as my prison, so it must be that the world is a place where I can be set free. I will look at the world this way, and see it as a place where I can find my Freedom.

4. (34) 'I can perceive Peace instead of this.'

When I perceive the world as a place of Freedom, I will realize that it reflects God's Law, rather than the laws of chaos that the personal mind gives to it. I will understand that Peace, not war, abides in my mind where I perceive the world, and I will perceive that Peace abides in everything in the world.

5. (35) 'My mind is Part of God's Mind. I am very Holy.'

As I extend Peace to the world that I perceive, I learn that Peace comes from deep within me. The world takes on the Light of my forgiving and shines forgiveness back to me. In this Light, I see What my illusions about myself have kept hidden from my awareness. I begin to understand the Holiness of my mind where I perceive a world, because it is One with me.

Lesson 58

Today's review covers the following ideas:

1. (36) 'My Holiness envelopes everything that I perceive.'

My Real Perception comes from my Holiness. By forgiving my perception that separation from God is real, I no longer see myself as guilty. I accept the Innocence that is the Truth about me. Seen through a Perception that understands the Truth, all I perceive is Holiness, because I can only perceive thoughts that I have about myself.

2. (37) 'My Holiness blesses the world that I perceive.'

My perception of my Holiness does not bless me alone in a personal identity; everything that I perceive in Its Light shares in the Joy It brings to me. There is nothing that is apart from this Joy, because there is nothing that does not share my Holiness. As I recognize my Holiness, It extends to the world that I perceive, and shines forth to fill my entire mind.

3. (38) 'My Holiness can undo any discord that I perceive.'

My Holiness is Limitless in Its power to heal all of the discord that I perceive, because It is limitless in Its power to save me from my illusions. Illusions are only my false ideas about myself. My Holiness undoes them all by asserting the Truth about me. In the Presence of my Holiness, Which is God's Holiness, all idols vanish from my mind.

4. (39) 'My Holiness is my salvation from hell.'

My Holiness saves me from all guilt, so my recognizing my Holiness is my salvation from the hell that I have made. It is also the salvation of my mind where I perceive a world. Once I have accepted my Holiness, I will be afraid of nothing. And when I am no longer afraid, my entire mind will share in my fearlessness, because One mind is God's Gift to me.

5. (40) 'I am blessed in my Oneness with God.'

This is my claim to All that is Good and only Good: I am blessed in my Oneness with God. All Good Things are mine, because God intends Them for me. I cannot suffer any loss or deprivation or pain, because of What I am. God supports, protects, and directs me in all things. God's Love for me is Infinite and with me Forever. I am Eternally blessed in my Oneness with God.

Lesson 59

Today's review covers the following ideas:

1. (41) 'God is with me, wherever I perceive myself.'

I cannot feel limited, when God is always with me. I cannot be doubtful or unsure of myself, when Perfect Certainty is with me in God. I cannot be disturbed in anything, when God rests in me in Absolute Peace. I cannot suffer, when Love and Joy surround me in God. I will not cherish illusions about myself. I am Perfect, because God is with me, wherever I perceive myself.

2. (42) 'God is my Strength. Real Perception is God's Gift to me.'

I will not use the personal mind's perception today. I am willing to exchange its pitiful illusion of perception for the Real Perception of my Christ Mind, Which is God's Gift to me. I call upon this Gift today, so that today I understand Eternity.

3. (43) 'God is my Source. My perception has no Reality apart from God.'

I can really only perceive what God wants me to perceive. Anything else I perceive is only an illusion. I choose illusions when I think I perceive apart from God, and when I try to perceive through the body's eyes. But the Real Perception of my Christ Mind has been given to me to replace illusions. It is through my Real Perception that I choose to perceive.

4. (44) 'God is the Light of my Real Perception.'

God is the only Light; without God I perceive in darkness. I can only perceive Truth through God's Light. I have tried to make something else to perceive, but I have been mistaken. Now I understand that God is the Light of my Real Perception. I welcome my Real Perception, and What I will perceive through It.

5. (45) 'God is the Mind with Which I really think.'

I have no real thoughts apart from God, because my mind is One with God. As Part of God's Mind, my Real Thoughts are God's Thoughts.

Lesson 60

Today's review covers the following ideas:

1. (46) 'God is the Love in Which I forgive.'

God does not forgive me, because God has never condemned me. Innocence does not blame, so It sees nothing to forgive. So my forgiving is the means by which I will recognize my Innocence. My forgiving reflects God's Love in my perception that I am in a world. It will bring me near enough to Heaven that I will ascend into God.

2. (47) 'God is the Strength in Which I trust.'

It is not the personal self's 'strength' through which I forgive; I forgive through the Strength of God within me, Which I am remembering as I forgive. As I begin to use my Real Perception, I recognize God's Reflection in my mind where I perceive a world. I forgive all that I perceive, because I feel God's Strength within me. I remember the Love that I chose to forget, but Which has not forgotten me.

3. (48) 'There is nothing for me to fear.'

How safe the world will appear to me when I perceive it with my Real Perception! It will not look anything like I imagine it now. Everyone and everything will be a blessing to me. I will recognize in all a dearest Friend. I have nothing to fear in a world that I have forgiven my illusions, and through which I therefore forgive myself.

4. (49) 'The Holy Spirit speaks to me all through the day.'

Every moment, the Holy Spirit calls on me to forgive to save myself from my illusion of separation from God. Every moment, the Holy Spirit directs my thoughts, guides my actions, and leads my feet. I am walking steadily on toward Truth. There is nowhere else I can go, because the Holy Spirit is the only Guide that has been given to me by God.

5. (50) 'I am sustained by the Love of God.'

As I listen to the Holy Spirit, I am sustained by God's Love. As I open myself to my Real Perception, God's Love lights up my entire mind for me. As I forgive, God's Love reminds me that I am Innocent. And as I extend my Real Perception, Which comes to me from God, to my mind where I perceive a world, I remember that I am One with God.

Lesson 61

'I am the Light of the world that I perceive.'

1. Only you can be the Light of the world that you perceive. Today's idea, then, is only a statement of the Truth about you. It is not pride, arrogance, or self-deception to know this about yourself. It does not describe you in your identification with a personal self, and it does not refer to any of the characteristics with which you have endowed your idols. It refers to you in your Oneness with God.

2. To the personal mind, today's idea is the height of self-glorification. But the personal mind does not understand true humility, which it confuses with self-debasement. With true humility, you accept your role in saving your mind from its illusions, and you take no other role. It is not humility for you to insist that you are *not* the Light of the world, because being the Light is the function that God gives to you. It is arrogance for you to assert that this function cannot be for you, and only the personal mind can be arrogant.

3. Today, with true humility, you will accept today's idea, because the Holy Spirit tells you that it is true. This is the first step in your accepting your function, as the Holy Spirit perceives it, in your perception that you are in a world. It is a giant step toward you taking your rightful place in saving your mind from its illusions. It is a positive assertion of your right to be saved from your illusions, and an acknowledgement of the Power that God gives you to save the part of your mind where you perceive a world.

4. Think about today's idea as often as possible today. It is the perfect answer to all of your illusions, and to all of your temptation to believe that illusions are real. It brings all of the images that you have made about yourself to the Truth, and helps you leave them behind in Peace, frees you of worry, and makes you certain of your purpose.

5. Take as many practice periods as possible today, each one for no more than a minute or two. Begin them by telling yourself:

'I am the Light of the world that I perceive. This is my only function in my perception that I am in a world.'

Then think about these statements for a while, with your eyes closed if the situation permits. Let a few related thoughts come to you, and repeat today's idea to yourself if your mind wanders away from the central thought.

6. Be sure to begin and end today with a practice period. You will awaken with an acknowledgement of the Truth about yourself, you will reinforce It throughout the day, and you will go to sleep reaffirming your only purpose in your perception that you are in a world. Your first and last practice periods may be longer than the rest, if you find them helpful and you want to extend them.

7. Today's idea goes far beyond the personal mind's limited ideas of what you are and what your purpose is. This is obviously necessary, as your role is to save your mind from limitations. This is the first of a number of giant steps that you will take in the next few weeks. Today, build a firm foundation for these advances. You are the Light of the world that you perceive. God's plan for your salvation from your illusions is built on you.

Mentor's Notes

In lesson 44, the use of the word 'Light' is introduced as a symbol for God. For you to be the Light of the world that you perceive, then, is for you to be the source of God-awareness in your perception of the world. It is the same as you saying, 'I am the Christ Mind.' Only you can bring God-awareness to your perception of the world, because the world is in your mind. In God, your Function is to extend God. In your perception that you are in a world, your function is to bring God back into your awareness by extending It to be all that you perceive.

Lesson 62

'Forgiving is my function as the Light of the world that I perceive.'

1. It is through your forgiving your illusions that your perception of a world of darkness is brought to the Light. It is through your forgiving your illusions that you recognize the Light of your Real Perception. It is through your forgiving your illusions that you demonstrate that you are the Light of the world that you perceive. It is through your forgiving your illusions that the Truth about you returns to your mind. So, in your forgiving your illusions lies your salvation from them.

2. Your illusions about yourself and the world are the same, and that is why forgiving is a gift that you always give to yourself. Your goal is to find out What you are, because you have denied your Identity by 'attacking' your Oneness with God. Now you are learning how to remember the Truth. Your 'attack' must be replaced by forgiveness, so that Life may replace death in your mind.

3. Remember that in every attack you make, you call upon the weakness of the personal mind, and that every time that you forgive, you call upon the Strength of your Christ Mind. Begin to understand what forgiving will do for you: It will remove all the sense of weakness, strain, and fatigue in your mind. It will take away all of your guilt, fear, and pain. It will restore to your awareness the Invulnerability and Power that God gives to you in Oneness with you.

4. Be happy to begin and end today by practicing today's idea, and to use it as frequently as possible throughout the day. This will help to make you as happy today as God wants you to be. Your happiness will extend to be all that you perceive.

5. As often as you can, with your eyes closed if possible, say to yourself today:

'Forgiveness is my function as the light of the world that I perceive. I want to fulfill my function, because it will make me happy.'

Then spend a minute or two considering your function, and the happiness and release it will bring to you. Let related thoughts come freely to you. Deep within you, you will recognize these words, and your mind will know that they are true. If your attention wanders, repeat today's idea and add:

'I want to remember this, because I want to be happy.'

Mentor's Notes

Remember, truly forgiving means recognizing that only God is Real, so it follows that, as the Light of the world that you perceive, your only function is to forgive, or to let go of, what is not-God. Only this can make you happy, because you are One with God. By forgiving the illusion that you are not-God, you reclaim your True Self.

Lesson 63

'Through my forgiving, the Light of the world extends Peace to my entire mind.'

1. How Holy you are that you can extend Peace to all that you perceive! How blessed you are that you can learn to let this be done through you! What purpose could bring you greater happiness?

2. You are indeed the Light of the world that you perceive with a function like this. Your Christ Mind looks to you for Its redemption from your illusions. It is yours to extend to all that you perceive, because it belongs to you. Do not accept any trivial purpose or meaningless desire in its place, or you will forget your function and leave yourself in hell. This is no idle request being asked of you. You are asked to accept salvation from your illusions, so that you can extend it to your entire mind.

3. If you recognize the importance of this function you will be happy to remember it very often today. Begin the day by acknowledging your function, and close the day by thinking about it again. Throughout the day, repeat this as often as you can:

> 'Through my forgiving, the Light of the world extends Peace to all that I perceive. I am the means that God has appointed for the salvation of my entire mind.'

4. In the minute or two that you give to related thoughts, you will probably find that they come to you easier with your eyes closed. Do not, however, wait for an opportunity to close your eyes. Do not waste any chance to reinforce today's idea. Remember, your Christ Mind looks to you to save It from your illusions. And through Christ, you are One with God.

Mentor's Notes

Your entire mind is what you think of as 'you' and everything that you perceive. Nothing that seems outside of you is really outside of you, so when you accept Peace for your mind, you accept Peace for everything that is in your mind as well.

Lesson 64

'I will not forget that my function is forgiving.'

1. Today's idea is another way of saying, 'I will not wander into temptation'. The purpose of the world, as the personal mind perceives it, is to obscure your function of forgiving your illusions. It tempts you to forget your function by seeming to justify your abandonment of your Identity in God to identify with a physical form. This world is what you perceive through the body's eyes.

2. It is the purpose of the body itself to tempt you to forget your Identity in God. But the Holy Spirit has another use for the illusions that you have made, so It sees another purpose for them. To the Holy Spirit, the world that you perceive is a place where you learn to forgive yourself what you think of as your 'sin' of separating from God. Through Its Perception, the physical world is not a place that tempts you to believe that your separation from God is real; it becomes a place where you save yourself from this temptation.

3. To review your last lessons, your function in your perception that you are in a world is to be the Light of the world, a function that is given to you by God. It is only the arrogance of the personal mind that leads you to question this, and only the fear of the personal mind that makes you think that you are unworthy to fulfill the task assigned to you by God. The salvation of the your mind where you perceive a world awaits your forgiving it, because through this you who are One with God escape all illusions and all temptations to believe that you are separate from God.

4. You can only be happy by fulfilling the function that God gives to you, because your function is to be happy by using the means by which your happiness becomes inevitable. There is no other way for you to be happy. Therefore, every time you choose whether or not to forgive your illusions, you are choosing whether or not to be happy.

5. Remember this today. Remind yourself of it when you get up in the morning, before you go to bed tonight, and all through the day. Prepare yourself in advance for all of the opportunities to decide for

forgiveness that you will have today by remembering that they are all very simple, because each one will lead you to happiness or unhappiness. Such a simple decision cannot be difficult for you to make. Do not let the form of decision deceive you, because a complex form does not imply a complex content. Every decision that you make in the world has the content of this one simple choice. It is the only choice that the Holy Spirit sees, so it is the only real choice there is.

6. Practice, today, with these thoughts:

> 'I will not forget that my function is forgiving. I will not substitute a function from the personal mind for God's function for me. I will forgive and be happy.'

At least once today, devote ten or fifteen minutes to reflecting on this statement. Related thoughts will come to help you if you remember the crucial importance of your function for your entire mind.

7. In your frequent applications of today's idea throughout the day, devote several minutes to reviewing these thoughts. Think about them, and nothing else. This will be difficult for you at first, since your mind is not yet disciplined. You may need to repeat, 'I will not forget my function' quite often to help you to concentrate.

8. You have two forms for your shorter practice periods today. Sometimes, do the exercises with your eyes closed, concentrating on the thoughts that you are using. At other times, keep your eyes opened after reviewing the thoughts, then look slowly and randomly around you, telling yourself:

> 'It is my function to forgive my mind where I perceive a world to save my entire mind.'

Mentor's Notes

Your perception that you are separate from God is never more than a *temptation*, because it can never be made a fact.

Lesson 65

'My only function is the one that God gives to me.'

1. Today's idea reaffirms your commitment to your salvation from illusions. It reminds you that you have no function *but* that. Both of these thoughts are necessary for your total commitment, because, obviously, if you have other functions, then your salvation is not your *only* function. So your full acceptance of your salvation as your only function entails two phases: The recognition of your salvation as your function; your relinquishment of all the other goals that you have invented for yourself.

2. This is the only way for you to take your rightful place as savior of the world that you perceive. This is the only way that you can say and mean, 'My only function is the one that God gives to me.' This is the only way that you can find Peace of mind.

3. Today, and for subsequent days, set aside ten to fifteen minutes for a more sustained practice period, in which you attempt to understand and accept the idea for the day. Today's idea offers you escape from all of the difficulties that you perceive. It places in your own hands the key to the door of Peace, which you have closed on yourself. It gives you the answer to all of the searching that you have done.

4. If possible, take the daily extended practice period at the same time each day. Choose it in advance, and then stick to it as much as possible. The purpose of this is for you to set apart time for God among all of the trivial purposes and goals that you pursue. This is part of a long-range plan of discipline for your mind, so that the Holy Spirit can use it consistently for the purpose of your salvation, which It shares with you.

5. For the longer practice period, begin by reviewing the day's idea. Then, close your eyes, repeat the idea once more, and watch your mind for whatever thoughts cross it. At first, do not make any attempt to concentrate only on thoughts that relate to the day's idea. Instead, try to uncover every idea that interferes with it. With

detachment, notice each one as it comes, dismissing each one by telling yourself:

> 'This thought reflects a goal that prevents me from accepting my only function.'

6. After a while, you will find interfering thoughts are harder to find. Continue a moment or so longer in an attempt to find a few idle thoughts, but do not strain or make an effort in doing this. Then tell yourself:

> 'On this clean slate I will let my true function be written for me.'

You don't need to use these exact words, but get a sense of being willing to have your illusory goals replaced by truth.

7. Finally, repeat today's idea once more, and spend the rest of the practice period focusing on its importance to you, the relief its acceptance will bring to you by resolving your conflicts, and the extent to which you really want to be saved from your illusions, in spite of your foolish ideas to the contrary.

8. In shorter practice periods at least once an hour, use this form in applying today's idea:

> 'My only function is the one that God gives to me. I have no other, and I want no other.'

As you practice this, sometimes close your eyes, and sometimes keep your eyes open as you look around you. What you perceive will be totally changed when you completely accept today's idea.

Mentor's Notes

Paragraph 2 introduces you to the concept that you are the 'savior of the world'. Though it may be hard for you to understand this at this point, the world is only in your mind. And remember, your mind is more than just the personal mind with which you are used to identifying. Your mind includes what you think of as 'you' and all that you perceive. So, who else could be the 'savior' of the world that you perceive, but you who perceive it? Further lessons will emphasize that your salvation and the world's salvation are one and the same.

Lesson 66

'My Happiness and my function are One.'

1. You may have noticed an emphasis in recent lessons connecting your fulfilling your function and your attaining Happiness. This is because you may not really see the connection. But there is more than a connection between them; they are the same. Their forms are different, but their Content is completely One.

2. The personal mind constantly battles with the Holy Spirit on the fundamental question of your function, so it does constant battle with the Holy Spirit over your happiness. This is not a two way battle, because the personal mind attacks, but the Holy Spirit does not respond. The Holy Spirit knows what your function is, and It knows that your function is your Happiness.

3. Today, you will go past this meaningless battle and arrive at the truth about your function. You will not engage in senseless arguments about what it is, you will not become hopelessly involved in defining what it is, or in determining the means for attaining it. You will not listen to the personal mind's attacks on the Truth. You will merely be grateful that you can find out what the Truth is.

4. In today's longer practice period, you have the purpose of accepting that there is not only a very real connection between the function that God gives to you and your Happiness, but that they are identical. God gives you only Happiness, so your function must be Happiness, even if it appears different. In today's exercises, you will go beyond their difference in appearance, and recognize their common Content of Truth.

5. Begin your ten to fifteen minute practice period by reviewing these thoughts:

> 'God gives me only Happiness. God has given my function to me. Therefore, my function must be Happiness.'

Try to see the logic in this sequence, even if you do not accept its conclusion. Only if the first two thoughts are wrong is the conclusion wrong. As you are practicing, think about these premises for a while:

6. The first premise is that God gives you only Happiness. This could be wrong, of course, but only if God is not God. Love cannot give evil, and what is not Happiness is evil. God cannot give what God does not have, and God cannot give what God is not. So unless God gives you only Happiness, God is evil. This is what you believe, if you do not accept this first premise.

7. The second premise is that God has given you your function. You have seen that there seems to be two parts of your mind. One part is the personal mind that you have made, and which is an illusion in your mind. The other is the Holy Spirit, Which is your True Mind. You have no other guides to choose between, and the only results your choice of guide can lead to are the fear that the personal mind always engenders, or the Love that the Holy Spirit always inspires.

8. So your function is either established by God through the Holy Spirit in you, or is made by the personal mind you made to replace God. Which is True? If God does not give you your function, then your function must come from the personal mind. But the personal mind is an illusion, and can offer you only an illusion of function.

9. Think about this during your longer practice period today. Also, think about the many illusions of function that the personal mind has offered to you, and the many ways that you have tried to find salvation from pain under its guidance. Did you find it? Were you happy? Did they bring you Peace? Be very honest with yourself today. Be fair as you remember the results of your listening to the personal mind, and ask yourself if it is reasonable for you to expect Happiness from anything that the personal mind proposes. The personal mind is your only alternative to the Holy Spirit.

10. You will listen to madness, or you will hear Truth. Try to make this choice as you think about the premises on which the conclusion above rests. You can share the conclusion with your

Christ Mind, but nothing else, because God shares it with you. Today's idea is another giant step in your perception that all illusions are the same, and that Truth is different from illusions. Realize today that only the Truth is True.

11. Twice an hour, for your shorter practice periods, use this form of today's idea:

> 'My Happiness and my function are One, because God has given me both.'

It will take only a minute, maybe less, to repeat these words slowly to yourself, and to think about them a little as you say them.

Lesson 67

'Love created me like Itself.'

1. Today's idea is a complete and accurate statement about you. It is why you are the Light and savior of the world that you perceive. Today, you will make every effort to reach this Truth, and to realize fully, if only for a moment, that it is the Truth.

2. In your longer practice period today, think about your Reality and Its wholly Unchanged and Unchangeable nature. Begin by repeating the Truth about you stated above, then spend a few minutes adding some relevant thoughts, such as:

'Holiness created me Holy.'
'Kindness created me Kind.'
'Helpfulness created me Helpful.'
'Perfection created me Perfect.'

Any attribute of God as God really is, is appropriate for you to use for this exercise. You are trying to undo the personal mind's definition of God, and to replace it with God's Real Definition. You are also emphasizing that you are Part of God.

3. After you have gone over several related thoughts, let all thoughts drop away for a brief interval, then reach past all the images and preconceptions that you hold about yourself to reach the Truth in you. Love created you like Itself, and this Self is in you. It is in your mind for you to find.

4. As necessary, repeat today's idea to replace distracting thoughts. If this is not enough, add other thoughts that are related to the Truth about you. Perhaps today you will go past all that, and through the interval of no-thoughts to an awareness of the blazing Light in Which you recognize yourself as Love created you. Whether you feel you have succeeded or not, you can be confident that you have done much today to bring that awareness nearer.

5. Practice today's idea as often as you can. You need to hear the

Truth about yourself as often as possible, because your mind is so preoccupied with false self-images. At least four or five times an hour, it will be of great benefit to you to remind yourself that Love created you like Itself. This is the Truth about you.

6. In your shorter practice periods, realize that it is not the personal mind that tells you this. This is the Holy Spirit reminding you of your Oneness with God. This is the Holy Spirit replacing what the personal mind tells you about yourself with the simple Truth. You were created by Love like Itself.

Mentor's Notes

'To create', as this course uses the term, means 'to be One with'. God 'creates' by extending Itself Infinitely and Eternally. As God's 'Creation' you are God's Extension. There is only God; despite your illusions, you are not, and can never be, apart from God.

Lesson 68

'Love does not hold onto resentment.'

1. You were created by Love like Itself, so you cannot hold onto resentment and know your True Self. For you to hold onto resentment is for you to forget What you are; it is to see yourself as a body/personal self. For you to hold onto resentment is for you to let the personal mind rule your mind, and condemn you to death in a body. Perhaps you do not yet realize what holding onto resentment does to your mind: It seems to split you off from God, and to make you unlike God. It makes you believe that God is like what you have made of yourself, because you cannot conceive of your Source as something unlike you.

2. While you seem shut off from your True Self, Which is Eternally aware that It is One with God, it seems like your Mind has gone to sleep, and the part of It that dreams appears to you to be what is awake. This is what seems to be happening when you hold onto resentment. When you hold onto resentment, you deny that you were created by Love, and you become afraid of God in your dream of hate. You cannot dream that hatred is real and not fear God.

3. It is certain that when you hold onto the personal mind's resentments, you will redefine God in its image, just as it is certain that God created you like God, and defines you as Part of God. It is certain that when you hold onto the personal mind's resentments, you will feel guilty, just as it is certain that when you forgive your illusions, you will find Peace. It is certain that when you hold onto the personal mind's resentments, you will forget What you are, just as it is certain that when you forgive your illusions, you will remember What you are.

4. You will be willing to relinquish the personal mind's resentments when you believe all of this is true. Perhaps you think that you cannot let go of resentment, but this is just a matter of motivation. Today, you will try to find out how you will feel without

them. If you succeed by even a little, you will have no problem being motivated ever again.

5. Begin today's extended practice period by searching your mind for those against whom the personal mind holds what you regard as major resentments. You will find these easily. Then, think of the personal mind's resentments that you consider minor that you hold against those that you like, and even think that you love. It will quickly become apparent to you that there is no one against whom you do not cherish resentment of some kind. In your perception of yourself as a personal self, this has left you feeling all alone.

6. Determine now to see all these people as your friends. In your mind, say to them one at a time:

> 'I want to see you as my friend, so that I remember that you are a part of my mind, and come to know myself.'

Spend the rest of the practice period thinking of yourself at Peace with everyone and everything, safe in a world that protects you and loves you, and that you love in return. Feel Safety surrounding you and holding you up. Believe, if only briefly, that nothing can harm you in any way. At the end of the practice period, tell yourself:

> 'Love does not hold onto resentment. When I let all of the personal mind's resentments go, I will know that I am Perfectly Safe.'

7. Your short practice periods should include a quick application of today's idea in this form, whenever any resentment arises in you against anyone, present or not:

> 'Love does not hold onto resentment. I will not betray my True Self.'

Also, repeat today's idea several time an hour in this form:

'Love does not hold onto resentment. I will awaken to my True Self by laying aside all of the personal mind's resentments.'

Mentor's Notes

It is the Law of Mind that Mind only knows Itself. Even the personal mind cannot escape this Law. In your identification with a personal mind, you must believe that God is like the personal mind. So you never really fear God; you fear the god that you have made in the personal mind's image.

It is important for you to realize that the personal mind will always attack, and it will always harbor resentment. Repressing these thoughts is just another way to hold onto them, and fighting them only gives them more power in your mind. Instead, let those thoughts come up, then let them go. They only define you in your mind if you hold onto them. By letting them go, you make room for your Real Thoughts, and, therefore, your Real Identity.

Lesson 69

'The personal mind's resentments hide the Light of the world in me.'

1. The personal mind's resentments hide the Light in your mind. Because they hide the Light in your mind, the world that you perceive seems dark to you. As you lift the veil of the personal mind's resentments from your mind, the part of your mind where you perceive a world is released with you. Share your salvation with the world that seemed to share hell with you. You and the world that you perceive are One in the Light that saves you both.

2. Today, you will make another real attempt to reach the Light in your mind. Before you do this in your extended practice period, take several minutes to consider what you are about to do. You are literally trying to get in touch with the salvation of the part of your mind where you perceive a world. You are trying to get past the veil of darkness that keeps your salvation hidden from you. Let the veil be lifted, and see your tears disappear in the Light.

3. Begin your longer practice period with the full realization that this can be so, and with a real determination to reach What is dearer to you than anything else. Your salvation from illusions is your only need. You have no other purpose or function to fulfill in your perception that you are in a world. Learning salvation is your only goal. Finish your endless searching for salvation today by finding the Light in you, and hold It up to be all that you perceive.

4. Very quietly, with your eyes closed, let go of all the thoughts that fill your mind. Picture your mind as a vast circle that is surrounded by a layer of heavy, dark clouds. You seem to be standing outside the circle, and you see only the clouds.

5. From where you stand outside the clouds, you see no reason to believe that there is a brilliant Light beyond them. The clouds seem to be reality, because they seem to be all that you can see. So you have not attempted to go through them, which is the only way that you can be convinced that they lack substance. You will go through

them today.

6. After you have thought about the importance of what you are doing for your entire mind, settle into perfect stillness, remembering how much you want to reach the Light today. You want to reach It right now! Determine to go past the clouds; visualize yourself reaching out and touching them. Brush them aside with your hand, and feel them touching your cheeks and forehead and eyelids as you go through them. Go on; clouds cannot stop you.

7. If you are doing this exercise properly, you will have a sense of being lifted and carried through. Your little effort and small determination call on the Power of God to help you, and God will raise you from the darkness into the Light. Your will is lined up with God's Will; you will not fail, because your will is God's Will.

8. Be confident in God today, and be certain that God has heard you and answered you. You may not recognize God's Answer yet, but you can be sure that It is here, and that you will receive It. As you go through the clouds into the Light, hold this confidence in your mind. Remember, you are joining your will to God's Will. Keep clearly in your mind the awareness that what you undertake with God must succeed. Then let the Power of God work in you and through you, so that your will joined with God's Will is done.

9. In your shorter practice periods, which you want to do as often as possible because of the importance of today's idea to you and to your happiness, remind yourself that the personal mind's resentments are hiding the Light of the world from your awareness. Remind yourself that you are not alone in searching for the Light, and that you know where to look for It. Say to yourself:

> 'The personal mind's resentments hide the Light of the world in me. I cannot see What they hide from me, but I want It revealed to me, for the salvation of my entire mind.'

Also, if you are tempted to hold anything against anyone today, be sure to tell yourself:

'If I hold onto this resentment, the Light of the world will be hidden from me.'

Lesson 70

'My salvation from guilt comes from me.'

1. Your temptation to pursue goals in the world is a form of denying today's idea. You look for salvation everywhere but within yourself. Guilt, too, seems to be everywhere but in you. You do not yet see that guilt and your salvation from guilt are in your own mind, and nowhere else. When you realize that all guilt is solely an invention of your own mind, you will realize that your salvation from guilt must also be in your own mind. In understanding this, you are saved.

2. The seeming 'cost' of your acceptance of today's idea is this: Nothing outside of you will save you; nothing outside of you will bring you Peace. But this also means that nothing outside of you can hurt you, disturb your Peace, or upset you in any way. Today's idea places you in charge of the universe that you perceive, which is proper, because of What you are. You cannot only partially accept this role, and you must surely begin to see that accepting it is your salvation from guilt.

3. You may not, however, see why recognizing that guilt is in your mind means that your salvation from guilt is also there. In Truth, your Mind is One, so your error of perceiving yourself as separate from God is in your mind with its Correction. But this is not the way that the personal mind works.

4. The personal mind is the opposite of God, and it uses distorted and fantastic means to keep the Correction away from your error to maintain your perception that you are separate from God. The personal mind intends to ensure that correction does not occur, but God, being in your mind Eternally, ensures that correction has already occurred.

5. Today, you will practice realizing that God's Will and your will are the same. God wants you to be corrected and restored to full awareness of God, and you do not really want to live in your mistaken identity, because it makes you unhappy. So, by accepting

today's idea, you are in agreement with God.

6. Today you are ready for two longer practice periods, each of them ten to fifteen minutes. You may decide when to take them. You will follow this practice for a number of lessons, and you should decide in advance when would be a good time for your exercises, and you should adhere to your own decision in this as closely as possible.

7. Begin these practice periods by repeating today's idea, adding a statement that indicates your recognition that your salvation from guilt comes from you. You might put it to yourself this way:

> 'My salvation from guilt comes from me. It cannot come from anywhere else.'

Then spend a few minutes, with your eyes closed, in reviewing some of the things to which you have looked for salvation from the pain of guilt: other people, possessions, situations, and self-concepts that you sought to make real. Recognize that your salvation is not in them, and tell yourself:

> 'My salvation from guilt cannot come from any of these things; my salvation comes only from me.'

8. Now try to reach the Light in you, Which is Where your salvation is. You cannot find it in the clouds that hide the Light, and it is in them that you have been looking for it. Remember, you will have to go through the clouds to reach the Light, but that you have never found anything in the clouds that have endured, or that you really wanted.

9. Since all illusions of salvation have failed you, surely you do not want to continue looking for idols in the clouds when you can easily walk into the Light of real salvation. Try to pass the clouds by whatever means appeals to you. If it helps, picture yourself holding the hand of, and being led by, Jesus, or some other Representative of

the Holy Spirit. This will not be an idle fantasy.

10. For your short and frequent practice periods today, remind yourself that your salvation comes from you, and that only your own thoughts can hold you from it. You are free from all external interference. You are in charge of your salvation from guilt; you are in charge of saving the part of your mind where you perceive a world. Say to yourself, then:

> 'My salvation from guilt comes from me. Nothing outside of me can hold me back. Within me is the salvation of my entire mind.'

Mentor's Notes

All the pain that you experience comes from the guilt that you feel in your identification with a personal self. That misidentification is your belief that you have attacked God, and that God will punish you. You cannot believe that the personal self is you and not feel the pain of guilt and fear of punishment, and you will always seek for salvation from this pain. You are seeking for salvation every time you think someone, something, or some circumstance can make you happy, peaceful, or whole. The personal mind advises you to seek outside yourself for salvation. But, logically, if the source of your guilt and pain is your perception that you are separate from God, then the way to undo them is to turn within to God and undo your perception of separation from God. Your Oneness with God is the Correction of your error of perceiving yourself as separate from God.

Lesson 71

'Only God's plan for my salvation from guilt will work.'

1. You may not yet realize that the personal mind has set up a plan for your salvation from the pain of guilt that is the opposite of God's plan for you. It is this plan in which you believe, so you must believe that to accept God's plan would leave you in hell. This sounds preposterous, of course, but after you consider just what the personal mind's plan is, you will realize that you do believe this.

2. The personal mind's plan for your salvation revolves around you holding onto its resentments. When you do, you are asserting that, if someone else were different, or if some external circumstance were changed, you would be saved from your pain. So, in your identification with the personal self, you constantly perceive the source of your salvation as outside of yourself. Every resentment of the personal mind to which you hold on is your declaration, 'If this is changed, I will be saved from pain.' Therefore, you demand that everyone and everything change for your salvation, except your own mind.

3. The role that the personal mind assigns to your mind in its plan is to determine what, other than your mind, must change if you are to be saved. According to this insane plan, any source of salvation that you perceive is acceptable, as long as it is not the real Source of your salvation. This ensures that your fruitless search will continue, because, although everything outside of you has failed you so far, you will still have a hope that something else that you have not yet tried might work: another person, another thing, another situation.

4. This is the personal mind's plan for your salvation. You can certainly see how it is in accord with the personal mind's strict doctrine, 'Seek, but do not find.' Searching for your salvation where it is *not* will surely guarantee that you will not find it.

5. But God's plan for your salvation from guilt works, because you will find your salvation where it *is*. But if you are to succeed, as God guarantees you will, you must be willing to seek for your

salvation *only* where it is. Otherwise, your purpose will be divided as you attempt to seek for your salvation in two plans that are diametrically opposed in all ways. This will bring you confusion, misery, a deep sense of failure, and despair.

6. Today's idea is your simple escape from this. Only God's plan for your salvation from guilt will work. There is no real conflict of plans, because only God's plan can work. Only God's plan is certain, and must succeed.

7. Today, you will practice this certainty. Rejoice that there is an answer to what seems to be a conflict without a resolution for you. Only what God Wills is possible, and your salvation is certain, because it comes from God.

8. Begin your two longer practice periods today by thinking about today's idea. Realize that it contains two parts, each contributing equally to the whole: God's plan for your salvation will work; other plans cannot. Do not allow yourself to become depressed by or angry at the second part, because it is inherent in the first part. The first part is your release from all of the personal mind's insane proposals for your salvation. *Those* have led to your depression and anger. But God's plan will succeed, and it will lead to your freedom from guilt, and to Joy.

9. Remember this, and spend the rest of the extended practice periods asking God to reveal Its plan to you. Ask God very specifically:

'What do You want me to do?'
'Where do You want me to go?'
'What do You want me to say, and to whom?'

Give God full charge of the rest of the practice period, and let God tell you what you need to do in God's plan for your salvation. You will hear God in direct proportion to your willingness to hear God. Do not refuse to hear. The fact that you are doing these exercises proves that you have some willingness to listen. This is enough for you to claim God's answer to you.

10. In your shorter practice periods, tell yourself often today that only God's plan for your salvation will work. Be alert to your temptation to listen to the personal mind's resentments today, and respond to them with this form of today's idea:

'My holding onto the personal mind's resentments is the opposite of God's plan for my salvation, and only God's plan will work.'

Remember today's idea six or seven times an hour. There is no better way for you to spend a half minute or less than to remember the Source of your salvation, and to see your salvation where it is.

Mentor's Notes

It is important for you to realize that it is not what you do, where you go, or what you say that is important in itself. But the process of stepping away from the personal mind and choosing to come from God is how you remember that you are One with God. This is how the Holy Spirit uses your perception that you are in a world to remind you that you are One with God.

Lesson 72

'My holding onto the personal mind's resentments is an attack on God's plan for my salvation from guilt.'

1. While you may recognize that the personal mind's plan for your salvation is the opposite of God's plan, you may not yet recognize that it is an active attack on God's plan, and a deliberate attempt to destroy it. In this attack, God and the personal mind switch places in your perception: You perceive God with the personal mind's attributes, and you perceive the personal mind with God's attributes.

2. The personal mind's fundamental wish is to replace God in your mind. The body is the physical embodiment of this wish, and it is this wish that makes it seem like your mind is surrounded by a body, separate and alone, unable to reach the part of your mind that you perceive as a world, except through a body that is meant to limit it. A limit on your mind cannot be the best means to extend it, but the personal mind wants you to believe that it is.

3. Although it is obvious here that the body/personal self is meant to limit you, you may not yet see why holding onto its resentments is an attack on God's plan for your salvation. But consider the things for which you are likely to hold onto resentment. They are always something associated with the body/personal self: Someone says something that it does not like, does something to displease it, or betrays their hostile thoughts toward it with their behavior.

4. Here, you are not dealing with the fact that a 'person' is really a projection from your split mind. You are exclusively concerned with bodies/personal selves, and you are not doing anything to free yourself from the perception that bodies/personal selves are real. In fact, you are actively holding onto a body/personal self as your reality. You are attacking God in this, because, in your mind, you are reducing God's Creation, Which is One with God, and Limitless like God, to separate bodies, with separate minds, in a separate world. You are bound to think that God is like a body/personal self, because

a creator cannot be unlike its creation.

5. If God is a body, what could God's plan for your salvation be but your death? God would be deceiving you in trying to present Itself as Life and not as death. God would be a liar, full of false promises, and an illusion of 'life' that is really death. When you believe that a body is your reality, this view of God is your belief. In fact, if bodies are real, it's difficult to see how you could escape these conclusions. And every resentment of the personal mind that you cling to insists that bodies are real, and entirely overlooks What is really in your mind. You condemn everything that you perceive to death, asserting that salvation must be in death, and you project this attack onto God, and hold God responsible for it.

6. In this carefully planned scenario, where it seems everyone seeks for victims, and mercy cannot enter, the personal mind comes to save you, saying, 'So God made you a body? Very well; accept it and be glad. Do not let yourself be denied anything that the body can get you. Grab every little scrap you can for yourself, because God has given you nothing. Only the body can save you. It is the death of God, and your salvation.'

7. This is the belief fostered by the world that the personal mind makes. You may hate the body and try to hurt and humiliate it, or you may love the body and glorify and exalt in it. But while the body stands at the center of your concept of yourself, you are attacking God's plan for your salvation, and holding resentments against God and what is really One with God, so that you won't hear the Holy Spirit and welcome It as your Friend. The body, your chosen 'savior', takes the Holy Spirit's place instead, and you believe that the Holy Spirit is your enemy, and that the body is your friend.

8. Today, you are going to stop these senseless attacks on your salvation, and you will welcome it instead. Your upside-down perception has destroyed your Peace of mind. You see yourself in a body, and you see the Truth as not part of you, blocked from your awareness by the body's limitations. Now you are going to see this differently.

9. The Light of Truth is in you, because you are One with God. It is the body that is really not a part of you, and that is not really your concern. To be without a body is your natural state of Being. When you recognize the Light of Truth in you, you recognize yourself as you are. To see your True Self apart from a body is to end your attack on God's plan for your salvation, and to accept it instead. When you accept God's plan, it is already accomplished.

10. Your goal in today's longer practice periods is to become aware that God's plan for your salvation is already accomplished in you. You have merely been attacking What you do not understand. Now you are going to lay all judgment aside, and ask God what God's plan is for you:

> 'God, what is my salvation? I do not know. Tell me, so that I will understand.'

Then wait in quiet for God's answer. You have attacked God's plan for your salvation without knowing what it is. You shout the personal mind's resentments so loudly that you cannot hear the Holy Spirit. You have used them to close your mind to God.

11. Now you are ready to open your mind and learn. 'God, what is my salvation?' Ask, and you will be answered; seek it, and you will find it. You are no longer asking the personal mind what your salvation is, or where to find it; you are asking Truth. You can be certain that the answer that you receive is true, because you are asking God.

12. Whenever you feel your confidence fade or your hope of receiving an answer diminish, repeat your question, remembering that you are asking the Infinite, Which created you like Itself.

> 'God, what is my salvation? I do not know. Tell me, so that I will understand.'

God will answer, so be determined to hear.

13. One or two shorter practice periods an hour will be enough for today, because the practice is longer than usual. Begin these exercises with this:

> 'My holding onto the personal mind's resentments is an attack on God's plan for my salvation. I will accept God's plan instead. God, what is my salvation?'

Then wait a minute or so in silence, preferably with your eyes closed, and listen for God's answer.

Mentor's Notes

Of course, your attack on God or God's plan has no effect on God, but it does have an effect on you. Attacking God leads you to guilt and fear of punishment, no matter that God does not think this way. It is the Law of Mind that a mind always sees itself. Because, in your identification with a personal self, you think in terms of attack-guilt-punishment, you think that God thinks this way.

Paragraph 5 introduces the association of bodies with death. This association may not be obvious to you, but bodies *are* death, because they are not Eternal. If you believe that God is a body, and that God made bodies in Its own image, then you think that God is death and cannot be Life. God's assertion that It is Life, then, becomes a lie. This is what the personal mind wants you to believe, and it counsels you (paragraph 6) to squeeze everything you can out of the body/personal self's brief 'life', because God lies to you and has abandoned you to ultimately die. And it tells you to shut the Holy Spirit out (paragraph 7), because God wants you dead. In this scenario, the body is your 'salvation' from God, and so, temporarily, from death.

Paragraph 6 also introduces the idea that the personal mind sees the body, and ultimately the body's death, as 'proof' that it has overcome God. It believes that it has reduced God (you) to a body, and the body's death is its ultimate victory over God. The personal mind often holds onto multi-layered, and sometimes even contradictory, concepts like these. Here, it tells you to resent God for limiting you to a body and killing you, while it rejoices in the body's death as *its own* victory over God! The personal mind has no problem with you perceiving the first part, where it has projected its own motivation (your death) onto God. But the second part it means to keep out of your awareness, because the guilt it produces in you might cause you to seek for Real Relief.

The personal mind wants to kill God in you; it cannot acknowledge that you are really only God, and that if it were even possible to kill you, its own source would be gone. This is because the personal mind believes it is wholly independent of any source; it believes it is a god itself. That's why it is in conflict with God.

Lesson 73

'It is my Will to perceive the Light of God.'

1. Today, you will consider the Will that you share with God. This Will is not the same as the personal mind's idle wishes, which result only in darkness and nothingness in your mind. The Will that you share with God has all the Power of God's Infinite Extension. The personal mind's idle wishes are limited to a personal 'you', so they have no power at all. In a sense, the personal mind's wishes are not 'idle' in that they have resulted in a world of illusions, and your belief in this world is very strong. But relative to God's Infinite Extension, Which is Reality, they are idle, because they make nothing Real.

2. The personal mind's idle wishes and resentments are co-makers of the world that you perceive. The personal mind's wish to be separate from God gives rise to the world and its resentments, which are necessary to maintain its world, and it peoples the world with figures that seem to attack you, and that call for your 'righteous' judgment against them. These attacking figures stand in the way of your awareness that only Christ is really in your mind. In your perceiving these attacking figures, you do not perceive an extension of your True Self instead.

3. Your Will is lost to your awareness in this constant exchange of guilt between you and an attacking world, and the personal mind's resentments increase with every exchange. This world could not be created by you in your Oneness with God, and God could not create this for you, who are One with God. Creation is God's Will in Oneness with you. God could not create a world that means to kill God.

4. Today, you will reach for your Real Perception, Which will reveal an awareness that is in accord with your Will. God's Light is in your Real Perception, because It does not oppose God's Will. Your Real Perception is not Heaven, but the Light of Heaven shines in It. Darkness will vanish from your mind as the personal mind's idle

wishes are withdrawn from it. The Light that shines in your Real Perception reflects your Will, so you must look for It within you.

5. What you perceive can only mirror what is in your mind. Neither God's Light, nor the darkness of your denial of God, can be found outside of you. When the personal mind's resentments darken your mind, you look out on a dark world. But your forgiving the personal mind's resentments lifts the darkness from your mind, reasserts your Will, and lets you perceive Light. It has been emphasized that you can easily pass the barrier of the personal mind's resentments, and they cannot stand between you and your salvation. The reason is very simple: You do not really want to be in hell; you do not really want to weep and suffer and die.

6. Forget the personal mind's arguments that the world that you perceive is really Heaven. You know it is not so, and you cannot want this for yourself. There is a point beyond which illusions no longer deceive you. Suffering is not Happiness, and you really want Happiness. This is your Will in Truth, so your salvation from suffering is your Will as well. You want to succeed today, so undertake your exercises with your blessing and happy willingness.

7. You will succeed today if you remember that you want to be saved from hell. You want to accept God's plan, because it is *your* plan. You have no will that can really oppose it, and you really don't want to do so. Above everything else, you want the freedom to remember What you really are. Today, it is the personal mind that is powerless before your Will. Your Will is Free, and nothing can prevail against It.

8. So today, undertake your exercises in happy confidence, certain that you will find What it is your Will to find, and you will remember What it is your Will to remember. No idle wishes will detain you or deceive you with an illusion of strength. Today, your Will is done, and you will end your insane belief that you want hell over Heaven.

9. Begin your longer practice periods by recognizing that *only* God's plan for your salvation is your Will. God's plan is not an alien

will that is forced on you; it is the one plan on Which you and God agree. You will succeed today, which is the time appointed to release your entire mind from the hell of the personal mind's idle wishes. Your Will is restored to your awareness when you willingly perceive the Light, and are saved from dark denial of God.

10. After reminding yourself of this, determine to keep your Will clearly in mind, and tell yourself with gentle firmness and quiet certainty:

> 'It is my Will to perceive the Light of God. I will behold the Light that reflects God's Will and mine.'

Then, let God's Will within you assert Itself, and put the rest or your practice period under God's guidance. Let God lead the way.

11. In your shorter practice periods, again declare what you really want. Say:

> 'It is my Will to perceive the Light of God. Denying God is not my will.'

Repeat this several times an hour today. It is most important to apply today's idea in this form when you are tempted to hold onto the personal mind's resentments in any form. This will help you to let them go, instead of to cherish and hide them.

Lesson 74

'There is only God's Will.'

1. You can regard today's idea as the central thought toward which all of the exercises in this Workbook are directed. There is only God's Will. When you recognize this, you will recognize that your will is God's Will, and your belief in conflict will be gone. Peace will replace your strange belief that you are torn between conflicting goals. As an Expression of God's Will, your only Goal is God.

2. Great Peace awaits you in today's idea, and today's exercises are directed toward your finding It. The idea is itself wholly true, so it cannot give rise to illusions. Without illusions, you cannot experience conflict, because then you have nothing to conflict with Truth. Recognize this today, and experience the Peace this recognition brings to you.

3. Begin today's longer practice periods by repeating these thoughts several times slowly, with firm determination to understand what they mean, and to hold them in your mind:

'There is only God's Will. I cannot be in conflict.'

Then spend a few minutes adding some related thoughts, such as:

'I am at Peace.'
'Nothing can disturb me; my will is God's Will.'
'My will and God's Will are One.'
'God wills Peace for me.'

During this introductory phase of the exercise, be sure to deal quickly with any thoughts of conflict that cross your mind. If they arise, tell yourself immediately:

'There is only God's Will. These thoughts of conflict are

meaningless.'

4. If you have certain thoughts of conflict that seem particularly difficult to resolve, single them out for special consideration. Think about the issue briefly, but very specifically. Identify any particular people or situations involved, and tell yourself:

'There is only God's Will, and I share It with God. My conflict about ______ is not real.'

5. After you have cleared your mind in this way, close your eyes, and experience the Peace to Which your Reality entitles you. Sink into It, and feel It closing around you. You may mistake this for attempting to withdraw, but you can easily detect the difference between withdrawal and Peace. Peace brings you a deep sense of Joy, and an increase in alertness; withdrawal takes the form of weariness and drowsiness.

6. Joy is a characteristic of Peace. You will know that you have reached Peace when you feel Joy. If you feel yourself withdrawing, quickly repeat today's idea. Do this as often as necessary. You definitely gain by refusing to withdraw, even if you do not yet experience the Peace that you seek.

7. In your shorter exercise periods of one or two minutes every half hour, say to yourself:

'There is only God's Will. I seek God's Peace today.'

Then find What you are seeking.

Lesson 75

'God's Light has come into my awareness.'

1. God's Light has come into your awareness. You are healed and you can heal; you are saved and you can save. You are at Peace, and you bring Peace with you wherever you perceive yourself. Darkness, turmoil, and death have disappeared. God's Light has come into your awareness.

2. Today, you celebrate the happy ending of your long dream of disaster. You have no dark dreams now, because God's Light has come into your awareness. Today, the time of Light begins for you and all that you perceive. It is a new era, in which a new Perception is born in you. The old perception leaves no traces as it passes. Today, you perceive differently, because God's Light has come into your awareness.

3. Your exercises today will be happy ones, in which you offer thanks for the passing of the old perception and the beginning of your Real Perception. No shadows from the personal self's past remain in your mind to darken your perception and hide the Real Perception your forgiving your illusions offers to you. Today, you accept your Real Perception as What you want to see. You will be given What you want. You will see God's Light, because God's Light has come into your awareness.

4. In your longer practice periods, look through the Real Perception that your forgiving shows you. This, and only This, is What you want to perceive. Your single Purpose makes your Goal inevitable. Today, your Real Perception rises before you, grateful at last to be seen. Your Real Perception is here, now that God's Light has come into your awareness.

5. You do not want to perceive with the personal mind's shadow across your mind today. You see God's Light, and in It you see Heaven's Reflection lie across all that you perceive. Begin your longer practice periods by telling yourself of the good news of your release from illusions:

'God's Light has come into my awareness. I forgive the personal mind's perception of the world.'

6. Do not dwell on the personal self's past today. Keep your mind completely open, washed of all past ideas, and clean of every concept of the personal mind. You forgive the personal mind's perception of the world today, and you can perceive the world now as if you never saw it before. You do not yet know how to use your Real Perception to see it; you only have to wait and this Perception will be shown to you. While you wait, repeat to yourself several times slowly, and in complete patience:

'God's Light has come into my awareness. I forgive the personal mind's perception of the world.'

7. Realize that your forgiving entitles you to your Real Perception. The Holy Spirit always gives you the Gift of Real Perception when you forgive. Believe that the Holy Spirit will give It to you now. You have forgiven the personal mind's perception of the world, and the Holy Spirit is with you as you watch and wait, and It will show you how to perceive the world with your Real Perception. This is the Holy Spirit's Will, and you have joined your will with It. Wait patiently for the Holy Spirit; It is here. God's Light has come into your awareness; you have forgiven the personal mind's perception of the world.

8. You know that you cannot fail when you trust in the Holy Spirit. Remind yourself that you wait in certainty to see the world with your Real Perception, as the Holy Spirit promises you. From this moment on, you will perceive differently. Today, God's Light has come into your awareness. You will see with your Real Perception, Which has been with you since you made time, and Which ensures the end of time.

9. Your shorter practice periods, too, will be joyful reminders of your release. Remind yourself every fifteen minutes that today is a

time for special celebration. Give thanks for the Love of God. Rejoice in the power of your forgiving to heal your perception completely. Be confident that today is a new beginning for you. Without the darkness of the personal mind's past on your mind, you will not fail to see with your Real Perception today. You will welcome What you see so much that you will gladly extend today forever.

10. Say, then:

> 'God's Light has come into my awareness. I forgive the personal mind's perception of the world.'

If you are tempted to be pulled back into a dark world today, say to it:

> 'The Light of God has come into my awareness. I forgive you.'

11. Dedicate today to the Serenity in Which God wants you to be. Keep It in your awareness of yourself, and in all that you perceive. Celebrate the beginning of your Real Perception, and the world that you perceive through It, which has come to replace the world of the personal mind that you thought was real.

Mentor's Notes

The personal mind perceives the world in ways that make the world real to you. Your Real Perception releases you from the world. Only the Holy Spirit knows how to release your mind in a form that is meaningful for you. Your Real Perception will evolve over time, as you become more and more willing to accept that only God is Real.

Lesson 76

'I am under only God's Law.'

1. You have already been shown how you look for your salvation from illusions in other illusions that cannot save you. Each limits you with 'laws' that are as illusory as themselves, but you are not bound by them. To understand this, though, you first must realize that your salvation does not lie in them. While you seek for your salvation in illusions, you bind yourself to illusory laws. These 'laws' are how the personal mind tries to 'prove' that you can find salvation where it is *not*.

2. Today, you will be glad that the personal mind cannot prove this. If it could, you would forever seek for your salvation and never find it. Today's idea reminds you again how simple your salvation is: Look for it where it is, and you will find it.

3. Think how free you will feel when you recognize that you are not bound by the strange and twisted 'laws' that the personal mind has set up to save the body! It has you believe that the body will starve, unless you have stacks of paper strips and metal disks. It has you believe that swallowing a small pellet, or having fluids pushed into the body's veins through a needle, will ward off disease and death. It has you believe that you are alone, unless another body is near the body with which you identify.

4. These beliefs are insanity. The personal mind calls them 'laws', and puts them under different names in a long catalogue of rituals that serve no real purpose. The personal mind has you think that you must obey the 'laws' of medicine, economics, health, etc. It teaches you that if you protect the body, *you* are saved.

5. These are not 'laws'; they are insanity. The body is endangered by your mind, which does not want to see that it is the victim of itself. The body's suffering is a mask your mind wears to hide that it is really your mind that suffers. You identify with a body to deny that you are your own enemy, that you attack yourself, and that you want to die. This awareness is what the personal mind's 'laws' are

meant to 'save' you from.

6. But the only law is God's Law. You need to repeat this over and over, until you realize that it applies to everything that you have made to oppose God's Will. Your magical solutions are illusions; the body that they are meant to save does not exist. Only What they are meant to hide will save you.

7. God's Law can never be replaced. Devote today to rejoicing that this is true. You no longer want to hide the Truth, because it is Truth that keeps you Eternally Free. Magical thinking limits you, but God's Law restores you to an awareness of your Limitlessness. God's Light has come into your awareness, because the only law is God's Law.

8. Begin your longer practice period today with a short review of the different kinds of 'laws' that you have believed you must obey. For example, the 'laws' of nutrition and medicine for the body's protection, as well as other laws, like the 'laws' of friendship, or 'good' relationships in general. You may even believe in 'laws' that set forth how God wants you to live in the world, which many of the split mind's religions teach. These latter 'laws' may even damn you in God's name if you don't obey, but they are no stranger than the other 'laws' that you believe you must obey to stay safe.

9. The only law is God's Law. Dismiss all foolish beliefs in magic today, and hold your mind in silent readiness to hear the Holy Spirit speak the Truth to you. The Holy Spirit will tell you that there is no loss under God's Law. You will not have to make payment, nor will you make any exchanges, because there are no substitutes in God, Where All is One. God's Law forever extends God, and never needs to take anything.

10. Hear the Holy Spirit, and realize that the 'laws' that uphold the world that you perceive are foolish. Then listen further; the Holy Spirit will tell you more: About God's Love for you, about the Endless Joy God offers to you, and about God's Oneness with you, Which seems to be blocked by your belief in hell.

11. Open your mind to God today, and let God's Will extend

through you back to God. This is how Creation is Endlessly Increased. The Holy Spirit will speak to you of this, as well as of the Joys of Heaven, Which God's Law keeps Eternally Limitless. Repeat today's idea until you have understood that the only law is God's Law. Then, at the end of the practice period, say to yourself:

'I am under only God's Law.'

12. Repeat this dedication at least four or five times an hour today. Use it throughout the day in response to any temptation to believe that you are subject to any other 'laws'. It is your statement of freedom from all danger and tyranny. It is your acknowledgment that you are One with God, and that you are saved.

Mentor's Notes

As God is Mind, God's Law is like the Law of Mind that Mind only knows Itself. God's Law is that God only knows God. Since God is All, only God is Real. It is not 'wrong' or 'bad' or 'sinful' for you to seek for salvation in other 'laws' (magical thoughts); it is only misguided, because they are not real, and they deal with protecting or enhancing a body/personal self that is not you.

The personal mind may tempt you with today's lesson by reading into it that, if you learn how to transcend the world's 'laws' and accept God's Limitlessness, you can find a way to manifest in the world everything that the personal mind wants you to have: physical health, material wealth, worldly 'success', etc. This is a distortion of what is being stated here, because this lesson, as with all the lessons, is not concerned with a personal self or the world, but rather with your forgiving your perception that you are a personal self in a world. For you to state that you are under only God's Law is for you to state that you recognize that you are not a personal self in a world; you are in God.

Lesson 77

'I am entitled to experience miracles.'

1. You are entitled to experience miracles because you are One with God, you *will* experience miracles because you are One with God, and you will *extend* miracles because you are One with God. Again, this is how simple your salvation is! It is merely you reclaiming your Identity, and it is this that you will celebrate today.

2. Your claim to the experience of miracles does not lie in the personal self, it does not depend on any magical powers that you may have, nor in any rituals that you may have devised. Your claim to the experience of miracles is inherent in the Truth of What you are, is implicit in What God is, is ensured by God's extension of God to you, and is guaranteed by God's Law.

3. Today, you will claim your right to experience miracles. You have been promised full release from the world that you made, and you have been assured that God is within you, and can never be lost to you. You ask for nothing more than what belongs to you in Truth. Today, you will also make sure that you are not content with less.

4. Begin your longer practice periods by telling yourself, with confidence, that you are entitled to experience miracles. Close your eyes, and remind yourself that you are asking for only what is rightfully yours. Remind yourself that the experience of miracles is not given to you alone in a personal identity, and that, in asking for it, you are asking for miracles for your mind where you perceive a world as well. Miracles do not obey the 'laws' of the world; they merely follow the Law of God.

5. After a brief introductory phase, wait quietly for the assurance that your request is granted. You have asked for your own salvation, and this means the salvation of your entire mind. You have requested the *means* for your salvation; be assured that you are answered, because you are asking that God's Will be done.

6. But you are not really asking for anything with today's idea; you are stating an undeniable fact. The Holy Spirit can only assure

you that it is so. When you accept today's idea, it will be so in your awareness. There is no room for doubt or uncertainty today.

7. Have frequent practice periods today that you also devote to today's simple fact:

> 'I am entitled to experience miracles.'

Ask for miracles in situations where they are called for; you will recognize these. Since you are not relying on the personal mind to find miracles, you will receive them whenever you ask.

8. Remember, too, to not be satisfied with less than the perfect answer. If you are tempted, tell yourself:

> 'I will not trade away the experience of miracles for resentments. I want only what belongs to me, and God has established miracles as my right.'

Mentor's Notes

'Oneness' is another way to state both the Law of Mind and the Law of God. Remember, a miracle is an extension of God's Love in your awareness. It is a shift in your perception, away from separation, toward Oneness. A miracle is always an internal experience; it may or may not manifest in the world that you perceive.

Lesson 78

'I will let miracles replace the personal mind's resentments.'

1. Perhaps it is not yet clear to you that every choice that you make is one between a resentment of the personal mind and the experience of the miracle. All resentments are obstacles to miracles. When you hold onto resentment, you cannot experience God's Love. Yet, all the time It waits for you in the Light of God in your mind.

2. Today, you will go beyond the personal mind's resentments to experience miracles instead. You will undo the way that you are used to thinking with a personal mind by not allowing your Real Perception to stop before you are aware of It. You will not hold onto hate, but you will let it go, and gently perceive Christ.

3. Your Christ Mind waits for you behind the personal mind's resentments, and as you let them go, you will see It shining where the resentments were. Your every resentment is a block to your Real Perception, and as you let them go, you will see Christ where It has always been. It is in the Light of God in your mind, where the personal mind is in your dark denial of God. All resentment makes the darkness of your mind deeper, and you cannot perceive Truth in the dark.

4. Today you will see Christ. You will not be blind to It; you will not perceive resentment. This is how the personal mind is undone: You look toward Truth, and away from fear. Today you will select one person that you have used for the personal mind's resentment, and you will lay the resentment aside as you perceive them. This may be someone you fear or hate; someone you love, but who has made you angry; someone you call a friend, but whom you may see as difficult, demanding, irritating, or untrue to the role that you think that they should fulfill.

5. You know the one to choose; you have already thought of them. It will be of this seeming 'other' that you ask to see Christ. By looking past the resentment that you hold against them, you will learn What is behind the personal mind's perception of everyone.

One who was enemy becomes more than friend to you when you perceive them through the Holy role that the Holy Spirit assigns to them. Let this one be your savior from illusions today. This is their role in God's plan for your salvation.

6. In your longer practice periods today, you will see this one person in this role. Hold them in your mind, first as you see them through the personal mind. Review their 'faults', your difficulties with them, the small and large hurts that you perceive they caused you, and their neglect of you. Regard their body with all of its flaws and better points; think of their mistakes and 'sins'.

7. Then, ask the Holy Spirit, Which knows your Christ Mind is your Reality, to help you forgive this perception so you can perceive Christ in its place. Ask the Holy Spirit:

> 'Help me to perceive Christ beyond the personal mind's perception of this one, whom you have appointed as the one to lead me to the Holy Light of my mind.'

With your eyes closed, think of this person whom you resent, and let yourself be shown the Light beyond the personal mind's resentments.

8. What you ask for is not denied to you. Your Christ Mind has been waiting long for this, and wants to be free, and to make Its Freedom yours. The Holy Spirit reaches you through this one other, seeing no separation between your mind and what it perceives. What you perceive through the Holy Spirit will free your entire mind. Be very quiet now, and look on Christ shining in your mind. No dark resentments obscure your perception of It. You have allowed the Holy Spirit to express through you the Role that God gives to the Holy Spirit to save you from your illusion of separation from God.

9. God is grateful to you for these quiet times, in which you lay aside the personal mind's images to perceive the miracle of God's Love that the Holy Spirit shows you in their place. With Heaven, the part of your mind in which you perceive a world thanks you,

because all of God's Mind must rejoice as you are saved from illusions.

10. Remember this throughout today, and take the role that God assigns to you as part of God's plan for your salvation. Your temptation to believe that you are separate from God will fall away as you allow each seeming other in the world that you perceive save you by refusing to hide God's Light behind the personal mind's resentments of them. Allow everyone you meet, or that you remember from the personal mind's past, to be your savior, so that you become the savior of yourself. For your entire mind, pray:

'I will let miracles replace the personal mind's resentments.'

Mentor's Notes

Only you can choose hell for yourself, so only you can be your own savior. This is the theme of this Workbook. Others are your 'attacker' or 'savior', not because of who they are, or what they do, but because you choose how you will perceive them. They are never separate from you; they are, along with what you think of as 'you', your entire mind.

Lesson 79

'I will recognize my only problem, so that it can be solved.'

1. You cannot solve a problem if you do not acknowledge what it is. Even if it has already been solved, you will not recognize the solution if you don't acknowledge the problem in the first place. This is your situation. Your *only* problem is that you perceive yourself as separate from God, and this has already been solved, because it can never be. But you don't recognize the Solution because you have not recognized your problem.

2. In your perception that you are in a world, you and everyone that you perceive seem to have your own special problems. But they are all the same, and you must recognize this to accept the One Solution for all of them. You will not see a problem is solved if you think that the problem is something else, because you will not recognize the relevance of the Solution.

3. This is the position in which you find yourself now. You have the Solution, but you are still uncertain what your problem is. You seem to be confronted by a long series of different problems, and as one seems to be settled, another arises. There seems to be no end to them. There is no time in which you feel completely free of problems and at Peace.

4. Your temptation to perceive many problems is your temptation to keep your perception of separation from God uncorrected. The world that you perceive seems to present you with a vast number of problems, each requiring a different solution. This perception puts you in a position where your problem-solving is inadequate, and your failure is inevitable.

5. No one could solve all of the problems that the world that you perceive seems to hold. They seem to occur on so many levels, and in such varying forms and contents, that they confront you with an impossible situation. It is inevitable that you experience dismay and depression. Some problems spring up unexpectedly, just as you think that you've resolved other problems. Others, you hide in

denial, and they rise to haunt you now and then, only to have you deny them again, and leave them unresolved.

6. All of this complexity is the personal mind's desperate attempt to keep you from recognizing your real problem and solving it. If you accept that, no matter what form a problem takes, it is always only your perception of separation from God, you will accept its Solution, because you will see the Solution's relevance. By perceiving the one underlying problem in all seeming problems, you will understand that you have the Means to solve all of them. And you will use the Means, because you will recognize your only problem.

7. In your longer practice periods today, ask the Holy Spirit what your only problem is, and what the answer to it is. Do no assume that you already know. Free your mind from all of the many different kinds of problems that the personal mind tells you that you have. Realize that you have only one problem, which until now you have failed to recognize. You will be told what your problem is, and What the Solution to it is.

8. You will succeed with today's exercises to the extent that you do not insist on defining the problem with the personal mind. It is not necessary that you let go of all of the personal mind's ideas. All that is necessary is for you to doubt the personal mind's version of what your problems are. By recognizing your only problem, you are trying to recognize that you already have the Solution, so that your problem can be undone by the Solution, and you can be at Peace.

9. Your shorter practice periods should be set by need, instead of by time. You will perceive many problems today, but direct your efforts toward recognizing that there is only one problem, and only One Answer. All of your problems are solved when you recognize this. This is your Peace.

10. Do not be deceived by the forms that problems take today. Whenever any problem seems to arise, quickly say to yourself:

'I will recognize my only problem, so that it can be solved.'

Then suspend all judgment of what the problem is. If possible, close your eyes and ask what it is. You will be answered.

Mentor's Notes

Obviously, if you did not identify with a personal self, you would not have the problems that a personal self perceives. So all problems that you perceive rest in your one error of perceiving yourself as separate from God. The only solution for all problems, then, is for you to accept that you are One with God.

This lesson states what your problem is, and what its Solution must be. So when it says to ask the Holy Spirit to tell you your only problem and its Solution, it means to let the Holy Spirit into your *experience.*

Lesson 80

'I recognize that my one problem has been solved.'

1. When you are willing to recognize your one problem, you will recognize that you have no problem, because you will recognize that you have its Solution. Therefore, you must be at Peace. Your salvation depends on you recognizing that your one problem is your perception that you are separate from God, understanding that this is a mistake, and accepting that you are Eternally One with God. One problem, one Solution - your salvation is accomplished. You are free from conflict. Accept this fact, and you take your place in God's plan for your salvation.

2. Your only problem has been solved! Repeat this over and over again to yourself today, with gratitude and conviction. Recognize your only problem, and open the way for the Holy Spirit to show you the Solution. Lay aside self-deception, and see the Light of Truth. Accept salvation for yourself by bringing your one problem to Truth. Recognize the One Solution, because you have identified your one problem.

3. Today, you are entitled to Peace, because the one problem that has troubled you is resolved. Only, do not forget that all of the problems that you perceive have been resolved. You will not be deceived by their many forms if you remember this: one problem; One Solution. Accept the Peace this simple statement can give to you.

4. In your longer practice periods, claim the Peace that is yours, because your one problem and its Solution have been brought together. Your Oneness with God is the Solution, and It cannot fail you. The Solution is inherent in the problem. Accept the Solution, and you are saved from the problem.

5. Accept the Peace that the Solution brings to you. Close your eyes, and receive It. Your one problem has been solved; you have no conflict. You are free and at Peace. You have one problem, it has One Solution; the simplicity of salvation is the guarantee that it will

work.

6. Assure yourself often today that all problems have been solved in this one. Repeat the idea frequently, and with deep conviction. Be sure to apply today's idea to any specific problem that seems to arise. Quickly say to yourself:

'I recognize that this problem has been solved.'

7. Be determined to not collect resentments today. Be determined to be free of problems that do not exist. The means is simple: Do not deceive yourself about what your one problem is, and you will recognize that it has been solved.

Mentor's Notes

If you find yourself resistant to accepting that you have only one problem, and that it has already been solved, it is not because you are deceived by many problems, or because this concept is too hard for you to understand. This lesson shows you just how easy your salvation is. If you are resistant to accepting it, it's because you do not yet want the Solution to your one problem. This is not a 'sin', so there is no need to feel guilty. You will, in an instant, undo your attachment to a personal self and return to God. Getting motivated for that moment is the process that you are engaged in doing this Workbook. Any resistance that you feel will pass away as you undo many layers of the personal mind's defenses, which you have accepted as your own.

Review 2

Introduction

1. You are now ready for another review. You will begin where the last review left off, but this time you will be covering only two ideas each day. The early part of the day you will devote to one idea, and the latter part of the day you will devote to the other idea. In addition to a long practice period for each idea, you will have frequent short ones.

2. Your longer practice periods of fifteen minutes each will follow this general form: Begin by thinking about the idea and the comments that are included with them. Devote three or four minutes to reading them slowly, several times if you want, then close your eyes and listen.

3. If you find your mind wandering, repeat the first phase of the exercise period. Try to spend most of the time listening, quietly and attentively. There is a message from God waiting for you; be confident that you will receive it. Remember, it belongs to you, and you want it.

4. Do not allow your intent to waver because of distracting thoughts. Realize that, whatever form the thoughts take, they have no meaning and no power. Replace them with your determination to succeed. Do not forget that your Will has power over all fantasies and dreams. Trust It to see you through them, and to carry you beyond them all.

5. Regard these practice periods as your dedication to the Christ in you. Refuse to be detoured by illusions and thoughts of death. You are dedicated to your salvation from illusions. Everyday, be determined to fulfill your function.

6. In the shorter practice periods, re-affirm your determination, using the original form of the idea for general application, and more specific forms when needed. Some specific forms are included in the comments that follow the ideas. These, however, are only suggestions. It is your intent, not the words you use, that matter.

Lesson 81

Today's review covers the following ideas:

1. (61) 'I am the Light of the world that I perceive.'

How Holy I am, because I have been given the function of extending God's Light in my mind where I perceive a world. I am still before my Holiness. In Its Calm Light, all of my conflicts disappear. In Its Peace, I remember What I am.

2. Some specific forms for applying today's idea when special difficulties arise might be:

'I will not hide the Light of the world in me.'
'The Light of the world shines through this appearance.'
'This shadow will vanish before God's Light.'

3. (62) 'Forgiving is my function as the Light of the world that I perceive.'

By accepting that my function is forgiving my illusions, I perceive God's Light in me. In this Light, I perceive my function clearly. My accepting my function does not depend on my understanding what true forgiveness is, but I trust that, in God's Light, I will come to understand it.

4. Specific forms for this idea might include:

'This will help me to learn what forgiving means.'
'I will not separate my function from my True Will.'
'I will not use this for an alien purpose.'

Lesson 82

Today's review covers the following ideas:

1. (63) 'Through my forgiving, the Light of the world brings Peace to my entire mind.'

My forgiving my illusions is the means through which God's Light finds expression in my perception that I am in a world. My forgiving is the means through which I become aware of God's Light within me. My forgiving heals me and the part of my mind where I perceive a world, so I forgive the world that I perceive to heal my entire mind.

2. Some specific forms for applying today's idea are:

'Peace extends from my mind to you, ______ (name).'
'I share God's Light with you, ______ (name).'
'By forgiving what is appearing, I can see What is really here instead.'

3. (64) 'I will not forget that my function is forgiving.'

I will not forget that my function is forgiving, because I want to remember my Self in God. I cannot fulfill my function if I forget what it is. Only if I fulfill my function will I experience the Joy that God intends for me.

4. Specific forms for today's idea are:

'I will not use this to hide my function of forgiving from me.'
'I will use this opportunity to fulfill my function by forgiving.'
'This may threaten the personal mind, but it cannot change my function in any way.'

Lesson 83

Today's review covers the following ideas:

1. (65) 'My only function is the one that God gives to me.'

The only function that I have is the one of forgiving that God gives to me. Recognizing this releases me from all conflict, because I have only one goal. With only one purpose, I always know what to do, what to say, and what to think. All doubt disappears as I acknowledge that my only function is the one that God gives to me.

2. Specific applications might take this form:

'The personal mind's perception of this does not change my function.'
'This does not give me a function that replaces the one that God gives to me.'
'I will not use this to justify a function that God does not give to me.'

3. (66) 'My Happiness and my function are One.'

All that comes from God is One. What comes from Oneness, I must receive as One. Fulfilling my function is my Happiness, because both my function and my Happiness come from God. To find my Happiness, I must learn the function that makes me happy.

4. Some specific applications of today's idea are:

'This cannot separate my Happiness from my function.'
'That my Happiness is my function is not changed by this.'
'This is not my function, and it can bring me only an illusion of happiness.'

Mentor's Notes

Remember, your Function in Heaven is to extend God, so your function in your perception that you are in a world is to forgive your illusions, so that you can extend the Light of God in your awareness.

Lesson 84

Today's review covers the following ideas:

1. (67) 'Love created me like Itself.'

I am One with God. I cannot suffer, I cannot experience loss, and I cannot die. I am not a body. I recognize my Reality today. I will not worship idols, or raise my own self-concept to replace my Self in God. I am One with God; Love created me like Itself.

2. You might use these specific forms in applying today's idea:

'I will not see an illusion of myself in this.'
'As I look on this, I remember God.'
'God did not create what I perceive with a personal mind.'

3. (68) 'Love does not hold onto resentment.'

The personal mind's resentments are completely alien to Love. They attack Love, and they keep Its Light hidden from me. If I hold onto resentments, I am attacking Love. Therefore, I am attacking my True Self, making my True Self an alien to me. Today, I am determined to not attack myself, so that I can remember What I am.

4. Use these specific forms for applying today's idea:

'This is not a justification for denying my True Self.'
'I will not use this to attack Love.'
'I will not be tempted to attack my True Self.'

Lesson 85

Today's review covers the following ideas:

1. (69) 'The personal mind's resentments hide the Light of the world in me.'

The personal mind's resentments show me what is not here, and they hide What I want to perceive. So, for what do I want resentments? They keep my mind in darkness, and they hide God's Light within me. Resentment and Light cannot go together, but God's Light is the Source of my Real Perception. For me to use my Real Perception, I must lay all of the personal mind's resentments aside. I want to use my Real Perception, and letting go of resentment is the means by which I will succeed.

2. You might make specific applications of today's idea in these forms:

'I will not use this to block my Real Perception.'
'The Light of the world will shine all of this away.'
'I have no need for this. I want to Perceive Truly.'

3. (70) 'My salvation from guilt comes from me.'

Today, I will recognize that my salvation from guilt lies in me, because its Source is in me. My salvation has not left its Source, so it cannot have left my mind. I will not look for salvation outside of myself, because salvation is not found outside, then brought within. But from within me, it will extend, and everything that I perceive will reflect the Light of God that shines within me, and in all that my mind perceives.

4. These forms of today's idea are suitable for specific applications:

'This will not tempt me to look outside of myself for my

salvation.'
'I will not let this distract me from my awareness of the Source of my salvation within me.'
'This cannot remove my salvation from within me.'

Lesson 86

Today's review covers the following ideas:

1. (71) 'Only God's plan for my salvation from guilt will work.'

It is senseless for me to search around wildly for salvation from the pain of guilt. I thought that I saw salvation in many people, things, and situations, but when I reached for it, it was not there. I have been mistaken about where salvation is, and I will stop this futile searching. Only God's plan for my salvation from guilt will work. I rejoice, because God's plan cannot fail!

2. These are some suggested forms for applying today's idea:

'God's plan for my salvation will save me from this perception.'
'God's plan for my salvation can be applied everywhere.'
'I perceive this in the Light of God's plan for my salvation.'

3. (72) 'My holding onto the personal mind's resentments is an attack on God's plan for my salvation from guilt.'

My holding onto the personal mind's resentments is my attempt to prove that God's plan for my salvation from guilt will not work. But only God's plan *can* work. By holding onto resentments, I exclude from my awareness my only real hope of salvation. I will no longer defeat what is truly for my own good in this insane way. I will accept God's plan for my salvation and be happy.

4. You might use these specific forms for applying today's idea:

'I am choosing between misperception and salvation as I look at this.'
'If I see a justification for resentment here, I will not see a justification for my salvation.'
'This calls for salvation, not for attack.'

Lesson 87

Today's review covers the following ideas:

1. (73) 'It is my Will to perceive the Light of God.'

Today, I use the Power of my True Will. It is not my Will to grope around in the darkness denying God, afraid of shadows; afraid of unreal things. God's Light will guide me today. I will follow It where It leads me, and I will perceive What It shows me. Today, I will experience the Peace of my Real Perception.

2. These forms of today's idea will be helpful for specific application:

'This cannot hide the Light I will to see.'
'______ (name), you stand with me in God's Light.'
'In God's Light, this looks different.'

3. (74) 'There is only God's Will.'

Today I am safe, because I recognize that there is only God's Will. I can only be afraid when I believe that there is another will. I attack only when I am afraid; I attack only when I believe that my Eternal Safety is not real. Today, I recognize that separation from God has not occurred. I am safe, because there is only God's Will.

4. Some useful forms for applying today's idea are:

'I will perceive this through God's Will.'
'It is God's Will that you, ______ (name), and I are One with God.'
'Whatever I perceive, I am Part of God's Will.'

Lesson 88

Today's review covers the following ideas:

1. (75) 'God's Light has come into my awareness.'

When I choose salvation over attack, I merely choose what is already here. My salvation is already done. Attack and resentment are not really here for me to choose, that is why I am always choosing between Truth and illusion; between what is here and what is not. God's Light has come into my awareness. I can really only choose the Light, because there is nothing else. Light replaces darkness, and the darkness is gone.

2. Here are some useful forms of today's idea for specific application:

'I cannot perceive this in darkness, because God's Light has come into my awareness.'
'______ (name), God's Light in you is all that I want to see.'
'I want to see in this only What is really here.'

3. (76) 'I am under only God's Law.'

This is the perfect statement of my freedom: I am under only God's Law. With the personal mind, I am constantly tempted to make other laws, and to give them power over me. I suffer, because of my belief in them. But they have no real effect on me at all; I am only affected by God's Law. God's Law is the Law of Limitlessness.

4. Some specific forms for applying today's idea are:

'My perception of this shows me that I believe in laws that do not exist.'
'I see only God's Law at work in this.'
'I will allow God's Law to work in this.'

Lesson 89

Today's review covers the following ideas:

1. (77) 'I am entitled to experience miracles.'

I am entitled to experience miracles, because I am under only God's Law. God's Law releases me from the personal mind's resentments, and replaces them with the experience of miracles. I will accept miracles in place of resentments, which are only illusions that hide the miracles beyond them. Now, I will accept only what I am entitled to under God's Law, so that I can use it on behalf of the function of forgiveness that God has given to me.

2. Some suggestions for specific applications:

'Behind this is a miracle to which I am entitled.'
'I will not hold onto resentment against you, ______ (name). Instead, I extend a miracle to you.'
'If I perceive this through Truth, it offers me a miracle.'

3. (78) 'I will let miracles replace the personal mind's resentments.'

With this idea, I unite my will with the Holy Spirit's Will, and recognize that they are One. With this idea, I accept my release from hell. With this idea, I express my willingness to have all of my illusions replaced with Truth, which is God's plan for my salvation from guilt. I will make no exceptions and no substitutes. I want All of Heaven, and only Heaven, as God wills for me.

4. Some useful specific forms for today's idea may be:

'I will replace this resentment with my salvation.'
'______ (name), let our resentments be replaced by miracles.'
'Beyond this is a miracle, which will replace all of the personal mind's resentments.'

Lesson 90

Today's review covers the following ideas:

1. (79) 'I will recognize my only problem, so that it can be solved.'

Today, I realize that any problem that I perceive is always some form of the personal mind's resentment, which I cherish. I also realize that the solution to the problem is always a miracle, which I will let replace the resentment. Today, I remember the simplicity of my salvation by reinforcing the lesson that I have only one problem, and it has only One Solution. I invite the Solution to come to me through my forgiving the personal mind's resentments, and my acceptance of the miracle to take their place.

2. Some useful forms for applying today's lesson are:

'This presents a problem that I want resolved.'
'The miracle behind this resentment will solve this problem for me.'
'The solution to this problem is the miracle that it conceals.'

3. (80) 'I recognize that my one problem has been solved.'

I only seem to have problems, because I perceive myself in time. I believe that the problem comes first, and that time must elapse before it is resolved. I do not see that a problem and its solution are simultaneous. This is because I do not yet realize that God has corrected my one problem, and that it is not separated from its Solution by time. I am willing to let the Holy Spirit teach me this. I understand that I cannot have a problem that has not already been solved.

4. Use ideas like these for your specific applications:

'I do not have to wait for this to be resolved.'
'The Solution to this problem has already been given to me. I

only have to accept It.'

'Time cannot separate this problem from its Solution.'

Mentor's Notes

Lesson 79 states that your only problem is your perception of separation from God, and that its only Solution is your Oneness with God. The first part of lesson 90 states that your only problem is a form of resentment, and that its solution is a miracle. This is not a contradiction. Lesson 90's approach is practical. On a daily basis, you experience your separation from God in the form of the personal mind's resentments, and you correct it by allowing yourself to experience a miracle, which reaffirms your Oneness with God.

The second part of lesson 90 recalls what it says in the Text about the idea of separation from God: The moment it occurred, it was undone. God, being All-encompassing, cannot have an opposite. So the idea of God's opposite is undone, really, before it occurs. This is why all the problems that you perceive are really not here.

Lesson 91

'I perceive miracles through God's Light.'

1. It is important for you to remember that your experience of miracles and your Real Perception go together. This needs frequent repeating. This is the center of your new thought system, and the Perception that it produces: *A miracle is always here.* Its presence is not caused by your Real Perception; its absence is not caused by your failure to use your Real Perception. Only your *awareness* of miracles is affected by your using or not using your Real Perception. You perceive miracles through God's Light in your mind; you cannot see them when you deny God's Light in your mind.

2. For you, then, learning that God's Light is within you is crucial. While you remain in the darkness of the personal mind, you cannot perceive miracles, so you are convinced that they are not here. This follows from the premise which darkens your mind: Deny God's Light within you, and you will fail to perceive It. Your failure to perceive God's Light leaves you in the darkness of the personal mind. God's Light is there within you, but It is useless to you when you deny It, and the seeming reality of the personal mind makes God's Light meaningless to you.

3. It must seem like insanity to you to read that What you do not see is here. But you must recognize that it *is* insanity to *not see* What is really here and *to see* what is not really here. You do not doubt that the body's eyes can see, and you do not doubt that the images that they show you are reality. Your faith lies in the personal self, not in God. How can this be reversed? In your identification with a personal self it is impossible, but you are not a personal self.

4. Your efforts, no matter how little they may be, have Strong Support. If you realized how great the Strength is within you, your doubts about God would vanish. Today, you will devote yourself to feeling God's Strength within you. When you have felt this Strength, Which places all miracles within your easy reach, you will not doubt It. The miracles that your belief in a weak personal self hides will

leap into your awareness as you feel the Strength of God within you.

5. Three times today, set aside ten minutes for quiet time in which you leave the weak personal mind behind. This is accomplished very simply: Tell yourself that you are not a body. Your faith goes to what you want, and you automatically instruct your mind accordingly. Your will is your teacher, and your will has all the strength to do what it desires. If you choose, you can escape the limitations of a body and experience God's Strength within you.

6. Begin your longer practice periods with this logical statement, and a question:

> 'I perceive miracles in God's Light, but it is not the body's eyes that perceive God's Light, so I am not a body. What am I?'

For your exercises today, you need the question with which this statement ends. What you think you are is a belief that you must undo, and you must allow What you really are to be revealed to you. The belief that you are a body is a mistake that calls for correction. The Truth of What you are calls on the Strength of God in you to bring into your awareness What your mistake conceals.

7. If you are not a body, then what are you? You need to become aware of Something Else, Which the Holy Spirit uses to replace the image of a body in your mind. You need to feel Something to put your faith in, as you remove your faith from a body. You need an experience of Reality, Which you will value more than the body.

8. If you are not a body, then what are you? Ask this in honesty, then spend several minutes allowing the attributes of your mistaken identity to be corrected by the Attributes of your Real Identity. For example, say:

> 'I am not weak; I am Strong.'
> 'I am not helpless; I am All-Powerful.'
> 'I am not limited; I am Limitless.'
> 'I am not doubtful; I am Certain.'

'I am not an illusion; I am Reality.'

'I cannot use my Real Perception in dark denial of God, but I can use It in the Light of God within me.'

9. In the second phase of your exercise periods, try to experience these Truths about you. Pay particular attention to the experience of Strength. Remember, all of your sense of weakness comes from your identification with a body, a mistake that does not deserve your faith. If only for a moment, try to remove your faith from it. You will become more accustomed to putting your faith in What is Worthy of your faith as you go along.

10. Relax for the rest of your practice period, confident that your efforts, no matter how small, are fully supported by the Strength of God within you. It is from This that your Strength will come; it is through Its Strong Support that you will feel Strength within you. God's Strength unites with you in this practice period, in which you share God's Purpose. God is the Light in Which you see miracles, because God's Strength is yours. God's Strength becomes your Means of perceiving, so that you can Perceive Truly.

11. Five or six times an hour, at as regular intervals as you can manage, remind yourself that you perceive miracles in God's Light. Meet any temptation to believe that separation from God is real with today's idea. This form will be helpful for this purpose:

'I perceive miracles in God's Light. Because of this, I will not choose darkness.'

Mentor's Notes

You are not asked to give up your identification with a personal self and be without an identity. The miracle is an experience of your Real Identity, with Which you will replace the personal self. But your Real Identity is not like a personal identity; It is not limited to form of any kind, nor to an image. Pure Being is Pure Experience; It is Limitless Love, Peace, and Joy. The experience of the miracle is a taste of This in your perception that you are in a world. As you experience the miracle more and more, it will be apparent to you that the value of this experience is much greater than anything that the personal self has to offer, and you will let the personal self go automatically.

Lesson 92

'I perceive miracles through God's Light, and God's Light and Strength are One.'

1. Today's idea is an extension of yesterday's idea. You do not think of God's Light in your mind as Strength, and the personal mind's dark denial of God as weakness, because you do not understand that you are Mind or the nature of your Mind. Your idea of 'perception' is tied up with the body's eyes and brain. You even believe that you can change your perception by putting little bits of plastic or glass in front of your eyes. These are forms of magical beliefs that come from your belief that you are a body, and that the body's eyes are the source of your perception.

2. You also believe that the body's brain can think! If you understood the nature of thought, you would laugh at this insane idea. It is as if you think you hold the match that provides the sun's warmth, or that you hold the world in your hand. These ideas are just as foolish as thinking that the body's eyes 'perceive' or that the brain can 'think'.

3. It is God's Strength in you that is the Light of your Real Perception, just as It is God's Mind with Which you really think. God's Strength undoes the personal mind's weakness in you. It is weakness to use a body to perceive. All it can show you is dark images like itself: the small, the weak, the sick, the dying, the needy, the sad, the poor, the afraid, and the unhappy. This is what you perceive with a body's eyes, which cannot bless.

4. God's Strength in you overlooks these appearances, and It keeps a steady eye on the Light beyond them. It unites with Light, of Which It is a Part; It sees Itself. It shows you the Light in Which to see your True Self. In dark denial of God, you perceive a self that is not here. God's Strength is the Truth about you; the personal mind's weakness is an idol that you worship and adore to dispel God's Strength in you, so that darkness can rule in your mind where God has put Its Light.

5. God's Strength in your mind comes from Truth and shines with God's Light; the personal mind's weakness reflects the darkness of its maker. The personal mind is sick, and it perceives sickness. Truth is a Savior, and It can only will Happiness and Peace in your mind where you perceive a world. It gives Its Limitless Strength to you when you ask for It. It recognizes that if lack is real anywhere, it is real in you, so It extends Its Light so that your entire mind may benefit as One. Truth's Strength extends to bring a miracle to all that you perceive, so that your entire mind unites in one purpose of forgiving illusions and of Love.

6. The personal mind's weakness is that it cannot see a purpose in forgiveness and Love. It looks on a world that it believes is real, but separate from itself, and it wants to extend nothing of itself to the world. It judges and condemns, but it does not love. It hides in dark denial of God, and dreams that it is strong and a victor over limitations that really only increase in its darkness.

7. The personal mind fears and attacks and hates you, and its darkness covers everything that you perceive with it, making its illusions as fearful as itself. No miracles occur in the personal mind; only hate. It separates itself from everything that you perceive, where God's Light and Strength in your mind extend to everything that you perceive. The Light of God's Strength is not like the light that you see with a body's eyes. It does not change or flicker or go out. It does not shift from night to day, and back again.

8. The Light of God's Strength is Constant, is as Sure as Love, and is Forever happy to extend Itself, because It knows that It can only extend *to* Itself. You cannot ask in vain to share Its Perception, and you cannot enter into Its Light without experiencing a miracle, and God's Strength and Light within you.

9. God's Strength in you offers you Its Light, and guides your perception, so do not dwell on the idle shadows that the personal mind uses to deceive you with the body's eyes. God's Strength and Light unite within you, and where They meet is your True Self. This is the Meeting Place that you will find and rest in today, because the

Peace of God is Where your True Self, Which is One with God, is waiting to meet Itself and be One again.

10. Give twenty minutes twice today to entering this Meeting Place, and to allowing yourself to be brought to your True Self. Its Strength will be the Light in Which your Real Perception is given to you. Leave the darkness of the personal mind for a little while today, and practice perceiving with the Light of God. Close the body's eyes, and ask Truth to show you how to find the Meeting Place Where you join with your True Self again, and Where God's Light and Strength are One.

11. Practice this morning and this evening. After your morning meeting with your True Self, use the day to prepare for the time at night when you will meet your True Self again. Repeat today's idea as often as you can, and recognize that you are being introduced to your Real Perception, and led away from dark denial of God to God's Light, Where you can perceive only miracles.

Mentor's Notes

This lesson makes a very clear distinction between Truth and illusion; What you are and what you are not. Its pointing out how the personal mind deceives you about what is real perception, however, does not mean that you should not wear contacts or glasses if you need them! Simply understand that what you see with the body's eyes is not Truth. You can only see Truth within yourself, and then extend It in your perception through your mind.

Since it is the Law of Mind that mind only knows itself, both the personal mind and the Truth in you only perceive themselves. The difference is that the personal mind projects what is in its mind and pretends that what it sees comes from something else; the Truth in you knows Itself, and happily and automatically extends Itself to keep Itself in Its awareness.

Lesson 93

'God's Light and Peace and Joy abide within me.'

1. You think that deep within you are evil, darkness, and sin. You think that if anyone could see this evil truth about you, they would be repelled, and they would recoil from you as from a poisonous snake. You think that if the evil truth about you was revealed to you, you would be struck with a horror so intense that you would kill yourself, because it would be impossible for you to live with what you saw.

2. These beliefs, which come from the personal mind, but which you have taken as your own, are fixed so firmly in your mind, that it is difficult for you to accept that they are based on nothing. It is obvious that, in your identification with a personal self, you have made mistakes, you have sought for salvation in strange ways, you have been deceived, you have deceived, you are afraid of foolish illusions, and you have bowed down to idols made of dust. This is all true, according to what you now believe about yourself.

3. Today, you will question all of this, not from the point of view of the personal mind, but from a very different Reference Point, from Which these idle thoughts are meaningless. These thoughts about yourself do not come from God, and God does not share them with you. This should be enough to prove to you that they are wrong, but you do not perceive this yet.

4. You should be overjoyed to learn that all of the evil that you think that you did has never been done, that all of your 'sins' are nothing, that you are Pure and Holy as Part of God, and that God's Light and Peace and Joy abide within you. The personal mind's image of you cannot stand up to the Will of God. In your identification with a personal self, you think that this is death. You think that God will destroy you, but God saves you.

5. The self that you made is not One with God, so it does not exist at all. Anything that it does or thinks is nothing. It is neither good nor bad; it is not real. It does not fight with God in you; it does not

hurt or attack God's Peace. It has not changed God's Extension of God to you, nor reduced your Eternal Innocence to guilt, or Love to hate. The self that you made does not possess any power that can contradict the Will of God.

6. Your Innocence is guaranteed by God. You must repeat this over and over until you accept that it is true. Your Innocence is guaranteed by God. Nothing can touch It, or can change What God created Eternal. The self that you made, which you perceive as full of 'evil' and 'sin', is meaningless. Your Innocence is guaranteed by God, and God's Light and Peace and Joy abide within you.

7. Your salvation from guilt requires that you accept only one thought: You are One with God, not with what you have made. Whatever 'evil' that you think you did, you are One with God. Whatever mistakes that you have made, the Truth in you is unchanged. What is One with God is Eternal and Unalterable. Your Innocence is guaranteed by God. You are, and will Forever be, One with God. God's Light and Joy and Peace abide within you, because you are One with God.

8. In your longer practice periods, which should be the first five minutes of every hour, begin by stating the Truth about you:

> 'God's Light and Peace and Joy abide within me. My Innocence is guaranteed by God.'

Then put away your foolish self-images, and spend the rest of the practice period experiencing What God gives to you in place of what you have made for yourself.

9. You are either One with God, or with what you made. One Self is True; the other self is not here at all. Experience the Unity of your One Self. Appreciate Its Holiness and the Love with Which It is One. Do not interfere with the Self Which is One with God by hiding Its Majesty behind the tiny idols of 'evil' and 'sinfulness' that you have made to replace It. Let your True Self come into your awareness: This is you. God's Light and Peace and Joy abide within you,

because this is so.

10. You may not be willing, or even able, to give the first five minutes of every hour to today's exercises, but try to do so whenever you can. At least, remember to repeat this thought every hour:

> 'God's Light and Peace and Joy abide within me. My Innocence is guaranteed by God.'

Then spend a minute or so with your eyes closed, realizing that this statement is the Truth about you.

11. If a situation arises that disturbs you, quickly dispel the illusion of fear by repeating this thought again. If you are tempted to become angry with someone that you perceive, say to them silently:

> 'God's Light and Peace and Joy abide within you. Your Innocence is guaranteed by God.'

You can do much to save your entire mind today. You can do much to bring you closer to the part in your salvation that God has assigned to you. And you can do much today to become convinced that the idea for today is true.

Mentor's Notes

You might not accept that deep down you think that you are 'evil' and 'sinful', but you are identified with a personal self or you wouldn't be doing these lessons, and those beliefs are inherent in a personal identity, because a personal identity is the opposite of God in every way. A personal identity is the belief that you have attacked God and taken part of God for yourself, and you fear that God is going to punish you for this. Without these beliefs, you would Joyfully be wholly aware of God again. And the evidence of these beliefs, even if you can't find them in your conscious mind, is there in your perception that the world is real. If you cannot access those beliefs, it is because your guilt is so great that you are afraid to look at it, just as it is stated in the first paragraph above. In that case, you need this lesson more than ever.

Remember, your mind is one, and you will believe that you are like what you perceive. So, whether you see 'evil' or 'sinfulness' in you or the world, it is in your mind, and it needs to be corrected.

Lesson 94

'I am as God created me.'

1. Today you continue with the one idea that brings you complete salvation, and that makes powerless all forms of temptation to believe that you are separate from God; it is the one thought that renders the personal mind silent, and which undoes it: You are as God created you. The sights and sounds of the world disappear, and all thoughts that you have ever had about the world are wiped away forever by this one idea. Here is your salvation accomplished, and your Sanity restored.

2. God's Light is Strength, and Strength is Innocence. You are as God created you, so you must be Strong, and God's Light must still be within you. God guarantees your Innocence, so God must guarantee Its Strength and Light are yours as well. You are as God created you. The personal mind's dark denial of God cannot obscure your Glory. You stand in God's Light, Strong in the Innocence in Which God created you, as you are Forever.

3. Today, you will spend the first five minutes of each waking hour experiencing the Truth within you. Begin with:

'I am as God created me. I am Eternally One with God.'

Now, reach within to the Christ in you. This is the Self that has never 'sinned', nor made an image to replace Its Reality. This is the Self that has never left God to perceive itself in an uncertain world. This is the Self that does not fear, and cannot conceive of loss or suffering or death.

4. The only thing required for you to reach this Goal is for you to lay aside all of the idols and self-images that you have made; to go past all attributes that you ascribe to the personal self, both 'good' and 'bad'; and to wait in quiet expectancy for the Truth. God has promised that God will be revealed to you if you just ask for God. You are asking now, and you cannot fail, because God cannot fail.

5. If you cannot practice for the first five minutes of every hour, at least remind yourself hourly:

'I am as God created me. I am Eternally One with God.'

Remind yourself frequently today that you are One with God. And when the part of your mind that you perceive as a world outside of you seems to irritate you, be sure to respond with these words:

'You are as God created you. You are Eternally One with God.'

Make every effort to do the hourly exercises today. Every one that you do will be a giant step toward your release from limitations, and a milestone in your learning the thought system which this course sets forth.

Mentor's Notes

Remember, in this course, *to create* means *to be one with*. God's *Creation* is God extending God Infinitely. As God's Creation, you extend God Infinitely.

Again, you see at the end of this lesson that you are to include what you perceive in a statement that originally seems to be only about you. You cannot exclude what you perceive from your change of mind about yourself, because what you perceive is in your mind. The perception that there is a 'you' and a world outside of you is the first error that you must correct, because as long as you see the world as separate from yourself, you will not understand that Mind is One, and, therefore, God is One. It will seem as though there are two realities: God and the world.

Lesson 95

'I am One within my True Self; I am One with God.'

1. Today's idea accurately describes you in God. You are One within your True Self, and you are One with God. This is the Unity of God's Creation; God's Limitless extension of God. Your Perfect Unity makes change in you impossible. You do not accept this, and you do not realize that it must be so, because you believe that you *have* changed yourself.

2. The personal self is a ridiculous parody of 'creation': weak, vicious, ugly, sinful, miserable, in pain. This is its version of you; a self conflicted within itself, separate from God, and barely held together by an erratic and capricious maker, to which you pray. But the personal mind cannot hear your prayers, because it is deaf to you. It does not see the Oneness in you, because it is blind to you. It does not understand that you are One with God, because it does not understand anything Real.

3. Today, you will be aware only of What can really hear and see you, and What makes Perfect Sense. You will again direct your exercises toward reaching your One Self, Which is One with God. Try again today, in patience and in hope.

4. Using the first five minutes of every hour for practicing has special advantages for you at this stage of your learning. It is still difficult for you to focus when you undertake a longer practice period. You have certainly recognized by now the extent of your lack of mental discipline, and of your need to train your mind. It is necessary that you recognize this, because it does slow down your progress.

5. Frequent, but shorter, practice periods also have other advantages for you at this time. Besides your inability to maintain your focus, you must also have noticed that, unless you are reminded of your purpose frequently, you tend to forget about it for long periods of time. You often forget the short applications for the day, and you have not yet formed the habit of using the day's idea as an automatic

response to temptation to believe that separation from God is real.

6. So structure is necessary for you at this time. It is planned to include frequent reminders of your Goal, and regular attempts to reach It. It is not ideal for your salvation that any ritual of time be practiced, but it is advantageous while your motivation is inconsistent, and you are still resistant to learning Truth.

7. Therefore, you will keep to the five minutes an hour practice periods for a while. Omit as few as possible. Using the first five minutes of the hour is particularly helpful, because it imposes a firmer structure. Do not, however, use forgetting an hour or so to be an excuse to not return to the exercise as soon as possible. Do not regard the day as 'lost' because you have failed to do as required. This is only your unwillingness to correct your mistake.

8. The Holy Spirit's teaching is not delayed by your mistakes. The only thing that can hold the Holy Spirit at bay is your unwillingness to let go of your mistakes. Be determined, particularly for the next week or so, to forgive yourself your lapses in practicing these exercises. This tolerance for weakness will enable you to overlook it, rather than give it power to delay your learning. If you give it this power, you believe that it is your strength, and you confuse weakness with strength.

9. When you do not comply with the requirements of this course, you are merely making a mistake. This calls for correction, and nothing else. To allow a mistake to continue is only another mistake, which perpetuates the first mistake. Lay this process aside, because it is just another way in which you defend illusions against the Truth.

10. Let all these errors go by recognizing what they are for: to keep you unaware that you are One Self, Part of God; One with God's Total Extension of God, and with God's Limitless Power and Peace. This is the Truth, and only this is the Truth. Today, you will reaffirm this Truth, and reach again for the Place in you Where there is no doubt that only this is True.

11. Begin today's practice periods with this assurance, which you

should offer to your mind with all of the certainty that you can muster:

'I am One within my True Self; I am One with God. I am at One with God's Total Extension, and Limitless in Power and in Peace.'

Then, close your eyes, and tell yourself again, slowly and thoughtfully, so that the words sink into your mind:

'I am One within my True Self.'

Repeat this several times, attempting to feel the meaning that the words convey.

12. You are One Self, United and Secure in God's Light and Joy and Peace. You are One with God, One Self, with One Creator and One Goal: to extend this awareness to your entire mind, so that God's Extension may be Complete in your mind. You are One Self, Complete and Whole, with the power to lift the veil of darkness from your mind where you perceive a world, and to let God's Light come through you to extend the Truth about you in your perception.

13. You are One Self, in Perfect Harmony with All that there is. You are One Self, the Holy Christ, united within your Self with all that you perceive; united with God in God's Will. Feel this One Self in you, and let It shine away all of your illusions and doubts. This is your True Self, Christ, as Innocent as God, with God's Strength within you, and God's Love yours Forever. You are One Self, and you can feel this Self within you, and you can cast away all illusions from the One Mind that is your Self, the Holy Truth within you.

14. Today, do not forget. Your little part brings happiness to your entire mind. Heaven looks to you in Confidence that you will succeed today. Share Its Confidence, because It is yours. Be vigilant, and do not forget your Goal today. Repeat today's idea as frequently as possible, and understand that each time that you do so, the Voice of Hope, a stirring of Truth, the gentle rustling of the wings of Peace,

extends to your entire mind.

15. Your acknowledgement that you are One Self, One with God, extends to make the world One with you. To everyone that you meet today, be sure to extend the promise of today's idea with these words in your mind:

'You are my One Self; One with God. I honor you because of What I am and What God is. God loves my entire mind as One.'

Mentor's Notes

You might wonder who the 'you' is in the second paragraph that prays to the personal mind, but that the personal mind cannot really know. You are One with God, but you identify with a personal self. The part of your mind where this split occurs is the 'decision maker'. It is the part of your mind that can choose to identify with What It is in Truth or with what it made (the personal self). This course always addresses you as the decision maker.

Certainly, the paragraphs concerning the format for these lessons were directed specifically at Helen Schucman, who scribed this course. However, most students struggle with maintaining their focus during extended meditations, and most students forget to practice the idea for the day throughout the day, unless they have had some previous experience with meditation; they have already, through some other means, worked through many layers of resistance to God; or they are highly motivated. If one of these describes you, you will still benefit by following the lessons as written.

Lesson 96

'My salvation from guilt comes from my One Self.'

1. Although you are One Self, you experience yourself as two selves: Good and evil, Loving and hating, Mind and body. This sense that you are split into opposite selves produces acute and constant conflict in your mind, and leads to your frantic attempts to reconcile the contradictory aspects of your split self-perception. You have looked for many solutions, and none of them has worked. The opposites that you experience within yourself will never be compatible, because only one of them exists.

2. If you want to be saved from guilt, you must accept that Truth and illusion cannot be reconciled, no matter how hard you try, what means you use, or where you see the problem. Until you accept this, you will attempt to reach an endless number of goals that you cannot reach. This will result in a series of senseless expenditures of your time and effort, and of vacillations between hopefulness and doubt. Each goal will be as futile as the one before, and will fail you as much as the next one.

3. Problems that have no meaning cannot be resolved. Two selves that are the opposite of each other in every way cannot be brought together, and Good and evil cannot be reconciled. The self that you made cannot be your True Self, and your True Self cannot be split in two and still be the Oneness that It is and must Forever be. You cannot be both a Mind and a body, because each denies that the other is real. If you are physical form, where is your mind? If you are Spirit, then a physical body is meaningless to your Reality.

4. Spirit uses the Mind as a means for Self-expression. A Mind that serves Spirit is filled with Peace and Joy. Its Power comes from Spirit, and It Happily fulfills Its Function when It serves Spirit. But the Mind can also see Itself as separate from Spirit, and confuse Itself with a physical form. Then it is without its Function, it has no Peace, and Happiness is foreign to it.

5. Mind apart from Spirit cannot think. It denies its Source of

Strength, and perceives itself as helpless, limited, and weak. Separated from its function, it thinks that it is alone, attacked by an outside world, and it hides in a body's frail support. Then it tries to reconcile what can never be reconciled, and this is what it thinks that it is for.

6. Do not waste anymore time on this. You cannot resolve the senseless conflicts which occur in the illusions that the personal mind perceives. The resolutions, if possible, would be meaningless in Reality. What purpose would they serve? Your salvation does not make your illusions real, nor solve problems that do not exist. Maybe you hope it can, but you don't really want God's plan for your release from limitations to limit you and bring you pain.

7. Your True Self retains Its Real Thoughts, and They remain within your mind and in God's Mind. The Holy Spirit holds your salvation in your mind, and offers it the way to Peace. Your salvation is a Thought that you share with God, because the Holy Spirit in you has accepted it and made it so. Salvation is kept among the Thoughts that your One Self holds dear and cherishes for you.

8. Today, you will find this Thought, the Presence of Which is guaranteed by the Holy Spirit, Which speaks to you from your One Self. Your hourly-five-minute-practice will be a search for the Holy Spirit in your mind. Your salvation comes from your One Self through the Holy Spirit, Which is the Bridge between your mind and your One Self. Wait patiently, and let the Holy Spirit speak to you about your One Self, and what your mind can do when it is restored to your One Self and is free to serve Its Will.

9. Begin your practice by saying to yourself:

> 'My salvation from guilt comes from my One Self. Its Thoughts are mine to use.'

Then seek for Its Thoughts, and claim Them as your own. These are your own Real Thoughts, Which you have denied to let your mind wander in an illusion of a world. These are the *only* Real

Thoughts that you have. Your salvation is among Them; find your salvation Here.

10. If you succeed, the Thoughts that come to you will tell you that you are saved from guilt, and that your mind has found its Function of serving Spirit, which it tried to lose. Your One Self will welcome your mind, and give it Peace. Restored to Strength, your mind will extend *from* Spirit *to* Spirit, everywhere. Your mind will bless all that it perceives. Your confusion will be over, and your Mind will be restored, because you will have found your One Self.

11. Your One Self knows that you cannot fail today. Perhaps your mind remains a little uncertain for a little while, but do not be dismayed by this. Your One Self will save for you the Joy It experiences, and you will one day be fully aware of It. Every time that you spend five minutes of the hour with the Holy Spirit, you offer the Holy Spirit another Treasure to keep for you.

12. Every time today that you remind your frantic mind that salvation comes from your One Self, you add another Treasure to your growing store of Treasures. All of your Treasure is extended when you ask for It and accept It. Think, then, of how much is given to you to give yourself today!

Mentor's Notes

God, Christ, One Self, True Self, Holy Spirit, Real Thoughts; They are all really the Same in that they are all really God, but there is a reason for the different labels. At the level of your mind that *perceives*, you can only *perceive* God, but you cannot *know* God. Only in God can you *know* God, because in God there is only God. But the level of *perception* is the level of seeming choice. You think, at this level, that there is something else besides God to choose to perceive. At this level, the Part of your mind that is fully aware of God is called *Christ*, Which is the highest that your mind can go in perception. When you have fully attained Christ Consciousness, you will be ready to leave perception behind and know only God again.

The *Holy Spirit* is the teaching aspect of your *Christ Mind.* It functions as a 'Bridge' in that it is aware of both your Christ Mind and of you as you see yourself now. Your *One Self,* or *True Self* are different terms for your Christ Mind. They are used to distinguish your Christ Mind from the personal *self* that you made. Your *Real Thoughts* are the Thoughts of your Christ Mind, and they reflect the Truth that you are One with God. God's Thought in you is the Holy Spirit.

Lesson 97

'I am Spirit.'

1. With today's idea, you identify with your One Self. You do not accept a split identity, or try to unite opposing self-concepts. Today's idea simply states the Truth. Practice today's Truth as often as you can, because it will lead your mind away from conflict, and fold it quietly in Peace. No chill of fear can enter here, because your mind is released from madness by your letting go of a split identity.

2. Today, you state again the Truth about your Self, the Christ Mind that rests within you, Which returns you to Sanity. You are Spirit, Lovingly endowed with all of God's Love and Peace and Joy. You are the Spirit Which completes God, and extends God as God extends God. God is always with you, as you are always with God.

3. Today, you practice bringing Reality closer to your awareness. Each time that you practice, your awareness is brought a little nearer Reality, and you save time. The minutes that you use are multiplied over and over, because the miracle uses time, but is not ruled by it. Your salvation from guilt is the first and the last miracle.

4. You are the Spirit in the Mind of Which is the miracle where time stands still. The miracle is where a minute spent in using the ideas in this Workbook becomes Timelessness. Give these minutes willingly to the Holy Spirit, Which has promised to lay Timelessness within them. The Holy Spirit will offer all of Its Strength to every little effort that you make. Today, give the Holy Spirit the minutes that it needs to help you understand that *you* are the Spirit Which abides in the Holy Spirit, and that calls through the Holy Spirit to your entire mind, that extends Its Perception to all that you perceive, and that replaces your error with the simple Truth.

5. The Holy Spirit will be glad to take five minutes of each hour from you, and extend them to the aching part of your mind where you perceive a world, where pain and misery seem to rule. The Holy Spirit will never overlook your mind when it is open to accept Its healing Gifts, and the Holy Spirit will extend Its Gifts wherever you

welcome Them in your perception. They will increase in healing power each time that you accept Them as your own Thoughts, and you use Them to heal.

6. Each gift of five minutes that you give to the Holy Spirit will be multiplied a thousand-fold. And when the gift is returned to you, it will surpass in Might the little gift that you gave. The Steady Brilliance of the Light it brings to your awareness will remain with you, and lead you out of dark denial of God. You will never get lost again.

7. Begin your happy exercises with these words that the Holy Spirit gives to you, and let them echo around the world that you perceive through the Holy Spirit:

> 'I am Spirit, One with God. I am Limitless, Safe, and Whole. I am free to forgive the world that I perceive.'

Expressed through you, the Holy Spirit will accept this gift that you received of It, increase its power, and give it back to you.

8. Offer every practice period today to the Holy Spirit. The Holy Spirit will speak to you, reminding you that you are One Spirit, One with God, and with all that you perceive. Listen for the Holy Spirit's Assurance every time that you speak the words that the Holy Spirit offers today. Let the Holy Spirit tell your mind that they are true. Use them against any temptation to believe that you are separate from God, and avoid the sorry consequences of that belief. The Holy Spirit gives you Peace today; receive the Holy Spirit's words, and offer them back to the Holy Spirit.

Mentor's Notes

You may not always *hear* the Holy Spirit; you may *experience* the Holy Spirit instead. You may experience the Holy Spirit as a still, quiet Voice that speaks words; as unformed thoughts; as gentle promptings; as an intuition that comes from a deeper part of your mind than the personal mind's 'gut feeling'. In time, you will sort out the Holy Spirit from the personal mind's cacophony of voices and myriad experiences. The Holy Spirit is always charge-neutral, quiet, still, and comes from a deeper place within you than the personal mind. What you hear or experience from the Holy Spirit will never frighten *you,* though the personal mind my resist or object to what you hear and feel.

Lesson 98

'I accept my part in God's plan for my salvation from guilt.'

1. Today is a day of special dedication as you take a stand on one side of your split mind. You will side with Truth and let go of illusions. You will not vacillate between the two, but take a firm position with the One. You will dedicate yourself to Truth today, and to your salvation from guilt, as God plans it. You will not argue that your salvation is something else; you will not seek for it where it is not. Happily, you will accept it as it is, and take the part that God assigns to you.

2. How happy you are to be certain! Lay all your doubts aside today, and take your stand with certainty of purpose, and with gratitude that doubt is gone and confidence has come. You have a mighty purpose to fulfill, and you are given everything that you need to reach your goal. No mistake stands in your way, because you have been absolved of your errors. All of your 'sins' are washed away as you recognize that they were only mistakes.

3. In your Innocence, you have no fear, because you are Safe, and you recognize your Safety in God. You don't need to appeal to magic, or to invent escapes from illusions of threat. You rest in Quiet Certainty that you will do what it is given to you to do. You do not doubt your own ability, because you know that your function will be filled completely in the perfect time and place.

4. The stand that you take today extends backwards and forwards in time, undoing guilt for all time. You do not choose for the personal self alone today, but for your entire mind.

5. Isn't it worth five minutes of every hour to accept the Happiness that God gives to you, and to recognize your special function in your perception that you are in a world? Five minutes is a small amount for you to give to gain a Reward so Great that It has no measure. You have made at least a thousand losing bargains before this.

6. Here is an offer that guarantees you your full release from pain

of every kind, and a Joy that the world that you perceive does not contain. You will exchange a little of your time for Peace of mind and certainty of purpose with the promise of complete success. Since time has no meaning, you are being asked for nothing in return for Everything. Here is a bargain in which you cannot lose! What you gain is Limitless indeed.

7. Every hour today, give the Holy Spirit the tiny gift of five minutes. The Holy Spirit will give to the words with which you practice today the deep conviction and certainty that you still lack. The Holy Spirit's words will join with yours, and will make your every repetition of today's idea a dedication of faith that is as Perfect as the Holy Spirit's Faith in you. The Holy Spirit's Confidence in you will bring God's Light to all the words that you say, and you will go beyond their sound to what they really mean. Today, as you practice with the Holy Spirit, say:

'I accept my part in God's plan for my salvation from guilt.'

8. The Holy Spirit will accept your words in each of the five minute intervals that you spend with the It, and It will give them back to you Bright with Faith and Confidence so Strong and Steady that they will light your perception with hope and gladness. Do not lose one chance to be the glad receiver of the Holy Spirit's Gifts, so that you can extend Them in your mind where you perceive a world.

9. Give the Holy Spirit the words, and the Holy Spirit will do the rest. The Holy Spirit will enable you to understand your special function, and will open up your way to Happiness. Peace and trust will be the Holy Spirit's Gifts to your words. The Holy Spirit will respond with Faith and Joy and Certainty that what you say is True. You will have the Conviction of the Holy Spirit, Which knows the function that you have in your perception that you are in a world and in Heaven. The Holy Spirit will be with you during each practice period that you open to the Holy Spirit, and It will exchange Timelessness and Peace for every instant of time that you offer to It.

10. Throughout the remainder of every hour, let your time be spent in happy preparation for the next five minutes that you will spend again with the Holy Spirit. Repeat today's idea often, while you wait for the happy time to come again. As you repeat it often, do not forget that you are preparing your mind for the happy time to come.

11. When the hour has passed, and you are aware of the Holy Spirit again, be grateful, and lay down all worldly tasks, all little thoughts, and all limited ideas. Tell the Holy Spirit once again that you accept the part that It wants you to have, and that It will help you fulfill. The Holy Spirit will make you certain that you want this choice, which you have made with the Holy Spirit.

Lesson 99

'My salvation is my only function in my perception that I am in a world.'

1. Your salvation and your forgiving are the same. They both imply that something is wrong, that there is something for you to be saved from and forgiven for, and that something that is not God's Will needs correction. Both terms imply something that is impossible, but that seems to have occurred, resulting in a state of conflict within you between What *is* and what can never be.

2. In your mind, Truth and illusion are equal, because it seems that both are real, so you must forgive yourself, and save yourself from, the impossible. Your salvation, then, is the borderland between Truth and illusion. It reflects the Truth, because it is the means by which you escape from illusion, but it is not the Truth, because it undoes what has never happened.

3. Both Heaven and the world exist in your mind, but they cannot be reconciled. You see illusions, and you think that they are real, and they have a type of existence in that they are thoughts. But they are not Real, because the mind which thinks these thoughts is separate from God, Which is Reality.

4. What joins with God's Mind in Oneness the part of your mind that thinks it is separate from God? What can hold the Truth in your mind, while recognizing the need for correction that you have in your belief in illusions? What will undo your belief in illusions without attack or causing you pain? Only the Holy Spirit in your mind, through Which you overlook what never happened, and you forgive 'sins' which were never real.

5. The Holy Spirit in your mind holds God's plan for your salvation. The Holy Spirit is apart from time in that Its Source is Timeless, but It operates in your mind in time, because you believe that time is real. The Holy Spirit looks on the sin, pain, death, grief, separation, and loss that you perceive without being disturbed. It knows that God is still Love, and that these things are not God's Will.

6. The Holy Spirit in you brings illusions to Truth by seeing them as appearances behind which is the Changeless and the Sure. The Holy Spirit within you saves you and forgives your illusions, because it has no faith in what God did not create. It is the Holy Spirit's function within you to save you from guilt by teaching you that Its function is yours. In the Holy Spirit, you are entrusted with the plan for your salvation. The Holy Spirit has one answer to all appearances, no matter the form, size, depth, or attributes that they seem to have:

> 'My salvation is my only function in my perception that I am in a world. God is still Love, and this is not God's Will.'

7. You, who will one day work miracles, be sure to practice well with today's idea. Perceive the Strength in these words, in which you find your freedom from guilt. God loves you; the world of pain is not God's Will. Forgive yourself the idea that God made the world for you, and let the Holy Spirit, with Which God has corrected all of your mistakes, enter the dark places of your mind where you have thoughts that are not God's Will.

8. Practice with the Holy Spirit today, and let the Holy Spirit's Light seek out and lighten all the dark places in your mind, to join them to the rest of your mind. It is God's Will that your mind be One with God's Mind; It is God's Will that God have only One Extension; It is God's Will that *you* are God's Extension. Think of these things when you practice today, and start today's lesson with this instruction to yourself:

> 'My salvation is my only function in my perception that I am in a world. My salvation and my forgiving are the same.'

Then turn inward to the Holy Spirit, Which shares your function in your perception that you are in a world, and let the Holy Spirit teach you what you need to learn to lay all fear aside, and know your True Self as Love. There is no opposite in you.

9. Forgive all thoughts which oppose the Truth of your Completion, Oneness, and Peace. You cannot lose What God gives to you; you do not want to be another self. Your only function is the one that God gives to you; forgive yourself the one that you think that you made. Your forgiving and your salvation are the same. Forgive what you have made, and you are saved.

10. Today, you have a special message that has the power to remove all forms of doubt and fear forever from your mind. If you are tempted to believe that doubt and fear are true, remember, with these words, that appearances cannot stand up to Truth:

> 'My salvation is my only function in my perception that I am in a world. God is still Love, and this is not God's Will.'

11. Your only function tells you that you are One. Remind yourself of this between your five minute practices with the Holy Spirit. Say to yourself:

> 'My salvation is my only function in my perception that I am in a world.'

This is how you forgive the personal mind, and you lay aside all fear, so that Love can take Its rightful place in your mind, and show you that you are One with God.

Lesson 100

'My part is essential to God's plan for my salvation from guilt.'

1. Just as your extension of God completes God, so your part in God's plan for your salvation from guilt completes God's plan. Your salvation reverses your mad belief in separate thoughts and separate bodies that lead separate lives in a world of separation. One function for your mind extended to all that you perceive unites your mind in one purpose, which is essential for your salvation.

2. God's Will for you is Perfect Happiness. Why choose to go against God's Will? Your part in God's plan restores you to God's Will. Your part is as essential, as is your Happiness. Your Joy must be complete to let God's plan be extended to your entire mind.

3. You are indeed essential to God's plan. Without your Joy, God's Joy is incomplete. Without Joy in you, you cannot extend It in your perception of a world. While you are sad, the Light that God appoints to save the part of your mind where you perceive a world is dimmed, and you do not perceive the Joy that is yours.

4. You are indeed essential to God's plan. Just as your Light increases God's Light in Heaven, so, in your perception that you are in a world, your Joy extends to that world to replace sorrow and separation. As a Joyous messenger of God, your Joy will heal sorrow and despair in your perception. When you accept God's Gifts as your own, you will be proof that God wills Perfect Happiness.

5. Do not let yourself be sad today. If you are, you will fail to take your part, which is essential to God's plan, as well as for your Real Perception. Your sadness will be a sign that you want another plan instead of God's plan. You will fail to extend to your mind where you perceive a world the Great Happiness that God wills for you, so you will not recognize that It is yours.

6. Today, understand that Joy is your function in your perception that you are in a world. If you are sad, your function is unfulfilled, and your mind where you perceive a world will not be joyous either. God asks you to be Happy, so that you can extend God's Love in

your perception, and know that God does not will sorrow or fear. You are God's messenger today; you extend God's Happiness and Peace to all that you perceive.

7. Prepare yourself for this in your five-minute-practice periods today by feeling Happiness arise within you. Your Happiness is God's Will and your will. Begin today's exercises with today's idea, and realize that your part is to be Happy. Only this is asked of you when you take your part as God's messenger. Think about what this means: You have been wrong in your belief that God asks you for sacrifice. You only receive in God's plan; you never lose, sacrifice, or die.

8. Now, find the Joy that proves God's Will to you. It is your function that you find It within, now. This is what you have been seeking; let today be the day that you succeed in finding It. Go deep within yourself, and don't be affected by all the little thoughts and foolish goals you pass as you ascend to your Christ Mind.

9. Christ is here, and you can reach It now. What would you rather perceive? No little thought or foolish goals can hold you back when God calls to you.

10. God is here; you are essential to God's plan. You are God's messenger today, and you must find What God wants you to extend. Do not forget today's idea between your hourly practice periods. It is your True Self that calls to you today. And it is your True Self that you answer every time that you tell yourself that you are essential to God's plan for your salvation.

Mentor's Notes

In your identification with a personal self, when you feel happiness it is only within you, and it goes no further. Even if you think that you are 'happy for another', the experience remains only in you. But when you experience God's Joy, It automatically extends from your mind outward in your perception.

Remember, you are both teacher and student; you are always teaching yourself. So as God's 'messenger', you are both sending and receiving God's message for yourself.

Lesson 101

'God's Will for me is Perfect Happiness.'

1. Today, you will continue with the theme of Happiness. This is essential to your understanding what your salvation from guilt means. You probably still believe that *salvation* means that you must suffer punishment for your 'sins'. This is not so, but while you believe that sin is real and that you have sinned, you will believe this.

2. If sin is real, then punishment is just, and you cannot escape it. Your salvation, then, would be through suffering. If sin is real, then happiness is an illusion, because sin and happiness cannot both be true. If you are 'sinful', then you deserve pain and death, and you ask for them. You will know that they wait for you, and that they will seek you out and find you sometime, in some form that evens your account with God. Afraid, you will want to escape God, but God will pursue you, and you will not be able to escape forever.

3. If sin is real, then your salvation is through pain, and you can never escape suffering. If sin is real, then you will fear salvation, because it will kill you slowly, taking everything away from you before it grants you death. If sin is real, salvation's wrath is boundless and merciless, but wholly just.

4. Why would you seek out such savage punishment? Of course you would flee from salvation, and try in everyway to deny the Holy Spirit within you, because It offers salvation to you. If sin is real, it offers you death, which it metes out in a cruel form to match the vicious wishes which give birth to your sin. If sin is real, salvation is your bitter enemy, the curse of God upon you for attacking part of God.

5. You need today's practice periods, because they teach you that sin is not real, and that the punishment that you expect will never happen, because it has no cause. Accept Atonement with an open mind that no longer cherishes a belief that you have made a devil of yourself. There is no sin. Practice this thought as often as you can

today, because it is the basis for today's idea.

6. God's Will for you is Perfect Happiness, because you cannot sin, and your suffering has no cause. Joy is Just, and pain is only a sign that you have misunderstood yourself. Do not fear God's Will. You can turn to It in confidence that It will set you free from all of the consequences of guilt that you have feverishly imagined. Say to yourself:

> 'God's Will for me is Perfect Happiness. There is no sin, so it has no consequences.'

This is how to start your practice periods. Then find the Joy that these thoughts will introduce into your mind.

7. Gladly give five minutes an hour to the Holy Spirit today to remove the heavy load that you carry in your belief that you have sinned. Escape from madness today. You are on the road to your freedom from guilt, and today's idea will speed you to your Goal of Peace. There is no sin. Remember this today, and tell yourself as often as you can:

> 'God's Will for me is Perfect Happiness. This is the Truth, because there is no sin.'

Lesson 102

'I share God's Will for my Happiness.'

1. You do not want to suffer. You may think that suffering buys you something, and you may still believe that it buys you something that you want. But surely this belief is shaken in you by now, enough for you to question it and suspect that it really does not make sense. It is not gone yet, but it is no longer securely rooted in the dark and secret places of your mind.

2. Today, you will loosen its hold even further, and realize that pain has no purpose, is without a cause, and has no power to accomplish anything. It cannot purchase anything for you, it offers you nothing, and it does not even exist. Everything that you think it offers you also does not exist. You have been bound by nothing. Be free today, and join the Happy Will of God.

3. For several days, you will continue to spend your practice periods practicing exercises that are designed to help you reach the Happiness that God's Will places within you. Your Happiness is your Home, your Safety, your Peace, and your salvation. There is no fear here, and you can rest at last.

4. Begin your practice periods by accepting God's Will for you:

> 'I share God's Will for my happiness. I accept Happiness as my function.'

Then seek your function deep within your mind; it is there, waiting for you to choose it. You will not fail to find it when you learn that it is your choice to share God's Will.

5. Be Happy, because your only function is Happiness. You have no need to be less Loving to yourself than God is, because you are One with God. Besides your five-minutes-an-hour rest periods, pause frequently today to tell yourself that you have now accepted Happiness as your one function. You can be sure that you are joining with God's Will.

Mentor's Notes

What do you think that pain can buy you? Deep down you hope that by punishing yourself you may lessen God's punishment of you. But on the surface, pain can also get much that the personal self desires: attention, pity, an excuse to withdraw from situations that it doesn't want or doesn't want to face.

Lesson 103

'Since God is Love, God is also Happiness.'

1. Happiness is an Attribute of Love, so It cannot be apart from Love or be experienced where Love is not. Love is Limitless, so Joy is Everywhere also. You have denied this, and you believe that there are gaps in Love where separation brings pain instead of Joy. By this strange belief, you have redefined Love as something limited. This limited 'love' would be the opposite of Real Love, Which is Limitless, so It has no opposite.

2. By limiting Love, you confuse Love with fear. Fear, then, is the consequence that you live with in your belief that you really have limited Love. The images of a world that this conjures up in your mind have no reality, but they witness to your fear of God. You have forgotten that, being Love, God must also be Joy. So today, you will bring this basic error to Truth and teach yourself:

> 'Since God is Love, God is also Happiness. If I am afraid of God, I am afraid of Joy.'

Begin your practice periods with this association, which corrects your false belief that God is fear. It also emphasizes that Happiness is yours because of What God is.

3. Allow this one correction to come into your mind every hour today. Then welcome the Happiness that it brings as Truth replaces fear, and Joy becomes what you *expect* to take the place of pain. Since God is Love, this is what you will experience. Bolster this expectation frequently throughout the day, and quiet all of your fears with this kind and wholly True assurance:

> 'Since God is Love, God is also Happiness. Happiness is What I seek today. I cannot fail, because I seek the Truth.'

Mentor's Notes

Remember from the Text that *fear* is the perception of the absence of Love. If you do not experience Love everywhere, always, you have allowed the belief that Love can be absent into your mind, which makes you fearful. So the limited 'love' of the personal mind, being inconstant, is really a form of fear. Since you confuse love with fear, you confuse God with fear.

Lesson 104

'I seek for only What belongs to me in Truth.'

1. Today's idea continues to remind you that Joy and Peace are not idle dreams; They are your Right, because of What you are. They come to you from God, Which extends Its Will to you Eternally. But your mind must be ready to receive God's Gifts, because you will not welcome Them gladly when you hold onto other 'gifts' that you have made to substitute for God.

2. Today, you will remove all of the meaningless self-made 'gifts' that you have placed in your Holy mind where God's Gifts belong. God's Gifts are yours in Truth, and They have been with you since before you conceived of time, and They will be with you after you have let go of time. God's Gifts are within you now, because they are Eternal. You don't have to wait for Them, because They belong to you.

3. Choose Them now, and know that in choosing Them in place of what you have made, you are recognizing that your will is God's Will. Your longer practice periods of five-minutes-an-hour, which you give to Truth for your salvation from guilt, should begin with this:

> 'I seek for only What belongs to me in Truth. Joy and Peace are mine.'

Then lay aside the conflicts of the world that you perceive, which offers only illusory 'gifts' and goals.

4. Seek instead for That Which is Truly yours, as you seek to recognize What God gives to you. Clear a Holy Place within your mind, Where God's Gifts of Peace and Joy are welcome. Come in confidence to this Place, aware that What belongs to you in Truth is extended to you from God. Wish for nothing else, because nothing else belongs to you in Truth.

5. You clear the way for God today by simply recognizing that

God's Will is done, and that Joy and Peace belong to you as God's Eternal Gifts. Do not let yourself lose sight of Them in the remainder of each hour. Use this reminder as often as you can:

> 'I seek for only What belongs to me in Truth. God's Gifts of Joy and Peace are all that I want.'

Lesson 105

'God's Peace and Joy are mine.'

1. God's Peace and Joy are yours. Today you will accept Them, knowing that They belong to you. Try to understand that These Gifts increase as you receive Them. They are not like the 'gifts' that the personal self gives, in which the giver loses and the receiver gains. What the personal self gives are not *gifts*, but *bargains* that it makes with guilt. With a True Gift there is no loss, because loss would mean that the Gift is limited.

2. The personal self's gifts are a bid for a more valuable return. You are supposed to get something worth more than what you give. This strange distortion of what *giving* means pervades all of the levels of the world that you perceive. It strips all real meaning from the 'gifts' that you give, and leaves you nothing in the 'gifts' that you take.

3. A major goal of this course is to undo this view of giving, so that you will be open to truly receive. Giving has become such a source of guilt and fear for you that you avoid receiving anything Real. But accept God's Gifts of Joy and Peace, and you will learn to look at *giving* differently. God's Gifts do not lessen as God gives Them; They increase.

4. Heaven's Peace and Joy intensify when you accept Them as God's Gift to you, and God's Joy intensifies when you accept God's Peace and Joy as yours. Truly giving is Truly creating. It is the extension of the Limitless to the Limitless, of Eternity to Eternity, of Love to Love. It adds to All that is already Complete, not in the sense of adding *more*, because that implies it once was *less*. Truly creating means the Limitless fulfilling Itself by extending All that It is to secure All that It is for Itself Forever.

5. Today, accept God's Peace and Joy as yours. Let God complete God as God defines Completion. You will understand that What completes God completes you as well. God cannot give through loss anywhere; neither can you. Receive God's Gift of Joy and Peace

today, and God will thank you for this gift to God.

6. Today, your practice periods will begin a little differently. Begin by thinking of those others in the world that you have denied an extension of Joy and Peace. As part of your mind, they have an equal right to Them, and you deny Them to yourself when you deny Them to any part of your mind. Here you will claim Joy and Peace as your own.

7. Think of these 'enemies' a little while, then say to each one in your mind:

> 'I extend Peace and Joy to you, so that I will have God's Peace and Joy myself.'

This is how you prepare yourself to recognize God's Gifts to you, and you free your mind of all that could prevent success today. Now you are ready to accept the Gift of Peace and Joy that God gives to you. You can say, 'God's Peace and Joy are mine', because you have given What you want to receive.

8. You will succeed today if you prepare your mind as suggested, because you will be lifting your obstacles to Peace and Joy, and What is yours will be able to come into your awareness at last. Tell yourself, 'God's Peace and Joy are mine', and close your eyes for a little while. Let the Holy Spirit assure you that the words that you speak are true.

9. Spend your five-minutes-an-hour with the Holy Spirit like this today. Do not think that less time is worthless when you cannot give the Holy Spirit more time. At least remember hourly today to say the words that call the Holy Spirit to give to you What the Holy Spirit wills to give to you, and that you will to receive. Be determined to not interfere with What the Holy Spirit wills. If you are tempted to not extend Peace and Joy to another today, view it as an opportunity to let yourself receive God's Gifts as yours. Then gratefully bless them as you say to yourself:

'I extend Peace and Joy to you, so that I will a have God's Peace and Joy myself.'

Mentor's Notes

To give, to teach, to extend all mean the same thing in this course, and they all refer to *ideas* and *experiences,* not *things.* You give, teach, or extend an idea or experience to strengthen it in your mind. This increases it in your awareness.

There is no corollary in the world for what is meant in this course by 'creating', because there is only God in God. 'Creation' is God's extension of God Infinitely and Eternally; 'creating' is the process of God extending God; God is the 'Creator', because God is the Source of the extension of God; you are God's 'Creation' because, in Truth, you are God's Extension. You are God's co-Creator, because God's Extension extends God. All of this explains the term 'God is One'.

Since this course uses Light as a metaphor for God, picture a Light that extends everywhere without limit, and in Which there is nothing but Light. That is what God and God's Creation are like.

As in parts of the Text, paragraph 4 mentions 'adding to' God. The Infinite Nature of God means God is Everywhere, and 'increasing' is meaningless in this Context. The idea only has meaning in the context that God's extension of God seems blocked in your mind by the illusion that not-God is real. In that context, when God flows over the block, God is increasing, not by adding *more* to God, but by fulfilling Its Infinite Nature where once It could not.

Lesson 106

'I will be still and listen to the Truth.'

1. Today, if you set aside the personal mind's voice, no matter how loud it is; if you don't accept its petty 'gifts', which give you nothing that you really want; if you listen with an open mind that has not already decided what your salvation is, then you will hear the Holy Spirit's Voice speaking the Truth to you, with Quiet Power and Confidence in Its message.

2. Listen, and hear God speak to you through the Holy Spirit, Which silences the thunder of the meaningless, and speaks to you of the way to Peace. Be still and listen to the Truth. Do not listen to the voices of death, which tell you that they are life.

3. Do not be afraid to circumvent the voices of the world. Walk lightly past your temptation to be persuaded by them, and do not hear them. Be still today, and listen to the Truth. Go past all the things that do not speak of the Holy Spirit, Which holds your Happiness, and offers It to you in Love. Hear only the Holy Spirit today, and do not wait any longer to reach for It.

4. Today, God's Promise is kept; be silent and hear It. The Holy Spirit wants to speak to you, and It comes with miracles that are a thousand times happier and more wonderful than those of which you've dreamed. The Holy Spirit's miracles are True; they will not fade when you no longer dream that you are separated from God. Instead, they end your dreaming. They last Forever, because they come to you from God.

5. Hear the Holy Spirit today, and listen to the Word that lifts the veil across the part of your mind where you perceive a world. God extends through you in your perception. God needs you to extend God to the world that you perceive to make your mind One again. Hear the Holy Spirit today, and offer It your mind to extend God.

6. Be ready for your salvation today, because it is here. You will learn your function from the Holy Spirit. Listen today, and you will hear the Voice Which will resound throughout the world through

you. The Holy Spirit needs you to receive miracles first, so that you can Joyously extend them in your perception.

7. This is how your salvation begins and ends: When you have accepted Everything True, and you have extended Everything True, then Everything True will remain in your awareness Forever. Today, you will practice giving, not the way that the personal mind understands it, but as it truly is. Every hour your exercises should begin with this request for your enlightenment:

> 'I will be still and listen to the Truth. What does it really mean to give and to receive?'

8. Ask this, and expect an answer. The answer to this question has been waiting long to be received by you. It will begin your mission by freeing your mind from the idea that giving is losing. It will prepare you to understand and receive the Truth.

9. Be still and listen to the Truth today. Every five minutes that you spend in listening extends Truth to your entire mind.

10. Today, the Holy Word of God is kept through your receiving It and extending It so that you can learn what giving means. Do not forget to reinforce your choice to hear and to receive the Word by this reminder, as often as possible today:

> 'I will be still and listen to the Truth. I am God's messenger today. I will extend What I receive.'

Lesson 107

'Truth corrects all of the errors in my mind.'

1. Only Truth can correct illusions, and your errors are only illusions that you do not recognize as illusions. When Truth enters your mind, your errors disappear without a trace. They are gone, because, without your belief in them, they have no life. Without your belief in them, you recognize that they are, and have always been, nothing. Then only Truth remains in your mind.

2. Imagine a state of mind without illusions: Try to remember when there was a moment, maybe only a minute or less, when nothing interrupted your Peace, and you were certain that you were loved and safe. Now imagine that moment extending to the end of time, and beyond into Eternity. Let the Quiet that you felt be multiplied a hundred times a hundred.

3. Now you have the barest hint of the State in Which your mind will rest when it knows only Truth. Without illusions, you feel no fear, no doubt, and no attack. When Truth comes into your awareness, all of your pain is over, because there is no room for transitory thoughts and dead ideas. Truth fills your mind completely, freeing you from all beliefs in the temporary, because Truth is Everywhere, Forever.

4. When Truth comes into your awareness, It does not stay only a little while, then disappear or change into something else. It does not shift or alter; It stays exactly as It always is. You can depend on Truth in every circumstance, and trust It through all the seeming difficulties that appear in your perception that you are in a world. These will blow away as Truth corrects the errors in your mind.

5. When Truth comes into your awareness, It brings the Gift of Perfect Constancy, and a Love Which does not falter in the face of pain, but looks beyond it. This is the Gift of healing, because Truth does not need to be defended, so no attack is involved. Illusions can be brought to Truth to be undone, but Truth cannot be brought to illusions to turn illusions into Truth.

6. Truth does not come and go, nor shift and change, nor does It appear in this illusion, then in that one. Truth does not hide, but It stands in the open, obvious and accessible. If you truly seek for Truth, you will succeed in finding It. Today belongs to Truth; give It Its due, and you will be given What is due to you. You are not meant to suffer and die. God wills that your illusions be undone; let Truth correct all of them.

7. You are not asking for What you do not already have; you are only asking to recognize What belongs to you. Today, you practice with a Certainty that comes from Truth. The shaky, unsteady footsteps of illusions are not your approach today. You can be certain of success. Do not doubt that you walk with Truth today, and depend on It to enter into all of your exercises.

8. Begin by asking the Holy Spirit to be in your awareness. You are not flesh and blood and bone, but you are One with the Holy Spirit in God. God knows you and the Holy Spirit are the Same. You are asking your True Self to be in your awareness; the Holy Spirit cannot ever be absent from you.

9. Truth corrects all of the errors in your mind, which teach you that you are separate from the Holy Spirit. Make a pledge to the Holy Spirit to let It fulfill Its function through you today. For you to share the Holy Spirit's function is for you to share the Holy Spirit's Joy. The Holy Spirit's Confidence is in you as you say:

> 'Truth corrects all of the errors in my mind. I rest in the Holy Spirit, Which is my True Self.'

Then let the Holy Spirit lead you to Truth, Which will envelop you with a Peace so Deep and Tranquil that you will reluctantly return to perceiving a world.

10. But you can be glad to return to perceiving a world, because you bring with you the promise of changes that the Truth will extend to the world through you. These changes will increase with your small gift of five-minutes-an-hour, as you let the errors that

surround your perception of the world be corrected.

11. Do not forget your function today. Every time that you tell yourself with confidence, 'Truth corrects all of the errors in my mind' you speak for your entire mind, and for the Holy Spirit. The Holy Spirit will release your mind from the world and set you free.

Lesson 108

'In Truth, to give and to receive are the same.'

1. Your Real Perception depends on today's idea. The Light of Truth is in it, because the Truth reconciles all seeming opposites. Truth, being Peace, resolves all of your conflicts, and transforms your thoughts to reflect Truth. But even those thoughts will disappear as the Truth beyond them takes their place in your mind. The illusion that you are separate from God will be over then, and you will be at Peace Forever.

2. The Light of Truth that makes your Real Perception possible is not the light that the body's eyes see. It is a State of Mind that is so Complete that there is no darkness in it. In this Light, What is the Same is seen as One, and what cannot be reconciled with Truth is overlooked, because it is not there.

3. The Light of Truth cannot reveal opposites, and your Real Perception, being whole, has the power to heal your mind. This Light extends your Peace in your perception, to make you glad that you are One with what you perceive. This Light heals your mind, because It produces a unified perception based on one Frame of Reference, from Which It derives One Meaning.

4. In the Light of Truth, you recognize that both *giving* and *receiving* are different aspects of God's Extension, Which is One. The Truth of God's Extension does not depend on whether the giving or the receiving seems to come first. In the Light, you understand that both occur together, so that God's Extension remains Whole. Understanding this, all opposites are reconciled, because you perceive them from the same Frame of Reference, Which unifies Its Own Extension.

5. One Idea, completely Unified, unifies all thought. This is the same as saying that you need only one Correction to be wholly corrected, or that for you to wholly forgive the personal mind's projections on one other is enough to bring salvation to your entire mind. These are special applications of the Law of Mind, Which is

One, where what you learn in a specific situation can be generalized to extend to your entire mind.

6. It is especially useful for you to learn that giving and receiving are the same, because you can easily test it and learn that it is true. When you apply this lesson to individual perceptions and find that it always works, you will then generalize it to all other perceptions. From there it will extend to the One Idea that is behind every perception.

7. Today, you will practice giving and receiving. You will not miss the results of this obvious, simple lesson. To give is to receive. Today, offer Peace to everyone, and learn how quickly Peace returns to you. In the Light of Peace is your Real Perception.

8. Begin your practice periods with this instruction:

'In Truth, to give and to receive are the same. I receive what I am giving now.'

Then close your eyes, and think of what you want to extend to everyone, so that you can have it. For example, you might say:

'I extend quietness to everyone.'
'I extend Peace of mind to everyone.'
'I extend gentleness to everyone'

9. Say each one slowly, then pause, expecting to receive the gift you offer. You will experience it to the degree to which you give it. You will find that you have exact return of what you give. It might be more helpful to think of someone in particular to whom to give your gifts. This one will represent everyone else, and through them you give to everyone else.

10. Today's very simple lesson will teach you much. You will understand cause and effect much better now, and you will make much faster progress. Think of today's exercises as quick advances in your learning each time that you say, 'In Truth, to give and to receive

are the same.'

Mentor's Notes

Giving and *receiving* are the same, because there is only One Mind. This is another way of approaching the Law of Mind that Mind only knows itself. Whatever you extend in your perception, *you* are the one who experiences it immediately.

In today's exercises, it will be helpful for you to feel what you are extending, and maybe for you to visualize. For example, feel quietness as you extend it outward in your perception, and picture a ripple of quietness passing over everyone that you perceive.

Lesson 109

'I rest in God.'

1. Today, you are asking for a Rest and a Quietness that are unshaken by the world's appearances. You are asking for Peace and Stillness in the midst of all of the turmoil of conflicting illusions. You are asking for Safety and Happiness, even though it seems like you look on danger and sorrow. Today's thought is the answer to what you are asking for.

2. 'I rest in God.' This thought brings you the Rest and Quietness, the Peace and Stillness, and the Safety and Happiness that you seek. 'I rest in God.' This thought is powerful enough to wake the sleeping Truth in you, Which sees beyond appearances to the same Truth in all that you perceive. Here is the end of suffering for your entire mind, for all time. Here is the thought in which Christ is born again in your awareness.

3. 'I rest in God.' This thought will carry you through all storms and strife, completely undismayed; past misery and pain, past loss and death, and inward to the Certainty of God. There is no suffering it cannot heal; there is no problem that it cannot solve. Every appearance will be transformed by Truth, when you rest in God.

4. This is a day of Peace. You rest in Peace, and while the world seems torn by hate, you remain completely undisturbed. Yours is the rest of Truth, and appearances cannot intrude on you. You extend rest to all that you perceive, because you rest in God.

5. In God, you have no cares, no concerns, no burdens, no anxiety, no pain, and no fear for the future or regrets for the past. You rest in Eternity, while time goes by without touching you, because your rest can never change in any way. Rest today, and close your eyes as you sink into stillness. Let these periods of Rest and Respite reassure your mind that all its feverish illusions have passed. Let your mind be still, and gratefully accept its healing. Now that you rest in God, you will have no more frightening illusions. Take the time today to slip away from illusions and into Peace.

6. Every hour in which you take your rest, Life is restored to part of your mind. The part of your mind where you perceive a world is born again in Peace every hour that you remember to bring God's Peace with you into your perception of it, so that it can rest with you.

7. Every five minutes that you rest today, your mind is nearer to waking from its dream of separation from God, and a time when Rest will be all there is comes closer to your weary mind. Hope is reborn, and energy is restored to your entire mind.

8. You rest within the Peace of God today, and you call on all that you perceive to rest with you. You will be faithful to your trust today, and you will forget no one and nothing as you bring everything into the Holy Sanctuary of Peace with you. Extend Rest to all that you perceive today.

9. You rest within the Peace of God today, quiet and unafraid. Extend Rest to all that you perceive to receive it for yourself. This is how your Rest is made complete. What you give today, you have already received. Time is not the guardian of what you give today. The Rest that you give extends across all time as you say to the part of your mind where you perceive a world, 'I rest in God.'

Lesson 110

'I am as God created me.'

1. You will repeat today's idea occasionally, because this one thought is enough to save your entire mind if you believe that it is true. It means that you have made no real changes in yourself, nor replaced God with fear, evil, misery, and death. You are as God created you, so fear has no meaning, evil is not real, and misery and death do not exist.

2. Today's idea is all that you need to let your mind be completely corrected, and to let your Real Perception heal all of the mistakes that any part of your mind has made at any time or place. Today's thought is enough to undo the past and free the future, and to bring you into the present. It is enough to make time the means for your entire mind to escape from time. In today's idea, every change that time appeared to bring passes away.

3. You are as God created you, so appearances cannot replace the Truth, a split mind cannot replace One Mind, death cannot replace Life, and fear cannot replace Love. You only need today's thought to let your mind where you perceive a world be lit by redemption, and be freed from its past story.

4. In today's thought, the personal self's past is undone, and your present quietly extends into a timeless future. You are as God created you, so there is no separation between your mind and God's Mind, and no split between your mind and the world that you perceive. Your mind is One.

5. The healing Power of today's idea is Limitless. It is the source of all miracles; it restores the Truth to your entire mind. Practice today's idea with gratitude. It is the Truth that sets you free from limitations; it is the Truth that God promises to you. Today's lesson is the Word in Which all of your sorrow ends.

6. For your five-minutes-an-hour practice periods, begin with this:

'I am as God created me. What is One with God cannot suffer.'

7. With this statement firmly in your mind, discover your Christ Self.

8. Seek within you the Christ that is One with God and the part of your mind where you perceive a world. This is the Savior that is forever saved, with the Power to save when you ask for It to do so.

9. You are as God created you. Honor your True Self today, and do not worship the graven images (bodies) that you have made instead. Deep in your mind, the Holy Christ in you is waiting for your acknowledgment that It is you. You are lost and do no know yourself while you do not acknowledge Christ as you.

10. Seek for and find Christ within you today. Christ is your Savior from all of the idols that you made. When you find Christ, you will understand that the idols and images that you thought were you are nothing and worthless. Today, you will make a great advance to Truth by letting go of idols and opening yourself to God.

11. You will remember Christ throughout the day with gratitude and Loving Thoughts for everyone you meet today. This is how you remember Christ in you. So that you remember that Christ is in you and in the part of your mind that seems to be a world outside of you, say:

'I am as God created me.'

Declare this Truth as often as you can. This is God's Word, Which sets you free. This is the key that opens up the Gate to Heaven, and that lets you enter into the Peace and Eternity of God.

Review 3

Introduction

1. Your next review begins today. You will review two recent lessons every day for ten days, and you will be observing a special format that you are urged to follow as closely as you can.

2. Of course, it may be impossible for you to do what is suggested as optimal for every hour of the day. Your learning will not be hampered if you miss a practice period because it is impossible at the appointed time, and it is not necessary that you make an excessive effort to be sure that you catch up. Your goal is not to make a ritual of this, which would defeat your goal of salvation from guilt.

3. But your learning *will* be hampered when you skip a practice period because you are unwilling to devote time to it. Do not deceive yourself in this and conceal your unwillingness behind situations that you pretend that you cannot control. Learn to distinguish situations that are not suited for practice from those situations that you make to hide your unwillingness.

4. Those practice periods that you have not done because you did not want to do them should be done as soon as you have changed your mind about your goal of salvation. You are unwilling to practice salvation only when it interferes with goals that you think are more valuable. When you withdraw the value that you give to these goals, allow your practice periods to replace your devotion to them. Those goals give you nothing, but your practicing offers you Everything. Accept Everything, and be at Peace.

5. The format for these reviews is this: Spend five minutes, or longer, twice a day to consider the thoughts assigned for the day. Read over the ideas and comments, then think about them while letting your mind relate them to your seeming needs, problems, and concerns.

6. Place the ideas in your mind, and let your mind use them as it chooses. Have faith that your mind will use them wisely as it is helped by the Holy Spirit. What can you trust but What is in your

mind? Have faith in these reviews that the means that the Holy Spirit uses will not fail. The Wisdom of your mind will come to your assistance. Give direction at the beginning, then let your mind use the ideas that were given to it.

7. You have been given these ideas in Perfect Trust that you will use them well for yourself. Offer them to your mind in the same Trust. Your mind will not fail, because it is the means that the Holy Spirit uses for your salvation. Since the Holy Spirit trusts your mind, surely your mind deserves your trust as well.

8. Ideally, you will use the first and last five minutes of your day for your five-minute practice periods. If you cannot do this, at least try to divide them so that you do one in the morning and the other in the hour before you go to sleep.

9. The exercises that you will do throughout the day are equally important, and maybe even more important. You have been inclined to practice only at appointed times, and then to go on to other things without applying what you have learned to them. As a result, your lessons have had little reinforcement, and you have not given your learning abilities a fair chance to prove what they can give to you. Here is another chance to use them well.

10. During these reviews, do not let your learning lie idle between your longer practice periods. Give your daily two ideas a brief, but serious, review each hour. Use one on the hour and the other on the half-hour. You only need to give each one a moment. Repeat the idea, then allow your mind to rest a little in Silence and Peace. Then turn to other things, attempting to keep the thoughts with you. Let the day's ideas help you keep your Peace throughout the day.

11. If you are shaken for some reason, think of the day's ideas again. These practice periods are designed to help you form the habit of applying what you learn to everything that you do each day. Do not repeat the idea and then lay it down. Its usefulness is limitless to you, and it is meant to serve you in all ways, at all times and places, and whenever you need help of any kind. Try, then, to

take it with you in the business of the day, and make the day Holy and worthy of you who are One with God.

12. Each day's review will conclude with a restatement of one thought to use each hour and the other thought for the half-hour. Do not forget them. This second chance with each idea will bring you such large advances that you will emerge from these reviews with learning gains so great that you will continue on more solid ground, with firmer footing, and with stronger faith.

13. Do not forget how little you have learned, and how much you have to learn. And do not forget that God needs you as you review these thoughts that come from God.

Lesson 111

For morning and evening review:

1. (91) 'I perceive miracles through God's Light.'

I cannot perceive truly when my mind is dark from denying God. I let the Light of Holiness and Truth light up my mind, so that I can see the Innocence within me.

2. (92) 'I perceive miracles through God's Light, and God's Light and Strength are One.'

I perceive truly through God's Gift of Strength to me. My weakness is the dark that God's Gift dispels by giving me God's Strength to take its place.

3. On the hour:
'I perceive miracles through God's Light.'

On the half-hour:
'I perceive miracles through God's Light, and God's Light and Strength are One.'

Lesson 112

For morning and evening review:

1. (93) 'God's Light and Peace and Joy abide in me.'

I am the home of God's Light and Peace and Joy. I welcome Them into the home that I share with God, because I am One with God.

2. (94) 'I am as God created me.'

I am Forever Changeless like God, because I am One with God.

3. On the hour:
'God's Light and Peace and Joy abide in me.'

On the half-hour:
'I am as God created me.'

Lesson 113

For morning and evening review:

1. (95) 'I am One within my True Self; I am One with God.'

Serenity and Perfect Peace are mine, because I am One Self, Complete and Whole, One with God and God's extension of God.

2. (96) 'My salvation from guilt comes from my One Self.'

In my One Self, the Knowledge of Which remains in my mind, I see God's perfect plan for my salvation fulfilled.

3. On the hour:
'I am One within myself; I am One with God.'

On the half-hour:
'My salvation from guilt comes from my One Self.'

Lesson 114

For morning and evening review:

1. (97) 'I am Spirit.'

I am One with God. A body cannot contain my Spirit, nor impose limitations on me.

2. (98) 'I accept my part in God's plan for my salvation from guilt.'

My function can only be to accept God's plan, because I am Forever One with God.

3. On the hour:
'I am Spirit.'

On the half-hour:
'I accept my part in God's plan for my salvation from guilt.'

Lesson 115

For morning and evening review:

1. (99) 'My salvation is my only function in my perception that I am in a world.'

My function in my perception that I am in a world is to forgive all of the errors that I have made. This is how I am released from them and from the world.

2. (100) 'My part is essential to God's plan for my salvation from guilt.'

I am essential to God's plan to save the part of my mind where I perceive a world. God gave me Its plan to save my entire mind.

3. On the hour:

'My salvation is my only function in my perception that I am in a world.'

On the half-hour:

'My part is essential to God's plan for my salvation from guilt.'

Lesson 116

For morning and evening review:

1. (101) 'God's Will for me is Perfect Happiness.'

God's Will for me is Perfect Happiness. I can suffer only from the belief that there is another will apart from God.

2. (102) 'I share God's Will for my Happiness.'

I share God's Will for me, because I am One with God. I want only What God gives to me, because What God gives to me is All that there is.

3. On the hour:
'God's Will for me is Perfect Happiness.'

On the half-hour:
'I share God's Will for my Happiness.'

Lesson 117

For morning and evening review:

1. (103) 'Since God is Love, God is also Happiness.'

I remember that Love is Happiness, and that nothing else brings me Joy, so I will not choose a substitute for Love.

2. (104) 'I seek for only What belongs to me in Truth.'

Love and Joy are mine, because I am One with God. I accept these Gifts of God as mine in Truth.

3. On the hour:
'Since God is Love, God is also Happiness.'

On the half-hour:
'I seek for only What belongs to me in Truth.'

Lesson 118

For morning and evening review:

1. (105) 'God's Peace and Joy are mine.'

Today, I accept God's Peace and Joy in exchange for all of the substitutes that I have made for Them.

2. (106) 'I will be still and listen to the Truth.'

I quiet the feeble voice of the personal mind so that I can hear the Holy Spirit assure me that I am Perfect, because I am One with God.

3. On the hour:
'God's Peace and Joy are mine.'

On the half-hour:
'I will be still and listen to the Truth.'

Lesson 119

For morning and evening review:

1. (107) 'Truth corrects all of the errors in my mind.'

I make a mistake when I think that I am hurt in any way. I am One with God; my True Self rests safely in the Mind of God.

2. (108) 'In Truth, to give and to receive are the same.'

I forgive everything today, so that I learn how to accept the Truth in me, and how to recognize that I am Innocent.'

3. On the hour:
'Truth corrects all of the errors in my mind.'

On the half-hour:
'In Truth, to give and to receive are the same.'

Lesson 120

For morning and evening review:

1. (109) 'I rest in God.'

I rest in Quiet and Certainty today, as I let God work in me and through me.

2. (110) 'I am as God created me.'

I am as God created me. Today, I put aside all sick illusions of myself and let God tell me What I really am.

3. On the hour:
'I rest in God.'
On the half-hour:
'I am as God created me.'

Lesson 121

'Forgiving is my key to Happiness.'

1. In today's idea is the end of your search for Peace, your key to meaning in a world that makes no sense, your way to Safety in the midst of apparent threats that make you doubt you will ever find Quiet and Peace, and the answer to all of your questions. Today's idea ensures the end of your uncertainty.

2. An unforgiving mind is full of fear and has no room for Love to extend Its Peace and lift it above the turmoil of the world that it perceives. An unforgiving mind is sad and without hope for release from pain. An unforgiving mind suffers and lives in misery, and looks around at nothing, but is certain that it sees danger lurking there.

3. An unforgiving mind is torn with doubt, confused about itself and all that it perceives. It is afraid and angry, weak and blustering. It is afraid to go ahead, afraid to stay, afraid to wake up, afraid to go to sleep, afraid at every sound, more afraid of the Quiet, terrified of darkness, but more terrified by God's Light. It can only perceive its own damnation, and 'proof' that all of its 'sins' are real.

4. An unforgiving mind cannot see mistakes, only 'sins'. It looks without Real Perception, and it shrieks as it sees its own projections rising to attack its miserable parody of a 'life'. It wants to live, but wishes it were dead. It wants forgiveness, but it sees no hope of it. It wants to escape, but cannot conceive of it, because it sees sin everywhere.

5. An unforgiving mind is in despair, because it sees a future that offers only more despair. It regards its judgments on the world that it perceives as unchangeable, and it does not see that it condemns itself to despair. It thinks that it cannot change, because what it perceives bears witness that its judgments are correct. It does not ask how to perceive the world, because it thinks it knows how. It does not question what it perceives, because it is certain that it is right in its perception.

6. Forgiving is a skill that you learn, because it is not inherent to your mind, which cannot sin. *Sin* is an idea that you taught yourself through the personal mind, which is an unforgiving mind, so you must now be taught to forgive by the Holy Spirit. Through the Holy Spirit, you learn how to forgive the self that you think you made, so that it can disappear from your mind. This is how you return your mind to God through the Holy Spirit, Which is your True Self, and can never 'sin'.

7. Every unforgiving mind that you perceive presents you with an opportunity to teach yourself how to forgive the unforgiving mind in you. Perceive each one looking to you for Heaven, and release them from hell, here and now. As you extend hope to other minds that you perceive, you accept hope for yourself. The part of your mind that does not forgive must learn, through your forgiving it, that it has been saved from hell. As you teach salvation, you learn salvation, but only when your teaching is from the Holy Spirit within you.

8. Today, you practice forgiving. If you are willing, you can take this key to your Happiness and use it on your own behalf. Devote ten minutes in the morning and ten minutes at night to giving and receiving forgiveness.

9. An unforgiving mind does not believe that giving and receiving are the same. But, today, you will learn that they are one by forgiving one whom you think of as an 'enemy' and another whom you think of as a 'friend'. As you learn to see them both as one, you will extend today's lesson to yourself and see that their escape from guilt is your escape from guilt.

10. Begin your longer practice periods by thinking of someone that you do not like. This can be someone who merely irritates you, whom you regret meeting, that you actively despise, or that you simply try to ignore. The form of your anger does not matter. You have probably already thought of someone; they will do.

11. Now, close your eyes, and picture this person clearly. Let go of the ugly picture that you have of them, and visualize God's Light in them. Extend the Light until it surrounds them and your picture of

them is Beautiful and Good.

12. Observe this changed perception for a while, then turn your mind to the one that you call 'friend'. Transfer the Light that you saw around your former 'enemy' to your friend. Perceive your friend as more than friend, because in the Light their Holiness is your Savior, and you are healed and Whole.

13. Then, allow your friend to extend the Light to you. Let your enemy and friend join in the Light to bless you with What you gave to them. Now, you are one with them, and you have been forgiven by yourself. Throughout the day, do not forget the role that forgiving plays in bringing Happiness to an unforgiving mind in whatever form it takes, whether it is 'yours' or 'another's'. Every hour, tell yourself:

> 'Forgiving is my key to Happiness. I will awaken from the dream that I am mortal, fallible, and full of sin, and know that I am Perfect, because I am One with God.'

Mentor's Notes

There is really only one mind that seems to be split between God and not-God. Its great deception is that it has projected itself into many forms (personal minds). But this is why, no matter where you forgive an unforgiving mind, you forgive it in yourself.

Lesson 122

'My forgiving offers me Everything that I want.'

1. Everything that you really want, your forgiving gives to you. Do you want Peace, Happiness, a Quiet mind, a sense of purpose, awareness of your Inestimable Worth, and Beauty that transcends what you perceive in the world? Your forgiving offers you all of this. Do you want to feel a Security that is Eternal, a Quietness that cannot be disturbed, Gentleness that can never be hurt, and a Deep Rest so Perfect that It can never be upset?

2. Your forgiving offers you all of this, and more. It gives you Joy throughout the day, and comforts you while you sleep undisturbed by nightmares. And when you awaken again, it offers you another day of Peace and Happiness.

3. Your forgiving lifts the veil of unforgiving that hides your Christ Mind from your awareness. As you recognize Christ, It wipes away all of the dead thoughts in your memory, so that you can remember God again. What else could you want? What other gifts are worthy of your seeking? What do you imagine has more value for you than What your forgiving brings into your awareness?

4. Don't seek for an answer other than the answer that answers everything. In your forgiving, you find the perfect answer to your imperfect questions, meaningless requests, and half-hearted willingness, effort, and trust in Truth. Your forgiving is the answer, so do not seek for another answer.

5. God's plan for your salvation cannot change or fail. Be thankful for this. It stands before you like an open door to a warm and welcome home that you are invited to enter and make your own. This is where you belong.

6. Your forgiving is the answer, so do not stand outside while Heaven waits for you within. Forgive, and you are forgiven; as you give, you receive. This is the only plan for your salvation. Rejoice today that this is true, because here you have your answer; clear, plain, and beyond deceit in its simplicity. All of the complex illusions

that the personal mind weaves disappear before the power and majesty of today's simple statement of the truth.

7. Forgiving is your answer, so do not turn away to wander aimlessly again. Accept your salvation from guilt now. Your salvation is God's gift to you; it does not come from the world that you perceive. You will not value any 'gift' that the world offers to you when your mind receives What God gives to you who are One with God. It is God's will that you are saved today, and that you are no longer deceived by the intricacies of your illusions.

8. Use your Real Perception today, and look on Happiness, Safety, and Peace. Your forgiving is the means by which They come to take the place of hell in your mind. In Quietness, They rise up in your awareness to fill you with the Deep Tranquility of Truth. What you remember with Them, you will not be able to describe, but It is What your forgiving offers to you.

9. Remembering the Gifts that your forgiving brings to you, practice today with hope and faith that today will be the day of your salvation. Sincerely and gratefully seek for your salvation, aware that you hold the key to it in your forgiving. Accept Heaven's answer to the hell that you made, and that you no longer want.

10. Morning and evening, gladly give fifteen minutes to the search that guarantees the end of hell for you. Begin hopefully, because you have reached the turning point at which the road will become far easier for you. There is not much further to go; you are close to the end of your illusions.

11. Sink into Happiness as you begin your practice periods, because they hold out the rewards of your forgiving. Today, you will feel the Peace that your forgiving offers to you, and the Joy that lifting the veil of unforgiving brings to you.

12. In God's Light, the world will fade today until it disappears from your mind and you perceive Something Else that you will have no words to describe. Walk directly into God's Light, and receive the Gifts that God has kept for you.

13. Your forgiving offers you Everything that you want. Today,

Everything is given to you. Do not let your Gifts recede from your mind as you return to a perception of a the world of constant change and bleak appearances. Hold onto your Gifts in clear awareness as you perceive the Changeless beyond the changing, and the Light of Truth beyond appearances.

14. Do not be tempted to let your Gifts slip away as you drift into forgetfulness. Hold onto Them by thinking of Them for at least one minute every quarter of an hour. Use this time to remind yourself of how Precious your Gifts are. Use these words to hold your Gifts in your awareness throughout the day:

> 'My forgiving offers me Everything that I want. Today, I accept this truth, and I receive the Gifts of God.'

Lesson 123

'I thank God for Its Gifts to me.'

1. Be thankful today, because you have come to a gentler, smoother road. You don't have to think of turning back, and your resistance to the Truth is no longer immovable. You might waver a little, object a little, or hesitate a little, but you can be grateful for your gains, which are far greater than you realize.

2. Devoting a day to gratitude will give you some insight into the real extent of all of the gains that you have made and of the Gifts that you have received. Be lovingly thankful that God has not left you alone in the darkness that you made. Be grateful that God saves you from the self that you thought that you made to take the place of God.

3. Thank God for not abandoning you and for Its Love, Which shines on you Forever, and cannot change. Thank God that *you* are Changeless in your Oneness with God. Be grateful that you are saved, and that you have the function of extending your awareness of your salvation in your mind where you perceive a world. Be thankful that your Value far transcends the meager 'gifts' of the personal mind, and its petty judgments on you who are One with God.

4. In gratitude, lift your heart above despair, and lift your eyes, thankful to be no longer looking downward in the dust. Be thankful today to honor your True Self, Which is One with God. Smile on everyone that you see as you lightheartedly attend to what the Holy Spirit appoints for you to do today.

5. You do not walk alone, so give thanks to God for the Holy Spirit, Which speaks God's saving Word to you. And thank yourself for listening to the Holy Spirit, because otherwise the Holy Spirit goes unheard. In thanking the Holy Spirit, you thank your True Self. A message that you do not hear will not save you, no matter how Mighty the Voice that speaks it; no matter how Loving the message.

6. Thanks to you for becoming a messenger who extends God's

message in your mind where you perceive a world. Receive God's Thanks to you as you give thanks to God. God receives your gifts in Loving Gratitude, and gives them back to you a thousand times over. God blesses your gifts by extending them to you, so that they grow in power and strength, until they fill all that you perceive with Happiness and gratitude.

7. Twice today, for fifteen minutes each, receive God's Gratitude and offer yours to God. As you thank God and God thanks you, you will realize that you and God are One. This holy half-hour that you give to God will save much time in the salvation of your entire mind.

8. Receive God's Thanks, and you will understand how Lovingly God holds you in Its Mind, how Deep and Limitless is God's Care for you, and how Perfect is God's Gratitude to you. Remember to think of God every hour, and thank God for Everything that God gives to you, so that you can rise above the world that you perceive and remember your Self in God.

Mentor's Notes

Besides thinking of everything mentioned here, use today to be thankful for how far you have come since you began these lessons a few months ago. You are a third of the way through these lessons now. Think of the miracles that you have had, and of the guidance and Peace that you have experienced. Consider how much lighter your mind is since you began, and how you now have tools to use to lighten it when it gets dark again. Think of how much you have learned about Truth through reading this course, and how much fear of God it has already helped you undo. Use today's lesson to recognize that you have already benefited from these lessons, so that you will be motivated to continue with less resistance.

Lesson 124

'I remember that I am One with God.'

1. Today, you will again be grateful for your Identity in God. Your Home is Safe, you are always protected, and God's Power and Strength are available to you in all that you do. You cannot fail. Everything that you touch is lit with a Light that blesses and heals. At One with God and God's Extension, you go forward rejoicing in the awareness that God is with you wherever you perceive yourself.

2. How Holy is your mind! Everything that you perceive reflects the Holiness within your mind, which is One within itself, and One with God. Your errors easily disappear, and death gives way to Everlasting Life. Your footprints point the way to Truth, because God is your Companion as you continue to walk for a little longer in a perception that you are in a world. Your Light remains within you as It extends into the part of your mind where you perceive a world.

3. The Eternal Gifts that you receive from God extend throughout time, undoing it. God loves as One 'you' and the part of your mind that you perceive as a world, and offers you the Happiness that you extend to the world.

4. Today, do not doubt God's Love for you, or question God's Protection and Care. Do not let meaningless anxieties come between your faith and your awareness of God's Presence. Remember today that you are One with God. Feel God in your heart, know that your mind contains God's Thoughts, and look upon God's Loveliness in all that you perceive. Today, perceive only the Loving and the Lovable.

5. Choose to perceive Peace instead of appearances of pain. Perceive Tranquility in place of the frantic, the sad, the distressed, the lonely, and the afraid. Perceive Life instead of the dying and the dead. You can perceive all of these Aspects of Love in the world when you first perceive Love in yourself.

6. When you know that you are One with God, you cannot be denied a miracle. Your Thoughts of God have the power to heal all

forms of suffering, anywhere that you perceive them, past, present, or future, because your Thoughts of God come from beyond time and space.

7. Join in this awareness as you say that you are One with God. In these words, you say that you are saved and healed, and that you are willing to extend salvation and healing, because you want to keep God's Gifts to you. Today, experience yourself as One with God, so that your entire mind can recognize Reality. In this experience, you set your mind free from the world. As you deny that you are separate from God, your entire mind is healed.

8. Peace is yours today. Maintain your Peace by practicing the awareness that you are One with God. Whenever it is best today, spend a half-hour with the thought that you are One with God. This is your first extended practice period where you will have no rules or special words to guide your meditation. Simply trust the Holy Spirit to speak to you; It will not fail you. Give the half-hour to the Holy Spirit, and the Holy Spirit will do the rest.

9. If it seems that nothing happens, you may not be ready to accept the gains that today's exercise can bring to you. But, at some time, they will come to you, and you will recognize them. Every minute of today's half-hour is valuable, because it frames your Christ Mind.

10. If not today, then at another time you will recognize Christ in this Holy half-hour. When you are ready, you will find It within your mind. Then, you will remember this half-hour, and be grateful that you spent it on this Goal.

11. If not today, then at another time you will look into your mind and understand that the Innocence and Loveliness that you see there is you. Count today's half-hour as your gift to God, and be certain that God will return to you Love and Joy so deep that you will not understand Them. But you can be sure that one day you will understand.

12. Add greater value to the half-hour that you practice today by repeating to yourself every hour:

'I remember that I am One with God and with the world that I perceive, in Everlasting Holiness and Peace.'

Mentor's Notes

If you do nothing else, simply opening your mind to God every day will be enough to transform your experience. The value of an exercise like today's cannot be overestimated.

Lesson 125

'Today, I receive God's Word in quiet.'

1. Today is a day of stillness and of quiet listening for you. God wills that you hear God's Word today, and calls to you from deep within your mind. Hear God today. Total Peace is not possible for you until you hear God's Word everywhere by quietly listening for and accepting the message that you must extend to your entire mind.

2. Your perception of the world can only change through you; nothing else can save your mind. God's plan is simply this: As Part of God, you are free to save yourself. You have Forever within you God's Word, the Holy Spirit, to be your Guide to God through your own free will. You cannot be led by force, but only by Love. God does not judge you, but knows that you are Holy.

3. In stillness, hear the Holy Spirit today, without the intrusion of the personal mind's petty thoughts and desires, and without judging the Holy Spirit. Do not judge yourself today, either, because What you are cannot be judged. Stand apart from all of the judgments that the personal mind makes on you who are One with God. It does not know you. Simply wait in silence for the Word of God.

4. Hear God, with Which you are One, speak to you. The Holy Spirit gives you God's Holy Word to extend salvation and Peace in your mind where you perceive a world. Come today to the Quiet Place within your mind Where God is Forever, in the Holiness that is One with God, and Which God can never leave.

5. God does not wait for you to give your mind to God to give the Holy Spirit to you. God does not hide from you while you seem to have wandered off from God. God does not cherish the illusions that you hold about yourself. God knows you as Part of Itself, and wills that you remain Part of God, regardless of your illusion that your will is not God's will.

6. God speaks to you today. The Holy Spirit waits for you to be quiet, because God's Word cannot be heard by you until your mind is still for a while, and you have put aside meaningless desires. Wait

for God's Word in quiet, and call on the Peace within you to help you make your Holy mind ready to hear That with Which it is One.

7. Set aside ten minutes three times today to stop listening to the personal mind and to listen to the Word of God instead. The Holy Spirit speaks to you from nearer than your heart; It is closer than your hand. The Holy Spirit's Love is Everything that you are; you and the Holy Spirit are One.

8. It is your Voice that you hear when the Holy Spirit speaks. It is your Word that the Holy Spirit speaks to you. It is the Word of Limitlessness and Peace, of One Will and Purpose, of the One Mind of God and you. In quiet, listen to your True Self today, and let It tell you that God has never left you, and you have never left your True Self.

9. Just be quiet; you need no other rule for today's practicing to lift you above the personal mind's thoughts, and to free your perception from the body's eyes. Just be quiet, and you will hear the Word in Which your will joins in God's Will. No illusion can come between what is Wholly One and True. At every hour today, be still a moment and remind yourself that you have a special purpose for today: To receive the Word of God in quiet.

Mentor's Notes

Remember from the Text that in God *to have* and *to be* are the same. So the Holy Spirit within you not only *has* God's Word but *is* God's Word. The Holy Spirit *speaks* God's Word to you and *embodies* God's Word for you.

Also remember that the personal mind always speaks first, so let it. Do not fight it or repress it; these only give it more power in your mind. Simply let what it says go by and sink into the Quiet in your mind.

Lesson 126

'All that I give, I give to myself.'

1. Today's idea is completely alien to the personal mind and its world, but it is crucial to the thought reversal that this course will bring about in you. If you believe today's statement, you will have no problem completely forgiving, and you will be certain that you will attain your goal of freedom from guilt. You will understand that your forgiving is the means by which your salvation is accomplished, and you will not hesitate to use it now.

2. Consider what you do believe: It seems to you that the other people that you perceive are apart from you, and that your perception of their behavior has nothing to do with you. So you think that your attitudes do not affect your perception of them, and that their calls for help have nothing to do with your own call for help. You think that you can judge their 'sins' without affecting your perception of yourself, and you think that you can be unaffected by your condemnation of them and be at Peace.

3. You believe that when you 'forgive' a 'sin' that there is no gain to you. You think that you are merely giving charity to one who is unworthy of it, so that you can appear 'better' than the one that you forgive. This 'sinner' has not earned your charity, because their 'sins' have made them beneath you, so they have no claim to your forgiveness, which you give as a gift, but which holds nothing for you.

4. From this view, forgiveness is insane; it is a charitable whim for the undeserving, which you sometimes bestow and you sometimes withhold. Since your forgiving is not deserved, you are just in withholding it, and you think that it is unfair that you suffer when you don't forgive, because the sin that you forgive is not your own. Someone separate from you has committed it, and if you are gracious enough to give them the forgiveness that they don't deserve, then the forgiveness that you give is no more yours than their sin is yours.

5. If all this were true about forgiveness, then your forgiving

would have no dependable justification. It would only be an eccentric giving of undeserved reprieve for others that you sometimes indulge in. It would remain your right to not let the sinner escape paying for their sin. Do you really think a Loving God would allow your salvation to depend on this? God would hardly care for you if your salvation rested on a *whim*.

6. You do not understand forgiveness if this is your view of it. In this view, it is only a disguised attack on another, because it does not require that *your mind* be corrected. If you perceive forgiveness like this, it cannot bring you Peace. It does not release you from something that you perceive in someone else, but that is really in your mind. It does not restore to your awareness that the other that you perceive is not separate from you. It is not what God intends for forgiveness to be.

7. When you don't give to God what God asks of you, then you do not recognize God's Gifts to you, and you think that God has withheld Them from you. But God only asks from you what can be turned into a Gift to you. God is not satisfied with the empty gesture of the personal mind's form of forgiveness, and God does not evaluate such petty gifts as worthy of you who are One with God. God's means of salvation for you is a better gift than this. True forgiving is the means by which you attain salvation, and it heals your mind when you give it, because giving is receiving. What you do not accept for yourself, you cannot give; what you give, you must have accepted for yourself.

8. Today, understand the truth that the giver and the receiver are the same. You need Help to make this meaningful to you, because it is alien to the way that you are used to thinking with a personal mind. The Help that you need is here in the Holy Spirit. Give the Holy Spirit your faith today, and ask the Holy Spirit to join you in practicing Truth. If you catch only a tiny glimpse of the freedom for you that lies in today's idea, then this is a glorious day for your entire mind.

9. Give fifteen minutes twice today to understanding today's

idea. It is the thought by which your forgiving takes its proper place at the top of your priorities. It is the thought that releases you from every obstacle that you have to understanding what forgiveness really is, and lets you see its value for you.

10. In silence, close your eyes on the world that does not understand forgiveness, and seek sanctuary in the Quiet Place within you, Where your thoughts are changed, and you put aside false ideas. Repeat today's idea, and ask the Holy Spirit to help you understand what it really means. Be willing to be taught. Be happy to hear the Holy Spirit speak of Truth and healing, and you will understand the Holy Spirit, and recognize that It speaks your words to you.

11. As often as you can, remind yourself throughout the day that today you have a goal of special value to you, and to your mind where you perceive a world. Do not forget the goal for long by telling yourself:

> 'All that I give, I give to myself. The Help that I need to learn that this is true is with me now. I trust the Holy Spirit.'

Then, spend a quiet moment opening your mind to the Holy Spirit's correction and Love. What you hear from the Holy Spirit you will believe, because what the Holy Spirit gives to you, you will receive.

Mentor's Notes

Paragraph 2 mentions 'calls for help', which you will remember from the Text is what occurs when you are not Loving. What isn't Love is a call for Love. It does not matter if you perceive a call for Love within yourself or in 'another'; you perceive it, so it is in your mind, and it is your call for Love.

You can only understand true forgiveness if you accept that what you perceive is occurring in your mind. You truly forgive by letting go of the personal mind's projections on others and the world, and by allowing the Holy Spirit to give you a Loving Perception in their place. You receive the forgiveness that you give, because you free your mind from its illusion that it is separate from God.

Lesson 127

'The only Love is God's Love.'

1. Maybe you think that there are different kinds of love: a love for this, a different love for that, one type of love for one person, another type of love for another. But Love is One; It has no separate parts or degrees, no types or levels, no divergences or distinctions. It is like Itself throughout Itself, and It never changes. It is not changed by a person or a situation. Love is the Center of God, and of you who are One with God.

2. Love's meaning is obscure to you when you think that it can change. A Love that changes is impossible, but your belief that Love can change is what makes you think that you can sometimes love and sometimes hate. You think that you can extend Love to some but withhold Love from others, and that Love will still remain Whole in your awareness. If you believe these things, then you do not understand Love. If Love could make distinctions, it would have to judge between the 'righteous' and the 'sinner'; It would perceive the Mind that is One with God in separate parts.

3. Love cannot judge, because It is One Itself and can only look on Love. Love's very Meaning lies in Its Oneness, and It is lost to your awareness if you think of It as partial or in parts. The only Love is God's Love, and all of Love is God's. There is no other Principle; Love is a Law without an opposite. Love's Wholeness is the Power that holds Everything in Oneness; Love is the Link that holds you and God in Oneness.

4. This course, which has the purpose of teaching you to remember What you really are, can only emphasize that there is no difference between What you really are and What Love is. Love's Meaning is your Meaning; It is the Meaning that you share with God, because you are What God is. The only Love is God's Love, and What God is, is Everything that is. God has no limits, so neither have you.

5. Nothing in the world that you perceive can help you understand Love's Meaning. You made the world to hide Love's Meaning

from yourself as a dark secret. Every principle that the world that you made upholds violates the Truth of What Love is, and of What you are as well.

6. Do not seek in the world that you perceive for your True Self. Love is not found in darkness and death, but Love is perfectly apparent to a mind that is open to Love's Voice. Today, you will practice freeing your mind from all of the laws that you think it must obey, all of the limits under which you think that it must live, and all of the changes that you think are part of its 'human destiny'. Today, you take the single largest step that this course requests of you as you advance toward its goal of releasing you from guilt.

7. If you achieve even the faintest glimmer of Love's Meaning today, you will save yourself time beyond measure in your release from guilt. Be happy to give this time to God today, and understand that there is no better use for time than this.

8. For fifteen minutes twice today, escape from every law in which you now believe. Open your mind, and rest in God. You can escape the world that seems to limit you if you do not value it. Withdraw all of the value that you have given to its meager offerings and 'gifts' to you, and let the Gift of God replace them all.

9. Call on God, and be certain that God's Holy Spirit will answer. God has promised this, and God will place a Spark of Truth in your mind wherever you give up a false, dark belief about your own reality and the meaning of Love. God's Light will shine through your idle thoughts today, and help you understand the Truth of Love. In Loving Gentleness, God will stay with you as you allow Its Holy Spirit to teach Love's Meaning to your open mind. God will bless this Lesson with Its Love.

10. Today, years of waiting for your salvation disappear before the Timelessness of What you learn. Be grateful that you will be spared a future like the past that the personal mind taught you. Today, you leave that past behind you, and you never have to remember it again. Perceive a different present unlike the past in every way, and it will extend into the future.

11. A new Perception is born in you, and you will watch It grow in health and strength to bless your perception of the world, which was made in hate to be Love's 'enemy'. Now your entire mind is free, and all that you perceive is One with you in God's Love.

12. Throughout the day, remember your mind where you perceive a world, because you cannot leave part of yourself outside of Love and know your True Self. At least three times an hour, think of one 'other' who seems to make the journey with you, and to whom you must extend what you are learning. As this one comes to mind, extend to them this message from your True Self:

> 'I bless you with God's Love, in Which you and I are One. I want to learn that there is only God's Love, Which encompasses everything that my mind perceives.'

Mentor's Notes

It might seem a contradiction that this course tells you to not accept what the world that you perceive teaches you, yet it also tells you to perceive Love in the world. But remember, you always look within first. If you look *to* the world as something apart from you to learn What you are, it cannot show you, because you will be looking at an empty projection of a personal mind. But if you first look within yourself to the Love that is there and then *extend* It outward, you will see the Love within you reflected back to you. Projection and extension are the same mechanism of mind seeing itself. *Projection,* however, is what your mind uses when it wants to perceive separation from God as 'reality', and does not want to see that it is the source of this idea. Such a projection can not be real, so it can only show you false ideas, like an illusory 'love' unlike God's Love. But when you are willing to see God's Love within you, you happily extend It to the world to keep It in your awareness.

Lesson 128

'The world that I perceive holds nothing that I want.'

1. The world that you perceive offers you nothing that you need, nothing that you can use in any real way, and nothing that serves to bring you Joy. Believe this, and you are saved from years of misery, countless disappointments, and from hopes that will turn to bitter despair. If you want to leave behind the limitations of the world, you must accept today's thought.

2. Everything that you value in the world that you perceive limits you to the world. Your valuing *anything* in the world serves only the purpose of limiting you. But the world serves the purpose that you give to it, and you can give it another purpose. The only purpose worthy of you is forgiveness. You can let go of the world, and you can stop delaying your salvation from guilt by perceiving some justification for hope in it. Do not be deceived anymore: The world that you perceive holds nothing that you want.

3. Today, escape from the limitations that you put on your mind when you think that the world offers you salvation. What you value you perceive as part of the self that you believe you are. Everything that you seek in the world to make yourself greater in your self-perception only limits you further, hides your True Worth from you, and presents another obstacle to your awareness of your True Self.

4. Do not let thoughts about the body/personal self delay your salvation from guilt, and don't hold yourself back by believing that the world holds anything that you want. There is nothing for you to cherish in the world; nothing that is worth one instant of pain or one moment of doubt. The worthless offers you nothing, and you cannot find your True Worth in what is worthless.

5. Today, let go of all of the value that you have given to the world that you perceive. Do not give purpose to any aspect of it or to its dreams. Release your mind from all that you wish that the world was, and set yourself free from the world with its little values and tiny goals.

6. Be still and be at Peace for a while, and see how far your mind rises above the world when you release it from the world's limitations. Let your mind find the Level Where it is at Home. Your mind will be grateful to be free for a while, because it knows Where it belongs. Let it rise in Joy to its Holy Purpose of Oneness with God. Let it rest in God, Where it is restored to Sanity, Limitlessness, and Love.

7. Give your mind ten minutes of rest three times today. When you open your eyes afterward, you will not value anything that you perceive in the world as much as you did before. Your whole perspective on the world will change every time that you let your mind escape its limitations. The world is not where your mind belongs, and you belong Where your mind wants to be, and Where it goes to rest when you release it from the world. Your Guide is with you. Open your mind to the Holy Spirit; be still and rest.

8. Protect your mind's rest throughout the day as well. When you think that you see some value in any aspect or image in the world, refuse to limit yourself, and tell yourself with quiet certainty:

> 'This will not tempt me to delay my salvation from guilt. The world that I perceive holds nothing that I want.'

Lesson 129

'Beyond my perception of a world is a Perception that I want.'

1. This thought follows from the one that you practiced yesterday. You cannot stop with the idea that the world that you perceive is worthless, because, unless you perceive something else to hope for, you will be depressed. You are not being asked to live in a void, but to exchange the world that you perceive for a Perception that is far more satisfying, and that is filled with Joy and Peace. The world that you perceive cannot offer you These.

2. Give a little more time to thinking about the value of the world that you perceive. Maybe you will concede that there is no loss for you in giving up all that you thought had value in the world. The world that you perceive is merciless, unstable, cruel, unconcerned with you, quick to avenge, and pitiless in its hate. It gives only to take back, and takes away everything that you have loved. No lasting love can be found in the world, because none is there. The world is bound by time, and all things in it come to an end.

3. There is no loss for you in perceiving What cannot lose, Love that is Eternal, and a Place Where hate does not exist, and vengeance has no meaning. There is no loss for you in perceiving All that you really want, and in knowing that It will never end, and will remain always the same throughout time. Yet, you will exchange even This for Heaven, Where there are no words to describe What Heaven is, but in Deepest Silence you understand It.

4. In Heaven, Communication between you and God is Clear and Limitless for Eternity. What is communicated between you and God has no words, because It cannot be limited to symbols. Your shared Knowledge with God is direct and Wholly One. You are far from This when you limit yourself to a world, but you are very near to This when you exchange the world for your Real Perception.

5. From your Real Perception, your return to God is certain; you are an instant away from Eternity. You can only look forward Here, and you can never look back to the world that you do not want. Your

Real Perception takes the world's place in your mind as you free it from the little things that you once valued in the world. Do not value them, and they will disappear from your mind; value them, and they will seem real to you.

6. This is your choice. There is no loss for you in choosing to not value nothingness. The world that you perceive holds nothing that you really want, but What you can choose instead you do indeed want! Accept your Real Perception today. It waits for you to choose It to take the place of all of the things that you once sought, but that you do not really want.

7. Practice your willingness to make this change for ten minutes, three times today: morning, evening, and once in-between. Begin with this:

> 'Beyond my perception of a world is a Perception that I want. I choose my Real Perception over the world, because the world offers nothing that I really want.'

Then close your eyes to the world, and, in the silent darkness, watch God's Light fill your mind until It is all that you perceive.

8. Today, the Light of Heaven shines in your mind as you rest beyond the world of darkness. This is a Light that the body's eyes cannot see, but that your mind can see and understand plainly. Today, you are given a day of Grace, so give thanks. Today, realize that what you feared to lose was loss itself.

9. Now you understand that there is no loss, because you have seen the opposite of loss. Be grateful that you have made the choice for your Real Perception. Remember your decision every hour by taking a moment to confirm your choice. Lay aside whatever thoughts you are having, and dwell briefly on this:

> 'The world that I perceive holds nothing that I want. Beyond my perception of a world is my Real Perception, Which I do want.'

Mentor's Notes

Your Real Perception can show up as the physical world transformed by Love, or as a Perception of Something beyond the world that defies description. You may have one or both of these experiences. In either case, you will be aware that What you are perceiving is in your mind, unlike when you perceive the world with a personal mind. In other words, with your Real Perception, Content overtakes form to such an extent that it renders form irrelevant, where in the personal mind's perception, form is all that there is.

Your Real Perception will come to you when you are ready for It. You will know without a doubt when you experience It.

Lesson 130

'It is impossible for me to use my Real Perception when I perceive the world as real.'

1. Perception is consistent. What you perceive reflects your thoughts, and your thoughts reflect what you want. Your values determine what you perceive, because you value what you believe is real. You will not perceive what you do not value, and you can only perceive what you do value and want.

2. You do not perceive both what you hate and what you love; you only perceive what you love. You do not want God to be Reality, so you are afraid of your Real Perception. Your fear of God makes you blind to It. What you love you perceive, but your fear hides What is really here from your awareness.

3. In your fear of God, you project nothingness onto a world to hide the Truth in your mind, and you perceive illusions. What could you want that fear shows to you? Why would you want to keep illusions?

4. Your fear of God has made everything that you perceive in the world: separation, distinctions, differences. They are not there; they were made by the 'enemy' of Love. But Love cannot have an 'enemy', because Love is all-encompassing, so your illusions have no cause, no being, and no consequence. You can value them, but that does not make them real. You can seek for salvation in them, but you will never find it in them. Today, you will not waste your time seeking for salvation where it cannot be found.

5. Since they cannot overlap, it is impossible for you to perceive the world as real and still use your Real Perception. If you want one, the other will disappear for you. This is your range of choice: You can only decide between the unreal and the Real.

6. Today, you will not try to make a compromise where a compromise cannot be made. The fact that you perceive a world is proof that you have already made a choice as all-encompassing as its opposite. What you will learn today is more than just that you cannot

perceive the world as real and still use your Real Perception. You will also learn that what you perceive is consistent within itself, because it reflects its source: fear or Love.

7. In gratitude, six times today happily give five minutes to the thought that ends all compromise and doubt. These are the same thing, and you will go beyond them. Do not try to make a thousand meaningless distinctions among illusions in an attempt to make some of them real as you devote your mind to finding Reality.

8. Begin by opening your mind to your Real Perception by asking for the Strength of God in recognition that you seek Reality. You do not want illusions, and you come to these five minutes with a mind that is empty of meaningless values for the world. Wait for God to help you as you say:

> 'It is impossible for me to use my Real Perception when I perceive the world as real. I accept the Strength that God offers to me, and I see no value in the world, so that I can be free of limitations.'

9. God is here for you. You have called on the Great Unfailing Power, Which takes this giant step with you in gratitude. You will see God's Thanks to you expressed in a tangible Perception of Truth. You will not doubt It when you perceive It, because though it is *perception,* it is not the kind of seeing that you are used to with the body's eyes. You will know that God's Strength upholds you when you choose your Real Perception.

10. Whenever it arises, dismiss the temptation to believe that the world is real by merely remembering the limits of your choice: The unreal or the Real. Your perception is consistent with your choice, and you will experience either hell or Heaven, never both together.

11. Accept any part of hell as real, and you will curse yourself with a perception of hell. But your release to Heaven is still within your range of choice. It can replace everything that your choice of hell shows to you. All that you need to say to hell, in whatever form

it appears to you, is simply this:

> 'It is impossible for me to use my Real Perception when I perceive the world as real. I want to be free from limitations, and this is not part of what I want.'

Lesson 131

'I will reach the Truth that I seek.'

1. Failure is all around you as you try to attain goals where they cannot be attained. You look for Permanence in the impermanent, for Love where there is none, for Safety in danger, and for Immortality in an illusion of death. You can not succeed in finding these Goals in an unstable setting that contradicts Them.

2. You cannot attain Real Goals in an illusion, because the means you would use to reach Them are illusions, too. Pursuing Real Goals in an illusion is a type of death, because you are searching in nothingness. You seem to be looking for Life, but you are asking for death. You look for Safety and Security, but in your heart you are praying for vulnerability by trying to protect the little illusion that you made.

3. It is inevitable that while you perceive yourself in a world of lack, you will search for What you gave away when you caused the lack. You made the world to be a place where you seek and do not find What you seek, so of course that is what you do there. But the world does not dictate *where* you seek, unless you give it the power to do so. You are free to search for your Goals beyond the world, in a Place within you that seems new, but was yours before time. It is a Place that holds Everything that you really want.

4. Be glad to learn that you are searching for Heaven, and that you will find It, because you really want It. You are One with God, so you cannot search in vain for Heaven, though you can delay and deceive yourself by believing that hell is Heaven. But when you are mistaken, you will find Correction; when you wander from your Goal, you will be led back.

5. You cannot remain in hell, because you cannot really abandon God, or affect God's Perfect, Eternal, Unchanging Love for you. You *will* find Heaven; everything else that you seek will fall away, not because it will be taken from you, but because you do not want it. It is as certain that you will reach the Goal that you really want as it is

that you are Innocent in God.

6. Why wait for Heaven? It is here right now. Time is the great illusion that makes you believe that Heaven is in the past or the future. But this cannot be, because Heaven is Where God wills you to be, and the Will of God cannot be in the past or the future. What God wills is *now*, because Eternity is Time*less*ness.

7. Heaven is the One Alternative to the strange world that you made, and to all of its ways: Shifting patterns, impossible means for your Goals, painful 'pleasures', and tragic 'joys'. God is One and does not make contradictions. What denies itself and attacks itself is not of God. God did not make two minds, one of Which is Heaven, and the other the opposite of Heaven in every way.

8. God is One and does not suffer from conflict. Nor are you, who are One with God, split in two. You cannot be in hell when you are One with God in Heaven. You cannot lose what your Eternal Will gives to you as your Home Forever. Do not try to impose an alien will on God's Single Purpose. God is here, because God wills to be here, and What God wills is present now, beyond the reach of time.

9. Today, you will not choose a paradox in place of Truth. You who are One with God have not made time to undo the Will of God. When you think that you have done so, you deny yourself and contradict What has no opposite. You think that you have made a hell by opposing Heaven, and you think that you live in what does not exist, while Heaven is the Place that you seek for and cannot seem to find.

10. Today, leave behind foolish thoughts like these, and turn your mind to True Thoughts instead. You will reach the Truth that you seek today. Devote ten minutes three times today to asking for your Real Perception to replace the foolish images that you value. Let True Ideas replace thoughts that have no meaning, no effect, no source, and no substance in Truth.

11. Start your practice periods with this:

'I ask to perceive differently, and to think thoughts that are different from those that I've made. The Real Perception that I seek comes to me from God; the thoughts that I want to think are God's Thoughts.'

Close your eyes, and for several minutes watch your mind, and see the senseless world that you have made. Also, review your thoughts about the world, which you think are true. Then let them all go, and sink into the Holy Place in your mind Where they cannot enter. Picture a door beneath these thoughts in your mind that you could never close off forever.

12. Before you open this door, remind yourself that beyond it you will find the Truth that you seek, and that you are requesting today. Only Truth has meaning for you now; you have no other Goal. You want only What lies beyond this door.

13. Put your hand on the door, and see how easily it opens with your single intent to go through it. God's Light shines on the other side; all darkness vanishes from your mind, and you are standing in a Light so Bright and Clear that you understand everything that you perceive. You might even experience a tiny moment of surprise as you realize that the Truth that you see with your Real Perception is familiar to you.

14. You will succeed today. The Holy Spirit has always been with you so that one day you could approach this door, and, with Its Help, slip effortlessly past the door and into God's Light. Today is that day. Today, God keeps Its Promise of Oneness to you, and you keep your Promise of Oneness to God. This is a day of Happiness for you, because you arrive Where you find the Goal that you have been futilely seeking in the world. Both the world and your seeking end as you pass through the door to Truth.

15. Remember often today that it is a day of special Happiness, and refrain from dismal thoughts and meaningless laments. It is time for your salvation from guilt. Heaven Itself sets today to be a time of Grace for your entire mind. If you forget this Happy Fact today, remind yourself with this:

'Today, I seek for and find all that I want, because my one purpose offers it to me. I will reach the Truth that I seek.'

Mentor's Notes

In this lesson, you revisit the idea that the world is hell. You may now be more willing to accept this idea than you were in earlier lessons. In essence, you are always seeking for the *experience* of Heaven in the world: Eternal Love, Peace, Joy, Wholeness, and Limitlessness. But, of course, the world cannot offer you these. Heaven is an awareness of your Oneness with God.

Paragraphs 7 and 8 address the concept of *duality*. Duality is the belief that there are two realities, or that you have two aspects: body and Spirit. This course reminds you of your non-dualistic nature, or that there is only One Reality, and that is God. That is why everything else is an illusion.

Lesson 132

'I release my mind from all that I thought that the world was.'

1. What limits you, but your beliefs? What can save you, but your Real Self? Your beliefs are powerful, the thoughts that you hold onto are mighty, and your illusions are as strong in their effects as is the Truth. It is insane for you to not doubt the reality of the world that you made, but you will not be persuaded by questioning your thoughts' effects. When you question the thoughts that are the *source* of their effects, you will at last have hope of freedom from limitations.

2. You can easily achieve your salvation, because you are free to change your mind, and when you do, all your thoughts will change with it. To change your mind means that you change the *source* of your thoughts, past, present, and to come. You free your perception of the past from all that you thought about it before with the personal mind, and you free your mind from projections of the personal mind's past on the future.

3. The present is the only time, and here in the present your mind is set free from all that you thought that the world was. As you let a personal past be lifted from your mind, and you release the future from the fears of the personal mind, you find your freedom, and you extend it in your perception of the world. You have perceived the world through all of your fears, doubts, and miseries. Death strikes the world everywhere, because you hold bitter thoughts of death in your mind.

4. The world is nothing in itself; your mind must give it meaning. What you see in the world are your wishes acted out so that you can perceive them and think that they are real. Maybe you think that you did not make the world, but came unwillingly to what was already made, and to what didn't need your thoughts to give it meaning. But, in truth, you find in the world exactly what you want to find.

5. What you perceive is not apart from what you want to perceive, and in this awareness lies your release. Change your mind

about what you want to perceive, and your perception will change accordingly. Ideas do not leave their source. This is the central theme often stated in the Text, and you must bear it in mind if you want to understand today's lesson. It is not the personal mind's pride that tells you that you made the world that you perceive, and that it changes as you change your mind.

6. But it is the personal mind's pride that argues that you are in a world that is separate from you, and that your perception of it is unaffected by what you think. There is no world! This is the central thought that this course teaches you. You might not be ready to accept this, but you will go as far in understanding this as you are willing to let yourself be led to Truth. You may approach Truth, then retreat, then approach It again.

7. But healing is the gift that you will receive when you accept that there is no world. You can accept it now. Your readiness will bring you this gift in some form that you will understand and recognize. You may see it at the moment of 'death', then choose to return to the world to continue to teach and learn. You may have an experience that is not of the world, in which you realize that there is no world, because you experienced the Truth, and It is wholly unlike the world.

8. Or you may find this gift in this course, and in today's exercises. Today's idea is possible, because the world does not exist. And since it only exists in your mind, you can release your mind from all that you ever thought the world was by merely changing all the thoughts that gave it those appearances. As you let go of all thoughts of sickness, sickness disappears; and death is undone when you let Thoughts of Life replace all of the thoughts you ever held of death.

9. An earlier lesson is stressed here again, because it contains the firm foundation for today's idea: You are One with God. There is no place where you can suffer, and no time that can change your Eternal State of Being. A world of time and place cannot exist, because you remain One with God.

10. Today's lesson is another way of saying that for you to know your True Self is the salvation of your mind where you perceive the world. If you change your mind about yourself, you free your mind from a perception of a world of pain. There is no world apart from your ideas, because ideas do not leave their source, and you maintain the world in your mind through thought.

11. Since you are One with God, you cannot think apart from God, nor really make what is unlike God. God's Attributes are not inherent in the world that you perceive, so it cannot be real. And, since *you* are Real, then the world that you perceive is false, because you are One with God, and the world is unlike *you* in every way. As it is by God's Thought that you are an Extension of God, so it is by your thoughts that the world was made, and by your thoughts you can release your mind from the world, so that you can know the Thoughts that you share with God.

12. Release your mind from the world! Your Extensions of God wait for you to release your illusions, so that they can show you that you are One with God, because you extend God. You are co-Creator with God, because God makes no distinction between God and God. What God extends is not apart from God, and there is no place where God ends and God's Extension begins as something separate from God.

13. There is no world, because it is a thought apart from God. It was made to separate God from Its Extension, and to break away a Part of God to destroy God's Wholeness. A world that rises from this idea cannot be real. It cannot be anywhere. Deny your illusions, and accept the Truth. Deny that you are a shadow that lies briefly on a dying world. Release your mind from all that you thought the world was, and you will see the world differently.

14. Today, your purpose is to free your mind from all the idle thoughts about the world and everything in it that it ever held. The world is not there, and you are not in it. You are at Home in God with your Extensions of God. You who are one with God, release from your mind your illusions about the world, and set your mind free.

15. Twice today practice for fifteen minutes, beginning them with:

'I am One with God, and I release my mind from all that I thought and the world was. I am Real, the world is not, and I want to know my Reality.'

Then merely rest, alert, but not straining, and let your mind be changed in Quietness so that your entire mind is freed.

16. You do not need to realize how healing extends to your entire mind as you extend these thoughts to bless all that you perceive. But you will feel your release, even though you may not fully understand yet that you can never be released without releasing the part of your mind that you perceive as a world.

17. Throughout the day, whenever you are tempted to deny the Power of your simple change of mind, increase the freedom that you extend by saying:

'I release my mind from all that I thought that the world was. I choose my own Reality instead.'

Mentor's Notes

This lesson fully encapsulates the central teachings of this course: The world exists only in your mind. Let it go, or forgive it, and *you* are free.

Paragraph 2 discusses 'changing your mind'. In this course, 'changing your mind' means that you literally change the mind, or thought system, with which you think. You let go of the personal mind so that your Real Mind, represented by the Holy Spirit, can take its rightful place. You do not have to seek for your Real Mind; you only have to remove the obstacle (the personal mind) to your awareness of It.

This lesson states that there is no world, yet it also tells you that you can see the world differently. The only way to see the world differently is to see that it is not real. This is what your Real

Perception shows you by overlooking appearances in the world and looking on God's Love instead. As was stated in the Mentor's Notes of Lesson 129, your Real Perception emphasizes the Content of your mind and its perception. It overlooks form, because it knows that form is not real.

Very importantly, paragraph 6 lets you know that you will understand that the world is not real to the extent that you are ready to accept Truth. This is not something that you can force, nor is it merely an intellectual realization. You cannot pretend that the world is not real to you when it is real to you. Do not try to force this realization, or you will become stressed and depressed. In time, as you are ready, you will have experiences of Truth, and you will see that the world is nothing, which will make it easy for you to let it go. These lessons, and the Holy Spirit's guidance, are what prepare you to experience Truth.

Lesson 133

'I will not value what has no value.'

1. Sometimes, after you have gone through theoretical lessons that seem far from what you think you know, there is a benefit to bringing you back to practical lessons. This is what today's lesson will do. Instead of dwelling on lofty, all-encompassing ideas, today's lesson is about what is of benefit to you.

2. You do not ask too much of life in a world; you ask far too little. When you let your mind be drawn to the body, to things to buy, to being recognized by the world, you are asking for sorrow, not for Happiness. This course is not trying to take away from you the little that you have. It is not substituting utopian ideas for the satisfaction that you think that you can find in the world. There is no satisfaction for you to find in the world.

3. Today's lesson lists the real criteria by which you should test all things that you think that you want. Unless something meets these sound requirements, it is not worthy of you, because then it will replace What offers you more. You cannot make the laws that govern your choices, nor make the alternatives from which you can choose. But you can, and must, do the choosing. So you must learn the laws that govern your choices, and you must learn what you really have to choose between.

4. You have already been shown that you have only two choices - Truth or illusion - even though illusions take so many forms it appears as though you have much more to choose between. Your range of choice is set and cannot be changed. It would not be generous to encourage you to believe that you have many alternatives, so that you can sift through every illusion until you have considered them all and learned that they *are* all illusions. It is kinder to make it clear to you now that you have only one choice to make between *two* alternatives.

5. A related law is that there can be no compromise between these alternatives. You cannot have just a little of each, because one choice

brings you Everything and the other brings you nothing. So if you learn the tests by which you can distinguish Everything from nothing, you will make the better choice.

6. First, if you choose something that will not last Forever, you are choosing something without value. A temporary value is not a real value. Time can never take away the Value of Something Real. What fades and dies is not really here, and it does not really offer you anything. If you think something temporary has value, then you are deceived by nothingness in a form that you think that you like.

7. Second, if you seek to take something from someone else, you will have nothing. This is because What has Real Value is Everywhere, and you deny that you already have Everything by thinking that another has something that you need. By seeking to get something from someone else, you are deceived by the illusion that the world that you perceive is real, and that you gain by getting something in it. But an unreal world can only offer you loss.

8. The third things for you to consider are questions on which the others rest. Why does something have value to you? What attracts you to it? What purpose does it serve? This is where it is easy for you to be deceived, because even the personal mind does not want to look at what it really wants. It does not even tell the truth as it perceives it, because it needs to protect its goal of keeping you separated from God with a veneer of 'innocent' goals.

9. But the goals that hide its real goal can deceive you only if you want to be deceived. Its goal is obvious if you care to look for it. Here, the personal mind's deception is doubled, because you feel that you have served worthy goals and do not perceive that you are experiencing loss.

10. But, even though you try to believe that you are reaching for worthy goals, you experience emptiness. You blame the emptiness on your being a 'sinner' and 'unworthy'. When you serve the personal mind, you do not believe in mistakes, but in sins, and your suffering is proof of this.

11. The final criterion for choosing what you want is probably the

hardest for you to accept, because its obviousness is obscured by many layers of complexity. If you feel any guilt about a choice you make, you have allowed the personal mind's goals to confuse you about your two simple alternatives: Truth or illusion. The guilt that you feel about the choice makes you afraid, and your fear makes you believe that your choice cannot be merely nothing.

12. All things are either valuable or invaluable, worthy or not worthy of being sought by you, entirely desirable or not worth your efforts to obtain it. This is why your choosing is easy. Complexity is only a smoke-screen that hides the fact that no decision is really difficult. Why do you need to learn this? It is for far more than teaching you that you can make choices easily and painlessly.

13. You will reach Heaven with a quiet and open mind that comes with nothing to find Everything and accept It as its own. You will reach this state today, laying aside self-deception, and with an honest willingness to value only What is Real and Truly Valuable. Begin your two extended practice periods of fifteen minutes each with this:

> 'I will not value what has no value. I seek for only What has Value, because That is all that I want to find.'

14. Then open yourself to receive What waits for you when you come to Heaven's Gate unencumbered by the personal mind's values. The Gate will swing open for you. If you find yourself valuing the valueless, or believing that you are facing a difficult decision, quickly use this simple thought:

> 'I will not value what has no value, because What is Truly Valuable belongs to me.'

Mentor's Notes

Here is an example of the type of situation that is referred to in paragraphs 11 and 12:

You very much want a particular position at work. You think, for various reasons, that it will make you happy, but you have multi-layered feelings about it: You feel hopeful, afraid, worthy, unworthy, determined, etc. Your mixed feelings about the position are an indication that you feel guilt about wanting something in the world. But the personal mind explains away your conflicting feelings with many different stories: You have a 'right' to the job, you've had feelings of unworthiness since you were a kid, you've 'earned' the position, it might be more than you can handle, etc. In other words, it obscures the real issue with complexity.

The real issue is that you are pursuing an illusion in the hopes that it will 'save' you (make you happy), and on some level you know that it cannot. You feel guilty, because your wanting this job to make you happy is further separation from God. This makes you afraid, and fear punishment from God. What you are not seeing is that both your wanting the job for happiness and the job itself are nothing. Your wanting the job for happiness is only a mistake, not a sin. You have the Source of Happiness within you, always. And the job's only value is to provide you with an income, and with teaching/learning situations in which you can practice forgiveness. You have confused what does not have value (the job for its own sake) with What does have Value (the Truth that is always within you). When you straighten this out in your mind, you can let go of the job and easily accept whatever outcome results.

It is going to be a long time before you stop valuing and wanting things in the world. It is not your wanting things that is your obstacle to Peace; it is your belief that they can give you something that they cannot (salvation) that is your obstacle to Peace. Do not deny or repress your desires; share them with the Holy Spirit to use for your goal of re-awakening to God. Remember, it is not your desire, but your attachment to the object of your desire, that is your obstacle. Acknowledge your desire, then let it go, recognizing that the object cannot bring you salvation. Keep your mind open, because you do not know what is truly useful for your salvation, but the Holy Spirit does know.

Lesson 134

'I will perceive forgiving as it is.'

1. It is time to revisit the true meaning of *forgiving*, because you are likely to distort it as something that entails the unfair sacrifice of your 'righteous anger', as a gift that you are unjustified in giving to someone who is undeserving of it, or as a complete denial of the truth. In this view of forgiving, it is an eccentric gesture that makes this course appear to teach you that your salvation rests on a whim.

2. This twisted idea of forgiving is easily corrected by your recognizing that true forgiving pardons the false, not the True. Forgiving is appropriate only for illusions. Truth comes from God, so there is no reason for you to forgive Truth. What is True reflects God's Law and radiates God's Love. What is Innocent and Eternally Benign does not need to be forgiven.

3. You find it difficult to truly forgive, because you still believe that what you are asked to forgive is true and not an illusion. You think that you are being asked to overlook what is real and true in order to deceive yourself into believing that God is All that is Real and True. This twisted view of forgiving only reveals the hold that the idea that you are really separate from God still has on you.

4. Because you think that you are really guilty of separating from God, you look on forgiving as a form of self-deception. It would be impossible for you to believe that separation from God is true and *not* believe that forgiving is a lie. Forgiving in this case is just another form of separation from God that seems to teach you that the true is false, and that you should look on sin as innocence, which can only result in self-deception. It seems that forgiving means that you are supposed to see as right what is plainly wrong, and to look on as good what is actually loathsome.

5. This view of forgiving offers you no way out of guilt; it merely points out that your sin of separating from God is unforgivable, and that forgiving only conceals, denies, or calls it another name, because forgiving is an attack on something true. If your guilt is real, then

you cannot be forgiven. If you have really sinned by separating from God, then your guilt is eternal. From this view that sin and guilt are real, those whom you forgive are mocked and condemned twice: first, by themselves for what they think that they did, then, by you who 'forgive' them because you think that what they did is real.

6. But it is the unreality of sin and guilt that makes your forgiving natural, wholly sane, and a deep relief and quiet blessing to you. True forgiving does not hold onto illusions, but sees through them with a gentle laugh as it compares them to Truth and watches them disappear.

7. In your illusion that you are in a world, your forgiving is the only thing that stands for Truth. Forgiving is your means of recognizing the nothingness of your illusions, and of looking straight through the thousands of forms in which they appear. It is the means by which you look on lies and are not deceived by them. It is the means by which you overlook guilt with quiet eyes that say, 'This is not the Truth.'

8. The Strength of true forgiveness is its honesty, which is completely uncorrupted, because it sees illusions as illusions, not as truth. Because of this, forgiving is the way that you are undeceived when faced with lies, and Truth is restored to your mind. By overlooking what is not here, it opens the way to Truth for you, which your illusions of guilt have blocked, freeing you to follow the way to Truth. If you forgive even one other your illusions about them, you open the way to Truth for yourself.

9. There is a way for you to find the open way to Truth through forgiving. When you are tempted to accuse another of sin in some form, do not dwell on what you think that they did, because then you deceive yourself. Ask yourself instead, 'Do I want to hold this against myself?'

10. This is how you will see alternatives that make your choosing to forgive or to not forgive meaningful to you. This is how you keep your mind free from guilt and pain as God intends it to be, and as it is in Truth. Condemnation only happens in an illusion; in Truth,

Innocence is all that there is. Your forgiving stands between illusions and the Truth, between the world that you perceive and Reality beyond it, and between the hell of guilt and Heaven's Gate.

11. Across the bridge that is your forgiving, which is as Powerful as the Love Which lays Its Blessing on it, all of your illusions of evil, hatred, and attack are brought to Truth to be undone by It. Truth will not keep them to grow and terrify you, who believes in them. Instead, you will be gently awakened to the awareness that what you thought was real was never there. You will know that escape from guilt was never denied to you.

12. You will know that you do not have to fight to save yourself, nor do you have to establish elaborate defenses to keep yourself safe. You can remove all of the protections that limited you to fear and misery. You can walk lightly on the way to Truth.

13. You have to practice forgiving, because you have forgotten its meaning in your perception that you are in a world, and the world cannot provide you with a guide to the beneficence of forgiving. There is no thought of the personal mind that can lead you to understand how true forgiving works, nor to the Thought that forgiving reflects. True forgiving is as alien to the world that you perceive as is your Reality, but it joins your mind with the Reality in you.

14. Today, you will practice truly forgiving, so that the time of joining your mind in Wholeness is not delayed any longer. You *want* to meet with your Limitless Reality in Peace. Your practicing lights the way for the part of your mind where you perceive a world to join you in Reality. Spend fifteen minutes twice today with the Holy Spirit, Which is your Guide to understanding true forgiving. Tell the Holy Spirit:

'I will perceive forgiving as it is.'

15. Then, choose one other as the Holy Spirit directs, and catalogue what you perceive as their 'sins'. Do not dwell on any one of them, but realize that you are using this other's 'offenses' to save

your entire mind from the idea of sin. As you briefly consider each of the 'evils' that you have thought of in connection with this person, ask yourself, 'Do I want to condemn myself with this?'

16. Free your perception of the other from all of the thoughts of sin that you have had of them, and you will free yourself of those thoughts. If you practice with willingness and honesty, you will feel a weight lifting from yourself, and a deep, certain feeling of relief. You can spend the rest of your practice period experiencing this freedom from the guilt that you tried to lay on another, but that you really laid on yourself.

17. Practice forgiving throughout the day, because there will be many times when you forget the meaning of forgiveness and attack yourself. When this occurs, look through the illusion as you tell yourself:

> 'I will perceive forgiving as it is. I do not want to condemn myself with this and bind myself with guilt.'

In everything that you do today, remember this:

> 'I cannot crucify myself or another without involving my entire mind, and I cannot enter Heaven without my entire mind.'

Mentor's Notes

You cannot truly forgive until you have had an experience that shows you that only God is True. Until then, your 'forgiving' is going to be an illusion that brings you no real relief. For example, let's say that you have found out that someone that you thought of as a friend at work has been spreading rumors about you that harm your chances of advancing in the company. If this makes you angry or feel betrayed, then you believe that something real has occurred. You believe that you are a personal self in a body in a world, and that the 'story' that you have for this personal self, including this 'betrayal', is your reality. Your 'forgiving' at this point will only be an illusion, because you will be trying to 'forgive' something that you believe really happened, and, since it happened, it cannot be undone. But, if you have had an experience that has shown you that only God is True, then you can access that experience, and you will recognize that what happens in the world is no more real than a story in your mind, and you will not have any personal feelings about it. You will forgive it.

But, while you may not yet have any real relief, this does not mean that practicing forgiving is wasted until you have had an experience that shows you that only God is Real. Often, it is through this practice that you invite the experience.

The personal mind teaches you that the world is separate from you, so that you can project guilt 'out there' and deny that it is an idea in your mind. But remember, it doesn't matter where you perceive guilt; if you perceive it at all, it's in *your* mind. However, it's also always only an illusion, no matter where you perceive it.

Lesson 135

'If I defend myself, I am attacking myself.'

1. You defend yourself only when you believe that you have been attacked, that the attack was real, and that your defense of yourself will save you. This is the folly of defense: First, you believe an illusion is real, then your defense reinforces this belief. Defending yourself adds illusion to illusion, making correction doubly difficult for you. When you make plans for the future, relive the past, or organize the present as the personal mind dictates, you are defending yourself and binding yourself to illusions

2. In your identification with a personal self in a world, you operate from the belief that you must protect yourself from whatever is happening, because it threatens you. Your feeling threatened is your acknowledgment that you believe that you are weak, and your belief that danger is real makes defending yourself seem appropriate. The world that you perceive is based on these insane beliefs. All of its structures, thoughts, doubts, penalties, weapons, legal codes, ethics, leaders, and gods serve only to preserve your sense of threat. You walk the world defensively, so you must be terrified.

3. Defending yourself frightens you, because it stems from fear, and your fear increases with each defense that you make. You think that defending yourself offers you safety, but all it does is make your fears real and justified to you. It is strange that you do not pause to ask, as the personal mind makes elaborate plans and denser protections for your safety, *what* you are defending, *how* you are defending it, and *against what* you are defending it.

4. First, consider what you are defending. It must be something that is weak and easily assaulted, that cannot protect itself, but that needs *your* protection. Only the body is so frail that it needs your constant care and watchful concern to protect its little 'life'. You are One with God, so only a body can seem to fail to protect you.

5. But a body cannot fear or be a thing of fear. It has no needs,

except those that you assign to it. It does not need a complicated health structure or health-inducing medicine. Really, it needs no care or concern at all. When you defend its 'life', or try to make it beautiful or shelter it, you are teaching yourself that your home is vulnerable to time and corruption. It is so unsafe that it must be guarded with *your* life.

6. This is frightening to you, and you cannot be at peace with a concept of your home like this. But only your belief endows the body with the right to serve you like this. It is your mind that gives the body all of the functions that you see in it, and that sets its value far beyond the pile of dust and water that it really is. You would not defend it if you saw that it is really nothing.

7. It cannot be emphasized too often that the body does not need to be defended. It will be strong and healthy if your mind does not abuse it by assigning it to fulfill roles that it cannot fulfill, to purposes beyond its range, or to exalted goals that it cannot attain. These ridiculous, but deeply cherished, aims that you have for the body are the sources of your many insane attacks on it, because it seems to fail your hopes, needs, values, and dreams.

8. This 'self' that you think needs your protection is not real. You only need to perceive the body as apart from you and it will be a healthy, useful instrument through which your Mind can operate until its use is done. You will have no use for it when it has finished serving your Mind.

9. You are Mind, so if you defend the body, you are identifying with it, and you are attacking your Mind by associating it with the body. You are assigning to your Mind the faults, weaknesses, limits, and lacks from which you think that the body needs to be saved. Because you do not see that the body is apart from your Mind, you impose on the body all of the pain that comes from perceiving your Mind as limited and fragile, separate from the part of itself where you perceive a world and from God.

10. The thoughts that result from your identification with a body instead of with your Mind are the thoughts that need healing, and

the body will respond with health when those thoughts have been corrected and replaced with the Truth. This is the body's only real defense. But this is not where you look for its defense. The kind of protection that you offer to the body in your identification with a personal self does not benefit it at all, but only adds to the distress of your mind. You do not heal, but you remove your hope of healing, when you do not see that your hope of healing really lies in your mind.

11. Your mind is not healed when it carries out the plans of the personal mind; it is healed when it carries out the plans that it receives from the Wisdom of the Holy Spirit. It waits until it has been taught what should be done, then proceeds to do it. When your mind is healed, it knows that it is adequate to fulfill the Holy Spirit's plans, and it is certain that no obstacle can stop it from accomplishing any goal that serves the larger plan of your salvation from guilt.

12. Your mind is healed when it lets go of the belief that it must use the personal mind to plan, because it recognizes that the personal mind cannot know the outcome that is best for you, the means by which it is achieved, nor the problem that must be solved. If you follow the personal mind, you will misuse the body with its plans, but when you have accepted that the personal mind cannot know what is best for you, then your mind is healed, and you let go of the body.

13. Binding the body to the plans that your unhealed mind sets up to save itself must make the body sick, because then it is not the means of helping a plan that far exceeds it, and which needs its service for a little while. The body's health is assured when it serves Your Mind's True Purpose, because everything that serves This functions flawlessly and with a strength given to it by your Mind.

14. Perhaps you do not realize that plans that you initiate with the personal mind are defenses. They are the means that you use to protect yourself in your fear, at the cost of Truth. Where your denial of Reality is obvious, it may not be difficult for you to realize that

some of your forms of self deception are for defense, but you often do not recognize that *all* planning with the personal mind is to defend *it*.

15. When your mind is occupied with planning for the personal self, it is occupied in trying to control the future, because you do not think that you will be provided for unless you follow the personal mind. You emphasize controlling the future based on experiences that you had in a personal past, and on your former beliefs. You overlook the present, because you think that the personal self's past has taught you enough to direct your future course.

16. When you plan like this, you are not acknowledging that you have changed your mind. What you learned in a personal past becomes your basis for future goals, and determines your choices for the future. You don't see that right now you have Everything that you need to guarantee a future unlike the personal past, and without its old ideas and sick beliefs continuing. You don't have to anticipate the future, because your confidence in What is present now will direct the future.

17. The plans that you make with the personal mind are actually defenses against the Truth. Your goal with them is to approve of what is compatible with your current beliefs about your reality, and to disregard what does not support these. But what remains is meaningless, because it is your actual Reality that is the 'threat' that your defenses attack, obscure, tear apart, and crucify.

18. If you can accept that everything that happens, past, present, and to come, is gently planned by the Holy Spirit, Which only has your good as Its purpose, then there is nothing that you will not accept. Perhaps you misunderstand the Holy Spirit's plan, because the Holy Spirit will never offer you pain. But your defenses do not let you perceive the Holy Spirit's blessing on every step that you have ever taken. While you made plans for death in your identification with a personal self, the Holy Spirit was there to lead you to Eternal Life.

19. Your present trust in the Holy Spirit is the defense that

promises you a future that is undisturbed by sorrow, and that is filled with the Joy that only increases as your life in the world becomes a Holy Instant representing Eternity in the midst of time. Let only your present trust direct your future, and your life in the world will become a meaningful encounter with Truth that your defenses would conceal.

20. Without defenses, you become a Light Which Heaven gratefully acknowledges as Its own. God's Light will lead you in ways that are appointed for your happiness, according to a plan that began the moment that you conceived of time. You will extend God's Light until the world that you perceive is wholly lit with Joy. All defenses that you perceive will fall, because they bring nothing but terror.

21. Anticipate that time with confidence today, because this is part of what is planned for you. Today, you can be sure that you have everything that you need to accomplish God's plan for your salvation from guilt. Do not make any plan for how this will be done, but realize that your defenselessness is all that is required for Truth to dawn on your mind.

22. Twice today, for fifteen minutes each, rest from senseless planning and every thought that blocks your awareness of Truth. Receive Truth in place of planning, so that you can extend Truth in place of organizing. You will receive Truth as you say:

> 'If I defend myself, I am attacking myself. But I am strong when I am defenseless, because I learn of What my defenses hide.'

23. That's all. If there are plans to make, you will be told. They may not be the plans that you think that you need, nor answers to the problems that you think that you have. But they are answers to your real question, 'What am I?', which remains unanswered for you until you accept the Real Answer at last.

24. All of your defenses have been aimed at not receiving What you receive today. In the Light and Joy of simple trust, you will

wonder why you ever thought that you must defend yourself against release. Heaven asks nothing of you; it is hell that demands that you sacrifice. You give up nothing today when, without defense, you present yourself to God as you really are.

25. God remembers you; today you will remember God. This is the time of your resurrection, and you will rise again from what seemed like death and hopelessness. The Light of Hope is reborn in you when you come to God without defenses to learn your part in God's plan for your salvation. No little plan or magical belief can still have value for you when you have received your function from God's Holy Spirit.

26. Try not to plan your day today, because you cannot conceive of all of the Happiness that will be yours when you don't plan. Learn this today, and your entire mind will take this giant step and celebrate your resurrection with you. Throughout the day, as foolish little things appear to tempt you to defend yourself and to weave plans, remind yourself that this is your special day for learning, and acknowledge it with this:

> 'This is the time of my resurrection, and I want to keep it Holy. I will not defend myself, because I am One with God, and I do not need to defend myself against my Reality.'

Mentor's Notes

This lesson states that the body is apart from you, yet it also states that the body is in your mind, and when it serves your Mind's True Purpose, it is healthy. This is not a contradiction. The body *is* an idea in your mind, but it is apart from you in the sense that it is *not you*. The error that you make that leads to an unhealthy body is your *identifying* with it. The body is an idea that can serve your salvation from guilt when you don't identify with it, but you identify with your True Self instead.

Paragraph 18 mentions the Holy Spirit's plan for everything that happens. This does not mean that your life in the world is pre-ordained by God. In paragraph 16, you are asked to acknowledge that you have changed your mind; you have put your life under the Holy Spirit's direction. This means that your life going forward *is* planned by the Holy Spirit. And the Holy Spirit has always been with you, even when you did not know it, ready to lead you back to God. Always, while you were busy developing a personal life, the Holy Spirit was right there with an alternative plan.

Another way to look at this is that the Holy Spirit sees a purpose for everything in the world that you perceive. On a practical level, the Holy Spirit knows that you have perceived needs in the world, and It will fill them for you in a way that supports your salvation if you step back and let It do so. And, ultimately, the Holy Spirit's plan for everything is for you to forgive it. Only the Holy Spirit knows the best way for you to understand this, and the best situations in which you can learn forgiving in such a way that you will generalize it to everything that you perceive.

Lesson 136

'Sickness is my defense against God.'

1. You cannot heal until you understand what purpose sickness is meant to serve, because then you will understand that its purpose is meaningless. You will learn that, being without a cause and without meaning, sickness cannot be real at all. When you see this, your healing is automatic, because, like all illusions, when it is compared to Truth it disappears.

2. Sickness is not an accident. Like all of the personal mind's defenses, it is an insane device that you use for self-deception. And, also like all of the personal mind's defenses, its purpose is to hide your Reality from you; to attack It, change It, make It powerless, distort It, twist It, or reduce It to a little pile of separate thoughts. The aim of all of the personal mind's defenses is to keep you from seeing that your Mind is One, so that you see each thought in your mind as though it is whole within itself.

3. The personal mind's defenses are not unintentional, nor are they made without your awareness. They are secret magic wands that you wave when God seems to threaten the personal mind that you want to believe is Real in place of God. They seem to be unconscious, because of how fast you choose them, but in the instant that you make the choice for a defense against God, you know exactly what you want to do, then you think that it is done.

4. Only *you* evaluate what is a threat to what you want, decide if escape is necessary, and then set up a series of defenses to reduce the threat that you have judged as real. You cannot do this unconsciously, but after you have done it, you forget that you did it. It seems to be something that comes to you from beyond your mind, and that seems to have real effects on you, instead of something that you have caused yourself.

5. Your quickly forgetting that you make your own 'reality' makes the personal mind's defenses seem to be beyond your control. But you can remember what you have chosen to forget if you are willing

to reconsider the decision that is doubly hidden by your choice to be oblivious of it. Your not remembering is only an indication that you want your decision to remain in force. Do not mistake the results of your hidden decision for Fact, because your defenses make Fact unrecognizable to you. This is their purpose.

6. Every defense that you make with the personal mind takes fragmented thoughts in your mind and assembles them without regard to your Mind's Oneness. This is how the personal mind's defenses construct an illusion of whole parts that are not really there. It is this process that really makes you feel threatened, not its result. When thoughts in your mind seem to be wrested from the Oneness of your Mind, and you see them as separate and whole within themselves, they become symbols to you of your attack on your Mind. You think that you have succeeded in attacking your Mind, and that you will never see It as Whole again. What you forget is that they only stand for your decision to choose for yourself what is real to take the place of What is *really* Real.

7. Sickness is your decision; it is not something that happens to you, that you didn't ask for, and that makes you weak and suffer. It is a choice that you make, a plan that you lay, when for an instant the Oneness of God rises in your deluded mind, and the world that you perceive seems to totter and prepare to fall. You are sick so that God will go away and no longer threaten what you have established as your home.

8. How does it seem to you that sickness can protect you from God? Sickness 'proves' to you that you are a body, so you must be separate from God. You suffer because the body suffers, and in this suffering you and the body are 'one'. This is how you preserve what you want to be your 'true' identity, and the strange, haunting thought that you might be Something beyond this little pile of dust and water is silenced. Because, look, this body can make you suffer and die and command that you cease to be!

9. So the body seems to you to be stronger than God, Which offers you Life, but cannot overcome your choice to die. The body

seems more powerful to you than Everlasting Life, hell seems stronger than Heaven, and God's plan for your salvation is opposed by your decision, which is stronger than God's Will. You who are One with God are dust, God is incomplete, and chaos takes God's Place.

10. This is your plan for your own defense. You believe that Heaven shrinks before these mad attacks, and that God is blinded by your illusions, Truth is turned into a lie, and your Mind is made a slave to laws that your will wants to impose on It. But only you who makes illusions believes in them and reacts to them as though they are the truth.

11. God doesn't know of your plan to change Its Will, your True Mind is not aware of the laws by which you thought to govern it, Heaven has not bowed to hell, and Life has not given in to death. You can only choose to *think* that you die, suffer sickness, or distort Truth, because What is Real is apart from all of this. Your defenses are plans to defeat What cannot be attacked. The Unalterable cannot change, and the Eternally Innocent cannot 'sin'.

12. This is the simple Truth, and God does not need power over you or to triumph over you. God does not command your obedience, nor does God seek to prove how pitiful and futile are your attempts to plan defenses that are meant to change God. God only wants to extend Happiness to you, because that is God's Purpose. Perhaps God sighs a little when you throw away Its Gifts, but God knows, with Perfect Certainty, that What It wills for you, you have received.

13. It is this Fact that demonstrates that time is an illusion, because time lets you think that What God gives to you is not the Truth *right now*, as It must be. God's Thoughts are apart from time, which is another meaningless defense that you have made against Truth. But What God wills is here, and you are still One with God.

14. God's Power is far beyond any defense that you can make against It, because no illusion remains when you allow Truth to enter your mind. God comes to your mind whenever you are willing to lay down your defenses and cease to play with meaningless ideas. You

can find God anytime; today, if you choose.

15. Finding God is your aim today. Give fifteen minutes twice today to opening your mind to God, so that It can free you from the limitations that you have made. God *will* come into your awareness, because It has never been apart from you; It only waits for your invitation. Begin your practice with a healing prayer that will help you rise above your defensiveness and let God be as It has always been:

> 'Sickness is my defense against God. I accept the Truth of What I am, so that my mind will be wholly healed today.'

16. Healing will flash across your mind as Peace and Truth take the place of war and illusions. There will be no dark corners left in your mind that sickness conceals and defends against the Light of God. There will be no dim figures from your illusions, or their obscure and meaningless pursuits with double purposes left in your mind. Your mind will be healed of all the sickly wishes that it tried to authorize the body to obey.

17. The body is healed when your mind is open to being healed. You will recognize that you have practiced well when you do not feel the body at all. You will have no sense of it feeling ill or feeling well, or of physical pain or pleasure. You will have no response at all to what the body does. Its usefulness for your salvation from guilt will remain, and nothing more.

18. Perhaps you do not realize that this removes the limits that you have put on the body with the personal mind's purposes for it. As you lay these aside, the body will always be strong enough to serve the truly useful purpose of your salvation. The body's health will be guaranteed, because it will not be limited by time, weather, fatigue, food, drink, or any laws that the personal mind made it serve before. You won't need to do anything to make it well, because sickness will be impossible.

19. This protection for the body can only be preserved by your

careful watching of your mind. If you let your mind harbor attack thoughts, yield to the personal mind's judgments, or make plans for the future, you will have again attacked the body by misidentifying with it with a sick mind.

20. If this occurs, correct it instantly by not allowing your defensiveness to hurt you any longer. Do not be confused about what must be healed, and tell yourself:

> 'I have forgotten What I really am by mistaking a body for myself. Sickness is my defense against God in me. But I am not a body, and my mind cannot attack, so I cannot be sick.'

Mentor's Notes

Be aware that the personal mind is going to use lessons like today's, which tell you that it is your mind that heals the body, to try and get you to heal the body for its own sake. What this lesson is saying is that when your mind is healed, the body is healed, not that you should use your mind to heal the body. If you do so, you are continuing in the error of putting your mind in the service of a body, and no true healing will occur.

The personal mind will also use any continuing illness or physical injury or pain to point out how you are failing as a student of this course. This course is a *process* of undoing your identification with a personal self. While you may sometimes experience spontaneous healing, real, complete healing will not occur until you have totally put aside all identification with a personal self. While you will do this in a single instant, it takes a long time to prepare to make this choice once and for all. Until then, you will continue to manifest physical symptoms of your misidentification with a body.

There is no reason for you to suffer, so as long as you believe that you are a body you can continue to use worldly remedies for physical illnesses and pain, though these remedies are only magical thoughts. To lessen the guilt that you will feel, ask the Holy Spirit to guide you as you seek relief from physical symptoms. This transforms the physical illness or injury into an opportunity for you to join with the Holy Spirit, and to extend the Holy Spirit into your encounters with health care providers, thereby healing your mind.

Lesson 137

'When I am healed, my mind is healed as One.'

1. Today's idea is the central thought on which your salvation from guilt rests. Healing is the opposite of all of the personal mind's thoughts, which dwell on sickness and separation as reality. In sickness you retreat into the isolation of a personal self, and you shut yourself off from the rest of your mind, which you perceive as a world outside of you.

2. Sickness is separation, because it validates you as a personal self that is feeling something that the rest of your mind, which you perceive as a world outside of you, does not feel. It gives power to the body to make separation real to you, and keeps your mind in a solitary prison, split apart from the rest of itself by a solid wall of sickened flesh, which it seems that it cannot surmount.

3. Your healing occurs apart from the laws of the world that you made for separation. It is impossible for you to heal apart from your entire mind. In sickness, you are apart and separate in a personal self, but healing is your decision that your mind be One again in your awareness, and that you accept your True Self with all of Its Parts intact. In sickness, your mind seems to be split between 'you' and a world outside of you, without the Oneness that is Its Life. But your healing is accomplished when you see that the body does not have the power to attack your Mind, Which is One.

4. The personal mind means for sickness to prove to you that lies are the Truth, but your healing demonstrates that only the Truth is True. The separation that sickness is meant to make real to you has never occurred. For you to be healed, you only have to accept the simple Truth, Which remains as It is Forever. But you are used to looking at illusions, and you must be taught that what you see is not true. So your healing, which is not needed by you in Truth, demonstrates that sickness is not real.

5. Your healing might be called a counter-illusion, because it cancels out the illusion of sickness in the name of Truth, but not

within Truth Itself, Where there are no illusions. Just as your forgiving overlooks all appearances of a separation that has never occurred, your healing removes illusions that have not occurred. Just as your Real Perception will rise to take the place of a world that has never been at all, your healing corrects imagined states of being and false ideas, which you have embroidered into a picture that you think of as truth.

6. Don't think that your healing is an unworthy function for you in your perception that you are in a world. In your belief that the world is real, anti-Christ is more powerful to you than Christ. The body seems more solid and stable to you than your Mind, and Love seems like the illusion, while fear is the one 'reality' that you can see and feel is justified and understandable.

7. Just as your forgiving shines away all 'sin', and your Real Perception takes the place of what you made, so your healing replaces the fantasies of sickness that the personal mind uses to block out Truth. When you see sickness disappear in spite of all of the world's 'laws' which say that it must be real, then all your doubts about Truth will be undone, and you will no longer cherish or obey the personal mind's laws.

8. Your healing is your freedom from limitations, because it demonstrates that illusions will not prevail against the Truth. Your healing is shared by your entire mind, and by this attribute it proves that the Law of Oneness is far more potent than the law that says that sickness is inevitable. Your healing is your strength, because through its gentleness you overcome weakness, and your mind, which seemed walled off within a body, is set free to join with the rest of itself to be Forever Strong.

9. Your healing, your forgiving, and your Real Perception are the means by which the Holy Spirit motivates you to follow It. The Holy Spirit's gentle lessons teach you that your salvation from guilt is easy, and that you only need a little practice to let Its Law replace the laws that the personal mind makes to bind you to death. The Holy Spirit's Life is your own as you expend the little effort that It asks of

you to free you from everything that ever caused you pain.

10. As you let yourself be healed, everyone and everything that you have ever perceived is healed with you. You might not recognize them all as part of your mind, or how great is what you offer to your entire mind when you allow healing to come to you, but when you are healed, your mind is healed as One. When you accept the gift of healing, it extends to your entire mind.

11. When you allow yourself to be healed, you become the instrument that extends healing to your entire mind. No time elapses between the instant that you are healed and your receiving the Grace of healing to extend. God has no opposite, and when you do not let the illusion of God's opposite occupy your mind, your mind becomes a haven of rest that extends to all that you perceive. This is where Truth is, and where all illusions are undone by Truth.

12. Don't you want to offer shelter to God's Will? You are only inviting your True Self to be at home, and your invitation cannot be refused. Ask the Inevitable to occur, and It will not fail. Your other choice is to ask what cannot be to be, and this can never succeed. Today, ask only the Truth to occupy your mind, so that healing thoughts will go forth from your healed mind to what you perceive must still be healed, in an awareness that healing occurs for both at once.

13. Every hour, remember that your function is to let your mind be healed so that you can extend healing, and exchange curses for blessings, pain for Joy, and your perception of separation from God for the Peace of God. It is well worth one minute every hour to give these gifts to receive these gifts. A little time is a small price for you to pay for the Gift of Everything.

14. But you must be prepared to accept such a Gift, so give ten minutes each to the beginning and the end of today with this:

> 'When I am healed, my mind is healed as One. I want to extend my healing to all that I perceive, so that sickness is banished from my entire mind, which is One with God.'

15. Let healing through you today, and as you rest in Quiet, give as you receive to hold onto what you give, and receive the Holy Spirit to take the place of all of the foolish thoughts that you ever imagined. Now your mind joins as One to heal all that was sick, and to offer blessing where once there was attack. You will not forget your function as every hour you remember your purpose with this thought:

'When I am healed, my mind is healed as One. I bless all that I perceive, because I am healed as everything that I perceive is healed with me.'

Lesson 138

'Heaven is the choice that I must make.'

1. In your perception that you are in a world, Heaven seems to be a choice, because you believe that there are alternatives to choose between. You think that all things have an opposite, and that you can choose which you want. You think that if Heaven exists, so must hell, because contradicting God is the way that you made the world that you perceive and think is real.

2. There is no opposite to God, but in the world, opposition is part of the world's 'reality'. It is this strange perception of what is true that makes choosing Heaven the same to you as relinquishing hell. This is not so, but you cannot understand What is True in God until you see some reflection of It in your perception while you perceive yourself in a world. Truth cannot come into your mind when you perceive It with fear, because your fear makes Truth an illusion to you. Your opposition to Truth makes It unwelcome in your mind, so It cannot come into your awareness.

3. The obvious escape for you from what appears as opposites is to make a choice between them. In the midst of what seems like conflicting goals, making a decision should be the aim of your time and effort. Without a decision, your time and effort are wasted. You spend them on nothing, accomplish nothing, and learn nothing.

4. You need to be reminded that you think that a thousand choices are confronting you, but there is really only One Real Choice that you can make, so It only *seems* to be a choice. Do not confuse yourself with the doubts that a myriad of choices induces in you. You only have one Thing to choose, and when you choose It, you will perceive that you had no choice at all, because Truth is True, and nothing else is True. There is no opposite for you to choose instead; nothing contradicts the Truth.

5. Your choice depends on what you learn, and you cannot *learn* Truth, you can only *recognize* It. When you recognize Truth, you accept It, and as you accept It, you know It. But Knowledge of Truth

cannot be taught within the framework of this course. This course can only teach you what Truth is, what It offers to you, and how you can reach It. Your decision is the outcome of what you learn, because your decision rests on what you accept as the truth about you and what you need.

6. In your insanely complicated world Heaven appears to be a choice, rather than All That is. Of all of the choices that you have tried to make, Heaven is the simplest and is the definitive choice that undoes all of your other seeming choices. If you could really choose anything else, you would not be choosing Heaven, but when you choose Heaven, all other choices, which take many forms, but which are all the same because they all conceal Heaven, are undone. Your final and only choice is to accept or deny Truth.

7. So you begin today considering the choice that time can help you make. This is time's Holy purpose, not the purpose that the personal mind gives to time. The personal mind uses time to demonstrate to you that hell and despair are real, and that Life Itself must in the end be overcome by death. From the personal mind's point of view, opposites are real, so life is conflict, and your salvation from conflict can only be your death.

8. These insane beliefs have an intense, unconscious hold on you, and they grip your mind with terror and anxiety so strong that you won't let go of the personal mind's ideas about what protects you. You think that you must be saved from God's version of salvation, that your Real Safety is a threat, and that you must find magical protections against the Truth. You keep these decisions out of your awareness to keep them safe and undisturbed; away from questions, sanity, and doubt.

9. But you choose Heaven *consciously*. You cannot make this choice until you have accurately seen and understood Its alternative. You must bring forth all of the beliefs that are hidden in the shadows of your mind to judge them with Heaven's Help, so that all of your mistakes in judgment can be open to correction, and the Truth can dismiss them as without cause. This is how you undo their effects.

You won't conceal them when you recognize that they are nothing.

10. Your consciously choosing Heaven is as certain as the end of fear for you when you stop denying it and bring it to God's Light within you. You cannot decide between What you clearly perceive and what you keep hidden, but you will make a clear choice when you can plainly see one choice is All Valuable and the other choice is a valueless, imagined source of guilt and pain. You won't hesitate to make this choice when it is clear to you; do not hesitate to make this choice today.

11. Make the choice for Heaven when you wake. Spend five minutes making sure that you make the one choice that is Sane. Recognize that you make a conscious choice between What is Real and what only has the appearance of truth. In the Light of Reality, you will see appearances as flimsy and transparent. They will not frighten you, because what you once saw as enormous, vengeful, and pitiless with hate is only frightening to you when it is hidden. In God's Light, you will see that they are only a foolish, trivial mistake.

12. Before you close your eyes to sleep tonight, affirm the choice that you have made every hour of the day. Give the last five minutes of your day to the decision that you made when you awoke. As every hour passes today, declare your choice again, in a brief, quiet time that you devote to maintaining your Sanity. Close the day with this, acknowledging that you have chosen What you want:

> 'Heaven is the choice that I must make. I make it now, and I will not change my mind, because It is the only thing that I want.'

Lesson 139

'I accept the Atonement for myself.'

1. Your accepting the Atonement, which is the correction of your perception that you are separate from God, ends all choices for you, because it is your decision to accept your Oneness with God. Your perception that you have choices is only your uncertainty about what you are; it is the source of all of your doubts and questions. All of your conflict entails the single, simple question, 'What am I?'

2. You only ask this question when you refuse to recognize your True Self, and only your refusal to accept your True Self can make this question seem sincere. The only thing that you can know for certain *is* What you are. From your True Self, you look on everything else as Certain as your Self.

3. Your uncertainty about what you are is self-deception on a scale so vast that you can hardly conceive of its magnitude. You are Life, so for you to not know your Self is for you to believe that you are really dead. *Life* is you being your Self, and only you are Life. So what can doubt what you are? What do you ask what you are, and what can answer you?

4. What has happened is that you have merely decided that you are not your Self and, therefore, supposedly being something else, you ask what that something else is. But you couldn't be alive at all unless you knew the answer to what you are. If you ask what you are, it is only because you don't want to be What you are. You are What you are because you are Life Itself, but you have judged against your Self and denied your worth, and you have decided that you do not know Life, though you are alive.

5. So you are uncertain of what you are because you have denied What you are, and it is this denial that needs correction. Your denial does not change What you are, but you seem to have split your mind into What knows what you are and what does not know what you are. There is no doubt that you are your Self, but you do doubt this. However, you don't ask what part of you can really doubt yourself.

It cannot really be a part of you that asks what you are, because it is asking it of What knows the Answer. If the unknowing part of you were really part of you, then no part of you could know what you are. You cannot both *know* and *not know* at the same time.

6. The Atonement, then, is the undoing of the strange idea that it is possible for you to be unsure of what you are. This idea is insanity, yet 'What am I?' is the universal question in the world that you perceive. But this only means that the world is insane. Don't share in the world's madness by believing that what is universal in the world is true.

7. Nothing that is taught in the world that you perceive is true. The purpose of the world is to be a place where you can seem to go to not know yourself. You will perceive it until you have fully accepted correction, and you have learned that it is impossible for you to not be aware of What you are.

8. You only need to *accept* What you are, because What you are is Forever in the Holy Mind of God, and in your mind. What you are is so far beyond all doubt and question that your asking what you are is proof that you believe the contradiction that you can *not* know What you *must* know. 'What am I?' is not really a question; it is a statement of Self denial. Do not occupy your Holy mind with these senseless thoughts.

9. You have a mission in your perception that you are in a world. It is not to reinforce the insanity that you once believed in. Do not forget the goal that you have accepted, because it is to gain Happiness for your entire mind. What you accept as yourself extends in your perception. Do not fail yourself. Look Lovingly on the part of your mind that you perceive as a world and know that it is a part of you.

10. This is what the Atonement teaches you, demonstrating that the Oneness of your Mind and your Oneness with God are not attacked by your belief that you don't know what you are. Today accept correction, by which you do not make your reality, but you accept your Reality, and you go forward rejoicing in God's Eternal

Love. This is all that you are asked to do, and this is all that you will do today.

11. Devote five minutes, in both the morning and the evening, to your assignment for today. Start with this review of your mission:

> 'I accept the Atonement for myself, because I am always One with God.'

You have not lost your Knowledge of God, and in your memory is the awareness that your entire mind, both what you perceive as 'you' and what you perceive as a world, is One in God's Love.

12. In gratitude to God for Its Extension of Itself Everywhere, rededicate yourself to your mission each hour today. Lay aside all thoughts that distract you from your Holy purpose, and spend several minutes with your mind cleared of all foolish thoughts about the world. Learn that the beliefs that seem to keep you unaware of your True Self are fragile as you say:

> 'I accept the Atonement for myself, because I am always One with God.'

Lesson 140

'Only my salvation from guilt can be said to 'cure' me.'

1. 'Cure' is a word that you cannot accurately apply to any remedy that you have accepted in your perception that you are in a world. What you perceive as therapeutic in the world is only what makes the body 'better'. When the world tries to heal a mind, it perceives it in a body, so the world's forms of healing are really illusions substituting for illusions. Healing in the world means that your belief in separation from God takes another form that you believe in, and then you perceive yourself as 'well'.

2. You are not healed in this case. All that's happens is that, in your illusion that you are separate from God, you had an illusion of being sick, and then an illusion that you found a magic formula to make yourself well. But you didn't undo the illusion that you are separate from God, so your mind remains in illusions as it was before. You did not perceive God's Light in your mind, which undoes your illusion of separation from God, and therefore all illusions in your mind. From the Perspective of Reality, the content of all illusions is illusion. You either perceive yourself in an illusion or in God; there is no compromise in this.

3. The Happy Illusions that the Holy Spirit brings to you are different from the personal mind's illusions in your perception that you are in a world. The personal mind's illusions foster your illusion of separation from God, but the Happy Illusions that you perceive through forgiving do not. Your Happy Illusions reflect your Oneness with God. They lead you out of illusions altogether, and gently into an awareness of Truth, so that all of your illusions fall away. This is how your Happy Illusions 'cure' you for all Eternity.

4. The Atonement, which corrects your perception of separation from God, heals you with Certainty, and cures all forms of perceived sickness. When you understand that sickness is nothing but an illusion, you will not be deceived by the forms that illusions take. Sickness always accompanies guilt, because it is the form that your

guilt takes in your perception that you are in a world. Correcting your perception that you are separate from God takes away the guilt that is the source of sickness. This is all that can be said to 'cure'. Sickness cannot return when guilt is gone.

5. Peace to you, who are cured in God, not in illusions. Your cure must come from your Holiness, and you cannot find your Holiness where you cherish separation from God. God abides in your Holy Mind; God cannot enter where you want to be separate from God. But God is Everywhere, therefore your perception that you are separate from God cannot be real. Holiness is Everywhere, so separation and sickness are nowhere.

6. This is the thought that cures you, because it does not make distinctions among illusions. It does not seek to heal the body as though it is not clear that it is the mind that needs to be healed. This is not magic; it is an expression of Truth, Which must heal, and heal Forever. It is not a thought that judges an illusion by its size, seeming gravity, or any other illusion of form. It focuses on What *is*, and knows that illusions are not real.

7. Today, do not seek to cure what cannot be sick. You must seek healing Where it is and apply it to your mind, which is what is sick, so it can be cured. No remedy in the world that you perceive makes any real change, but when you bring your illusions to be undone by Truth, your mind is truly changed. This is the only real change possible, because illusions do not differ from each other, except in empty form.

8. Today, you seek to change your mind about the source of sickness. Instead of shifting illusions around, you will seek a cure for all illusions. Find today the Source of healing within your mind, where God is. It is no farther from you than your True Self. It is as near to you as your thoughts; so close that you cannot lose It. You only need to look for It, and you will find It.

9. Do not be misled today by what appears to you as sickness. Go beyond appearances today, and reach the Source of healing, from Which no illusion is exempt. You will succeed to the extent that you

realize that there is no meaningful distinction between what is untrue and what is equally untrue. There are no degrees of existence; what does not exist is not truer in some forms than in others. All illusions are false and can be cured, because they are not true.

10. Lay aside your magical forms of healing in whatever forms they take. Be still, and listen to the Holy Spirit, Which is the Voice of healing, and Which will cure all of your ills as one, restoring you to Sanity. Only the Holy Spirit can cure. Today, hear this One Voice, Which speaks to you of Truth, Where all of your illusions end, and Peace returns to you who are the Eternal, Quiet Home of God.

11.When you awake, listen for the Holy Spirit, and let It speak to you for five minutes as your day begins. End the day listening to the Holy Spirit again for five minutes before you go to sleep. You only have to prepare by laying aside all interfering thoughts, not one-by-one, but all at once, because they are all the same. Don't make them different and delay the time when you will hear God again. Hear God now; come to God today.

12. With your mind free of attachments and listening, and your heart lifted to God, pray:

> *'Only my salvation from guilt can be said to 'cure' me. Speak to me, God, so that I am healed.'*

Feel your salvation cover you with soft protection, and with Peace so deep that no illusion disturbs your mind, or seems to be real. This is what you will learn today. Say your prayer for healing on every hour today, and take a minute to hear in Silence and Joy the Answer to your prayers. This is the day when healing comes to you. This is the day when your perception of separation from God ends, and you remember What you really are.

Mentor's Notes

Your perception that you are separate from God is the source of all of your guilt and sickness; it is also the source of all of your fears.

Because you feel guilty for separating from God, you expect punishment from God. The obvious remedy for this perception is for you to learn that you have never separated from God; you are Eternally One with God. When you fully accept this, your mind will be wholly healed, and the body will fall away from your awareness.

Review 4

Introduction

1. Now you have another review, this time in the awareness that you are preparing for the second part of learning how to apply the Truth. Today, you begin to concentrate on being ready for what will follow next, which is the aim of this review and the lessons that follow. So you will review your recent lessons and their central thoughts in a way that will facilitate the readiness that you now want to achieve.

2. The central theme that unifies every step in this review can be stated simply in these words:

'My mind holds only What I think with God.'

This is a statement of Fact that represents the Truth of What you are and of What God is. It is by what this thought states that God extends Itself to you, establishing you as co-Creator with God. It is by what this thought states that your salvation is guaranteed, because no thought can stay in your mind but the One that you share with God. You block your awareness of this by not forgiving your illusions, but it is Forever True.

3. Begin your preparation with some understanding of the many forms in which you carefully conceal your lack of true forgiving. Because they are illusions, you do not perceive them as they are: Your defense against recognizing your unforgiving thoughts. Their purpose is to show you something else, and hold off your correction through self-deception.

4. And yet, your mind holds only What you think with God. Your self-deceptions do not take the Place of Truth, anymore than a child can change the ocean's tides by throwing a stick into the sea. So start each practice period in this review by readying your mind to understand the lessons that you read, and the meaning that they offer to you.

5. Begin each day by devoting time to preparing your mind for learning each day's idea, and for accepting the Peace and Freedom that it offers to you. Open your mind, and clear it of all deceptive thoughts. Let this thought alone engage it fully:

'My mind holds only What I think with God.'

You only need five minutes with this thought to set your day along the lines that God appoints, and to place God's Mind in charge of all of the thoughts that you will receive today.

6. Your Thoughts will not come from the personal self, but from God, so Each will bring the message of God's Love to you, and return your Love to God. You will commune with God, as God wills. You are God's Completion, and you are Complete in God.

7. After you prepare, read each of the day's two ideas. Close your eyes and say them slowly to yourself. You do not have to hurry now, because you are using time as God intends it to be used. Let each word shine with the Meaning that God gives to it through the Holy Spirit within you. Let each idea that you review give you the Gift that God lays in it for you. Your only format for practicing is this:

8. Every hour of the day, bring to mind the thought with which you began the day, and spend a quiet moment with it. Then, repeat the two ideas for the day unhurriedly, with enough time to perceive the Gifts that they contain for you. Receive Them, because They are meant to be received by you.

9. Do not add other thoughts; let these messages be as they are. You need only this to give you Happiness and Rest, Endless Quiet and Perfect Certainty, and All that God wills that you receive from God. Every day, close the day as you began it, repeating first the thought that made the day a special time of Blessing and Happiness for you. Through your faith in God, your mind will be transformed from dark to Light, from grief to Joy, from pain to Peace, and from separation to Wholeness.

10. God gives thanks to you for practicing God's Word. As you

give your mind to the day's ideas again before you sleep, God's Gratitude will surround you in the Peace Where God wills you to be Forever, and Which you are learning to claim again as your own.

Lesson 141

'My mind holds only What I think with God.'

(121) Forgiving is my key to Happiness.
(122) My forgiving offers me Everything that I want.'

Lesson 142

'My mind holds only What I think with God.'

(123) I thank God for Its Gifts to me.
(124) I remember that I am One with God.

Lesson 143

'My mind holds only What I think with God.'

(125) Today, I receive God's Word in quiet.
(126) All that I give, I give to myself.

Lesson 144

'My mind holds only What I think with God.'

(127) The only Love is God's Love.
(128) The world that I perceive holds nothing that I want.

Lesson 145

'My mind holds only What I think with God.'

(129) Beyond my perception of a world is a Perception that I want.
(130) It is impossible for me to use my Real Perception and perceive the world as real.

Lesson 146

'My mind holds only What I think with God.'

(131) I will reach the Truth that I seek.

(132) I release my mind from all that I thought that the world was.

Lesson 147

'My mind holds only What I think with God.'

(133) I will not value what has no value.

(134) I will perceive forgiving as it is.

Lesson 148

'My mind holds only What I think with God.'

(135) If I defend myself, I am attacking myself.

(136) Sickness is my defense against God.

Lesson 149

'My mind holds only What I think with God.'

(137) When I am healed, my mind is healed as One.

(138) Heaven is the choice that I must make.

Lesson 150

'My mind holds only What I think with God.'

(139) I accept the Atonement for myself.

(140) Only my salvation from guilt can be said to 'cure' me.

Lesson 151

'All things reflect the Holy Spirit.'

1. You cannot judge correctly on partial evidence. To do so is not good judgment, but is merely to have an opinion based on ignorance. The seeming certainty in which you make judgments with a personal mind is only a disguise for your uncertainty. The personal mind's judgments are irrational, so they need an irrational defense. Your defense of them seems strong and convincing, because of the doubt that you feel underneath.

2. You do not seem to doubt the world that you perceive; you never really question what the body's eyes show you. You do not ask why you believe them, even though you have learned that the body's senses do deceive. When you consider how frequently they have been wrong, it is strange that you believe them to the last detail. But you trust them so completely because of your underlying doubt, which you hide with a show of certainty.

3. You cannot correctly judge with a personal mind when its judgment rests on what the body's senses witness to. There is no falser witness than this, but how else are you supposed to judge a world that you perceive with a personal mind? You pathetically place your faith in what the body's eyes and ears report, and you think that its fingers touch 'reality'. This is the awareness that you think you understand, and that is more real to you than What is witnessed to by God's Eternal Holy Spirit within you.

4. This cannot be your Real Judgment. You are often urged to give up judging with the personal mind, not because it is *right* that you should not judge, but because, with a personal mind, you *cannot* judge. Its judgments are always wrong: It guides the body's senses to prove to you how weak you are, how helpless and afraid you should be, and how you should fear the punishment that you deserve, because you are sinful and guilty.

5. Do not listen to the personal mind, because the witnesses that it uses to prove to you that *its* separation from God is *your own* are

false, and they speak with a certainty that they do not have. Your faith in them is blind, because you do not want to share the doubts that the personal mind cannot wholly banish. You think that when you doubt the personal mind, you doubt yourself.

6. But you must learn that for you to doubt the personal mind's witnesses clears the way for you to recognize your True Self, and let the Holy Spirit alone be the Judge of What is worthy of your belief. The Holy Spirit will not tell you to judge others by what the body's eyes see or hear or feel about them. The Holy Spirit overlooks these witnesses, which are not Reality. The Holy Spirit recognizes only What God loves and, in the Holy Light of God, all of the personal mind's illusions about you vanish in the Splendor that It perceives.

7. Let the Holy Spirit judge what you are, because the Holy Spirit has the Certainty in Which doubt is meaningless. Christ cannot doubt Itself, so the Holy Spirit can only honor you, rejoicing in your Perfect, Everlasting Innocence. When you accept the Holy Spirit's judgment on you, you will laugh at guilt, and refuse to play with the idea that separation from God is real. You will not heed the body's witnesses when you perceive your Christ Mind's Holiness instead.

8. This is how the Holy Spirit judges you. Accept the Holy Spirit's judgment of What you are, because the Holy Spirit witnesses to your Beautiful Extension of God, and to God's Mind, Which extends Its Reality to you. The body means nothing to That Which knows the Glory of God and you, who are One with God. The Holy Spirit cannot hear any whisper of the personal mind, nor anything that would convince It that your 'sins' are real. Let the Holy Spirit also judge everything that seems to happen to you in your perception that you are in a world. The Holy Spirit's lessons will enable you to bridge the gap between illusions and Truth.

9. The Holy Spirit will remove your faith in pain, disaster, suffering, and loss. The Holy Spirit gives you your Real Perception, Which looks beyond these grim appearances, and perceives your gentle Christ Mind instead. You will no longer doubt that only Good can come to you whom God loves, because the Holy Spirit will judge

everything that happens, and teach you the single lesson that they contain.

10. The Holy Spirit selects the elements in every situation that represent Truth, and disregards those aspects that represent illusion. The Holy Spirit reinterprets all that you perceive, and every situation in which you perceive yourself, through Its Frame of Reference, God. Through the Holy Spirit, you will see the Love beyond the hate, the Constancy in change, the Pure in 'sin', and only Heaven's blessing on all that you perceive.

11. This is your resurrection, because your Life is not a part of anything that you perceive. It is beyond the body and the world, past every witness to un-holiness; It is within the Holy, Which is as Holy as Itself. Through everyone and everything, the Holy Spirit speaks to you only of your True Self and God, with Which you are One. This is how you will see and hear your Holy Christ Mind in everything.

12. Today, you practice with words only at the beginning of the time that you spend with God. Introduce these times by repeating today's single thought slowly. Then watch your thoughts, appealing silently to the Holy Spirit, Which sees elements of Truth in all of them. Let the Holy Spirit evaluate each thought that comes to your mind, so that It can remove the illusory elements, and give them back to you as clear ideas that do not contradict God's Will.

13. Give the Holy Spirit your thoughts, and It will give them back to you as miracles that Joyously proclaim the Wholeness and Happiness that God wills for you, as proof of God's Eternal Love for you. As each or your thoughts are transformed like this, they will take on a healing power from the Mind Which saw the Truth in them and was not deceived by the illusions in them. All threads of illusions will be gone, and what will remain will be unified into a Perfect Thought that extends Its Perfection everywhere.

14. This is your resurrection, as you lay the Gift of your Innocence on all that you perceive to replace the personal mind's witnesses to your 'sin' and death. Your entire mind is redeemed

through your transfiguration, and is Joyfully released from guilt. Lift your resurrected mind happily and gratefully to God, Which has restored your Sanity to you.

15. Remember God, Which is your salvation and deliverance from guilt, every hour today. As you give thanks, all that you perceive will unite with you and happily accept the extension of your thoughts, which Heaven has corrected and made Holy and Pure. Your mission has begun at last, to extend in your perception the awareness that Truth is not an illusion, and that the Peace of God, through you, belongs to your entire mind.

Lesson 152

'The power of decision is mine.'

1. You can only suffer loss or pain if you choose to. You can only grieve, or fear, or think that you are sick if this is what you want. You even die only by your own decision. Everything that occurs to you represents your own wish, and anything that you want must occur. This is the basis of the world that you made, in all of its details. This is its whole 'reality' for you, and it is only in this awareness that you can find your salvation from it.

2. You may believe that what was just stated is extreme and includes too much to be true, but the Truth cannot have exceptions. You have Everything, so loss cannot be real. Pain cannot be part of Peace, grief cannot be part of Joy, and fear and sickness cannot be where there is Love and Perfect Holiness. Truth must be all-inclusive to be Truth. Do not accept any opposites or exceptions to Truth, or you contradict Truth entirely.

3. Your salvation is in your recognizing that the Truth is True, and nothing else is True. You have read this before, but you may not yet accept both parts. Without the first part, the second part has no meaning, and without the second part, the first part would not be True. Truth cannot have an opposite and be True. You cannot think about this too much. If what is not true is as true as What is True, then part of Truth is false, and Truth is no longer Truth. Only the Truth is True; what is false is false.

4. This is the simplest distinction, yet the most obscure to you, but not because it is a difficult distinction for you to perceive. You conceal it behind a vast array of choices that do not appear to be your own. So, to you, the Truth appears to have some aspects that are not consistent, and you do not see that the contradictions that you perceive are introduced by you.

5. In your Oneness with God, you must be Unchanging, and any transitory state is therefore false. This includes all shifts in feeling,

alterations in the body and the mind, and in your awareness and response. This is the All-inclusiveness that sets the Truth apart from the false, and keeps the false apart from the Truth.

6. It is strange that you believe that it is arrogant for you to think that you made the world. You can be sure that God did not make the world. God does not know of the ephemeral, the 'sinful', the guilty, the afraid, the suffering, the lonely, or a mind that lives in a body that must die. For you to believe that God made a world where these things are real is for you to accuse God of insanity. God is not insane, and only insanity makes a world like this.

7. It *is* arrogance for you to think that God made chaos, contradicts Its Own Will, invented opposites to Truth, and made death to triumph over Life. It is with humility that you can see at once that these things are not of God. You cannot perceive what God does not extend, and to think that you can is for you to believe that you can make what is not God's Will. There is nothing more arrogant than this.

8. Be truly humble today, and accept what you have made as the illusion that it is. The power of decision is yours. Decide to accept your rightful place as God's Extension, Which extends God as God extends God, and all that you think that you made will disappear. What will rise to your awareness is All that has ever been, and It will take the place of your self-deception, which you made to take the place of God in your mind.

9. Today you practice true humility by abandoning the personal mind's false pretense that true humility is arrogance. Only the personal mind can be arrogant. The Truth in you is humble when It acknowledges Its Strength, Its Changelessness, and God's Gift of God's Eternal, All-encompassing Wholeness to you. Lay aside the arrogance in which you say that you are a 'sinner': guilty, afraid, and ashamed of yourself. Instead, lift your heart in true humility to God, Which has created you Immaculate, and like God in Power and Love.

10. The power of decision is yours; accept of God That Which you are by humbly recognizing that you are God's Extension of God. For

you to recognize yourself as God's Extension you must lay aside all false self-concepts and perceive the personal mind's arrogance behind them. And in humility, Joyously accept the Radiance of your Christ Mind, Its Gentleness, Its Perfect Innocence, God's Love, and your Right to Heaven and release from hell.

11. Join your Christ Mind in glad acknowledgement that lies are false and only the Truth is True. Think only of Truth when you wake up, and spend five minutes practicing Its ways, encouraging your frightened mind with this:

> 'The power of decision is mine. Today, I accept myself as God's Extension.'

Then wait in silence, and give up all self-deception as you ask your True Self to reveal Itself to you. The Christ in you, Which has never left you, will come again into your awareness, gratefully restoring your mind to God, as it was meant to be.

12. Patiently wait for God throughout the day, and hourly invite God with the words of today's lesson. Conclude with the same invitation to your True Self. The Holy Spirit will answer, because It speaks for God and for you. The Holy Spirit will substitute the Peace of God for all of your frantic thoughts, the Truth of God for your self-deceptions, and God's Extension for your illusions of yourself.

Lesson 153

'My Safety lies in my Defenselessness.'

1. If you feel threatened by the changing world that you perceive, its twists of fortune, its bitter jokes, its brief relationships, and all of the 'gifts' that it offers to you only to take them away, then pay attention to this lesson. There is no safety in the world. Its roots are in attack, and any safety that you perceive in it is only an illusion. The world attacks and attacks, and no Peace of mind is possible for you in such a dangerous place.

2. You can only be defensive if such a world is real to you. The threats that you perceive in your identification with a personal self make you angry, and your anger makes your attacks seem reasonable, honestly provoked, and righteous in the name of self-defense. But your defensiveness threatens you itself, because it reinforces your sense of vulnerability, so it sets up a defense system that cannot make you feel safe. It makes it seem to you that there is treachery within you, as well as outside of you. This confuses you, and you don't know where to turn to find escape from these illusions.

3. It is as if you are trapped in a vicious cycle of attack-defense-attack-defense that fills your days, and makes escape seem impossible to you. There seems to be no break or ending in the ever-tightening hold attack and defense have on your mind.

4. Of all of the prices that you pay to identify with a personal self, your defenses are the costliest to you. Insanity lies in them in a form so grim that any hope of Sanity that you have seems to be an impossible dream. The sense of danger that the world that you perceive instills in you is so much deeper than the frenzy and intensity that you are aware of, that you cannot conceive of the devastation that it has wrought in your mind.

5. You are a slave to the world that you made. In your fear of it, you do not know what you do. You do not know how much you sacrifice to it; you do not realize that you sabotage the Holy Peace of

God within you to defend yourself against it. You, who are One with God, see yourself as though you are a victim of attack by your own illusions. You seem helpless in their presence, and you can only use other illusions to defend yourself, and to give yourself a sense of safety.

6. But your Defense*less*ness is your Real Safety, because It testifies to your awareness of the Christ within you. Perhaps you will recall that the Text says that your choice is always between Christ's Strength and the personal mind's weakness. In your Defenselessness you will never perceive yourself as attacked, because in It you will recognize a Strength within you that is so Great that the idea of attack will be foolish to you.

7. Your defens*ive*ness is weakness, because, through it, you proclaim that you have denied the Christ within you, and this makes you feel that you have attacked God, so you fear God's anger. In your defensiveness nothing can save you from your delusion of an angry god whose works you see in an evil world around you. Only illusions can seem to defend you when you are fighting illusions.

8. Today you will not play with foolishness, because your true purpose is to save your entire mind, and you do not want foolishness to replace the Endless Joy that your function offers to you. You do not want to let your Happiness slip by because a fragment of illusion happens to cross your mind, and you mistake what you see in it for Reality.

9. You will look past illusions today, and recognize that you don't need any defense, because in your Oneness with God, you are Unassailable, and you do not have any thought or wish or illusion in which attack has meaning. You will not fear, because you have left all fearful thoughts behind. In your Defenselessness you are Secure and Serenely Certain of your Safety; you are sure of salvation, and sure that you will fulfill your purpose in your mission to extend Its Holy blessing through all that you perceive.

10. Be still for a moment, and in Silence think of how your purpose is Holy, and how secure and untouchable you rest in it in

God's Light. As God's messenger, you have chosen that the Truth be with you, and nothing is Holier than you. You cannot be surer that your Happiness is fully guaranteed, or feel more Mightily protected. You cannot possibly need defense, because you are chosen by God's Will and your will to fulfill the purpose that God gives to you.

11. It is your function as God's messenger to extend in your mind where you perceive a world your choice to accept God's Will as your own. If you fail to teach this, your salvation will have to wait, and the darkness of guilt will have a grim hold on your entire mind. You will not learn that God's Light is with you, and that your escape from darkness has already been accomplished. And you will not see God's Light until you extend it to all that you perceive, and, as you see it there, you recognize It as your own.

12. Look on your salvation as a game designed by God, Which loves you, and wants to replace your fearful games with Joyous games that teach you that fear has gone. God's game teaches you Happiness, because there is no loser in it. If you play, you win, and in your winning everything that you perceive wins. You will gladly lay aside the game of fear when you see the benefits that salvation brings to you.

13. You have played a game where you have no hope, you are abandoned by God, you are left alone in terror in a frightening world that is insane with sin and guilt, but now you can be happy, because that game is over. A quiet time has come to you, in which you can put away your childish and quaint toys of guilt, and lock them away Forever from your Pure and Holy Mind, Which is One with God.

14. You will pause for a moment to play your final Happy game in your perception that you are in a world, then you will go on to take your Rightful Place, Where Truth abides, and games are meaningless. So the story of the world ends; let today bring the last chapter of the world closer for you, and learn that the tale of a terrifying destiny for you, defeat of all of your hopes, and a pitiful defense against a vengeful world that you could not escape, is only your own deluded illusion. As God's messenger, you have come to

undo the dark illusions that this story evoked in your confused, bewildered mind. You can smile at last as you learn that they are not true.

15. Today, you practice in a form that you will maintain for a while. Begin each day by giving your attention to the daily thought as long as possible. Five minutes is now the minimum that you give to this; ten minutes would be better, and fifteen minutes would be better than that. And as you become less distracted from your purpose, you will find that half-an-hour is too short a time to spend with God. Give the same amount of time each night, in gratitude and Joy.

16. Every hour will add to your increasing Peace as you remember to be faithful to the Will that you share with God. Sometimes, a minute or less will be all that you are able to offer as the hour strikes. Sometimes, you will forget. At other times, you will not be able to withdraw from the world for a little while to turn your thoughts to God.

17. But, when you can, observe the trust that you hold as a messenger of God, in an hourly remembrance of your mission and God's Love. Sit quietly and wait for God, listening for the Holy Spirit, and learn what God wants you to do in the hour ahead. And thank God for all of the Gifts that It gave to you in the one that just past.

18. In time, and with practice, you will never cease to think of God and hear Its Loving Holy Spirit guiding your footsteps into quiet ways, where you will walk in True Defenselessness. You will know that Heaven goes with you wherever you perceive yourself, and you will not want to keep your mind away from God for a moment, even though your time is spent in extending salvation in your mind where you perceive a world. God will make this possible for you, who have chosen to carry out God's plan to save you.

19. Today, your theme is your Defenselessness. Clothe yourself in It as you prepare to meet the day. Rise up strong in Christ, and let the personal mind's weakness disappear as you remember that

God's Strength abides in you. Remind yourself that God is beside you throughout the day, and that God never leaves you in weakness. Call upon God's Strength whenever you feel the threat of your defenses undermine your certainty of purpose. Pause a moment as the Holy Spirit tells you, 'I am here.'

20. Your practicing will now take on the earnestness of Love to keep your mind from wandering from its Intent. Do not be afraid or timid; there is no doubt that you will reach your final Goal. As a messenger of God, you cannot fail, because the Love and Strength and Peace that extends from you to all that you perceive comes from God. These are God's Gifts to you; your Defenselessness is all that you need to give to God in return. Lay aside what was never real to look on your Christ Mind and see your Innocence.

Mentor's Notes

In paragraph 1, it points out that the world's roots are in attack. The 'attack' that it is referring to is your perceived attack on God. You made the world to be a place where you can be separate from God, and every aspect of it is meant to support the idea that you have really done this. But, as you have learned from earlier lessons, you can interpret the world differently. The only other way to interpret the world is to forgive it your desire for separation from God by overlooking all 'evidence' of separation from God and perceiving God's Love instead. This process leads you to an awareness that only God is Real, and the world is only an illusion of separation from God.

You cannot willingly be Defenseless in the world that you perceive until you have a sufficient awareness of the Christ within you to feel Its Safety all around you. Until then, you will reinforce fear in your mind by pretending to feel a Safety that you do not yet feel. Simply accept that you will use the personal mind's defenses until you have experienced your Real Safety. It is not a 'sin' to do so; it is only a mistake that you are working to correct.

Lesson 154

'I am a messenger of God.'

1. Today, don't be arrogant or falsely humble; you have gone beyond such foolishness. You cannot judge yourself correctly with a personal mind, and you don't need to do so. Those judgments are only attempts to hold off making a decision for God, and to delay your commitment to your function of forgiveness. It is not the personal mind's job to judge your worth, nor can it know the role through which you will learn best. You cannot see the whole plan for your salvation from guilt, so you cannot understand your part. Your part is cast in Heaven, not in hell. What the personal mind has taught you is weakness is your Strength, and what it teaches you is your strength is often just arrogance.

2. Your role in the plan for your salvation is chosen by the Holy Spirit, Which speaks for God as well as for you. The Holy Spirit, knowing what your strengths are, and where they can best be applied, for what, toward whom, and when, chooses and accepts your part for you. The Holy Spirit does not work in you and through you without your consent, but It also is not deceived in what you are. The Holy Spirit listens only to Its Voice in you.

3. It is through the Holy Spirit's ability to hear the One Voice Which is Its Own that you will become aware that there is only One Voice in you. That One Voice appoints your function, relays it to you, and gives you the strength to understand it, to do what it entails, and to succeed in everything that you do that is related to it. God joins you in this, so you become a messenger of your Oneness with God.

4. It is your joining God through the Holy Spirit in you that sets your salvation apart from the world that you perceive. It is the Holy Spirit that speaks of the Law that the world does not obey, that promises you salvation from all perceived 'sin', and that abolishes guilt in your mind, which is Innocent, because it is One with God. This is how your mind becomes aware again of God and of its True

Self. Your True Self is the Reality through Which your will and God's Will are joined.

5. A messenger does not write the message that they deliver, nor do they question the right of the one who does write it, or ask why they were chosen to receive the message that they carry. They only have to accept the message and give it as directed to fulfill their role in its delivery. If they determine what the message should be, what their purpose is, or where they should deliver the message, then they are failing to perform their part as messenger.

6. There is one major difference between the world's messengers and you as Heaven's messenger that sets you apart. The Messages that you deliver are intended for you first. Only after you have accepted them for yourself will you be able to deliver them further, as you are directed. Like messengers in the world, you did not write the Messages that you carry, but you become the first receiver of the Messages in the truest sense, receiving Them to prepare yourself to extend Them.

7. A messenger in the world fulfills their role by giving all of their messages away. As God's messenger, you fulfill your role by accepting God's Messages for yourself, and then demonstrating that you have understood Them by giving Them away. You do not choose roles that are not given to you by God, so you gain by every Message that you extend.

8. You become God's messenger by *wanting* to become God's messenger. You are already appointed, yet you wait to extend the Messages that you have received, so you do not know that They are yours, and you do not recognize Them. You cannot recognize that you have received Them until you extend Them, because your extending Them is your own acceptance of What you have received.

9. You are now God's messenger, so receive God's Messages, because that is part of your role. God has not failed to offer you What you need, nor have you failed to accept It, because the Holy Spirit in you has accepted It for you. But the other part of your role is to accept It in your *awareness*, thereby to identify with the Holy Spirit

and claim your Identity.

10. It is your Oneness with the Holy Spirit that you seek to recognize today. Do not keep your mind apart from the Voice that speaks for you, because It is your Voice. Only the Holy Spirit can speak to you and for you, joining in One Voice the receiving and extending of God's Messages; the receiving and extending of God's Will.

11. Practice giving the Holy Spirit what the Holy Spirit wants, so that you can recognize the Holy Spirit's Gifts to you. The Holy Spirit needs your voice, so that It can speak through you; your mind to hold Its Messages, so that you can extend Them where the Holy Spirit directs; and your feet, so that you can go where the Holy Spirit directs, for you to be delivered at last from all perceptions of misery. The Holy Spirit needs your will united with Its Will, so that you become the True Receiver of the Gifts that the Holy Spirit gives.

12. Learn this lesson today: You will not recognize What you have received until you extend It. You have read this a hundred times in a hundred different ways, yet your belief in it is still lacking. You can be sure that, until you do believe it, you will receive a thousand times a thousand miracles, but you will not know that God gives you only What you already have, and that God has not denied you even the tiniest blessing. This won't mean anything to you until you identify with God.

13. Today's lesson is stated:

> 'I am a messenger of God, and I am grateful that I have the means to recognize that I am Limitless.'

14. The world will recede as these Holy words light up your mind, and you realize that they are true. This is the message that God gives to you for today. Now, demonstrate how it has changed your mind about yourself and what your function is. As you prove that you do not accept any will that you do not share with God, your many Gifts from God will spring into your sight and leap into your

hands, and you will recognize What you have received.

Mentor's Notes

Paragraph 8 ends by pointing out that you cannot know that you have received God's Messages until you extend them, because only by extending Them do you accept Them. This reflects the Law of Mind that Mind only knows Itself; Mind is One. You know what you believe you are by what you perceive. If you perceive that the world is real, then you believe that you are a personal self in a body in a world; you believe that you are separate from God. You have looked within and seen separation as real and projected it outward to perceive it in a world. But if, instead, you look within and see your Oneness with God, you will just as automatically extend God in your perception. The automatic extension of what is in your mind proves what you have accepted there.

God's 'Messages' to you always reflect your Eternal Oneness with God.

Lesson 155

'I step back and let the Holy Spirit lead the way.'

1. There is a way for you to live in your perception that you are in a world that is not really in the world, although it seems to be. Your appearance will not change, but you will smile more often; your forehead will be serene, and your eyes will be quiet. You will recognize Christ in others, though they will seem to see in you what they believe is in themselves.

2. The world that you perceive is an illusion. You project it to avoid your Reality, and to make the illusory world your reality instead. But when you realize that even though you perceive a world you can experience your Reality, then you can step back and let your Reality lead the way. This is the only real choice that you have to make in your perception that you are in a world. It is insane for you, who are Reality, to let illusions guide you, but it is sane for you to let your illusions sink behind your Reality, so that your Reality can be What It is.

3. This is the simple choice that you make today. The illusion of a personal self will remain with you for a while as you learn to extend only the Christ in your mind to the part of your mind where you perceive a world outside of you. That part of your mind can only return to Truth through your overlooking your illusions there.

4. If the Holy Spirit demanded that you give up the world, you would feel that you were being asked to sacrifice the personal self, which you have not yet wholly learned is not you. If you renounce the world while still believing that it is real, you will suffer from a sense of loss, and you will not be released from illusions. And if you choose nothing but the world, you will suffer from a sense of loss even deeper, without understanding why.

5. But there is a path between these two ways that leads you away from loss of every kind, because on it you leave behind all loss and deprivation. This is the way appointed for you. You will walk this path not seeming to be different from other personal selves in

the world that you perceive, but you will be. As you forgive your projections of personal selves, you forgive the illusion that you are a personal self. This is the way that God has opened for you to return your entire mind to God.

6. You will still seem to be part of illusions so you can undo them, but you will have stepped away from them. You will overlook illusions, because you will be perceiving from the Truth in you. Your new path leads you past illusions, and on your way you unite your entire mind: Both 'you' and what you perceive.

7. Any road that you take in the world would ultimately lead to this one, because sacrifice and deprivation are paths that lead nowhere. They are choices meant to 'defeat' God, and their goal is impossible. All of this falls back as you let the Holy Spirit come forth in you to lead your mind away from death and onto the path to Happiness. Your suffering is an illusion, but you need a Guide to lead you out of it, because you have mistaken illusions for the Truth.

8. This is all that your salvation asks of you: Accept the Truth, and let It go before you to light up your path of freedom from illusions. Your freedom does not have a price; you only gain from it. Illusions can only *seem* to limit you; it is from illusions that you are saved. As you let them fall back, you find your True Self again.

9. Walk safely, but carefully, because this path is new to you, and you may find that you are tempted to let the personal self walk ahead of Truth, and then illusions will be your guide. Walk with certainty of purpose to Truth by extending Truth to the part of your mind where you perceive a world, to guide your entire mind back to Oneness.

10. At the end of your journey there will be no gap between you and the Truth. All of the illusions that you perceive will be gone, and there will be nothing in your mind to keep you from God's Completion. Step back in faith, and let the Holy Spirit lead the way; without It, you do not know where you go.

11. When your illusions are gone, time is over, and miracles no longer have a purpose, you will make no more journeys. You will no

longer have a wish to be an illusion instead of Truth. You are stepping toward this as you walk the path upon which Truth leads you. This is the final journey for your entire mind; do not lose your way. As Truth goes before you, It leads your entire mind as One.

12. You walk to God. Pause and reflect on this. There is no path that is Holier, more deserving of your effort, your love, or your full intent. There is no path that can give you more than Everything, or offer you less and still content you, God's Holy Extension. You walk to God. The Holy Spirit, Which walks before you, is One with God, and It leads you to God. What other path could you want to choose instead?

13. You are firmly set upon the road that leads your entire mind to God. Do not look to paths that seem to lead you elsewhere. Illusions are not a worthy guide for you who are One with God. Do not forget that God's Holy Spirit is in you, and that God trusts you to extend It to all that you perceive. God is not deceived in you. God's Trust makes your path certain and your Goal secure. You will not fail to unite your entire mind in your True Self.

14. God only asks that you think of God for a while each day, so that God can speak to you, and tell you of Its Limitless Love for, and Great Trust in, you. In your recognition of your Oneness with God, gladly practice with this thought today:

> 'I step back and let the Holy Spirit lead the way, because I want to walk along the road to God.'

Mentor's Notes

The last line in paragraph 1 reflects again the Law of Mind that a mind always sees itself. The 'evidence' of your transformation will not be what others see in you, but what you see in others: When you identify with Christ, you will see only Christ and overlook everything else.

You cannot be without an identity, so as you let go of a personal self, you must have another identity to take its place. You only have two choices in identification: The personal self, which you made, and Christ, Which you are. But, because of your identification with a personal self, you still need to learn how to identify with Christ. This is what you are doing when you step back and let the Holy Spirit lead the way. Eventually, you will not feel that there is Something going ahead of you; the Holy Spirit will simply be What you are.

Lesson 156

'I walk with God in Perfect Holiness.'

1. Today's idea states the simple Truth that makes your thoughts of sin impossible. It promises that you have no cause for guilt, so guilt does not exist. It follows the basic thought mentioned in the Text: Ideas do not leave their source. Since this is true, you cannot be apart from God. Even in your perception that you are in a world, you do not walk apart from your Source.

2. There are no inconsistent thoughts in this lesson plan. Either Truth is True throughout or It's not True. Truth cannot contradict Itself, nor can it be partly certain and partly uncertain. Even in your perception that you are in a world you are with God, because God is your Life. Where you are, God is. There is only One Life, and you share It with God. You cannot be apart from God and live.

3. Where God is, there is Holiness as well as Life. You share every Attribute of God. You are as Holy as God, because what shares God's Life is part of Holiness, and you can no more choose to be sinful than the sun can choose to be ice.

4. There is a Light in you that cannot die; Its very Presence in you is so Holy that it blesses your entire mind, and everything that you perceive returns your gift to you in gratitude and gladness.

5. The Light in you is What you long to behold throughout your entire mind. The Light that you carry belongs to everything that you perceive, and you are the savior and the God of all that you perceive, because it is in your mind. Accept the reverence that belongs to Holiness Itself, Which walks with you, and transforms everything that you perceive with Its Gentle Light. It transforms everything into Its Likeness and Purity.

6. This is the way that your salvation is done: As you step back, God's Light in you steps forward and encompasses all that you perceive. This signals the end of sin, not through your punishment and death, but through your laughter as you see its quaint absurdity. *Sin* is a foolish thought; a silly illusion that is ridiculous, not fright-

ening. Do not delay an instant with this silly whim as you approach God.

7. Yet you have wasted many, many years on just this foolish thought. The past is gone with all of its illusions, and you are no longer limited by them. Your approach to God is near, and in the little interval of doubt that remains, you may still lose sight of your Companion and mistake It for the senseless illusion that has passed.

8. So, a thousand times a day you should ask yourself, 'Who walks with me?' until you are certain and at Peace. Today, let your doubting cease. God answers your question by giving you these words to use:

> 'I walk with God in Perfect Holiness. Holiness lights my mind and all that I perceive, which is One with me.'

Lesson 157

'I enter into Christ's Presence now.'

1. This is a day of silence and of trust for you. It is a special time of promise; a day that Heaven shines upon with Its Timeless Light, and in it you will hear reminders of Eternity. This day is Holy, because it ushers in a new experience for you. You have spent long days and nights celebrating death; today you learn to feel the Joy of Life.

2. Today brings another crucial turning point for you in this lesson plan. A new dimension will be added; a fresh Experience that will illuminate all that you have already learned, and that will prepare you for what you have yet to learn. This Experience will bring you right up to God, Where your learning ends, and you will catch a glimpse of God beyond this highest awareness that your learning can attain. You will stop here a moment, then go beyond, sure of your Direction and your Only Goal.

3. Today, you will feel a touch of Heaven, though you will return to an awareness of the world to continue your learning. Now you have come far enough along for time to alter, so that you can rise above its laws and walk in Eternity for a while. You will learn to do this more and more, as you faithfully practice every lesson and they bring you more swiftly to this Holy Place and leave you, for a moment, to your True Self.

4. The Holy Spirit will direct your practicing today, because What you ask for now is What the Holy Spirit wills. When you join your will with the Holy Spirit's Will, What you ask for must be given to you. You only need today's idea to light your mind, so that it can rest in Still Anticipation and in Quiet Joy, Where you quickly leave the world behind.

5. From today on, your mission takes on a genuine devotion and a Light that extends from you and blesses all that you perceive. Your Real Perception will touch on all that you perceive or even think of, and It will be returned to you. Your Experience today will so

transform your mind that it will be the Experience by Which you determine the Holy Thoughts of God from your other thoughts.

6. Your body will be sanctified today, because its only purpose now will be to bring the Real Perception that you experience today to Light the part of your mind where you perceive a world. You cannot convey What you experience today to what seems outside of you, but It will leave you with a Perception that you can extend to all that you perceive to bring closer your forgetting the world and your remembering Heaven.

7. As this Experience increases for you, and all goals but God become of no value to you, your experience of the world will come closer to ending. By bringing God's Light into your perception of the world, you will come to perceive God's Light more certainly, and your Real Perception will become more distinct. The time will come when you will no longer seem to have a form, because you will not need it, but now it has a purpose and can serve you well.

8. Today, you will embark upon a journey that you have never imagined, but the Holy Spirit, Which gives you the Happy Illusion, translates your perception into Truth, and is your Holy Guide to Heaven, has imagined this journey that you start today, with the Experience that this day holds out to you.

9. Enter into Christ's Presence now, serenely unaware of anything but Christ's Light and Perfect Love. The Perception of your Christ Mind will stay with you, but there will be a Holy Instant that transcends all perception, even the Holiest Perception. You will never teach yourself This, because you have not learned It; It is always yours. But your Real Perception reminds you of What you experience in that Holy Instant, and will surely wholly remember again.

Mentor's Notes

This lesson is about practicing the *Holy Instant*. Your fullest experience of the Holy Instant is a direct *Revelation* of God, Which is pure Experience and cannot be conveyed in words or any other symbols, because the Limitless cannot be limited. But, as this lesson emphasizes, the experience of the Holy Instant stays with you and changes your perception if you let it.

Paragraph 2 mentions the 'highest awareness' that your learning can attain. This is your Christ Mind; beyond your Christ Mind is God, Which you cannot learn, because you have never lost your Knowledge of God. It might seem to be a contradiction that you *learn* Christ's Perception but that you *know* God, but this is because *learning, perception,* and your *Christ Mind* only have meaning in your seeming separation from God. Only in your seeming separation from God do you seem to need to remember that you are One with God, and do you seem to have the choice to learn this or not. *Christ* is the label given to your awareness that you are One with God as long as you *perceive* instead of *know*. When you attain this awareness, you will be ready to leave behind all perception and learning and know only God again.

Lesson 158

'Today, I learn to give as I receive.'

1. What have you been given? The Knowledge that you are Mind, in God's Mind, Eternally Innocent, and wholly without fear, because you are One with Love. You have not left God; you are always One with God. This is the Knowledge that God extends to you, and Which you cannot lose. This is the Knowledge that is Life Itself.

2. You have received all of this, and it is as true for you as it is for the part of your mind where you perceive a world. But this Knowledge is not what you give, because this Knowledge is Creation, and you cannot learn It. So what are you to learn to give today? Yesterday's lesson evoked a theme found early in the Text: You cannot extend your direct Experience of God the way that you can extend your Real Perception. The Revelation that your entire mind and God are One will come in time, but that time is determined by your mind's readiness for the Revelation; the Revelation is not Something that you learn.

3. That time has already occurred, though it seems to you to be arbitrarily in the future. So there is no step along the road to God that you take that is up to chance. It seems like you have hardly embarked on the journey, but you have really already taken it. Time goes in one direction, but you are undertaking a journey that was already over before time. It only *seems* like you have a future that is unknown to you.

4. Time is a trick, a sleight of hand; a vast illusion in which illusory figures seem to come and go as if by magic. Yet, there is a plan behind these appearances that does not change. It is as though there is a script with the ending already written; the Experiences that will end your doubting have been set. There really is no journey, but you imagine that you are taking one, learning what you have really already learned.

5. You cannot teach the Experience of God, because you do not learn God; God is revealed to you when you are ready for the

Experience. But the Gift that you can give, or extend, is your Real Perception. The Knowledge of your Christ Mind is also not lost to you, and you can teach yourself through It, because Christ is in your perception. God's Will and the Will of your Christ Mind are joined in Knowledge, but your Real Perception comes to you from your Christ Mind through the Holy Spirit.

6. Through your Real Perception, your perception of a world of doubt and shadows is joined with a quiet place within you where your perception is made Holy through forgiving and Love. All contradictions are undone here, because your journey ends with your Real Perception. This is where you are wholly ready to go beyond to experience God, Which you do not learn, teach, or perceive. But this Experience is beyond your goal, because It transcends what you can attain. Your concern is with the Real Perception of your Christ Mind, Which you *can* attain.

7. The Real Perception of your Christ Mind has One Law. It does not look on bodies and mistake them for God's Creation. It perceives God's Light beyond bodies, and beyond what can be touched with a body. It perceives a Purity that is untouched by errors and fearful thoughts of guilt that come from illusions of sin. It does not see separation, and it looks on everyone, everything, and every situation without the Light It perceives fading.

8. This, you *can* teach and you *must* teach if you want to learn It. This only requires that you recognize that the world cannot give you anything that even faintly compares in value to your Real Perception, and that you do not set up any goal that will only disappear when you have perceived this. This is what you can give today: Do not see bodies, but see instead the Light of your Christ Mind, and acknowledge that the part of your mind where you see a world is One with you.

9. This is how you forgive your 'sins', because the Real Perception of your Christ Mind has the power to forgive sin wherever you perceive it. Unperceived by the Christ in you, sin merely disappears, because the Holiness of your Real Perception

takes its place. It doesn't matter what form these sins took, how enormous they seemed to be, or who seemed to be hurt by them. They are gone, and all the effects that they seemed to have are undone forever.

10. This is how you learn to give What you have received, and how you perceive *yourself* through the Real Perception of your Christ Mind. This lesson is not difficult to learn if you remember that what you perceive in the world you first see in yourself. If you perceive sin, then you believe that you are a 'sinner', but if you perceive God's Light, then you have forgiven yourself the idea of sin. Everyone you meet today provides you with an another chance to let the Real Perception of your Christ Mind shine on you and offer you the Peace of God.

11. It doesn't matter when a Revelation comes to you, because It is not of time. But in time, you still have a Gift to give in Which Knowledge of God is reflected in a way that is so accurate that Its image shares in Holiness and shines with Immortal Love. Practice seeing with your Christ Mind today, and, by the Holy Gifts that you extend, the Real Perception of your Christ Mind will look on you as well.

Mentor's Notes

Paragraph 2 says that a Revelation of God is not Something that you learn, but Something that occurs when you are ready for It. The purpose of your learning and your Real Perception is to prepare you for the Revelation. Paragraph 5 also mentions this distinction in learning. Remember, you always teach yourself, so your teaching and learning are simultaneous. Because you do not *learn* God, you cannot *teach* yourself God. What you can, and must, teach yourself and learn are the *conditions* for remembering God.

Paragraphs 3, and 4 are referring to the fact that the moment that the idea of not-God occurred it was undone, because God is All-encompassing and cannot have an opposite. But the idea of not-God contains the concept of *time*, and only in time does it seem that you separated from God in a distant past, and that you will return to God at an indefinite time in the future. Time is the illusion on which all other illusions rest. This is why the Experience of the Holy Instant is so important. In the Holy Instant, you step out of time and into Eternity, and you realize that you have never left God; there is no time, no world, and no journey. And when you return to time from a Holy Instant, it never again has the same hold over you.

The last two lines in paragraph 6 say that you cannot attain God, but that you can attain the Real Perception of your Christ Mind. *Attain* here does not mean that you can never *reach* God, but that you cannot *learn* God. Once you have wholly attained, or learned, your Real Perception, only God will be in your perception, which will then translate easily into Knowledge of God.

Lesson 159

'I give the miracles that I have received.'

1. You cannot give what you have not received; to give something you must have it in your possession. This law is true in both Heaven and in the world that you perceive. But then the laws of Heaven and the world separate. In the world, for you to continue to possess something, you must hold onto it. But, for your salvation, you must learn that it works another way for What God gives to you: Giving It away, or extending It, is how you learn that you have It. This 'proves' What you have.

2. You understand that you are healed when you extend healing, you accept forgiveness for yourself when you forgive, and when you recognize your True Self in the world that seems outside of you, you perceive that your Mind is Whole. You can give any miracle, because every miracle has been given to you. Receive them now by opening your mind where they are laid and by giving them away.

3. Your Christ Mind's Real Perception is a miracle. It comes from far beyond Itself, because It reflects Eternal Love, and in It you are reborn to the Love Which never dies, but Which you had hidden. Your Real Perception reflects Heaven, because It is so like Heaven that What is Perfect in God is mirrored There. The darkened glass that the world presents to you can only show you twisted images in broken parts, but your Real Perception pictures Heaven's Innocence.

4. Your Christ Mind's Real Perception is the miracle in which all other miracles are born. It is their Source, remaining with each miracle, and also with you, who extends the miracle. Your Real Perception is the bond by Which you, the giver, and the part of your mind that seems to be a world outside of you, which receives, are united in extension as your Mind is One in Heaven. Your Christ Mind does not perceive sin anywhere, and through Its Perception, your Innocent mind is One. The Holiness that It perceives is given by God and Itself.

5. Your Christ Mind is the Bridge between the world that you

perceive and your Real Perception. You can safely trust in Its Power to carry you from your perception of a world of separation to a Perception that is made Holy through your forgiving. Things that seem solid in the world that you perceive are only shadows in your Real Perception: transparent, sometimes forgotten, and never able to obscure God's Light, Which shines beyond them. In It, your Holiness is returned to your perception; where you were blind, you now can see.

6. Your Real Perception is the Holy Spirit's Single Gift to you. It is the Treasure House to Which you can appeal with perfect certainty for all that can contribute to your Happiness. Everything is already There for you, and you only have to ask to receive Everything. The door is never locked, and you will never be denied your smallest request or your most urgent need. Your every sickness has already been healed, your every lack has been filled, and your every need has been met within the Golden Treasury of your Christ Mind.

7. In your Real Perception, you remember What you lost when you made the world. Here, your perception is repaired and made new again, but in a different Light. The world that you made to perceive sin becomes the center of redemption and the hearth of mercy, where your suffering is healed and you are welcome. You will not be turned away from where your salvation waits; you are not a stranger there. The only thing that will be asked of you is that you accept your welcome.

8. Your Christ Mind's Real Perception is the Holy Foundation of your forgiving. This is its home. You bring your forgiving to the world that you perceive from your Real Perception, but it does not live in the world. Your forgiving needs the Light and Warmth and Kindly Care of your Christ Mind. It needs the Love with Which your Christ Mind perceives, and then your forgiving becomes the messenger that gives as it receives.

9. Take from the Storehouse of your Christ Mind, so that Its Treasure is increased. What you take does not leave Christ when you

carry It into the world that you perceive. It does not leave Its Source, but you carry Its beneficence with you and turn your perception into a reflection of Heaven. Now, you are twice blessed, because the messages that you brought from Christ are returned to you.

10. Behold the store of miracles set out for you to give! Aren't you worth this gift that God has appointed for you? Do not judge yourself, who are One with God, but follow the way that God has established for you. Your Christ Mind perceives an illusion in which the illusion is forgiven. This is Its Gift to you, in which you can make a sweet transition from death to Life, and from hopelessness to hope. Give an instant to sharing this Happy Illusion with your Christ Mind, because It awakens you to Truth. Your Christ Mind's Real Perception is the Means for your return to your Everlasting Sanctity in God.

Lesson 160

'My mind is at Home in God. Fear is the stranger in my mind.'

1. Fear is a stranger to the Ways of Love. When you identify with fear, your True Self is a stranger to you, and you think that you are another self that is real, but that is not your True Self. You cannot be sane in this situation. Only in insanity can you judge against your True Self and believe that you are what you are not.

2. There is a stranger in your mind, who comes from an idea so foreign to your Truth that it speaks a different language, looks on a world that Truth does not know, and understands illusions that have no meaning to Truth. Even odder, it does not know in whose mind it is, and yet it maintains that your mind belongs to it, so you have become the alien in your own mind. But how easy it would be for you to say, 'My mind is my home and I belong here. I will not leave, because an insane idea says I must.'

3. The only reason that you can have for not saying this is that you have asked this stranger into your mind, and you have let your True Self become a stranger to you. You can only have let yourself be dispossessed of your own mind so unnecessarily because you think that there is another home more suited to you.

4. Who is the stranger in your mind? Either fear or you are unsuited to the home Which God provided for you who are One with God. God did not make fear; fear is unlike God in every way, and it is not fear that completes God or that is completed by God. Love and fear cannot coexist, so your mind cannot be a home to both Love and fear. If you are real, then fear must be an illusion, but if fear is real, then you do not exist at all.

5. How simply, then, the question is resolved. In fear, you only deny yourself and say, 'I am a stranger in my own mind, so I leave it to something more like me than myself, and I give it all that I thought belonged to me.' Now you are exiled, not knowing who you are, uncertain of everything but this: You are not yourself, and you have been denied your home.

6. Now, you must search for a home. But, being a stranger to yourself, you cannot find one, no matter where you look, because you have made your return to your real home impossible. You have been lost, but now a miracle can find you and teach you that you are not a stranger in your own mind. The miracle will come, because your True Self is still in your mind. It did not ask a stranger to come into your mind, and It did not ask an alien thought to be Itself. Your True Self calls you to Itself, because It recognizes Its Own.

7. Who is the stranger in your mind? The one that your True Self does not call to. You have been unable to recognize this other self as the stranger because you gave it your rightful place, but your True Self is as certain of you as God is certain of your True Self. God is not confused about Its Own Extension, and no stranger can be interposed between God's Knowledge and the Reality of God's Extension. God doesn't know about strangers; God is only certain of you, Its Own Extension.

8. God's Certainty is enough. You who are One with God belong in God, Where God has placed you Forever. God has answered your question, 'Who is the stranger in my mind?' Hear the Holy Spirit assure you, Quietly and Confidently, that you are not a stranger to God, nor is God a stranger to you. You are joined with God Forever in Oneness; you are at Home in God, and no stranger to your True Self.

9. Today, thank God that Christ has come to your mind to find Its Self. Your Christ Mind's Real Perception does not see a stranger, but sees you who are One with Christ, and It joyously unites with you. You see the Christ in you as a stranger because you do not recognize your True Self, but, as you welcome Christ, you will remember. Christ leads you gently Home to God, Where you belong.

10. Christ does not forget any part of your mind, so It gives you a Perception of the part of your mind where you perceive a world for you to remember Christ, so that your mind can be as Complete and Perfect as it was established by God. Your Christ Mind has not forgotten you, but you will not remember It until you perceive only

Christ. When you refuse to extend Christ in your perception, you deny Christ in yourself, and you refuse the Gift by Which you clearly recognize your True Self, your Home, and your salvation.

Mentor's Notes

Remember, this course addresses you as the decision maker. You are really One with God, but you have made a personal self, referred to as 'fear' or the 'stranger' in this lesson. You have the choice to identify with What you are or with what you made.

Lesson 161

'Holy Extension of God, give me your blessing.'

1. Today, you will practice in a different manner and take a stand against your anger, so that your fears will disappear and offer room to Love. Your salvation is in today's simple words. Here, you answer your temptation to see yourself separate from God by welcoming Christ where fear and anger prevailed before. Here is your Atonement completed, the world is gone, and Heaven is restored to your mind. Here is the Holy Spirit's Answer.

2. The natural condition of your Mind is Complete Abstraction, but part of It is now unnatural. This part does not look on everything as One. Instead, it sees fragments of a whole, and this is how it invents the incomplete world that you perceive. The purpose of all perception is to show you what you want to see, and everything that you hear is what you want to hear.

3. This is how you made specifics, and the Holy Spirit must use specifics for your practicing. The Holy Spirit uses them for a purpose that is different from the purpose of separation that you gave to them. The Holy Spirit uses what you made to teach you from a different point of view, so you can see a different purpose for everything.

4. One person that you perceive can represent your entire mind, because your mind is One. This is the truth, and it should make clear to you the meaning of *extension*. These words can bring perfect clarity to you, or they can seem to you to be empty sounds that you find pretty, correct in sentiment, but not something that you fundamentally understand. You have taught yourself to think specifically so you no longer grasp *abstraction* in the sense that it is all-encompassing. You need to perceive a little, so that you learn a lot.

5. It seems to you that the body limits you, makes you suffer, and finally ends your life. But the body is only a concrete form of fear. Fear needs a symbol for you to respond to, though symbols can, and do, stand for the meaningless. Fear is false, so you attach it to specific

symbols to give it forms that make it seem real. But Love, being True, does not need symbols.

6. A body that seems to contain a separate mind can attack, but a Mind that is One cannot. This is why bodies are so easily the symbol of fear for you. You are often urged to overlook bodies, because they represent Love's 'enemy', and your Christ Mind's Real Perception cannot see them. A body is always the target for your attack, because you do not think in terms of hating a mind. But only your mind directs the body to attack. Only what thinks of fear can be the source of fear.

7. Hate is specific. You must attack *something*. You must perceive an 'enemy' in a form that can be touched, seen, heard, and ultimately killed. When you hate something, you are clearly calling for its death, as certainly as the Holy Spirit proclaims that there is no death. Fear is insatiable, consuming everything that it perceives, and seeing itself in everything, compelling it to turn on itself and destroy.

8. When you look on a body, you see fear and you attack, because what you perceive is your own fear externalized, poised to attack you, and longing to unite with you again. Do not mistake the intensity of the rage that your projected fear causes in you. It shrieks in wrath and claws the air, frantically hoping it can reach you and devour you.

9. This is what is in your mind when you look on a body, where Heaven sees Love and Perfection to cherish instead. The Reality of your mind is that it is Perfect in God. In the Real Perception of your Christ Mind, your Loveliness is reflected in a form so Holy and Beautiful that you will want to kneel before It. And you will join with this Perception, because you are One with It. Attack another, and you will make your mind an enemy to you, and you will not see that in your perception of them you could find your salvation. Extend salvation to replace your perception of a body, and you will receive salvation. Do not make another a symbol of fear, unless you want to ask the Love in you to destroy Itself. Instead, let Love reveal

Itself to you, and set yourself free.

10. Today, you will practice in a form that you used earlier. You are more prepared now, and you will grow closer to your Real Perception. If you are intent on reaching It, you will succeed today. Once you have succeeded, you will not be willing to accept the witnesses that they body's eyes see. What you will perceive will remind you of What you knew before. Heaven has not forgotten you; now you will remember Heaven.

11. Select one person to be a symbol for your entire mind, and seek salvation in them. See them clearly in the form that you are used to seeing. See their face, hands, feet, and clothing. Watch them smile, and use familiar gestures. Then think of this: What you are seeing now conceals from you the Real Perception that can forgive your 'sins' and remove your pain. Ask this of the one on whom you look so you can be free:

> 'Holy Extension of God, give me your blessing. I want to perceive with Christ's Real Perception, and to see my Perfect Innocence in place of a body.'

12. Your Christ Mind will answer your call, because It hears the Holy Spirit in you and answers you with your own Voice. Look where you used to see flesh and bone, and recognize that Christ is here. Today's idea is your safe escape from anger and fear. Be sure to use it instantly when you are tempted to attack another and see them as a symbol of your fear. You will see them suddenly transformed from enemy to Savior; from devil to Christ.

Lesson 162

'I am as God created me.'

1. This single thought, held firmly in your mind, can save you. From time to time you will repeat it as you reach another stage of learning. It will mean more to you as you advance. These words are sacred, because they are the words that God gives to you in answer to the world that you made. By these words, the world and all of the illusions in it disappear from your mind.

2. These words are the Word by Which you are God's Happiness, Love, and Completion. Here, you proclaim and honor God's Extension as you are. These words dispel from your mind every illusion and thought of separation from God. They herald the re-awakening of your entire mind to God. Hear them, and you will never look on death.

3. You are Holy indeed as you make these words your own as you arise in the morning, recall them throughout the day, and bring them with you as you go to sleep at night. Your dreams will be happy, your rest secure, your safety certain, and the body healed, because you sleep and awaken with the Truth in front of you. You bring with you the part of your mind where you perceive a world, because you extend these words of Truth to all that you perceive each time that you practice with them.

4. Today, you will practice simply, because these words are Mighty, and you do not need any words beyond them to change your mind. So completely can they change your mind that your mind will become the Treasury in Which God places all of Its Gifts and Love, to be extended by you, and therefore increased in your awareness. You keep God's Treasure Complete by sharing It without limit, and this is how you learn to think with God. Your Christ Mind's Real Perception restores your mind by saving it for God.

5. You honor yourself today. You have the Right to the Perfect Holiness that you accept now. By your acceptance, you save your entire mind, because you will not cherish the idea of sin when you

have Holiness and blessing to extend. You will not despair, because Perfect Joy is yours as a remedy for any appearance of grief, misery, or loss, and as complete escape from all thoughts of sin and guilt.

6. And you will be the redeemer for all that you perceive as all that you perceive will redeem and save you. Your Holiness will extend to all that you perceive, and you will feel welcomed by Love everywhere. You are One with God. These words dispel all darkness from your mind. God's Light has come into your mind today to bless all that you perceive, because you have recognized yourself as God's Extension, and you join your entire mind in this recognition.

Mentor's Notes

The past few lessons have been hammering home the awareness that you must see all that you perceive as you see yourself. This is because it is not the personal self that is One with God; your entire mind is One with God. Your entire mind is what you think of as 'you' along with what your mind perceives, because thoughts do not leave the mind of the thinker. Your Mind is One, so It is Everywhere. But the personal mind sees itself one way, and it perceives a world outside of itself that is different from it. If your experience of being One with God happens within you but does not extend in your perception, then you can be sure that you are not experiencing Oneness with God; you are experiencing the personal mind. When you truly experience your Oneness with God, it automatically extends in your perception. You can also invite the experience of Oneness by choosing to consciously overlook the world and extend God's Love and Peace and Joy in your awareness. Choosing to do this consciously expresses your willingness to have the actual experience.

Lesson 163

'There is no death. I am Limitless in God.'

1. Death is an idea that takes on many forms that you may not recognize: Sadness, fear, anxiety, doubt, anger, lack of faith and trust in God, concern for the body, envy, and all forms of your wishing to be what you are not. All of these thoughts reflect your worshiping death as your savior.

2. The idea of death seems strong to you as the embodiment of your fear, the host of your 'sin', your 'god' in your guilt, and the 'lord' of all of your illusions and deceptions. It seems to hold your 'life' in its withered hand, all of the personal mind's hopes in its blighted grasp, and you perceive all of the personal mind's goals through its sightless eyes. When you feel frail, helpless, and sick, you bow down before death, because you think it alone is real, inevitable, and worthy of your trust. Death alone seems certain to come to you.

3. In your identification with a personal self, everything but death seems uncertain; too quickly lost, no matter how hard to gain; apt to fail the hopes that they once engendered in you; and you are left with dust and ashes in place of your aspirations and dreams. But you can count on death, because it will certainly come in time and take all of 'life'.

4. Do you want to bow down to this idol? You perceive God's Strength and Might in death. It is this opposite of God that you proclaim the 'lord of creation', stronger than God's Will for Life, Limitless Love, and Heaven's Perfect Constancy. Death is meant to defeat God's Will and your Will, and to lay you who are One with God in a body to rest beneath a headstone.

5. In defeat, you are made unholy, because you become what death wants you to be. Your epitaph, written by death itself, says, 'Here lies a witness that God is dead.' This is written again and again while you, who worship death, agree with it.

6. It is impossible for you to worship death in any form and still

select a few forms in which you do not want to believe, because death is total. Either death or Eternal Life is real; no compromise is possible. Here again you see an obvious position that you must accept if you want to be sane: What contradicts a thought entirely is true only if the thought is false.

7. The idea that God is dead is so preposterous that even the insane have difficulty believing in it. It implies that a stronger will triumphed over the All-Powerful and that Eternal Life gave way to death. And since the Source of Life is dead, you died as well.

8. Worshiping death, you are afraid, but can these thoughts be frightening? If you see that it is only this that you believe, you will be released. And you can demonstrate this today. There is no death; for your own salvation, renounce it now in every form. God did not make death, so whatever form it takes is an illusion. Take this stand today, because you have it in you to look past death and see Life beyond it.

9. *'Dear God, bless my perception today. I am Your messenger, and I want to look on the Glorious Reflection of Your Love, Which shines Everywhere. I live and move only in You, because I am not separate from Your Eternal Life. There is no death, because death is not Your Will. I abide Where you placed Me, in the Life that I share with You, Who is All Life, to be like You and Part of You Forever. I accept Your Thoughts as my own, and my will is One with Yours. Amen.'*

Mentor's Notes

Really, all experiences of the personal self represent death, because the personal self inevitably 'dies', and it is meant to represent the 'death' of God in your mind.

The italicized quote at the end represents a prayer.

Lesson 164

'Now I am One with God, my Source.'

1. You can only recognize Truth *now*. The present is the only time that there is, and so today, this instant, *now*, you perceive What is Forever here, not with the body's eyes, but with your Real Perception. With your Christ Mind, you look past time to Eternity. The noise of the senseless, busy world fades into the background, because the Sounds of Heaven and the Voice of the Holy Spirit are closer and clearer to you, and What you hear from Them has more meaning for you.

2. The world fades away easily in your Real Perception. Its noise grows dim as a Sound from far beyond the world becomes more and more distinct to you. You hear a Timeless Call to Which your Christ Mind gives a Timeless Answer. You will recognize this Answer, because It is your answer to God's Call to you. Christ answers for you, because It is your Self, and It answers with your consent and accepts your salvation for you.

3. Your practicing will be Holy today, because your Christ Mind gives you Its Perception, and It hears and answers God's Call for you. How quiet is the time that you will spend with Christ beyond the world; how easily you will forget all of your seeming sins and sorrows! Today, you will lay aside grief, because a Perception and Sound that come from What is closer to you than the world that you perceive are now clear to you as you accept the Gifts that God gives to you.

4. There is a Silence upon Which the world cannot intrude, there is a Timeless Peace that you carry within you and have never lost, there is a Holiness in you that the thought of separation from God has never touched. You will remember all of This today. Your faithfulness in practicing today will bring you Rewards so great, and so completely different from all of the things that you sought before, that you will know that This is your Treasure, and Here you rest.

5. This is the day when your vain illusions part like a curtain in

your mind to reveal What lies beyond them. You will see What is really in your mind, while the darkness that seemed to hide It merely sinks away. The scale of judgment will be balanced as judgment is left to the Holy Spirit, Which judges True. In the Holy Spirit's Judgment, a Perception of Perfect Innocence will unfold before you, and you will see It through your Christ Mind, as the transformation of your mind is made clear to you.

6. This day is sacred for your entire mind. From your Real Perception, Which is given to you from beyond the world, you will look back on the world in a new Light. What you see will be your healing and your salvation. You will clearly perceive and recognize the Valuable and the valueless for what they are, and What is worthy of your Love will receive your Love, and nothing else will remain.

7. You will not judge with the personal mind today, but you will receive What is given to you from a Judgment that comes from far beyond the world. Your practicing today will be your gift of gratitude for your release from denial of God and misery. All that you will perceive will increase your Joy, because the Holiness that you will perceive will reflect your own. You are forgiven in Christ's Perception as you forgive the world that you perceive. Bless all that you perceive as you perceive in it the Light in Which your Christ Mind looks on you, and offer your entire mind the freedom that you receive from the forgiving Perception of your Christ Mind.

8. Open the curtain of your mind in your practicing today by merely letting go of all that you think that you want. Put away the trifling treasures that you seek with a personal mind, and leave a clean and open space within your mind where Christ can come and offer you the Treasure of salvation. Christ needs you to save your entire mind, and this is the only purpose worthy of you. The Real Perception of your Christ Mind is more worthy of your seeking than all of the world's unsatisfying goals.

9. Do not let today slip by without receiving and accepting the Gifts that it holds out for you. You can change your entire mind if you acknowledge Them. You may not see the value in your accep-

tance, but you surely want to exchange all suffering for Joy today. Practice in earnest, and the Gift is yours. God does not deceive you, and God's Promises cannot fail. Do not withhold so little, when God holds out complete salvation to you.

Lesson 165

'I will not deny the Thought of God.'

1. The only thing that makes the world that you perceive seem real to you is your own denial of the Truth that lies beyond it. Only your thoughts of misery and death obscure the Happiness and Eternal Life that God wills for you, only illusions can hide What cannot be concealed in Truth, and only your choice to deny What is here keeps you from accepting What you already have.

2. The Thought of God is your Source. It has not left you, nor have you been apart from It for an instant. It belongs to you; by It you live. It holds you One with It, and Everything is One with you, because It has not left you. The Thought of God protects you, cares for you, makes a Soft Resting Place for you, and, in your perception that you are in a world, It makes your path smooth, lighting your mind with Happiness and Love. Eternity and Everlasting Life shine in your mind, because the Thought of God has not left you and still abides with you.

3. You would not deny your Safety, your Peace, your Joy, your healing, your Quiet Rest, and your calm awakening if you recognized that They abide within you. You would instantly prepare to go within and abandon everything else that is worthless in comparison. And once you found Them, you would make sure that They stayed with you.

4. Do not deny Heaven; It is yours today if you ask for It. You do not need to perceive, before it comes to you, how great a Gift It is, nor how It will change your mind. Ask for Heaven, and It will be given to you. You will be certain of Heaven as you receive It; until then, you will doubt It. But God is fair, and your certainty is not required for you to receive the Certainty that only your acceptance of Heaven can bestow on you.

5. Ask with true desire, but you do not need to be sure that you are requesting the *only* thing that you want. Yet, when you receive It, you *will* be sure that you have the Treasure that you have always

sought. Then, there will be nothing that you will exchange for It. Nothing will induce you to let It fade from your ecstatic perception, because you will perceive that you exchanged deliberate blindness for the Real Perception of your Christ Mind. Your mind will have come to lay aside denial to accept the Thought of God that belongs to it.

6. All of your doubting will be past, the end of your journey will be certain, and you will be saved. Christ's Power will be in your awareness to extend healing as you were healed. You will take your place as the savior of your entire mind; your destiny lies here and nowhere else. God would never let you who are One with God remain forever in a perception of lack that deprives you of your Knowledge of your Wholeness because of your own denial. God's Abundance is within you, and self-deprivation cannot cut you off from God's Sustaining Love, and your Home.

7. Practice with hope today, because your hope is indeed justified. Your doubts are meaningless, because God is Certain. The Thought of God is never absent from you, and Certainty must be in you who are One with God. This course removes all doubts that you have interposed between God and your Certainty of God.

8. Count on God, and not on the personal mind, to give you Certainty. Practice in the Name of God, as God's Word directs you to. God's Sureness lies beyond every doubt in your mind. God's Love remains beyond your every fear. The Thought of God is still beyond all of your illusions, and is in your mind as God wills.

Mentor's Notes

The Thought of God is another name for the Holy Spirit.

Lesson 166

'God entrusts me with Its Gifts.'

1. All things are given to you. God's Trust in you is Limitless, because God knows you as One with God. God gives to you without exception, and holds nothing back that can contribute to your happiness, but unless your will is One with God's Will, you will not receive God's Gifts. What makes you think that there is a will other than God's?

2. This is the paradox that makes the world that you perceive. This world is not God's Will, so it is not real. So, if you think that the world is real, you must believe that there is another will, and one that leads to the opposite of God. This is impossible, of course, but when you look at the world and judge it as real, solid, and trustworthy, you either believe in two creators, or in one, yourself. But never in only One God.

3. When you hold such strange beliefs, the Gifts of God are not acceptable to you, because you believe that for you to accept God's Gifts, no matter how obvious They become, or how pressed you may feel to accept Them, is for you to be treacherous to yourself. You must deny Their Presence, contradict the Truth, and suffer to preserve the world that you made.

4. In this case, the world is the only home that you think you know, and the only safety that you think that you can find. You fear that, without the world that you made, you will be homeless and afraid. You do not realize that it is in the world that you are afraid and homeless, and wandering so far from your Real Home that you have forgotten Where you came from, where you are going, and even What you really are.

5. But, even in your lonely, senseless wanderings, God's Gifts go with you, though you don't recognize Them. You cannot lose Them, but you won't look at Them. You wander on, aware of the futility that you perceive everywhere in the world, watching the little that you have dwindle as you go nowhere. Though God goes with you, and

you have a Treasure so Great that everything in the world that you perceive is valueless before Its Magnitude, you wander on in misery and poverty.

6. You seem to be a worn and weary and sorry figure that walks a painful road. You see this tragic, hopeless story not just for yourself, but in some form for everyone that you perceive in the world. But is it really tragic, when you see that it is a choice, and you only need to realize that God is with you, and that all of God's Treasures are yours?

7. This is the story of your chosen self, the one that you made to replace your Reality. This is the self that you savagely defend against all sense and proof that shows you that it is not you. You do not heed the evidence, but you go the way that you have chosen with your eyes cast downward, so that you will not catch a glimpse of Truth and be released from self-deception.

8. You cower fearfully away from your Christ Mind and Its Gentle Direction to look on your Gifts, then you proclaim that you have been deprived and sent into exile. With your Christ Mind, you could only laugh at this perception of yourself. It undoes all of your self-pity, as well as the tragedy that you sought to make for yourself, whom God intended only for Joy.

9. Your old fear has come upon you now, and God's Justice has caught up with you at last! Your Christ Mind has come into your awareness, and you feel that you are not alone. You even think it's possible that the miserable self that you thought you were might not be your real identity. You think that perhaps God's Word is truer than your own, and God's Gifts to you are Real. Perhaps, God has not been wholly outwitted by your plan to keep yourself in deep oblivion by taking a road away from your True Self.

10. God's Will does not oppose; It merely is. It is not God that you have limited with your plan to lose your True Self. God doesn't know about a plan so alien to Its Will. You had a need that God did not understand, to which God gave an Answer; that is all. And you have no need but this Answer.

11. Now you live and cannot die. Your wish for death is answered, and the eyes that looked on death have been replaced by a Perception that sees that you are not what you have pretended to be. The Holy Spirit walks with you, and It gently answers all of your fears with this one merciful phrase: 'It is not real.' The Holy Spirit points to all of your Gifts each time that the thought of lack oppresses you, and It reminds you of Its Companionship every time you perceive yourself as lonely and afraid.

12. And the Holy Spirit reminds you of one more thing that you have forgotten: Its Presence in you has made you like Itself. The Gifts that you have are not for you alone in a personal self. What the Holy Spirit gives to you, you must now extend in your awareness. This is the lesson that the Holy Spirit's giving holds for you, because the Holy Spirit saves you from the solitude of a split mind that you tried to make to hide from God. The Holy Spirit has reminded you of all of God's Gifts to you, and speaks to you as well of what becomes your will when you accept these Gifts and recognize that they are your own.

13. God's Gifts are yours, entrusted to your care, to extend to the lonely world that is now behind you. The world was once your wish, but you can teach yourself now that you have learned of your Christ Mind that there is another way to walk. Teach by extending your Happiness in recognition of your Christ Mind and God's Gifts. Do not let sorrow tempt you to be unfaithful to your trust.

14. Your sighs and tears will now betray the extension of your Hope; if you are sick, you will not extend healing, and what you fear will justify the fearful world that you perceive. You can extend Christ to all that you perceive, and your change of mind can become the 'proof' that, when you accept God's Gifts, you cannot suffer from anything. You are entrusted with your entire mind's release from pain.

15. Do not betray this trust. Become the living proof of What your Christ Mind can extend everywhere. God has entrusted all of Its Gifts to you. Let your Happiness be the Witness to your transformed

mind, which has chosen to accept God's Gifts, and to be aware that it is Christ. This is your mission now, because God entrusted the extension of Its Gifts to you when you received Them. God shares Its Joy with you; now you can extend It to be all that you perceive.

Lesson 167

'There is One Life, Which I share with God.'

1. Just as with Truth, there are not different kinds of Life. Life does not have degrees; It is the One Condition of God's Extension. Like all of God's Thoughts, Life does not have an opposite. There is no death, because God's Extension shares God's Life; there is no death, because God does not have an opposite; there is no death, because God and God's Extension are One.

2. In the world that you perceive, Life seems to have an opposite, which you call *death*. And you have learned that death takes many forms; it is the one idea that underlies all feelings that are not Supreme Happiness. Death is signaled by anything that is not Perfect Joy. All sorrow, loss, anxiety, suffering, and pain; even a little sigh of weariness, a feeling of slight discomfort, or the tiniest frown, are your acknowledgement that death is real. This is how you deny that you live.

3. You think that death is of the body, but it is an idea that is irrelevant to physical form. An idea is in your mind, and you apply it as your mind directs. Where an idea originates is where it needs to be changed, if you want change to occur. *Ideas do not leave their source.* The emphasis that this course places on this idea is due to the crucial part it plays in your changing your mind about yourself. This idea is the reason that you can heal; it is the cause of your healing. It is why you cannot die. The truth of this idea establishes you as One with God.

4. Death is your 'proof' that you are separate from God. It is your belief that your Condition can change, and that your emotions can alternate, because of forces beyond your control. It is your belief that, as God's Idea, you can leave your Source, and take on qualities unlike your Source, become different from It, and apart from It in distance, time, and form as well.

5. But death cannot come from Life, and you remain united to your Source, Which is Life. So you can extend God's Life, and so

extend your True Self, but you cannot extend what was not given to you by God. What you extend must be What God extends to you. This is why you will return to God, Which is Where you come from.

6. You can think that you are unaware of God, but that is all. You cannot change What you are in God. You cannot make a body real, nor abide in a body. What is alien to your Mind in God does not exist, because it does not have a real source. God's Mind creates Everything that exists, and you cannot make attributes that God lacks, nor change your own Eternal State of Mind. You cannot make the physical real, so the death of a body is only a sign that you have chosen to be unaware of God.

7. Life does not have an opposite, so what seems to be the opposite of Life is only Life made into form. It can therefore be reconciled with Life. In the world that you perceive, Life may appear to be what It is *not*, but your mind is *mind*, whether you are aware of God or not. And your mind is not its own opposite, and neither is the world that you think that you make when you choose to be unaware of God.

8. The Mind that God extends is only aware of God. There is no Part of God's Mind that is unaware of God, or that makes conditions that It does not share with God. Your concept of death is not the opposite of Life, because God has no opposite, is Forever Changeless, and extends Itself Infinitely and Eternally.

9. Death, which seems to be the opposite of God, is only your denial of God. When you choose to be what you are not, to give your power to an alien will that does not exist, to enter into a state that is not real, and to live in a condition that is unlike God in every way, you are only going into denial. And, in your denial, you seem to live in time, where what seems to happen has never occurred, where the changes that occur are not really changes at all, and where everything that happens is an illusion. When you choose to become aware of God again, your Mind will simply go on as It was before.

10. Today, be One with Truth, and do not deny your Holiness. Your life is not what you are imagining that it is. You did not change

Life by denying It and making illusions. Do not ask for death in any form today, and do not let imagined opposites to Life abide in your mind, where Eternal Life has been placed by God.

11. Today, strive to keep your Mind, God's Holy Home, as God wills It to be Forever. God is in charge of what you think today, and in God's Thoughts, Which have no opposite, you will understand that there is One Life, Which you share with God and with God's Total Extension in Oneness. Life cannot separate from Life in death.

12. You have One Life, because you have One Source from Which your Perfection comes to you, remaining always Holy in your mind; as you were, are now, and will Forever be. You will put aside denial as you see that your own Perfection reflects God so Perfectly that It blends into God. Your mind will not remain only a Reflection of God, but will become God. You will no longer need perception when you are wholly aware again of God, because you will know your Source, your Self, and your Holiness.

Lesson 168

'God, You give to me your Grace; I claim It now.'

1. God speaks to you, so why don't you speak to God? God is not distant and does not try to hide from you. But you try to hide from God, and you suffer from your self-deception. God is entirely Accessible to you, because God is One with you. This is the only Thing that is Certain, and It is enough. God Loves you Eternally, even when you think that you deny God. And, when you are willing to be aware of God again, God's Love will still be Unchanged.

2. If you knew the Meaning of God's Love, you would have neither hope nor despair. You would not need hope or despair, because you would have Everything, so nothing to hope for, and nothing to be in despair about. God's Grace is God's Answer to your despair, because in It you remember God's Love. God gladly gives you the Means by Which you will recognize God's Will. You will experience God's Grace when you acknowledge It. The Memory of God returns to your mind when you ask for the Means that God gives to you to be aware of God again.

3. Today, ask God for the Gift that God has most carefully preserved in your mind, and Which is only waiting for your acknowledgment. This is the Gift by Which God reaches you and takes the final step in your salvation. Every other step you learn through the Holy Spirit, but in the end, God comes Itself and sweeps away all the loose threads of denial that remain in your mind. God's Gift of Grace is more than just an Answer. It restores to your mind All that you chose to forget; all Certainty of Love's Meaning.

4. God loves you as Part of God. Request of God the Means by Which the world will disappear from your mind. Your Real Perception will come first, and Knowledge of God an instant later. In Grace, you perceive God's Light covering all that you perceive in Love, and you watch all fear disappear. Nothing remains to delay Heaven an instant longer. There is nothing still undone when you forgive everything.

5. Today is a new and Holy day for you, because you receive What has been given to you. Rest your faith in the Giver of God's Gift, not in your own acceptance. You must acknowledge your mistakes, but God, Which does not know of error, is the One that corrects them by giving you the Means to lay them down and return to God in Gratitude and Love.

6. God comes to meet you as you go to meet God, and What God gives to you, you receive. This is God's Will, because God loves you, who extend God's Will. Pray to God today, returning to God the words that God gives to you through Its Holy Spirit:

'God, You give to me Your Grace; I claim It now. As I go to You, You come to me as I request, because You love me.'

Mentor's Notes

The way that this course uses the term, *Grace* is an awareness of God within you that hovers between Revelation and the miracle. It is the awareness of God's Love within you that you extend through the miracle, but It does not quite reach to Revelation, Which is a direct experience of God. Grace inspires the miracle, and it is also the State of Mind with which you return to an awareness of the world after Revelation.

Lesson 169

'I live by Grace; I am released from limitations by Grace.'

1. Grace is an Aspect of God's Love, and It is most like the State of Oneness in Truth. It is your most lofty aspiration in your perception that you are in a world, because It leads you beyond the world entirely. It is past what you can learn, but It is the Goal of your learning, because Grace can only come to your mind when you are prepared to accept Truth. Your experience of Grace is inevitable when your mind has been prepared, is clear of guilt and fear, and you are willing to receive It.

2. Your experience of Grace comes from your acceptance of God's Love while you perceive yourself within a hateful and fearful world. Through God's Grace alone, hate and fear disappear from your mind and all that it perceives, because Grace represents a State that is the opposite of all that you perceive in the world. When your mind is lit with the Gift of Grace, you will not believe that the world of fear is real.

3. You do not learn Grace, because It is the Final Step beyond all learning. You will not attain Grace through this course, but this course prepares you for Grace by teaching you to open your mind to God's Call. When your mind is not shut tight against the Holy Spirit, and you have become aware that there are Things that you do not know in your identification with a personal self, you will be ready to accept a State that is completely different from the experience of the personal mind that you find familiar and call 'home'.

4. This might seem to contradict an earlier statement, in Lesson 158, which says that the Revelation of your Oneness with God has already occurred. But that lesson also says that your mind has to be prepared for Revelation. You are urged to be a witness to the Holy Spirit to hasten your direct experience of the Truth, and to speed the awareness of Truth to your entire mind.

5. Oneness is simply the idea *God is*. God's Being encompasses All That is Real. In Truth, your mind holds only God. Say, *'God is'*,

then cease to speak, because in that Knowledge words are meaningless. There is no mouth to speak them, and no part of Mind that is separate and could feel that it is now aware of Something that is not itself. Mind is One, and, like God, it merely *is*.

6. You cannot speak or write or even think of This at all. God comes to your mind when you have totally recognized that God's Will is your will. Revelation returns your mind to the Endless Present, Where you cannot even conceive of *past* or *future*. It lies beyond salvation, past time, past forgiveness, and even past Christ Consciousness. You merely blend into God as God blends into you. The world has never been at all Where Eternity is the Constant State.

7. But What you are trying to hasten is beyond your current experience. Forgiving, which you teach and learn simultaneously, will bring you Experiences that witness that the time of Revelation is here now. So you cannot really hasten Revelation, because It is already here, only concealed, except from the Holy Spirit, Which teaches you what forgiving means.

8. All that you have to learn is already in the Holy Spirit in your mind, accomplished and complete. The Holy Spirit recognizes that you think that you are in time, and It gives time to you, so that, from the Holy Spirit within you, Which stands outside of time, you can determine when you want to be released to Revelation and Eternity. Remember, you seem to be making a journey that is already over.

9. Oneness must be here. To a Constant State that is Forever the Same, it is entirely irrelevant when you are ready for Revelation. You only *seem* to be taking part in a 'script' that the Holy Spirit has 'written' for your salvation in God's Name and your Name.

10. There is no need to clarify further what you cannot understand apart from God. When you experience Revelation of your Oneness with God, you will fully know and understand God. Now you have work to do, because in time you can teach and learn What is beyond time.

11. The Ending will remain obscure to you until you play your part in the Holy Spirit's 'script'. This does not matter, because your

entire mind depends on what you are learning *now*. As you play the 'role' assigned to you, salvation comes closer to your entire mind, where you do not yet perceive only God.

12. *Forgiving* is the central theme that runs throughout the 'script' for your salvation. It holds everything that you encounter in a meaningful relationship, directs the course you will take, and assures its outcome. Now is the time for you to ask for Grace, the final Gift that the plan for your salvation can bestow. The Experience that Grace provides you will end in time, because Grace foreshadows Heaven, but It does not yet replace time.

13. An interval of Grace is enough. It is in Grace that your miracles are laid from the Holy Instants that you receive. Through the Grace of your Experience of God, you will extend the Holy Instant to be all that you perceive. Your awareness of Christ is the result of your moment in Timelessness, and It brings back a Clear Reflection of the Oneness that you experienced to extend to all that you perceive. You cannot attain Christ while part of your mind still seems outside of you and in need of your extension of Truth.

14. Be grateful to return to an awareness of the world from Grace, and accept the Gifts that Grace provides you. You extend Them to your True Self. Revelation stands near; Its coming is ensured. Ask for the experience of Grace, and welcome the release that It offers to your entire mind. You are not asking for What you cannot ask for; you are not looking for more than Grace can give. The Grace that you extend is the Grace that you receive.

15. Your learning goal today does not exceed the prayer below. But, in your perception that you are in a world, there is nothing more that you can ask of the Holy Spirit.

'I live by Grace; I am released from limitations by Grace. I give by Grace; I will release my mind from limitations by Grace.'

Mentor's Notes

Paragraphs 7-9 revisit the ideas laid out in Lesson 158. Remember, only in time does time, and a story for time, have meaning. In Eternity, Which is Time*less*ness, and Which you enter in Revelation, time does not exist, even as a concept. So all that you seem to learn in time you already know in Eternity. From the Holy Spirit' Perspective, then, the purpose of time is not for you to attain a future State, but for you to prepare to enter Timelessness *now*.

The Holy Spirit's 'script' is merely another name for the Holy Spirit's 'plan'. This is the specific lesson plan that the Holy Spirit has designed for you to remember your Oneness with God.

At Its Ultimate, a *Holy Instant* is Revelation. Practicing the Holy Instant, then, is asking for Revelation. In practice, you will experience the Holy Instant in 'degrees', which don't really exist, because the Holy Instant is always Total. But you determine for yourself how much of God you want to experience in any given instant.

Lesson 170

'There is no cruelty in God, so there is none in me.'

1. You only attack with the intention of hurting, and there is no exception to this. When you think that you attack in self-defense, you teach yourself that to be cruel is protection, and you think that you are safe because you are cruel. You think that to hurt another brings you freedom, and that to attack is to exchange the state in which you perceive yourself for something better, safer, and more secure from invasion and fear.

2. It is thoroughly insane for you to believe that you need to attack to defend yourself from fear, because attacking is how you *perpetuate* fear and make it grow. This is how you protect fear, not escape from fear. Today, you will learn a lesson that can save you from more wasted time and needless misery than you can possibly imagine. This is it:

> You make what you defend yourself against. By your own defense against it, you make it real and inescapable to you. Only by laying down your defenses will you learn that what you perceive is not real.

3. It seems like there is an 'enemy' outside of you who attacks you, but your defenses set you up with an enemy within you: fear. Your mind then splits in two, part of it within you and part of it outside of you, which deprives you of Peace. Now, you who are Love have an 'enemy', an opposite, and fear, which now seems to be you, needs to be defended against What you really are.

4. Consider carefully the means by which your imagined self-defense proceeds, and you will perceive the premises on which it stands. First, it is obvious that you believe that ideas can leave the mind that thinks them, because you are the one who thinks of attack, then perceives it outside of you. You split your mind into 'you' and a world outside of you with perfect faith that this split is real.

5. Next, you bestow the Attributes of Love onto Its opposite, fear. Fear becomes your safety, the protector of your peace, your solace, your escape from doubts about your strength, and your hope of rest. Since you have stripped Love of the Attributes that belong to It alone, you now endow Love with the attributes of fear, because Love asks you to lay down all defenses in recognition that they are foolish. And your defenses *will* crumble into dust, because this is what they are, and knowing this scares you.

6. With Love as your enemy, cruelty becomes your god. The god of cruelty demands that you, who worship it, obey its dictates and refuse to question them. You are punished harshly if you ask if cruelty's demands are sensible or sane. Cruelty teaches you that its enemy, Love, is What is unreasonable and insane, while it is always merciful and just.

7. Today, you will look on this cruel god with detachment. Note that though its lips are smeared with blood, and fire seems to flame from it, that it is made of stone. It can do nothing, so you don't need to defy its power. It has none. When you see in it your safety, you have no guardian, no strength to call upon in danger, and no warrior to fight for you.

8. This moment can be terrible for you, but it can also be a time of release for you. Seeing this idol exactly as it is, you have a choice to make: Will you restore yourself to Love? Or will you make another idol to replace this one? The god of cruelty takes many forms, so you can always make another.

9. But do not think that you can escape from fear with fear. Remember what the Text stresses about your obstacles to Peace: The final fear, the hardest for you to believe is nothing, the obstacle that seems like an insurmountable block, is your fear of God. This is the basic fear that enthrones fear as a god for you, because you love fear when you worship it, and Love then seems to be cruel.

10. Where does your totally insane belief in vengeful gods come from? It is not Love that has confused Its Attributes with those of fear. When you worship fear, you perceive your own confusion in Love,

and you see cruelty in It. Then nothing is more frightening to you than God, the Source of Love Itself. Blood seems to be on God's lips, fire seems to be coming from God, God seems to be terrible above all else, cruel beyond conception, and ready to strike you down.

11. The choice that you make today is certain, because you look for the last time upon the stone god that you made, and you will no longer call it god. You have reached this place before, but you have chosen that this cruel god stay with you in another form, so the fear of God has remained with you. This time, you leave fear of God behind you, and you accept a new Perception, unburdened by fear.

12. Now, your perception belongs to your Christ Mind, and you see through It. Now, your voice belongs to God and echoes God's Voice. And now, you are at Peace Forever. You have chosen God in place of idols, and the Attributes that are given to you by God are restored to you at last. You heard God's Call, and you answered. Fear gives way to Love, as God replaces cruelty.

13. *'God, I am like You: There is no cruelty in me, because there is none in You. Your Peace is mine, and I bless all that I perceive with What I have received only from You. I choose again, and I make the choice for all that I perceive, knowing that my mind is One. I extend Your salvation as I receive it from You now. I give thanks for All that I perceive, because It makes me complete. I perceive Your Glory and my Peace everywhere. My entire mind is Holy, because Your Holiness sets it free. I thank You. Amen.*

Mentor's Notes

The 'god of cruelty' is another name for the personal mind, which believes that attack is real and necessary to defend itself. It may seem strange to say that you 'worship' cruelty and fear, but this is what you are doing when you defend the personal self.

The reason that you can put your defenses down and be safe is that only the personal self needs defense, so your identification with it is your only attack on yourself. When you put down your defenses, you put down the personal self, and your Identity in God is restored to you.

Review 5

Introduction

1. Now, you have another review. This time, you are ready to give more effort and time to what you are undertaking. Recognize that you are preparing for another phase of understanding. You want to take this step completely, so that you can go on again with more certainty, more sincerity, and with total faith. You have wavered and doubted, so your learning has been uncertain and slow, but now you will go on more swiftly if you approach this step with greater certainty about your Goal, and a firmer sense of purpose.

2. *'Dear God, steady me. You will quiet my doubts and still my Holy mind as you speak to me. I have no words to give to You, because I would rather listen to Your Word and make It mine. Lead my practicing as I take this path that I do not yet understand. I will follow You, sure that I am safe, because You lead the way for me.*

3. *I give my practicing to You. If I stumble, You will raise me up; if I forget the way, You will remember for me; when I wander off, You will call me back to You. Quicken my footsteps now, so that I may walk more certainly and quickly to You. I accept the Holy Spirit that you offer to me to unify my practicing as I review the thoughts that you have given to me.'*

4. Below is the thought that should precede the thoughts that you review. Each thought will clarify some aspect of this thought, help to make it more meaningful to you, more true, or more descriptive of your Holy Self, which you are preparing to know again:

'God is only Love, therefore so am I.'

Your Holy Self alone knows Love; your Holy Self alone is Perfectly Consistent in Its Thoughts, knows God, understands Itself, is Perfect in Its Knowledge and Love, and never changes from Its Constant State of Oneness within Itself and with God.

5. And It is your Holy Self that waits to meet you at the end of your journey. Every step that you take brings you a little nearer to

your Goal. This review will shorten time for you immeasurably if you keep in mind that your Holy Self is your Goal, and, as you practice, This is What you are approaching. Raise your mind from death to Life as you remember What is promised to you, and that this course opens up the path of God's Light to you, and teaches you, step by step, how to return to the Eternal Self that you thought that you had lost.

6. The Christ in you takes the journey with you. It shares your doubts and fears a little while as you are lead by It, because It recognizes the road by which you overcome all of your fears and doubts. Because you walk with the Christ in you, It must understand your uncertainty and pain, although It knows that they have no meaning. Your Savior must remain with you as It teaches you, perceiving what you perceive, but still holding in Its Mind the way out for you. You are crucified, until you walk with the Christ in you.

7. Christ is resurrected in your mind when It has led you to the Place Where your journey ends, and you have forgotten it. Christ is renewed in your mind every time that you learn that there is a way out of misery and pain. Christ is reborn in your awareness whenever you turn to the Light within you and you look for Christ. Christ has not forgotten you, so help Christ to lead you back to where your journey began, so that you can make another choice with It.

8. Release Christ in you as you practice again the thoughts that Christ has brought to you from God. Your Christ Mind sees your bitter need, and knows the Answer that God has given to It for you. Review these thoughts with your Christ Mind, and devote your time and effort to them. From Christ, you will extend them to be all that you perceive. God does not want Heaven to be incomplete. Heaven waits for you, as the Christ in you waits for you. Your Christ Mind is incomplete without you, and as you make Christ Whole, you return to your Eternal Home, Which was prepared for you before you conceived of time, has been kept unchanged by time, and will be just as Immaculate and Safe when you let go of time.

9. Let this review period be the gift that you give to your Christ

Mind. This alone is all that the Christ in you needs: That you hear the words that It speaks and extend them in your perception. You are your Christ Mind's voice, eyes, feet, and hands as you extend Christ in your perception to save your entire mind. The Self from Which Christ calls to you is your own. This Self is Christ and you together. Bring with you all that you perceive, because this is not a path that you walk as a personal self. In Christ, you walk with all that you perceive, because your entire mind walks with you. God Wills that you be One with God. All that lives is One with You.

10. Let this review period be a time in which you seem to have a new experience with Christ that is really older than time. You are Holy; your Glory is undefiled Forever. Your Wholeness, as God established It, is renewed in your awareness. You are One with God, completing God's Extension through your own extension of God. In this review, you practice a Truth that you knew before you made illusions. Remind yourself that your mind is free from illusions every time that you say:

'God is only Love, therefore so am I.'

11. Start each day of your review with this. Start and end each practice period with this as well. Go to sleep with this thought, and waken with it again to greet another day. Surround each thought in your review with it, and use those thoughts to hold it in your mind. Keep this idea clear in your mind throughout the day. This is how, when you have finished the review, you will come to recognize that these words are true.

12. These words are only aids. Use them only at the beginning and end of the practice periods to remind you of their purpose. Place your faith in the *experience* that comes from practice, not in the words and means that you use for practice. Wait for the experience, understanding that this is what will bring you conviction in the words. Go beyond the words to their Meaning, Which is far beyond their sound. The sound will grow dim and disappear as you approach the Source

of their Meaning. It is Here that you will find Rest.

Mentor's Notes

Paragraph 7 mentions returning to where your journey began so that you can make another choice. In essence, your journey is one that takes you from your identification with a personal self to an awareness that you are the one split mind, the 'dreamer of the dream' of separation from God. Only in this awareness can you act as the decision maker and make the choice between the personal mind, which you made, and your Christ Mind, Which you are.

Lesson 171

'God is only Love, therefore so am I.'

(151) 'All things reflect the Holy Spirit.'

'God is only Love, therefore so am I.'

(152) 'The power of decision is mine.'

'God is only Love, therefore so am I.'

Lesson 172

'God is only Love, therefore so am I.'

(153) 'My Safety lies in my Defenselessness.'

'God is only Love, therefore so am I.'

(154) 'I am a messenger of God.'

'God is only Love, therefore so am I.'

Lesson 173

'God is only Love, therefore so am I.'

(155) 'I step back and let the Holy Spirit lead the way.'

'God is only Love, therefore so am I.'

(156) 'I walk with God in Perfect Holiness.'

'God is only Love, therefore so am I.'

Lesson 174

'God is only Love, therefore so am I.'

(157) 'I enter into Christ's Presence now.'

'God is only Love, therefore so am I.'

(158) 'Today, I learn to give as I receive.'

'God is only Love, therefore so am I.'

Lesson 175

'God is only Love, therefore so am I.'

(159) 'I give the miracles that I have received.'

'God is only Love, therefore so am I.'

(160) 'My mind is at Home in God. Fear is the stranger in my mind.'

'God is only Love, therefore so am I.'

Lesson 176

'God is only Love, therefore so am I.'

(161) 'Holy Extension of God, give me your blessing.'

'God is only Love, therefore so am I.'

(162) 'I am as God created me.'

'God is only Love, therefore so am I.'

Lesson 177

'God is only Love, therefore so am I.'

(163) 'There is no death. I am Limitless in God.'

'God is only Love, therefore so am I.'

(164) 'Now I am One with God, my Source.'

'God is only Love, therefore so am I.'

Lesson 178

'God is only Love, therefore so am I.'

(165) 'I will not deny the Thought of God.'

'God is only Love, therefore so am I.'

(166) 'God entrusts me with Its Gifts.'

'God is only Love, therefore so am I.'

Lesson 179

'God is only Love, therefore so am I.'

(167) 'There is only One Life, Which I share with God.'

'God is only Love, therefore so am I.'

(168) 'God, You give to me Your Grace; I claim It now.'

'God is only Love, therefore so am I.'

Lesson 180

'God is only Love, therefore so am I.'

(169) 'I live by Grace; I am released from limitations by Grace.'

'God is only Love, therefore so am I.'

(170) 'There is no cruelty in God, so there is none in me.'

'God is only Love, therefore so am I.'

Introduction to Lessons 181-200

1. Your next few lessons make a special point of firming up your willingness, strengthening your commitment, and blending your scattered goals into One Goal. You are not yet being asked for total dedication all the time, but you are asked to practice in order to attain the sense of Peace that a unified commitment will bestow on you, even if only intermittently. It is your experiencing Peace that will motivate your total willingness to follow the way that this course sets forth.

2. Your lessons now are geared specifically toward widening your perception, and to direct approaches to the special blocks that keep your perception too narrow and limited for you to see the value of your Goal. You will be lifting these blocks, if only briefly. Words cannot convey the Limitlessness that you will experience when they are lifted. The Experience that you will have when you give up the personal mind's tight control over your perception will speak for Itself. Your motivation to practice will become so strong that you will not need words. And you will be sure of What you want and of what no longer has value for you.

3. So, you start your journey beyond words by first concentrating on what still impedes your progress. You will not experience the Peace that lies beyond the personal mind's defensiveness while you deny Peace. It is here, but you won't accept Its Presence. So you will go past all defenses a little while each day. This is all that is asked of you, because this is all that you need to do. This will be enough to guarantee that the rest will come.

Lesson 181

'I trust in the Oneness that I perceive.'

1. Your trusting in the Oneness that you perceive is essential to establishing and holding up your faith in your ability to transcend doubt about your True Self. When you attack anyone or anything in the world that you perceive, you proclaim that you are limited to a personal self. You do not look beyond your error of believing that separation from God is real, but you magnify it, and it becomes a block to your awareness of your True Self, Which lies beyond the personal errors and 'sins' that you perceive in 'yourself' and 'others'.

2. Your perception always has a goal, and it is this that gives consistency to what you perceive. Change your goal, and your perception will change with it. Your perception will shift now and give support to your Goal of God, Which has replaced the goal of separation from God that you held before. Remove from your mind the goal of perceiving sin, and you will experience the Peace that comes from having faith that Innocence is Real. Your faith in Innocence receives its support from the Oneness that you perceive beyond your perception of separation. When you focus on the sins of the world, you are witnessing to the sin that you believe is in you. You do not transcend your perception that separation from God is real and see your Innocence, Which lies beyond it.

3. Therefore, in your practice today, let these little goals give way to your great need to perceive your Innocence. Instruct your mind that Innocence, and only Innocence, is What you seek for just a little while. In this interval of time where you practice changing your goal, do not concern yourself with future goals, and forget what concerned you a moment ago. Seek for Innocence, and nothing else; seek for It with concern only for *now*.

4. A major impediment to your success has been your involvement with the personal mind's past and future goals. You have been preoccupied with how extremely different the Goal of God that this course advocates is from those that you had before.

You have also been dismayed by the depressing and restricting thought that, even if you should succeed on a certain day, you will inevitably lose your way again.

5. This does not matter. The past is gone, and you only imagine a future. Your concern with them is only a defense against changing the goal for your perception, and nothing more. Lay these pointless limitations aside for a while. Do not look to past beliefs, or imagine what you will believe in the future. Enter into your practice time with one intention: to look upon your Innocence within.

6. If anger blocks your way in any form, recognize that you have lost sight of your Goal. And if a perception of separation seems real to you, your narrowed focus will limit your perception and turn your mind to the personal self's mistakes, which you will call your own, magnify, and call sin. So, for a little while, without regard for the past or the future, transcend these blocks by instructing your mind to change its focus. Say to yourself:

> 'I do not want to look at this. I trust in the Oneness that I perceive beyond it.'

7. Also, use this thought to keep you centered in Peace throughout the day. Do not seek for long-range goals, which are only an obstruction that blocks your awareness of your Innocence now. Instead, seek for respite for a while from the misery that your goal of separation from God brings to you, and that will remain with you if you do not correct it.

8. You are not seeking for fantasies, because What you want to perceive is really here. As your goal goes beyond mistakes, you will perceive only Innocence. When This is all that you want to see, and when This is all that you look for, the Real Perception of your Christ Mind will inevitably come into your awareness again. Innocence will be the only thing that you will see within yourself, and It will therefore be reflected in your perception.

9. In the world where you once perceived your sins, you will see

the proof that you are Innocent. Your love for all that you perceive will attest to your remembering your Holy Self, Which does not know sin, and cannot conceive of anything without Its Own Innocence. Seek for this Memory as you practice today. Do not look backwards or ahead, but straight into the present. Trust the Experience that you are seeking for now. Your Innocence is God's Will, and, in this Holy Instant, your Will is One with God.

Lesson 182

'I will be still for an Instant and go Home.'

1. The world that you seem to live in is not your home, and Somewhere in your mind you know that this is true. A memory of your Real Home haunts you, as if It calls to you to return, although you do not recognize Its Voice, nor of What Its Voice reminds you. Yet, you feel like an alien in the world that you perceive, though from Somewhere that you don't seem to know. You don't feel anything so definite that you could say with certainty that you are an exile in the world, but you have a persistent feeling, no more than a tiny throb, that sometimes you hardly remember, and other times you actively dismiss, but is sure to come to your mind again.

2. You certainly know what these words are about. You may try to hide your suffering in games that you play to occupy your time to keep your sadness at bay. You may even deny that you are sad and not recognize your tears at all. Or you may think that this idea is the illusion, the fantasy. But, in simple honesty, and without defensiveness or self-deception, you cannot deny that you understand these words.

3. These words speak for you, who seem to walk in a world, because you are not at Home. You go about uncertainly seeking in darkness for a Home that you cannot find, not even recognizing that this is what you are doing. You make a thousand homes for yourself, but none of them settles your restless mind. You do not understand that you build in vain, because the Home that you seek you cannot make. There is no substitute for Heaven; all that you have ever made in the world is hell.

4. Maybe you think that it is the childhood home of the personal self that you want to find again. But the childhood of the body, and its place of shelter, are distorted thoughts in your mind that make a picture of a past that never happened. It is the Christ in you that seeks Its Home, and knows that It is an alien in the world that you perceive. This Life is Eternal, with an Innocence that endures

Forever. Where the Christ in you will go is Holy Ground. It is your Christ Mind's Holiness that lights up Heaven, and that brings to the world that you perceive the Pure Reflection of God's Light, Where your perception and Heaven are joined as One.

5. It is the Christ in you that God knows as One with God. It is the Christ in you that knows God. Christ desires to go Home so deeply and unceasingly that Its Voice cries to you to let It rest for a while. Christ asks you only for a few Instants of respite in which It can return to breathe again the Holy Air that fills Heaven. You are Christ's home as well, and you will return to an awareness of the world with Christ. Just give Christ a little time to be Itself within the Silence, the Peace, and the Love that is Its Home.

6. Your awareness of Christ in you needs your protection. Christ is far from Home, and you are so little aware of the Christ in you that you easily shut It out. Christ's Voice seems so tiny that you readily obscure It. Its Call to you is almost unheard by you amid the grating, harsh, rasping noises of the world that you perceive, but Christ knows that Its sure protection lies in you. You will not fail Christ. It will go Home, and you will go with It.

7. Your Christ Mind is your Defenselessness and Strength. Christ trusts in you and has come into your awareness, because you will not fail. Christ whispers to you of Heaven unceasingly, because Christ wants to take you back Home, so that It may stay There and not return to where It does not belong, and where It lives as an outcast among alien thoughts. The patience of your Christ Mind is Limitless, and It will wait for you to hear Its Gentle Voice within you calling for you to let It go in Peace with you to Where Christ and you are at Home.

8. When you are still for an Instant, when the world recedes from your mind, and valueless ideas cease to have value for you, then you will hear Christ's Voice. So poignantly does your Christ Mind call to you that you will not be able to resist It. In that Holy Instant, Christ will take you Home, and you will stay in Perfect Stillness, at Peace, beyond all words, untouched by fear or doubt, and sublimely

certain that you are at Home.

9. Rest in Christ frequently today. Christ is willing to come into your awareness so that you can learn how Strong you are without defenses, and when you extend only Christ's Love to a world that seems to be your enemy. Christ holds the Might of Heaven, and extends Its Strength in your perception, so that you will see that you are Christ. Your Christ Mind only asks that you protect your awareness of It, because Christ's Home is far away, and Christ will not return to Heaven without you.

10. Christ is reborn within you every time that you wander from Home, because you must learn that What you want to protect is your awareness of the Christ within you. Your Christ Mind is Defenseless and is protected by your Defenselessness. Go Home with Christ frequently today. You are as much an alien in the world that you perceive as Christ is.

11. Take the time today to lay down the defenses of the personal mind, which bring you nothing, and to lay down the methods of attack that you raise against an enemy that does not exist. You are One with Christ, and Christ asks your help in getting Home, Completed and Completely. Christ comes to you, asking for you to protect your awareness of Christ in you with Love. Your Christ Mind is All-powerful, yet It asks you unceasingly to return to Heaven with It, and to no longer make illusions your god.

12. You have not lost your Innocence. It is for This that you yearn; This is your heart's desire. Your Innocence is the Voice that you hear, and is the Call that you cannot deny. The Holy Christ is in you; Christ's Home is yours. Today, Christ gives you Its Defenselessness, and you accept It in exchange for all of the toys of war that you have made. Now, your way is open, and your journey's end is in sight at last. Be still for an Instant, go Home with Christ, and be at Peace for a while.

Mentor's Notes

This is another lesson for practicing the Holy Instant. You do not have to be afraid that you will be pulled back into Heaven before you are ready. Paragraph 5 reassures you that, from a Holy Instant, you will return to an awareness of the world. And, at the end of paragraph 11, you are reminded that while your Christ Mind is All-powerful, It cannot overpower you, who are One with It, and whose will is as free as Its Will.

The Holy Instant familiarizes you with the experience of God, so that you can learn that there is nothing to fear in God. You will not wholly return to God until you are wholly without fear of God.

Lesson 183

'I call on God's Name, therefore on my own.'

1. God's Name is Holy, but no Holier than yours. To call on God's Name is to call on your own Name. The Whole of God extends Its Attributes to every Part of God, so God shares Its Identity with every Part of God. And every Part of God is like every other Part of God, so shares in One Identity. The Name of God reminds you of What you are, even in a world that seems apart from Truth; even though you seem to have forgotten It.

2. You cannot hear God's Name without responding to It, nor can you say God's Name without It calling you to remember God. Say 'God', and you invite God's Thoughts to surround you, to keep you safe, and to shelter you from thoughts of the world that you perceive that would intrude on your Holiness.

3. Say God's Name, and you will respond by laying down your illusions. Every illusion that you have of the world that you hold dear will suddenly disappear, and where they seemed to be, you will find miracles of Grace. You will be healed of your thoughts of sickness, you will perceive the Truth, and you will hear the Voice for God. You will cast off your sadness, and your tears of pain will dry up as your happy laughter extends blessing to all that you perceive.

4. Say God's Name, and the little names that you have for things in the world will lose their meaning. What tempted you to believe in separation from God before will become meaningless to you. Say God's Name, and see how easily you forget the names of all of the gods that you made and valued. They will become anonymous to you, though you once worshiped them.

5. Say God's Name, and you call on your True Self, also named God. Say God's Name, and all the tiny, nameless things of the world will slip into proper perspective. When you call on God's Name, you cannot mistake the God-less for God, nor sin for Grace, nor bodies for What is One with God. And when you join in silence with the part of your mind where you perceive a world, and you extend God's

Name to it, you establish a connection in your mind to God and God's Extension.

6. Practice this way today: Say God's Name slowly again and again. Let go of every name but 'God'; hear only 'God.' Anchor all of your thoughts on 'God.' Say today's idea only at the beginning of your practice, then let God's Name become your only Thought, your only Word, the only Thing that occupies your mind, your only desire, the only sound with any meaning, and the Name of all that you desire to perceive and want to call your own.

7. This is how you extend an invitation that can never be refused. God will come and answer your invitation Itself. God cannot answer your little prayers for idols that want to make God what God is not, because they do no reach God. God cannot hear requests that God not be God, nor that you be something other than One with God.

8. Say God's Name, and you acknowledge God as the Only Reality. You also acknowledge that you are One with God, extending God as God extends God. Sit silently, and let God's Name become the all-encompassing Thought that fills your mind. Let go of all thoughts but This One. To all other thoughts, respond with 'God', and see God's Name replace the thousands of words that you give to your thoughts without realizing that there is only One Name for All That is.

9. Today, you can receive the Gift of Grace. You can escape from the limitations of the world that you perceive, and extend Limitlessness in your perception. You can remember What you forgot to perceive a world instead. You can accept the part that you play in your salvation, and therefore perfectly accomplish your salvation

10. Turn to the Name of God for your release from limitations, and it is done. This is the only prayer that is necessary for you, because all of your prayers are contained in it. Words are insignificant, and you have nothing to request when you call on God's Name. God's Thoughts become your own. You claim All that God extends to you always. You call on God to replace all the things that

you thought without God, and God's Holy Name becomes the measure of their worthlessness.

11. All little sights and sounds of the world that you perceive disappear now. There is only you calling on God, with Which you are One, and the Holy Spirit answers in God's Holy Name. In this Eternal, Still Relationship, in Which Oneness transcends all words with Limitlessness, is Eternal Peace. In God's Name, you want to experience this Peace today, and in God's Name, It is extended to you.

Mentor's Notes

This lesson and the next almost seem to be using the concept of God's 'Name' in a magical way, but they are really playing with a symbol that the split mind made to bring into focus your Oneness with God.

Paragraph 7 says that God cannot answer your little prayers for idols that want to make God what God is not, because they do not reach God. For example, praying to God for things or situations in the world to bring you Limitless Love, Peace, Joy, Security, and Wholeness. God extends These Things to you directly, not through the world. You have Them always. In this circumstance, you are in essence asking God to not be What God really is, and you are asking to be what you are not.

You can also read this to mean that when you say things like, 'God damn it!' you are again asking God to not be God since God does not damn. Those prayers never reach God.

Lesson 184

'The Name of God belongs to me.'

1. In the world that you perceive, you live by symbols. Your split mind has made up names for all of them, and each is a separate entity that is identified by its own name. This is how your split mind makes separation to replace the Oneness of your mind. It designates everything with special attributes, then sets it off from other things by emphasizing their separateness. It makes a space between all the things that it has given different names, it has put space and time between all situations, and it tells you to greet every body by a different name.

2. This separation between everything is the basis of your perception of a world that you think of as reality. You perceive things where there is really nothing, and you see this nothingness Where there is Oneness. You perceive a space between all things, and between you and all things. This is how your split mind thinks that it has given 'life' to separation. It makes you think that you are independent from everything else, that you are unified only within yourself, and that you have a will of your own.

3. Your split mind has given the names by which your 'reality' becomes a series of separate events and things, and bodies with separate consciousnesses. It establishes what you perceive by what you *want* to perceive. By naming things, your split mind gives them reality for you, because by naming them, it gives them meaning for you. They seem to be causes with true effects, and with consequences inherent in themselves.

4. This is how your split mind makes your so-called 'reality' through partial perception that purposefully overlooks Truth. The 'enemy' of your 'reality', then, is the actual Wholeness of your Mind. Your split mind imagines little things and you perceive them, and a Perception of Oneness becomes the threat that your perception must overcome, conflict with, and deny.

5. But the Perception of Oneness is still the natural direction for

your mind. It is hard to teach your mind thousands of different names, and yet this is what your split mind has taught you to believe that *learning* means. This is the essential learning goal of the personal mind, and how it thinks that communication is achieved and concepts are meaningfully shared.

6. A million different names is what your perception of a world bestows on you, and when you think that the world is real, you accept the symbols and the names that seem to make the world real. This is what they are for, because you do not doubt that what is named is here. You see what you anticipate seeing, and What denies your chosen 'reality' becomes the illusion in your mind. So to question this 'reality' becomes insanity, and to accept it becomes sanity.

7. This is what your split mind teaches you through the world that you perceive, and it is a phase of learning that you must go through in your perception that you are in a world. But the sooner that you perceive that this learning rests on nothing, that its premises are questionable, and that you can doubt its results, the sooner you will question its effects. If your learning stops with the world, it stops short of Real Meaning. Properly perceived, you can use learning to learn Something Else, to regain your Real Perception, and to undo the meaning of the arbitrary names that your split mind has bestowed.

8. Do not think that your split mind has made reality; it has made illusions. But What is True in your Perception and in Heaven is beyond the names that your split mind gives. When you call on another by name in the world that you perceive, you are appealing to a body. You hide your True Identity from yourself with the body that you believe is really there. Then a body seems to respond to what you call them, and the name that you gave them is validated. This is how you twice deny the Oneness of your Mind: First, you perceive a body as real, then you perceive validation by their response to you.

9. You are not being asked to go beyond all of the symbols of the

world that you perceive and forget them forever. But you are asked to take a teaching/learning function. You have a need for the symbols of the world for a while, but don't be deceived by them. They do not stand for anything at all, and in practicing this idea you will be released from them. The symbols of the world will be the means by which you communicate to yourself in your perception that you are in a world, but recognize that they are not the Oneness Where you will find True Communication.

10. So you need intervals every day in which you recognize that what you learn in the world is transitory, and that it is a limitation from which you must rest in Limitlessness. In these intervals, you will understand the Name Which God gives to you; the One Identity Which is All and Truth. Then you will return to limitations, not because they are real, but only to recognize their unreality in terms that still have meaning for you.

11. Use all of the symbols and their names which define the dark world that you perceive, but do not accept them as your reality. The Holy Spirit uses all of them, but the Holy Spirit does not forget that God's Extension has One Name, One Meaning, and One Source Which unifies All That is Real within Itself. Use all of the names that your split mind has bestowed on the world that you perceive for convenience, but do not forget that your entire mind shares God's Name.

12. In Reality, God has no name, but in your perception that you are in a world, in God's Name is the Final Lesson in Which you learn that All is One, and then your learning ends. You will perceive your entire mind as One as it reflects Truth. There will be no separation in your mind. The Name of God is What God gives to you, who have chosen to learn about illusions to replace Heaven. In your practice, your purpose is to let your mind accept What God has given in Answer to the pitiful world that you made.

13. You cannot fail when you truly seek the Meaning of the Name of God. Experience will come to supplement words, but first you must accept God as Reality, and realize that the many names that

you have given to parts of your mind have caused you to perceive distortedly, but they have not interfered with Truth at all. Bring One Name into your practice; use One Name to unify your perception.

14. Even though you use a different name for all that you perceive in the part of your mind that you perceive as outside of you, understand that your entire mind has only One Name, Which God has given to it. It is This Name that you will use in practice, and through Its use, all foolish perceptions of separation that kept you blind to Oneness will disappear. You are given Strength to look beyond them. Your perception is blessed with Blessings that you can extend, because you have received Them.

15. *'Dear God, your Name is Mine. In It, I am united with All Life and You, Who extend All Life, Infinitely and Eternally. What I made and call by many different names is only a shadow that I tried to cast across Your Reality. I am glad and thankful that I was mistaken. I give all of my mistakes to You, so that I will be absolved from all of the effects that my errors seemed to have. I accept the Truth that You extend to replace every one of them. Your Name is my salvation and escape from what I made. Your Name unites us in the Oneness that you extend to me in Peace. Amen.'*

Mentor's Notes

Your split mind is the one mind that is the source of all of the personal selves and the world that you perceive. You did not as a *person* make names for everything in the world. In fact, as a *person* you seem to have to learn all these names. This is how deep your denial goes. At the level of the split mind, you have made it all, but as a personal self, with which you are used to identifying, you seem to be a part of the world, not the source of the world. You will first take responsibility for your personal projections, then you will become aware that you are the one split mind, the 'dreamer of the dream' of separation from God. Only at that level, which is the source of the world, can you let go of the world.

Paragraphs 9 and 10 point out that you are not being asked to stop using names for people, things, and situations in the world. You are simply being asked to not think that they are reality. Stepping out of the world several times a day to practice your lessons helps you to do this.

Lesson 185

'I want the Peace of God.'

1. For you to say these words is nothing, but for you to mean these words is everything. If you mean these words for only an instant, then suffering in any form will become impossible for you. Heaven will be restored fully to your awareness, you will wholly remember God, and the resurrection of Christ within you will be fully realized.

2. If you mean these words, you will be healed. You will no longer play in illusions, or think that you are an illusion. You will not make hell, and think that it is real. When you wholly want the Peace of God, It will be given to you. When It is all that you want, It will be all that you receive. You may have said these words, but you did not really mean them. You only have to look out at the world that you perceive and realize that you did not. If you did, your perception of the world would be completely changed by your extending God's Peace to it.

3. When you join your entire mind with One Intention, it becomes so strong that it becomes the Will of God. Your mind can join itself only in Truth. In your illusion, your mind and the world that it perceives do not have the same intent. For you, and all the other personal selves that you perceive, the central character of the world's story is different, and no two want the same outcome. There is a constant shifting of gain and loss.

4. In your illusion, you and others can only compromise. Sometimes, this takes a form of union, but it is only a *form*. Real Oneness is not part of the illusion, but compromising is the goal of the illusion. In your illusion, your mind does not unite with what it perceives; it can only bargain with what seems separate from it, and no bargain in separation can give you the Peace of God. Illusions take God's Place in your mind, and God's Oneness is lost to you in your belief that for you to gain, something that your mind perceives must lose.

5. When you truly mean that you want the Peace of God, you will renounce all illusions. You cannot mean these words and want illusions and seek the means to make illusions. These words mean that you have looked on illusions and found them lacking, and now you seek to go beyond them, recognizing that one illusion is like all the others. You mean that you have learned that the differences among them are only differences of form, and that you know that one will bring the same despair and misery as all the rest.

6. When you truly mean that you want the Peace of God, you will join your mind as One, because this is how you obtain God's Peace. When your desire for Peace is genuine, the means for finding It will be given to you in a form that you can understand. If you are sincere in asking for Peace, the lesson will come to you in a form that you cannot mistake. But, if you are not asking for Peace sincerely, there is no form that that the lesson can take that you will accept and truly learn.

7. Devote your practicing today to recognizing that you really mean that you want the Peace of God. This is not an idle wish, and these words are not a request for another illusion. You are not asking for compromise, or for another bargain that you hope will succeed where no other illusion has. When you mean today's words, you are acknowledging that illusions are futile, and you are requesting the Eternal in place of shifting illusions that have no real content.

8. In your practice periods, search your mind to find the illusions that you still cherish. What are you really asking for? Forget the words that you use in making your request, but look at what you believe will comfort you and make you happy. Do not be dismayed by lingering illusions, because their form does not matter now. Do not make some illusions more acceptable, and some more shameful and secret. They are all the same, so you should ask this same question of all of them: 'Is this what I want in place of Heaven and the Peace of God?'

9. This is the choice that you make; do not deceive yourself that it is otherwise. There is no compromise possible in this. You either

choose God's Peace or you ask for illusions, and illusions will come to you as you request them. But God's Peace will come to you as certainly if you request It, and It will remain with you Forever. Unlike illusions, God's Peace does not leave you with every twist and turning of the road, only to reappear, unrecognizable, in forms that shift and change with every step that you take.

10. You want the Peace of God, and so does your mind where you perceive a world. When you ask for God's Peace with deep certainty, you are asking for your entire mind. This is how you reach the Peace that you really want above all else, and join your entire mind in Oneness. You have been weak and uncertain in your purpose at times; unsure of what you wanted, where to look for it, and where to turn for help in finding it. Help is given to you in the Holy Spirit. Claim It by extending It to be all that you perceive.

11. If you truly seek for God's Peace, you will find It, because you will be asking to no longer deceive yourself by denying What God Wills for you. You cannot remain unsatisfied when you ask for What you already have. You cannot be unanswered when you request What is yours to extend in your awareness. The Peace of God *is* yours.

12. God extends Peace to you as God's Eternal Gift to you. You cannot fail when you ask for What God wills for you, and your request cannot be limited to you as a personal self. God's Gift must be extended to your entire mind. It is this attribute that sets the gifts of God apart from every illusion that ever seemed to take the place of Truth.

13. No part of your mind can lose and another gain when you request and receive any of God's Gifts. God gives only in Oneness, so God does not understand the concept of taking away. When this concept is as meaningless to you, you will be sure that you share God's Will with God. And you will also know that you share God's Will in One Intent with all that your mind perceives.

14. It is this One Intention that you seek today, uniting your desire with the need of your entire mind, which calls with a hope

that is beyond despair, with Love that attack wants to hide, and in the Oneness that you sought to split up with hate, but Which is still One with God. With Help like this with you, you cannot fail today as you ask for the Peace that God gives to you.

Mentor's Notes

This is another lesson that highlights the differences between the two thought systems in your mind – the personal mind and your Christ Mind. In the world, you must make compromises, because form is limited and cannot be extended everywhere. But in God, Where All is One, compromise is impossible, because God is Formless and extends Everywhere. You are not being asked to make the world like God by not making compromises in it; you are being asked to no longer compromise by letting go of the world. You do this by extending Truth in your awareness from your Christ Mind, and overlooking the world. Your interactions in the world will always involve compromise, but you do not have to accept the world as your reality.

Lesson 186

'The salvation of the part of my mind where I perceive a world depends on me.'

1. Here is a statement that removes all of the personal mind's arrogance from your mind. Here is a thought of true humility, because it upholds only the function that has been given to you. It is your acceptance of the part assigned to you, without you insisting on another role. It is not a judgment on your proper role, but it acknowledges that God's Will is done in your perception that you are in a world, as well as in Heaven. It unites your will in Heaven's plan to save your entire mind, restoring it to Heaven's Peace.

2. Do not fight against your function; the personal mind did not establish it, and it is not its idea. You are given the means by which your function will be perfectly accomplished, and all that you are asked to do is to accept your part in genuine humility, and to not deny with self-deceiving arrogance that you are worthy. What it is given to you to do, you have the Strength to do. Your mind is perfectly suited to do the part assigned to you by the One that knows you well.

3. You might find today's idea sobering, but look at its meaning: All it says is that God still remembers you as you really are, and God offers you the Perfect Trust that God holds in What is One with God. It does not ask that you be different in any way from What you are. This is all that you can accept in true humility, and all that you can deny in the arrogance of the personal mind. Today, you will not shrink from your assignment on the superficial grounds that it outrages the personal mind's 'modesty'. It is only the personal mind's pride that wants to deny the Call of God.

4. Lay aside all false humility today, so that you can listen as the Holy Spirit reveals to you what It wants you to do. Do not doubt your adequacy for the function that the Holy Spirit offers to you. Be certain that the Holy Spirit knows your Strength, Wisdom, and Holiness. The Holy Spirit judges you as worthy, so you *are* worthy. It

is only the personal mind's arrogance that judges you otherwise.

5. There is only one way for you to be released from the limitedness of the personal mind's plan to prove that illusions are Truth: Accept the plan that the personal mind did not make instead. Do not judge your value to it. The Holy Spirit assures you that the salvation of your entire mind depends on your part, so you can be sure that this is so. The arrogant personal mind clings to words, afraid for you to go beyond them to the Experience that will offend it. But you are free in your true humility to hear the Holy Spirit, Which tells you What you are, and what to do to remember What you are.

6. The arrogant personal mind makes an image of you that is not real, and it is this image that quails and retreats in terror as the Holy Spirit assures you that you have the Strength, the Wisdom, and the Holiness to go beyond all images. You are not weak, ignorant, and helpless like this image of yourself. Sin does not tarnish the Truth in you, and misery cannot come near to you, the Holy Home of God.

7. All of this the Holy Spirit tells you, and as It speaks to you the image that the personal mind has of you trembles and seeks to attack a threat that it cannot know. But it does know that its whole basis is crumbling. Let it go. The salvation of your entire mind depends on you, not on this little pile of dust. It cannot tell you who are One with God anything Real. You have no need to be concerned with it at all.

8. And so you find your Peace. You will accept the function that God has given to you, because all of your illusions rest on your weird belief that you can make another function for yourself. But your self-made roles shift. They change from mourner to ecstatic 'lover'. They laugh or weep, and greet the day with welcome or with tears. When you identify with a personal self, your very being seems to change as you experience thousands of shifts in mood as your emotions rise high and then dash to the ground in hopelessness.

9. This is not What is One with God. God did not create such instability and call it One with God. God is Changeless, and God extends Its Attributes to Its Creation. All of the images that the

personal mind makes have no effect on What you are in Truth. They blow across your mind like wind-swept leaves that form a pattern for a moment, then break apart and group again. They are mirages rising from the desert.

10. When you accept the function that God gives to you, these insubstantial images that the personal mind has of you will go and leave your mind unclouded and serene. These images give rise to impermanent, vague, ambiguous, and conflicting goals. You cannot be constant in your efforts and concentrate your energies toward goals like these. The functions that the personal mind values are so uncertain that they change ten times an hour at their most secure. You cannot have any hope of gain with goals like these.

11. In Lovely contrast, and as certain as the sun's return every morning to dispel the night, your true function stands out clear and unambiguous. You cannot doubt its validity. It comes to you from God, Which does not know error, and God's Holy Spirit is as certain as the messages that It brings to you from God. These will not change, nor conflict. All of them point to One Goal; the only One that you can attain. The personal mind's plan is impossible, but God's plan cannot fail, because God is its Source.

12. Do as the Holy Spirit directs you, and if you think that It asks you to do something impossible, remember What is directing you, and what it is in your mind that denies It. Then, consider which is more likely to be right: The Holy Spirit, Which speaks for the Source of All, and Which knows all things exactly as they are; or the personal mind, which makes a distorted image of you that is confused, bewildered, inconsistent, and unsure of everything. Do not let the personal mind direct you, but hear instead the Certain Voice of the Holy Spirit, Which tells you of a function given to you by God, Which remembers you, and urges you to remember It.

13. The Holy Spirit is calling from the Knowing to the unknowing in you. God wants to comfort you, though God does not know sorrow; God wants to restore you, though God knows only Completion; God wants to give you a Gift, though God knows that

you have Everything. God has Thoughts that answer every need that you perceive, although God does not see them. Love must extend Itself, and What God extends takes on the form most useful to you in your perception that you are in a world of form.

14. These are forms that can never deceive you, because they come from Formlessness Itself. In Heaven, Love has no form, but in the world that you perceive, Love takes the form of forgiving. What you need in your perception that you are in a world is supplied as you need it. Through the form of forgiving, you can fulfill your function in the world, although What Love will mean to you when you have been wholly restored to Formlessness will be even greater. The salvation of the part of your mind where you perceive a world depends on you who can forgive it. This is your function in your perception that you are in a world.

Lesson 187

'I bless all that I perceive because I bless myself.'

1. You cannot give what you do not have. In fact, your giving is the proof of your having. This point has been made in this course before, and you don't find it hard to accept. You cannot doubt that you must first possess what you want to give; it is on the second phase that this course emphasizes that the personal mind and your Real Perception differ. In the world, you lose what you give away, but Truth emphasizes giving to increase What you have.

2. How is this possible? It is certain that, if you give a finite thing away, the body's eyes will no longer perceive it as yours. But, you have learned that things only represent the thoughts that make them. And you have seen it proven that, when you extend an idea, you strengthen it in your own mind. Maybe the form in which the thought seems to appear changes in your giving it, but it must return to you as the giver. Nor can the form that returns to you be less acceptable; it must be more acceptable.

3. You must first have an idea before you can give it away. To save the part of your mind where you perceive a world, you must first accept salvation for yourself. But, you will not believe that this is done until you see the miracles that you extend to the world. Here, the idea of giving is clarified and given meaning for you. Now, you can understand what you have is increased by your giving it.

4. Protect everything that you value by giving it away, and you will be sure that you will not lose it. And what you think that you do not have is also proven yours this way. But value is not in form, because this will change and grow unrecognizable in time, however much you try to keep it safe. No form endures; it is the thought behind form that is unchangeable.

5. Give gladly, because this is the only way to gain. Thoughts remain with you and grow and are reinforced by your giving them. Thoughts extend as they are shared, and you cannot lose them. With thoughts, there is no giver and receiver. You retain what you give, so

you are also the receiver. You gain in this seeming exchange, because the thought takes the form that is most helpful for you at the time. The idea that you seem to give, you will value less than what you gain.

6. Never forget that you give only to yourself. When you understand this, you will only laugh at the idea of sacrifice. Nor will you fail to recognize the many forms that sacrifice seems to take. You will laugh at pain and loss, at sickness and grief, at poverty, starvation, and death. You will recognize that sacrifice is the one idea that stands behind all of these, and, in your gentle laughter, they are all healed.

7. Illusions that you recognize as illusions must disappear from your mind. If you do not accept the idea of suffering, then you remove the idea of suffering from your mind. When you choose to see all suffering as it is, your blessing will lie on all appearances of suffering. The thought of sacrifice is what gives rise to all forms that suffering seems to take, and suffering is an idea that is so insane that Sanity dismisses it at once.

8. Never believe that you can sacrifice. There is no place for sacrifice in What has Real Value. If the thought of sacrifice occurs to you, its very presence means that you have made an error, and that you need correction. Your blessing will correct it. Given first to you, it is yours to extend. No form of sacrifice and suffering can endure for long when you forgive and bless yourself.

9. The forgiveness that you extend in your perception returns to your mind. You cannot fear to look on such Lovely Holiness. Before Purity, the great illusion of your fear of God diminishes to nothingness. Do not be afraid to look within. The blessedness that you behold will sweep away all thoughts of form, and leave instead the Perfect Gift that is Forever there, Forever to increase, Forever yours, and Forever extending.

10. Now, your mind is One in thought, because fear is gone. Before God, the One Creator, the One Thought, your entire mind stands as One. You are not separate from God, your Source, nor are

you distant from the part of your mind where you perceive a world, which with you is your One Self, in Which you are One in Innocence. You stand in blessedness, and you give as you have received. The Name of God is on your lips, and as you look within, you see the Purity of Heaven shine in the Reflection of God's Love.

11. Now you are blessed, and you bless the world. What you have seen within you want to extend, because you want to perceive It everywhere. You want to behold It shining with the Grace of God on all that you perceive. You do not want to withhold it from anything. To ensure that this Holy Sight is yours, you extend It to everything. Where you see It, It will be returned to you in a form of forgiveness that your mind can understand, making it a Home for Innocence Itself, Which dwells in you and offers you Its Holiness as yours.

Mentor's Notes

The first few paragraphs of this lesson make the point that, even in your perception that you are in a world, you are in Wholeness, because while form changes and falls away, it is always replaced by forms that are more useful and meaningful to you at the time. For example, you have a job that requires that you work long hours, and you are longing for more free time. You get laid off, and you find a job that pays less, but also requires less hours. Though you are making less money, the free time that you valued more has come to replace the long hours. If you look at your life honestly, you will find that you always get what you ask for, and you always ask for what you value. Your thoughts and desires shape what shows up in the world for you. The personal mind may complain because it wants it *all* right now, but time and space are limited, and only your strongest desires are manifested.

Lesson 188

'The Peace of God is shining in me now.'

1. Why wait for Heaven? By seeking the Light of Heaven, you are denying that It is in you now. *Enlightenment* does not change you; It is your recognition that God's Light is within you. God's Light is not of the world that you perceive, and you, who have It within you, are also alien in the world. God's Light goes with you in your perception that you are in a world, and stays with you, because It is yours. It is the only thing that you bring with you from God, your Source. It shines in you, because It lights your Real Mind, and leads you back to Where It came from, and Where you are at Home.

2. You cannot lose God's Light, so why wait to find It in the future, or believe that you have lost It, or that It has never been? You can look upon It so easily that your arguments that try to prove that It is not here are ridiculous. You cannot deny the Presence of What you can find within yourself. It is not difficult for you to look within; all of your perception begins there. All that you perceive, in illusions or through Truth, is a projection of what you see within yourself. Within you is where your perception starts, and where it ends. You are its only source.

3. The Peace of God is shining in you now, and from your center It extends to all that you perceive. It pauses to caress everything, and It leaves a blessing that remains Forever. What It gives is Eternal, and removes all thoughts of the temporary and valueless. It renews your tired mind, and Lights your Real Perception. You extend all of Its Gifts everywhere, and your gratitude is returned to you from all that you perceive for your receiving It.

4. The Peace shining in you extends in your mind where you perceive a world, and restores the Memory of Peace to your entire mind. From your salvation, salvation radiates with Gifts beyond measure that you give, and so receive. To you, who extend God's Gifts, God gives thanks, and, in God's Blessing, the Light in you shines brighter, adding to the Gifts that you have to extend to be all

that you perceive.

5. You can never contain the Peace of God. When you recognize It in yourself, It automatically extends in your perception. The means for extending are then within your understanding: You forgive your illusions, because you recognize the Truth in you. The Peace of God is shining in you now, and in your entire mind. In Quietness, you acknowledge It everywhere, because What you perceive within yourself becomes your perception of everything.

6. Sit quietly, and close your eyes; the Light within you is enough. It alone has the Power to give you the Gift of your Real Perception. Exclude thoughts of the world that seem outside of you, and let your thoughts fly to the Peace within you. They know the way, because your Honest Thoughts, Which are untainted by your illusion of a world, are the Holy Messengers of God.

7. These are the Thoughts that you think with God. They recognize Their home in you, and They point to Their Source, Where you and God are One. God's Peace shines on Them, but They are with you as well, because They are born in your Mind as your Thoughts are born in God. They lead you back to Peace, from Which they came to remind you of how to return to Peace.

8. These Thoughts listen to the Holy Spirit when you refuse to listen, and they gently urge you to accept What you are, instead of fantasies and shadows. They remind you that you are co-Creator of Life with God, because as the Peace of God shines in you, It must shine on Them.

9. Practice going closer to God's Light within you today. Take your wandering thoughts, and gently bring them back to Where they fall in line with all of the Thoughts that you share with God. Do not let your thoughts stray, but let the Light in your mind direct them Home. You have betrayed your Real Thoughts, ordering Them to leave you, but now you call Them back, and wash them clean of strange desires and disordered wishes. You restore Them to the Holiness that is Theirs.

10. Your mind is restored with Them. Acknowledge that the Peace

of God is still shining in you, and from you to all that you perceive. You will forgive all of your illusions, and absolve your mind from all that it thought that the world did to you. You have made a world to perceive as you want it, and now you choose to perceive Innocence and salvation. Lay your saving blessing on all that you perceive as you say:

> 'The Peace of God is shining in me now. I let all things shine on me in God's Peace, and I bless everything with God's Light in me.'

Mentor's Notes

Paragraphs 2 and 5 reiterate a point that is made early in the Text: You always look inward before you perceive outward. What you perceive is always a reflection of what you have seen within yourself, whether it is projected away by the personal mind, or is extended by your Christ Mind.

Lesson 189

'I feel the Love of God within me now.'

1. There is a Light in you that the personal mind cannot perceive, and with its eyes, you do not see this Light, because you are blinded by your perception of a world. Yet, you have the means to perceive It. It is in you for you to perceive; It was not placed in you to be hidden from you. This Light is a reflection of the thought that you practice today. To feel the Love of God within you is to perceive Innocence, Hope, and Blessing with Perfect Charity and Love.

2. You cannot feel fear with a Perception such as This. It welcomes you, rejoices with you, and sings your praises, as It keeps you safe from every form of danger and of pain. It offers you a warm and gentle Home in Which to stay for a while. It blesses you throughout the day, and watches as Silent Guardian of your Holy sleep. It sees salvation in you, and protects God's Light in you, in Which It sees Its Own. It offers you Beauty and Comfort in thankfulness for your Benevolence.

3. This is the Perception that the Love of God shows to you. It is so different from the world that you see through a perception that is dark with malice and fear, that each undoes the other. You can only perceive one of these, and the one you choose makes the other meaningless to you. A Perception in Which your forgiving shines on everything, and Peace offers Its Gentle Light to everyone, is inconceivable to you when you see a world of hatred that rises from attack, and is poised to murder and destroy.

4. But the world of hatred is equally invisible and inconceivable to you when you feel God's Love within you. Then, your Perception reflects the Quietness and Peace that shines in you, the Gentleness and Innocence that you know surrounds you, and the Endless Joy within you. What you feel within you, you perceive everywhere.

5. What do you want to see? It is your choice. Learn, and do not forget, this Law of Perception: You will perceive that which you feel is within you. If you feel hatred within you, you will perceive a

frightening world held cruelly in death's bony grasp; if you feel the Love of God within you, you will perceive Mercy and Love.

6. Today, you will pass illusions as you reach to What is True in you and feel Its all-encompassing Tenderness; Its Love, Which knows that you are as Perfect as Itself; Its Perception, Which is the Gift of Love that It bestows on you. You learn the way to Love today. It is as sure as Love Itself, because its simplicity avoids the snares that the foolish convolutions of the personal mind's 'reasoning' only hides.

7. Simply do this: Be still, and lay aside all thoughts that you have about what you are and what God is, all concepts that you have for the world that you perceive, and all images that you hold for yourself. Empty your mind of everything that it thinks is true or false, good or bad, worthy or shameful. Let everything go. Do not bring with you one thought that you learned in the personal mind's past. Forget the world, forget this course, and come with a wholly empty mind to God.

8. God knows the way to you; you do not need to know the way to God. Your part is simply to let all obstacles between you and God be quietly removed Forever. God does Its Part Joyfully and immediately. Ask and receive, but do not make demands, or make the road to God by Which you want God to come you. The way for you to reach God is simply for you to let God be. This is how you claim your Reality as well.

9. Today, you do not choose the way that you go to God, but you do choose to let God come to you. And, with this choice, you rest. In your quiet and open mind, God's Love will blaze Its pathway Itself. The Truth is here, and you can reach It, and you know this if you do not deny it. God knows you who are One with God. God knows the way to you, and God does not need you to show God how to find Its way. Through your open mind, God's Love shines outward from Its home within you, and lights your perception with Innocence.

10. *'Dear God, I do not know the way to You, but I have called and You have answered. I will not interfere. The way of my salvation is not mine*

personally, because it belongs to You, and it is to You that I look for it. My mind is open to receive Your Gifts. I have no thoughts that I do not think with You, and I cherish no beliefs about what I am or about You. Yours is the way that I want to find and follow. I ask only that Your Will, Which is also my Will, be done in me and in my perception, so that I can see that my entire mind is One with Heaven now. Amen.

Lesson 190

'I choose the Joy of God instead of pain.'

1. Pain is a mistaken perspective. When you experience pain in any form, it is proof that you are deceiving yourself. Pain is never a fact; in any form, it will disappear when you perceive correctly. Pain proclaims that God is cruel, so it cannot be real in any form. It is meant to witness to God's hatred of you, the sinfulness that God sees in you, God's insane desire for revenge on you, and for your death.

2. These projections can never be proven; they are wholly false. Pain only witnesses to your mistaken beliefs about yourself. It is an illusion of fierce retaliation for a crime that you could never commit: An attack on the Unassailable. It is your nightmare that you have been abandoned by Eternal Love, Which can never leave you, who are One with Eternal Love.

3. Pain is a sign that illusions reign in the place of Truth in your mind. It demonstrates that you are denying God, confusing God with fear, perceiving God as insane, and seeing God as a traitor to Itself. If God is Real, there is no pain; if pain is real, there is no God. Vengeance is not part of Love. Your fear denies Love and uses pain to 'prove' that God is dead; that death is victor over Life. Pain shows that you believe that you are a body, corruptible in death, and as mortal as the 'god' that you have slain.

4. Peace to your mind in place of such foolishness! The time has come for you to laugh at such insane ideas. There is no need for you to think of these ideas as savage 'crimes' or secret 'sins' with weighty consequences. Only in insanity can you conceive of them as the cause of anything. Their witness, pain, is as insane as they are, and not more to be feared than the insane illusions which it shields and tries to demonstrate is true.

5. It is your thoughts alone that cause you pain; nothing outside of your mind can hurt or injure you in any way. There is no cause outside of you to oppress you, and only you affect yourself. There is nothing in the world that you perceive that has the power to make

you ill or sad or weak or frail. But you have the power to dominate all things by recognizing what they are. As you perceive Harmlessness, all that you perceive will respond to your Holy Will. What you once saw as frightening, you will now see as Innocent and Holy.

6. You who are Holy, think of this: The world that you perceive does nothing; it has no effects at all. It only represents your thoughts, and it will change entirely as you elect to change your mind by choosing the Joy of God as What you really want. Your True Self is Radiant in this Holy Joy, Eternally Unchanged, Unchanging, and Unchangeable. Do not deny a little bit of your mind the Joy that belongs to it by making it a place for pain and sickness, where Life must come to die at last.

7. The world that you perceive may seem to cause you pain, but the world has no cause, so it has no power to cause. It is an effect, so it cannot make effects. As an illusion, it is only what you wish, and your idle wishes make its pains. Your strange desires make its evil dreams and your thoughts of death envelop it in fear, but your kind forgiving makes it reflect Life.

8. Pain is your belief in evil taking form and wreaking havoc in your mind. It is the ransom that you gladly pay to not be Limitless. In pain, you deny God Its Oneness with you. In pain, fear appears to triumph over Love, and time seems to replace Eternity and Heaven. The world becomes a cruel and bitter place to you, where sorrow rules, and little joys give way to the savage pain that waits to end all joy in misery.

9. Lay down your defenses, and come into the Quiet Place, Where Heaven's Peace holds your entire mind still at last. Lay aside all thoughts of danger and of fear. Let no thought of attack enter your mind, lay down the judgments that you hold against yourself, and put aside your withering assaults on your Holiness.

10. This is Where you will understand that there is no pain, and that the Joy of God belongs to you. In today's lesson, you can realize all of the power of your salvation. It is this: Pain is illusion; Joy is

Reality. Pain is your denial of God; Joy is your awareness of God. Pain is your self-deception; Joy is your Truth.

11. So, again, you make the only choice that you can ever make as you choose between illusions or Truth, pain or Joy, hell or Heaven. Let your gratitude to the Holy Spirit fill your heart as you are free to choose your Joy instead of pain, your Holiness instead of sin, the Peace of God instead of conflict, and the Light of Heaven for the darkness of the world.

Lesson 191

'I am God's Holy Extension.'

1. Here is your declaration of release from the limitations of the world, and here you release your perception of the world as well. You do not see what you have made of the world by making it your prison. How could you perceive the world as anything but vicious, frightening, punishing, wild, lacking all reason, blind, and insane with hate?

2. What have you done that this is what you perceive? When you deny your Real Identity, this is what remains. You perceive chaos and claim that it is you, and then everything that you perceive proves this to you. Every sound that you hear speaks of frailty within you and around you, every breath that you draw seems to bring you closer to death, and all of your hopes dissolve into tears.

3. When you deny your Real Identity, you cannot escape the insanity that induces this weird, unnatural, ghostly thought that mocks God's Extension and laughs at God. When you deny your Real Identity, you attack everything alone, and you are a friendless, tiny particle of dust up against legions of enemies. When you deny your Real Identity, you look on evil, sin, and death, and watch as despair steals every scrap of hope from you, leaving you with nothing but the wish to die.

4. But your denying your Real Identity is nothing more substantial than a game. You are One with God; anything else that you believe is folly. In this One Thought your entire mind is set free, in this One Truth all illusions are swept from your mind, and in this One Fact you proclaim your Innocence to be Forever Everything, the Central Core of Existence, and the Guarantee of Immortality.

5. Let today's idea find a place in your thoughts, and you will rise far above your perception of a world and all of your limiting thoughts about it. From this Place of Safety, you will return to an awareness of the world to let it go, because when you accept your Real Identity, you are truly saved from illusions. Your salvation is

then the gift that you extend in your mind where you perceive a world in gratitude to the Holy Spirit, Which guides you to the Happiness that changes your whole perspective on the world.

6. One Holy thought like this, and you are free: You are God's Holy Extension. And, with this Holy Thought, you learn that you have freed your mind from your perception of the world as well. You will have no need to use the world cruelly and then perceive this savage need in it. You will set your mind free from its limitations. You will not see a devastating image of yourself walking in a world of terror that twists in agony because you laid the mark of death on it with your fears.

7. Be glad today that you learn how easily hell is undone. Tell yourself:

> 'I am God's Holy Extension. I cannot suffer, be in pain, experience loss, or fail to do all that my salvation requires.'

In this thought, everything that you perceive is wholly changed.

8. A miracle will light up all of the dark corners of your mind, where death has lurked since you first conceived of time. Time will lose its hold on your mind, because Christ will have come into your awareness to forgive your perception of the world. You will not see the world as dark and sinful when Christ comes again into your awareness to free your mind from this perception.

9. In your identification with a personal self, you perceive yourself as weak, frail, with futile hopes and devastated dreams, born only to die and weep and suffer pain, but hear this: All Power is given to you in Heaven and in your perception that you are in a world. There is nothing that you cannot do. You play a game of death, of helplessness, of pitiful separation in a merciless world. But when you extend Mercy to the world, you will perceive Mercy shining on you.

10. Let your Oneness with God return to your awareness, and, with Its Holy Perception, bless the world that you made. Your

perception of a world began in error, but it will end in a Reflection of Holiness. Then, you will no longer deny God and believe in death. Join with your Christ Mind today; Its Glory is the Light that saves your entire mind. Do not withhold your salvation any longer. Look on the world in which you perceive suffering and know that you are willing to extend Rest in your perception instead.

11. The part of your mind where you perceive a world waits for your release, because it stays in illusions until you are free of them. You cannot extend Mercy to it until you find Mercy in yourself. You will perceive pain until you have denied its hold on you; you will perceive death until you have accepted your own Eternal Life. You are God's Holy Extension. Remember This, and your entire mind will be free; remember This, and your perception of the world will blend into Oneness with Heaven.

Lesson 192

'Forgiving is the function that God wants me to fill.'

1. It is God's Holy Will that you complete God; that you are God's Sacred Extension, Forever as Pure as God, and Forever receiving and extending God's Love. But what does this Function in Heaven mean for you in your perception that you are in a world of envy, hate, and attack?

2. You have a function in your perception that you are in a world that is in the world's terms, because you cannot understand Eternity in time. *Forgiving* is your function in the world. Forgiving was not created by God, because it is the means by which you undo illusion. You do not need to forgive Heaven, but in your perception that you are in a world, you need the means to let go of the world. God's Extension waits only for your *acknowledgment*, not for you to make It Complete.

3. In your perception that you are a personal self, you cannot even conceive of God's Extension, because It has no meaning in the world. *Forgiving* is the closest that you can come to God's Extension in the world. God's Extension is Formless, but the Holy Spirit has the power to translate the Formless into form. What the Holy Spirit makes are illusions, but of a kind that are so aware of God that God's Light shines in them, and your Real Perception beholds their Joyful offerings.

4. When you are forgiving, you look gently on illusions that are unknown in Heaven, and you watch as they disappear and leave your mind a clean slate. Then, they are replaced by Perceptions of the Holy Spirit. Forgiving is the means by which you overcome your fear of death, because death does not attract you when guilt is gone. Your forgiving lets you perceive the body as it is: not something that can change you, but a simple teaching aid that you will lay aside when your learning is complete.

5. Without perceiving itself in a body, your mind cannot make mistakes. It cannot think that it will die or be the prey of merciless

attacks. It cannot be terrified, so it cannot be angry. Fears cannot assail you when you have let go of the source of all attack, the core of anguish, and the seat of fear. Only by forgiving can you relieve your mind of thinking that a body is its home; only by forgiving can you restore to your mind the Peace that God intends for it; only by forgiving can you be persuaded to look on your Holiness.

6. When anger is gone from you, you will indeed perceive that no sacrifice was asked for you to receive the Gift of your Real Perception; only pain was lifted from your sick and tortured mind. Do you find this unwelcome and frightening? Or do you hope for it, and accept it Joyfully and thankfully? Your mind is One; you therefore give up nothing, but receive Everything from God.

7. But you need to forgive your illusions to perceive that this is so. Without the kindly light of forgiveness, you grope in darkness, using reason only to justify your rage and attack. Your understanding is so limited in your identification with a personal self that what you think you understand is only confusion that is born of error. You are lost in shifting and frightening illusions, and your mind is shut tight against God's Light. Your mind is engaged in worshipping what is not here.

8. You can be born again in Christ by forgiving everyone and everything that you see or think of or imagine. You cannot be free while you perceive part of your mind limited to a world, because your mind is not really split between 'you' and a world outside of you. So it is that by extending freedom to all that you perceive, you set yourself free.

9. Do not hold onto your illusions; let them go and set yourself free. The way is simple: Every time that you feel a stab of anger, realize that you hold a sword above your own head. It will fall on you or to the side, depending on whether you condemn or free yourself. Everyone and everything that tempts you to anger can be your savior if you choose. Then you will owe them thanks instead of pain.

10. Be Merciful today, because you are One with God and deserve

Mercy. It is the Christ in you that asks you to accept the way to freedom now. Do not deny Christ, because God's Love for Christ belongs to you. Your function in your perception that you are in a world is only to forgive your entire mind so that you can accept your Identity in Christ. Your Christ Mind is One with God, and you are Christ. Forgive your entire mind the sins that you perceive anywhere, and you will see that you are One with Christ.

Lesson 193

'All things are lessons in forgiving that God wants me to learn.'

1. God does not know of learning, but God's Will extends to what God does not understand in that God Wills that your Happiness be undisturbed, Eternally expanding in the Joy of Full Extension, and Wholly Limitless in God. So God's Will provides the Means to guarantee that This is done.

2. God does not see contradictions, but you believe that you see them, so you have a need for the Holy Spirit, Which can correct your mistaken perception, and give you your Real Perception to lead you back to Where perception ends. God does not *perceive* at all, but It is God That gives you the Means by Which your perception is made True and Beautiful with the Light of Heaven in it. It is God that answers the contradictions that you make, and it is God that keeps your Innocence Forever Safe.

3. These are the lessons that God wants you to learn. God's Will reflects on them all, and they reflect God's Loving Kindness to you who are One with God. Each lesson has the same central thought. Their form is different with different circumstances, characters, and themes, but the content of each lesson is fundamentally the same. It is this:

'Forgive this, and you will see it differently.'

4. You may not yet perceive that all distress is only a form of your not-forgiving, but that is the content beneath every form. It is this sameness that makes your learning certain, because the lesson is so simple that you cannot reject it in the end. You cannot hide from a truth that is so obvious that it appears in countless forms, but that you can recognize easily if you want to see it in each of them.

'Forgive this, and you will see it differently.'

5. These are the words that the Holy Spirit speaks to you in all of the tribulations, pain, and suffering that you perceive in any form. These are the words in which your temptation to believe in separation from God ends, and you abandon guilt, no longer revering it. These are the words that end your illusion that separation from God is real, and rid your mind of fear. These are the words by which salvation comes to your entire mind.

6. You will learn to say these words when you are tempted to believe that pain is real, or to choose death instead of Life. You will learn to say these words when you understand their power to release your entire mind from limitations. The meaning of these words gives you power over all events that seem to have power over you. You see every situation correctly when you hold the meaning of these words in your awareness and do not forget to apply it to everything and everyone that you look on in separation.

7. You can tell when you are perceiving incorrectly, and failing to learn the lesson that God wants you to learn, when pain seems real to you. This indicates that you are holding onto not-forgiving.

8. God does not want you to suffer, and God will help you to forgive yourself. You do not remember What you are, and God wants you to remember God's Love for you, and all of the Gifts of God's Love for you. Do not renounce your own salvation. Do not choose to fail the simple lessons that the Holy Spirit sets before you, so that pain may disappear from your mind, and you remember your Oneness with God.

9. All things are lessons in forgiveness that God wants you to learn. God does not leave an unforgiving thought uncorrected in your mind to hurt you. God ensures that your Holy Rest is untroubled and Serene in your Eternal Home. God wipes away your tears, and undoes the source of any tears that have yet to fall. God wills that your laughter replace every tear, and that you be free from pain again.

10. Today, you will try to overcome in one day what seems like a thousand obstacles. Let Mercy come to you quickly, and do not try

to hold It off another day, another minute, or another instant. This is how the Holy Spirit uses time; use it today for this purpose. Morning and night, use time to serve this purpose, and do not use time for meeting less than your deepest need.

11. Give all that you can today; then give a little more. Now you want to arise quickly and return to your Home in God. You have been gone too long, and you don't want to linger in illusions any longer. As you practice today, think of all of the problems and pains that you keep apart from healing to settle for yourself. Give them to the Holy Spirit, Which knows how to look at them, so that they disappear. Truth is the Holy Spirit's Message; Truth is What the Holy Spirit teaches you. Truth is the Lesson that God wants you to learn.

12. Every hour, today and in the days to come, spend a little time in practicing a lesson in forgiving in the form given for that day. Apply it to what has happened in the hour just past, so that the next hour is free of what happened the hour before. This is how you loosen the chains of time from around your mind: Do not let any hour cast its shadow on the one that follows, and when that one passes, let everything in that one go as well. This is how you will remain free from illusions, and in Eternal Peace in your perception that you are in a world of time.

13. This is the lesson that God wants you to learn. There is a way for you to look on everything that turns it into a step toward God and the salvation of your entire mind. To all of your perceptions of terror say:

'I will forgive this, and it will disappear.'

Repeat these words to every apprehension, every concern, and every form of suffering that you perceive. Then, you hold the key to Heaven that brings God's Love into your perception at last, to raise your entire mind up to Heaven. God takes the final step Itself; do not deny God the little steps that God asks of you.

Mentor's Notes

Your Function in Heaven is to extend God as God extends God to you. Your function in the world is to forgive, which extends God's Love in your awareness, so that God's Love becomes all that you perceive. When you have completely forgiven all of your illusions and you perceive only God's Love, then your function in the world blends into your Function in Heaven.

Throughout the Text, and in this Workbook, there is often a reference to God taking the 'last step', as it does in this lesson's last paragraph. This means that when all that you have in your perception is God, then God is all that is in your entire mind. Perception then disappears, and Knowledge of God takes its place in your mind. In other words, when there is only God in your mind, there is only God in your mind.

Lesson 194

'I place the future in the Hands of God.'

1. With today's idea, you take another giant stride toward your salvation. It encompasses a distance so great that it sets you down just short of Heaven, with God in your sight and all of your obstacles to God behind you. You stand just outside of Heaven, in a quiet place of Peace, where you wait in certainty for God to take the final step. How fast you are progressing away from your perception of a world! How close you are to your Goal! How short is the journey ahead of you!

2. If you accept today's idea, you will pass by all anxiety, the pits of hell, the blackness of depression, all thoughts of separation from God, and the devastation brought about by guilt. If you accept today's idea, you will release your entire mind from all limitations. You will be saved, and your salvation will become what you extend to all that you perceive, because you have accepted it.

3. In *this Instant* you do not feel depression, experience pain, or perceive loss. In *this Instant* you do not set sorrow on a throne and faithfully worship it. In *this Instant* you cannot even die. So each instant that you give to God, with the next one already given to God, is the Instant of your release from sadness, pain, and even death.

4. God holds your future, as God holds your past and present. They are one to God, so you can see them as one as well. But in your perception that you are in a world, the progress of time seems real to you, so you are not being asked to not perceive a sequence for time. You are asked instead to let go of the future, and place it in God's Hands. And you will learn through experience that you have placed the past and present in God's Hands as well. You will see that the past can no longer punish you when you no longer dread the future in the present.

5. Release the future, because the past is gone, and the present, freed from grief and misery and pain and loss, is the Instant in Which time and illusion slip away from the limits of an inevitable

course. Each instant that was a slave to time can become a Holy Instant, where God's Light, Which you hid, is freed to bless your entire mind. You can be free, and Christ can shine in your perception, and share in your Holiness.

6. If you recognize that today's lesson is your deliverance from illusions, you will not hesitate to give as much consistent effort as you can to making it a part of you. You will extend your learning to your entire mind as today's thought becomes the thought that rules your mind, a habit in your problem-solving repertoire, and a way to react quickly to the temptation to perceive yourself as separate from God. As you learn to see salvation in all things, you will perceive the part of your mind where you perceive a world as saved.

7. No worries will bother you when you give your future into the Loving Hands of God. You will not suffer, and nothing will cause you pain or bring you loss. You will not fear, and you will regard everything with Love. By escaping all fear of future pain, you will find the way to present Peace, and a certainty of Safety that the world cannot threaten. You will be sure that, when your perception is mistaken, it will be corrected. You will be free to choose again when you have deceived yourself, and to change your mind when you have made a mistake.

8. Place your future in the Hands of God, and call the Memory of God to come again into your mind to replace all thoughts of separation and evil with the Truth of Love. Your entire mind will not fail to gain by this, and all of your perceptions will be healed. When you entrust yourself to God, you also place the part of your mind where you perceive a world into the Hands to Which you appeal for Help and Comfort. You lay aside the sick illusions that you have of the world, and you offer Peace to your entire mind.

9. Now, you are saved indeed! In God's Hands, you rest untroubled, certain that only Good can come to you. If you forget, you will be gently reassured; if you accept an unforgiving thought, it will soon be replaced by a Reflection of Love; and if you are tempted to attack, you will appeal to the Holy Spirit, Which guards

your Rest, and makes the Choice for you that leaves far behind all of your temptations to perceive yourself as separate from God. The world that you perceive will no longer be your enemy, because you will have chosen to be its Friend.

Mentor's Notes

Paragraph 3 is referring to the fact that you can remember depression, pain, loss, sorrow, and death, or you can anticipate them in the future, but in *this Instant* none of them exists.

Lesson 195

'I am grateful that I walk the way of Love.'

1. It is hard for you to learn gratitude when you look at the world and think that it is real. The most that you can do then is see yourself as better off than some others and try to be content, because you perceive someone else suffering more. How pitiful and deprecating are those thoughts! You cannot have cause for thanks while you perceive justification for less cause for thanks. You cannot suffer less because you project suffering outside of your mind and onto a world. Your gratitude is due only to the Holy Spirit, Which makes the cause of sorrow disappear from your mind entirely.

2. It is insane for you to offer thanks because of suffering, but it is equally insane for you to fail to offer gratitude to the Holy Spirit, Which offers you the certain means by which you heal all pain, and you replace suffering with laughter and Happiness. Even in your partial-Sanity, you cannot refuse to take the steps that the Holy Spirit directs and follow in the way that the Holy Spirit sets before you to escape the limitations that you thought were real, but that you now perceive are not.

3. In your identification with a personal self, the world that you perceive is your 'enemy', because you see in it the rival for your peace; a plunderer that takes your joy away from you and leaves you nothing but a black despair that is so bitter and relentless that there is no remaining hope for you. This leaves you with only vengeance to wish for. Now, you can only try to make the world lie down in death with you, as useless as yourself, and with nothing left in its grasping fingers, like you.

4. You are not being grateful to God when you perceive a world that is more limited than you, nor are you saner when you are enraged when it seems less limited than you. Love does not make comparisons, and your gratitude is sincere only if you join it with Love. Offer thanks to God that, in you, the part of your mind where you perceive a world will be freed. It can never be that part of your

mind is Limitless while the other part is limited, because you cannot bargain away One Mind in the name of Love.

5. Give thanks to God, but sincerely. Let your gratitude make room for all of those perceptions with which you will escape from limitations: the sick, the weak, the needy, the afraid, the mourners, the sufferers, the hungry, the hating, and the dying. Do not compare yourself with them or you split your mind into 'you' and a world outside of you. Instead, be grateful that they give you the opportunity to perceive the Love in your mind beyond them.

6. Thank God for one thing: That you are not separate from the part of your mind that seems to be a world, therefore you are One with God. Rejoice that no exceptions to your Wholeness can ever be made, nor impair, nor change your Function of completing God, Which is Completion. Give thanks for your entire mind, otherwise you offer thanks for nothing, and you fail to recognize God's Gifts to you.

7. Extend rest to the part of your mind where you perceive a world, and offer thanks for it. If you can extend to it the Peace that you want, then the way is open to you at last. The door to Timelessness will swing open for you, and you will remember God's Word, Which gathers clarity as you become willing to hear It once again.

8. Be grateful that you walk the way of Love. You will forget hatred when you put all comparisons aside, and nothing will remain as an obstacle to Peace. The fear of God will be undone, and you will forgive without comparisons. You cannot choose to overlook some things that you perceive in the world, and to keep others that you lock away as 'sins'. When your forgiving is complete, you will have total gratitude, because you will see that your entire mind has the right to your Love, because it *is* Love. It is your Self.

9. Today, you learn to think of Love in place of anger, malice, and revenge. You have Everything, and if you refuse to acknowledge It, you are not entitled to bitterness and a perception that you are a personal self in a world that does not care for you and that pushes

you around. Substitute gratitude in place of this insane perception. God loves you, and you are One with God. What can there be that is more to you than This?

10. Your gratitude will pave the way to God for you, and shorten your learning time by more than you can imagine. Gratitude goes hand-in-hand with Love; where you find one, you find the other. Gratitude is an aspect of Love, Which is the Source of Creation. God thanks you for being What you are: God's Own Completion, and the Source of Love, along with God. Your gratitude to God is one with God's Gratitude to you. Love can only walk the way of gratitude, so gratitude is the way that you walk to God.

Mentor's Notes

Paragraph 5 brings to mind the idea in the Text which says that what isn't Love is a call for Love. You can use your perception of an absence of Love as a reminder of Love.

Love is Oneness. From Love, you can only perceive Love, so, of course, Love does not make comparisons, because it cannot perceive anything to compare.

Lesson 196

'It is only myself that I crucify.'

1. When you fully understand this statement, and you keep it fully in your awareness, you will no longer attempt to harm yourself, nor make the body a slave to vengeance. You will not attack yourself, and you will realize that to attack another that you perceive is to attack yourself. You will be free of the insane belief that to attack what your mind perceives saves you, and you will understand that the safety and healing that you can perceive instead is your own.

2. Maybe, at first you will not understand how you can find Limitless Mercy in today's idea. Because the personal mind is quick to site the Truth to save its lies when it feels threatened, you may interpret it to mean that you can never escape from punishment. But the personal mind does not understand the truth that it uses for itself. *You,* however, can learn to see these foolish applications of truth, and to deny the meaning that the personal mind sees in them.

3. This is also how you will teach yourself that you are not a personal self. The ways in which the personal mind distorts Truth will not deceive you for much longer. You will not believe that you are a body to be crucified, and you will see the Light of your resurrection in today's idea, which looks past all thoughts of crucifixion and death, to thoughts of liberation from illusions, and of Life.

4. Today's idea is one step that you take away from limitedness to Limitlessness. Take this step today, so that you will go quickly on the way of your salvation, relinquishing your burdens one-by-one. You do not need time for this, but willingness. What seems to you to need a thousand years, you can easily do in just one Holy Instant by the Grace of God.

5. You have been crucified by the dreary, hopeless thought of the personal mind that you can attack what your mind perceives and escape from attack yourself. Maybe you thought that this was salvation, but it only stands for your belief that your fear of God is justified. And what is this but hell? With the fear of hell on you, you

believe that God is your deadly enemy, separate from you, and waiting to kill you.

6. This is the form of insanity that you believe, if you accept the fearful thought that you can attack what you perceive and be free yourself. Until this changes, you have nothing for which to hope. You will not escape this idea until you see that it is entirely impossible. The fear of God is real to you when you think that it is true. You will not perceive its foolishness, or even that the idea is there, and question it.

7. For you to question this idea at all, you must allow its form to change enough to permit your fear of retaliation to abate, so that the responsibility for the idea is returned to you. From there, you can at least consider if you want to continue along this painful path. Until you experience this shift, you will not perceive that it is only your thoughts that bring you fear, and that your escape from fear depends on you.

8. Your next steps will be easy, if you take this one today. From here, you will go ahead quite rapidly, because once you understand that it is impossible for you to be hurt by anything but your own thoughts, your fear of God must disappear. You won't be able to believe that fear is caused by something outside of you. And you will welcome your awareness of God, Which you wanted to banish, back to your Holy mind, Which God never left.

9. You can sense your salvation from illusions in the idea that you practice today. If you only crucify yourself, then you did not hurt the world, so you do not need to fear its vengeance. You also do not need to hide in terror from the deadly image of God that you have projected. But the thing that you dread the most is your own salvation. You are Strong, and It is Strength that you want; you are Limitless, and glad of Limitlessness. Yet, you have sought to be both weak and limited, because you feared your Strength and Limitlessness, and your salvation is in Them.

10. When you realize, once and for all, that it is you that you fear, and your mind perceives itself as split, there will be an instant when terror will seem to wholly grip your mind, and you will feel that

escape from it is hopeless.You have concealed this awareness by believing that you could direct attack outward and be attacked yourself from outside of you. It seemed to you that you had an enemy outside of you that you had to fear, so a god outside of you became your mortal enemy, and the source of your fear.

11. For an instant, you will perceive a murderer within you that plots your punishment until it can kill you at last. Yet, in this instant, your salvation will come as well. Your fear of God will disappear, and you will call on God to save you from your illusions with God's Love, in recognition that you are One with God. Pray that this instant is soon; today. Step back from fear and advance to Love.

12. Every Thought of God goes with you to help you reach this instant and go beyond it, quickly, surely, and Forever. When your fear of God is gone, there will be no obstacles between you and the Holy Peace of God. How kind and Merciful is today's idea! Welcome it, because it is your release from fear. It is indeed only you that you can try to crucify, but your redemption comes from you, too.

Mentor's Notes

Today's idea is directly related to the other concept often stated in this Course: Thoughts do not leave the mind of the thinker. It does not matter where you perceive attack; if you perceive it at all, it is in your mind.

Paragraph 2 refers to the fact that the personal mind is not threatened by ideas that are meant to undo it, as long as it can distort them for itself. It will do this often with ideas in this course. You will recognize that this is what is happening when you feel guilt or fear in connection with this course. For example, the personal mind reads today's lesson to mean that you will always crucify yourself. It doesn't care how you are crucified, as long as you feel it is justified. Paragraph 7 points out that you will have to have a shift in how you read today's lesson in order to move fear out of the way enough for you to understand what today's lesson really means, which is stated in the last line of this lesson.

Lesson 197

'It can only be my gratitude that I earn.'

1. Here is the second step that you take to free your mind from your belief that there are outside forces pitted against you. You make attempts at kindness and forgiveness, but then you turn them to attack again if they are not met with external gratitude. So you think that God's Gifts are loans at best, and, at worst, deceptions meant to cheat you out of your defenses, so that when God strikes, It won't fail to kill you.

2. How easily you confuse God with guilt when you do not know what your thoughts can do! When you deny your Strength, you see weakness as your salvation; when you choose to see yourself as limited, limitation becomes your home. You will not leave the limitations of the world and claim your Strength until you no longer confuse guilt with salvation, but you see instead that your salvation is in your Limitlessness and Strength.

3. You will perceive gratitude when you release the world from your illusions, because then your perception of it will reflect your gratitude to yourself. Your gratitude is all that your gifts require for them to be a lasting offering to you from a thankful mind that is released from hell forever. But this is what you undo when you take back your gifts because they are not honored by someone that you perceive outside of you. It is only *you* who can honor your gifts and be grateful for them, because it is you who receive the gifts that you give.

4. It does not matter if another that you perceive in the world thinks your gifts are unworthy. Others are in your mind, so beyond the personal mind's projections onto them is your mind thanking you. It does not matter if your gifts seem lost and ineffectual in the world, because they are received within you where you truly give them. In *your* gratitude they are accepted everywhere and thankfully acknowledged by God. Don't take them back when God has gratefully accepted them.

5. God blesses every gift that you give to God, and every gift that you give *is* given to God, because you can only give to yourself. What belongs to God must be God's. But you will never realize that God's Gifts are sure, Eternal, Changeless, Limitless, Forever extending Love and adding to Joy, while you forgive only to attack again.

6. If you withdraw the gifts that you give, then you will think that what God gives to you has been withdrawn. But if you learn to let your forgiving take away the 'proof' of separation that you think that you see outside of yourself, then you will not think that God gives Its Gifts only for a little while before snatching them away from you in death. Death will have no meaning for you, then.

7. And with the end of your belief in death, fear will be forever gone from you. Thank your True Self for this, because It is grateful only to God, and God thanks God for you. Christ must come into your entire mind, because Christ *is* your Whole Mind. Christ's Being in God is Secure, because Their Will is One. Their gratitude to All that They extend together has no end, because gratitude is a part of Love.

8. Thanks be to you, who are One with God. As God extends Itself to you, you contain All of Reality within your True Self. You are always One with God, and you cannot dim the Light of your Perfection. In your mind is the Mind of God. God holds you dear, because you are God, and all gratitude belongs to you, because of What you are.

9. Give thanks as you receive thanks. Be free of any ingratitude to the part of your mind where you perceive a world, because it makes your True Self complete. Nothing is left outside of this Self. Give thanks for all of the countless channels through which you can extend your True Self. All that you do is given to your True Self; all that you think can only be the Thoughts of your True Self, Which are shared with God. By forgiving, claim now the gratitude that you denied yourself when you forgot the function that God has given to you. Never think that God has ever ceased to offer thanks to you.

Mentor's Notes

Since it is the Law of Mind that mind only sees itself, you will perceive God as you perceive yourself. If you are untrustworthy, that is how you will perceive God.

Paragraph 4 explains how detachment from the world is possible. If you give from Love, then you don't care how a seeming 'other' responds to your gift. They may seem to accept it, to disparage it, or to not notice it at all. But it won't matter to you, because you will have received the Love that you were extending. If, however, you require their gratitude to justify your gift, then you will learn that you were not giving from Love after all, but from the personal mind, which only gives to receive something in return. You can only be truly detached from the world by living in an awareness of Love's Constant Presence.

Lesson 198

'Only my condemnation can injure me.'

1. Injury to you is impossible, but illusion makes illusion. If you think that you can condemn, then you will think that you can be injured. If you believe that you can injure, then you will use what you have made against yourself until you lay it down in recognition that you don't want it, because it is unreal and without value. Then, your illusion will cease to have seeming effects, and those effects that it seemed to have will be undone. You will be free from injury, because you will extend the idea that injury is impossible, and you will receive the gift that you give.

2. Condemn, and you limit yourself; forgive, and you are freed of limitations. This is the Law of Perception. God does not understand this particular expression of the Law, because Limitlessness is part of God. Condemnation, then, is impossible in Truth. What seems to be the influence and effects of condemnation have not occurred at all, but you must deal with them as if they have occurred. Illusion makes illusion, with one exception: Your forgiving is an illusion that undoes all other illusions.

3. Your forgiving sweeps away all of your other illusions, and even though it is itself an illusion, it does not make any more illusions. All illusions but this one multiply, and your forgiving is where illusions end. It is the illusion where you become aware of God again, but it is not itself the Truth. It points to Truth, however, and directs you to It with the Certainty of God. It is the illusion in which you become aware again of your True Self and of God, and you know that They are One.

4. Forgiving is the only path that leads you out of disaster, past all suffering, and finally away from death. There is no other way; this one is the plan of God. You have no reason to oppose it, quarrel with it, seek for a thousand ways in which it must be wrong, or for a thousand other possible roads to salvation.

5. It is wiser for you to be grateful that you have the answer to

your problems. It is more intelligent to thank God, Which gives you your salvation, and to accept God's gift with gratitude. It is a kindness to yourself to hear the Holy Spirit, and to learn the simple lessons that It teaches you, instead of dismissing Its words and substituting the personal mind's words in their place.

6. The Holy Spirit's words will work; they will save you. The Holy Spirit's words contain all of the hope, all of the blessing, and all of the Joy that you can find in your perception that you are in a world. God is the Source of the Holy Spirit's words, and they come to you with Heaven's Love upon them. When you hear the Holy Spirit's words, you hear the sound of Heaven. It is in these words that your thoughts merge into one at last, and as they fade, the Word of God will take their place, because then you will remember It and love It.

7. The world that you perceive has many seemingly separate situations where Mercy has no meaning, and attack appears justified. But they are all one: a place where you offer death to the Christ in you, and to God. You may think that They accept this, but if you look again at the situations where you think that you see proof of Their death, you will perceive a miracle instead. How foolish of you to think that They could die! How foolish of you to think that you can attack! How insane of you to think that you who are One with God can be condemned to die!

8. The Stillness of your True Self is unmoved and untouched by thoughts like these, and It is unaware of any condemnation which could need forgiveness. Illusions of any kind are strange and alien to the Truth, and only Truth can build a Bridge for you to bring your illusions to Truth to be undone.

9. Today, you practice letting Limitlessness make Its home again in your awareness. The Truth gives these words to you, so that you have the idea that ends your suffering:

> 'Only my condemnation can injure me; only my forgiveness sets me free.'

Do not forget today that all forms of suffering that you perceive only hide an unforgiving thought, but also that all forms of pain are healed by your forgiving.

10. Accept the one illusion that proclaims that there is no condemnation in you who are One with God, and you will remember Heaven instantly. You will forget the world, and all of your weird beliefs about it, as your Christ Mind is revealed to you with this one illusion. This is the gift that the Holy Spirit holds for you from God. Celebrate today, in your perception that you are in a world, and in your Holy Home as well. Be kind to both, as you forgive yourself the trespasses that you projected onto them, and see your Innocence shining on you from your Christ Mind.

11. Now, the world that you perceive is silenced; now, there is a Stillness where there was a frantic rush of thoughts that made no sense. Now, there is a Tranquil Light in your perception, which is made Quiet without illusions; now, only the Word of God remains in your entire mind. You will perceive This only an instant, then symbols will be gone, and everything that you ever thought that you made will completely vanish from your mind, which God Forever knows as One with God.

12. There is no condemnation in your Christ Mind; you are Perfect in your Holiness. You don't need thoughts of Mercy, nor gifts, because you have Everything. You have no need to offer forgiveness to What is One with Innocence Itself, and Which is so like God that to behold It is to no longer perceive, but to know only God. In your Perception of the Christ in you, Which is so brief that not an instant stands between It and Eternity, you will perceive your True Self, and then you will disappear Forever into God.

13. Today, you come nearer the end of everything that stands between you and your Real Perception. Be glad that you have come this far, and recognize that the Holy Spirit, Which has brought you this far, will not forsake you now. The Holy Spirit gives to you the Gift that God gives to you through the Holy Spirit. Now is the time for your deliverance from illusions. The time has come today.

Lesson 199

'I am not a body; I am Limitless.'

1. You cannot feel free and Limitless as long as you perceive a body as you. The body is a limit on you, and you cannot find your Freedom in what is meant to limit you. But your mind *is* Limitless when it doesn't perceive itself as tied to a body and sheltered by it. If your mind was limited to a body, it would be vulnerable indeed!

2. When your mind serves the Holy Spirit, it is Eternally Limitless in every way, beyond the 'laws' of space and time, unbound by any preconceptions, and with the Strength and Power to do whatever it is asked. Attack thoughts cannot enter your mind, then, because it has been given to the Source of Love, and fear cannot enter your mind when your mind is One with Love. Your mind rests in God, and you cannot be afraid when your mind lives in Innocence and only loves.

3. It is essential for your progress in this course that you accept today's idea and hold it very dear. Do not be concerned that the personal mind considers it quite insane. The personal mind holds the body dear, because it thinks that it lives in it, and it is united with the home that it has made. It is part of the illusion that protects it from your finding that it is an illusion itself.

4. The personal mind hides in the body, and it is here that you can see it as the limit on you that it is. Declare your Innocence, and you are free of the body, because you have no need of it, except as the Holy Spirit sees it. For the Holy Spirit's purpose, the body is a useful form for what the mind needs to do. It becomes a vehicle which helps you to extend your forgiving to all that comes into your awareness, according to God's plan.

5. Cherish today's idea and practice it, today and everyday. Make it a part of every practice period you take. Every thought will gain power by it, and it will increase the gifts of every thought to you. This idea extends freedom in your mind where you perceive a world as well, and you are not exempt from the gift that you give.

6. The Holy Spirit is the Home of your Limitless Mind, Which you seek. When you find It in the Holy Spirit, the body, free of conflict and in clear response, will become a worthy servant of your Limitless Mind, and without the power to enslave It, which you had given to the body before.

7. Be free today, and extend your Freedom to overlook all of the bodies that you perceive. Be free, so that the Holy Spirit can use your escape from limitations to set free the part of your mind where you perceive a world. Let Love replace all perceptions of helplessness and fear through you. Accept your salvation now, and give your mind to the Holy Spirit, Which calls to you to make this a gift to It. The Holy Spirit wants to give you Perfect Freedom, Perfect Joy, and the hope that is fully satisfied in God.

8. You are One with God, and you are Eternally Immortal; return your mind to This. Practice well the thought that the Holy Spirit gives to you for today. Your entire mind is released with you in today's idea. All that you perceive is blessed with you, you will no longer weep, and Heaven thanks you for the increase of Joy that your practice brings even to It. God extends Its Love and Happiness every time that you say:

> 'I am not a body; I am Limitless. I hear the Holy Spirit, Which God gives to me, and it is only This that my mind obeys.'

Lesson 200

'The only peace is God's Peace.'

1. Do not seek any further; the only peace that you can find is the Peace of God. Accept this fact, and you save yourself the agony of more bitter disappointments, bleak despair, icy hopelessness, and doubt. Do not seek any further, unless you seek for misery or pain, because the only thing for you to find is the Peace of God.

2. This is the final point to which you must come at last. Lay aside all hope of finding Happiness where there is none, and of being saved by what can only hurt you; of trying to make Peace out of chaos, Joy out of pain, and Heaven out of hell. Do not try any longer to win through losing, or to live through dying. You are only asking for failure.

3.You can ask as easily for Love, Happiness, and Eternal Life in Infinite Peace. Ask for all This, and you can only win. You will only succeed when you ask for What you already have, but when you ask for illusion to be the Truth, you will only fail. Forgive yourself your futile imaginings, and don't seek any longer for what you cannot find. Nothing is more foolish than for you to seek again and again for hell when you only have to look into your mind to find that Heaven is here, and that It welcomes you.

4. Go Home, because you have not found your Happiness in a foreign place, and in alien forms that have no meaning to you, though you have sought to make them meaningful. The world that you perceive is not where you belong; you are a stranger there. But you have been given the means to no longer perceive the world as a limitation.

5. In the world where you once limited yourself you can find your Freedom, but you must change your mind about the purpose of the world to escape from it. You will be limited until you extend blessing to your mind where you perceive a world, free it from the projection of your mistakes, and honor it as your Self. You did not make yourself, and as you free one part of your mind, you accept the

other part as it is.

6. What does your forgiving do? In Truth, it has no function; it is unknown in Heaven. You only need to forgive in hell, where forgiving serves a mighty function. Isn't it a worthy purpose for you who are One with God to escape the evil dreams of hell that you have imagined? How could you hope for more while it appears to you that there is a choice to make between success and failure; between Love and fear?

7. The only peace is God's Peace, because you are One with God, and you cannot make a world that opposes God's Will, Which is your own. What could you hope to find in such a world? It cannot be real, because it is not of God, so is it there that you want to look for Peace? You can see, instead, that such a world deceives you, but you can also learn to perceive it differently, and find the Peace of God.

8. Peace is the Bridge that you will cross to leave the world behind. But Peace begins for you in your perception that you are in a world when you perceive it differently, and then, with your Real Perception, Peace leads you up to Heaven, and then beyond. Peace is your answer to conflicting goals; senseless journeys; frantic, pointless pursuits; and meaningless endeavors. Your way is easy as it slopes gently toward the Bridge Where your Freedom lies within the Peace of God.

9. Do not lose your way again today. You go to Heaven, and the path is straight. You will be delayed on thorny byways only if you try to wander. God alone is Certain, and God will guide your steps. God will not desert you, nor let you stray forever from your Home. God calls; you will hear. And that is all there is to what appears to be a world apart from God, where bodies have reality.

10. Now, there is Silence, so seek no further. You have come to where the road is littered with false desires, fallen from the hopelessness that you sought before. They are underfoot, but you look upward to Heaven. The body's eyes serve you only for an instant now. You already recognize Peace, and you can feel Its Soft Embrace surround your mind with Comfort and Love.

11. You will not seek for idols today, because Peace cannot be found in them. The Peace of God is yours, and this is all that you want and accept. Peace be to you today, because you have found a simple, happy way to leave behind the world of ambiguity, and to replace the personal mind's shifting goals and lonely illusions with a single purpose and Holy Companionship. Peace is Oneness, because It comes from God. Seek no further; you are close to Home, and you draw even closer as you say:

'The only peace is God's Peace, and I am glad and thankful that this is so.'

Review 6

Introduction

1. For this review period, you will take one idea each day and practice it as often as is possible. Besides the fifteen minutes that you give each morning and evening, and the hourly remembering that you make throughout the day, use the day's idea as often as you can. Any of these ideas alone is enough for your salvation, if you truly learn it. Any of these ideas is enough to release your entire mind from limitation, and invite the Memory of God to return to you.

2. With this in mind, you start your practicing, in which you carefully review the thoughts that the Holy Spirit has given to you in your last twenty lessons. Each one contains the whole lesson plan of this course, if you understand it, practice it, accept it, and apply it to everything that seems to happen throughout the day. One idea would be enough if you make no exceptions with it, so you need to use them all, so that they blend into one, as each is a part that contributes to the whole.

3. These practice sessions, like in your last review, center on a central theme with which you begin and end each lesson. It is this:

> 'I am not a body. I am Limitless, because I am Eternally One with God.'

Your day begins and ends with this, and you will repeat it every hour, or when you remember in between that you have a function that transcends the world that you perceive. Beyond this, and a repetition of the special thought that you practice for each day, you have no form of exercise, except a deep relinquishment of everything that clutters up your mind, and makes you deaf to True Reason, Sanity, and simple Truth.

4. You will go beyond all words and special forms of practicing for this review, because you will take a quicker path to the Serenity and Peace of God. You only have to close your eyes and forget all

that you thought that you knew and understood, because this is how your Freedom is given to you from What you did not know, and failed to understand, in your identification with a personal self.

5. There is only one exception to this lack of structure: Permit no idle thought to go uncorrected. If you notice one, deny it by quickly assuring your mind that this is not what you want. Then, gently let it go in exchange for the idea that you practice that day.

6. When you are tempted by illusions, quickly proclaim your freedom from temptation as you say:

'I do not want this thought. Instead, I choose ______.'

Then repeat the idea for the day, and let it take the place of what you were thinking. Beyond this special application for the day's idea, add only the day's few formal expressions or specific thoughts to aid your practicing. Then, give these times to the Holy Spirit, Which instructs you in Quiet, speaks of Peace, and gives your thoughts whatever meaning that they may have.

7. The Christ in you offers this review to the Holy Spirit for you, and places you in the Holy Spirit's charge to let the Holy Spirit teach you what to do, what to say, and what to think every time that you turn to the Holy Spirit. The Holy Spirit will always be here when you call on It for help. Offer the Holy Spirit the whole review now as you begin, and do not forget that you have given it to the Holy Spirit as you practice each day, and advance toward the Goal that It set for you. Allow the Holy Spirit to teach you how to go forward, and trust It completely to show you the way that each practice period can best become a Loving gift of Freedom for your entire mind.

Lesson 201

'I am not a body. I am Limitless, because I am Eternally One with God.'

1. (181) 'I trust in the Oneness that I perceive.'

Everything that I perceive is in my mind. I am blessed in Oneness with my entire mind, and with God, the Source of my Whole Mind, Which is my True Self.

'I am not a body. I am Limitless, because I am Eternally One with God.'

Lesson 202

'I am not a body. I am Limitless, because I am Eternally One with God.'

1. (182) 'I will be still for an Instant and go Home.'

I do not choose to stay an instant more where I do not belong, when God has given me the Holy Spirit to call me Home.

'I am not a body. I am Limitless, because I am Eternally One with God.'

Lesson 203

'I am not a body. I am Limitless, because I am Eternally One with God.'

1. (183) 'I call on God's Name, therefore on my own.'

The Name of God is my deliverance from every thought of 'evil' and 'sin', because It is my own as well as God's.

'I am not a body. I am Limitless, because I am Eternally One with God.'

Lesson 204

'I am not a body. I am Limitless, because I am Eternally One with God.'

1. (184) 'The Name of God belongs to me.'

God's Name reminds me that I am One with God. I am not a slave to time; I am free of laws which rule the world of sick illusions, I am Limitless in God, and I am Eternally One with God.

'I am not a body I am Limitless, because I am Eternally One with God.'

Lesson 205

'I am not a body. I am Limitless, because I am Eternally One with God.'

1. (185) 'I want the Peace of God.'

The Peace of God is Everything that I want. The Peace of God is my One Goal, the aim of my living in the world, the end I seek; my purpose, my function, and my life, while I abide where I am not at home.

'I am not a body. I am Limitless, because I am Eternally One with God.'

Lesson 206

'I am not a body. I am Limitless, because I am Eternally One with God.'

1. (186) 'The salvation of the part of my mind where I perceive a world depends on me.'

I am entrusted with the Gifts of God, because I am One with God. I want to extend God's Gifts to my entire mind, where God intends Them to be.

'I am not a body. I am Limitless, because I am Eternally One with God.'

Lesson 207

'I am not a body. I am Limitless, because I am Eternally One with God.'

1. (187) 'I bless all that I perceive, because I bless myself.'

God's Blessing shines on me from my Center, Where God abides. I only need to turn to God and every sorrow melts away, as I accept God's Boundless Love for me.

'I am not a body. I am Limitless, because I am Eternally One with God.'

Lesson 208

'I am not a body. I am Limitless, because I am Eternally One with God.'

1. (188) 'The Peace of God is shining in me now.'

I will be Still and perceive my entire mind as Still with me. In that Stillness, I will find the Peace of God, Which is my Center, and Which witnesses to God.

'I am not a body. I am Limitless, because I am Eternally One with God.'

Lesson 209

'I am not a body. I am Limitless, because I am Eternally One with God.'

1. (189) 'I feel the Love of God within me now.'

The Love of God created me, the Love of God is Everything that I am, the Love of God proclaims that I am One with It, the Love of God within me frees me from limitations.

'I am not a body. I am Limitless, because I am Eternally One with God.'

Lesson 210

'I am not a body. I am Limitless, because I am Eternally One with God.'

1. (190) 'I choose the Joy of God instead of pain.'

Pain is an idea in my split mind. It is not a thought of God, but one that I think apart from God's Will. God's Will is Joy, and only Joy, for me. I choose Joy instead of what I made.

'I am not a body. I am Limitless, because I am Eternally One with God.'

Lesson 211

'I am not a body. I am Limitless, because I am Eternally One with God.'

1. (191) 'I am God's Holy Extension.'

In Silence and true humility, I seek God's Glory within in my True Self, Which is One with God.

'I am not a body. I am Limitless, because I am Eternally One with God.'

Lesson 212

'I am not a body. I am Limitless, because I am Eternally One with God.'

1. (192) 'Forgiving is the function that God wants me to fill.'

I seek the function of forgiving that will set me free from all of the pointless illusions of the world. Only the function that God gives to me can offer me freedom. I seek only this, and I will accept only this as mine.

'I am not a body. I am Limitless, because I am Eternally One with God.'

Lesson 213

'I am not a body. I am Limitless, because I am Eternally One with God.'

1. (193) 'All things are lessons in forgiving that God wants me to learn.'

A lesson is a miracle that God offers to me to replace the thoughts of the personal mind, which I made, and which hurt me. The forgiving that I learn of God is the way that I am set free, so I choose to learn God's lessons and forget the personal mind's lessons.

'I am not a body. I am Limitless, because I am Eternally One with God.'

Lesson 214

'I am not a body. I am Limitless, because I am Eternally One with God.

1. (194) 'I place the future in the Hands of God.'

The past is gone; the future has not come. Now I am freed of both, because What God gives can only be Good. I accept only What God gives to me as What belongs to me.

'I am not a body. I am Limitless, because I am Eternally One with God.'

Lesson 215

'I am not a body. I am Limitless, because I am Eternally One with God.'

1. (195) 'I am grateful that I walk the way of Love.'

The Holy Spirit is my only Guide. The Holy Spirit walks with me in Love, and I thank the Holy Spirit for showing me the way to go.

'I am not a body. I am Limitless, because I am Eternally One with God.'

Lesson 216

'I am not a body. I am Limitless, because I am Eternally One with God.'

1. (196) 'It is only myself that I crucify.'

All that I do, I do to myself. If I attack, I suffer, but if I forgive, I am saved from suffering.

'I am not a body. I am Limitless, because I am Eternally One with God.'

Lesson 217

'I am not a body. I am Limitless, because I am Eternally One with God.'

1. (197) 'It can only be my gratitude that I earn.'

Only my True Self can be grateful for my salvation, and only through my salvation can I find the True Self to Whom I owe thanks.

'I am not a body. I am Limitless, because I am Eternally One with God.'

Lesson 218

'I am not a body. I am Limitless, because I am Eternally One with God.'

1. (198) 'Only my condemnation can injure me.'

My condemnation keeps my perception dark, and then I cannot perceive the Glory of my True Perception. But today, I choose to behold my Glory and be glad.

'I am not a body. I am Limitless, because I am Eternally One with God.'

Lesson 219

'I am not a body. I am Limitless, because I am Eternally One with God.'

1. (199) 'I am not a body; I am Limitless.'

I am One with God. I still my mind and think about this for a moment, then, when I return to an awareness of the world, I am not confused about the Self that God loves Eternally as One with God.

'I am not a body. I am Limitless, because I am Eternally One with God.'

Lesson 220

'I am not a body. I am Limitless, because I am Eternally One with God.'

1. (200) 'The only peace is God's Peace.'

I will not wander from the way of Peace, because I am lost on other roads. I will follow the Holy Spirit, Which leads me Home, then my Peace will be as Certain as the Love of God.

'I am not a body. I am Limitless, because I am Eternally One with God.'

Part Two

Introduction

1. Words will be of little use to you now, as you will use them only as a guide on which you will not depend. Now you are seeking direct experience of Truth. The lessons that remain are only introductions to the times that you leave the world of pain to enter into Peace. Now, you will begin to reach the Goal that this course has set for you, and find the End toward Which your practicing has been geared.

2. Now, the exercises will only be a beginning for you, because you will wait in quiet expectation for God, Which has promised to take the final step Itself. You can be sure that God keeps Its Promises. You have come far along the road to God, and now you only wait for God. You will continue spending time with God every morning and night for as long as you are happy. The time that you give to this will not be a matter of specific duration for you now; you will use as much time as you need for the Result that you desire. You will also use your hourly remembrances in between, and call on God when you are tempted to forget your Goal.

3. You will continue with a central thought for the rest of the lessons, and you will use that thought to introduce your times of rest, and then to calm your mind as needed. But you will not be content with simple practicing in the remaining Holy Instants that conclude this year that you give to God. You will say some words of welcome, and expect God to reveal Itself, as God has promised. God has promised that when you call on God, you will always be answered.

4. Now you go to God with only God's Word on your mind, and you wait for God to take the final step that God told you through the Holy Spirit that God will take when you invite God. God has not left you in your insanity, nor has God betrayed your trust in It. God's Faithfulness has earned God your invitation, which God seeks to make you Happy. Offer your invitation, and it will be accepted. This

is how your time with God will now be spent: You will say the words of invitation that the Holy Spirit suggests, and then you will wait for God to come to you.

5. Now, all ancient prophesies and promises are fulfilled and fully kept. No step remains for time to separate from its accomplishment, because now you cannot fail. Sit silently, and wait for God. It is God's Will that God will come to you when you have recognized that it is your will that God do so. You could not have come this far unless you saw, however dimly, that this is your will.

6. Your Christ Mind is so close to you that you cannot fail. '*Dear God, I give these Holy times to you in gratitude for your Holy Spirit, Which has taught me how to exchange the world of sorrow for its Replacement, Which you give to me. I will not look backward now; I look ahead to the End of my journey. Accept my little gifts of thanks as, with my Christ Mind, I behold a Perception beyond the world that I made, and I take It to be the full Replacement for the world.*

7. Now, I wait in silence, unafraid, and certain of Your coming. I have followed the Guide that you sent to me. I did not know the way, but You did not forget me. I know that you will not forget me now. I ask that You keep your Timeless Promises, Which it is Your Will to keep. I will with You in asking this. You and I are One, and Our Holy Will, Which created All that is Real, cannot fail in anything. In this Certainty, I undertake these last few steps to You, and I rest in Confidence upon Your Love, Which will not fail me.'

8. And so you start the final part of this Holy year, which you have spent with Christ in search of Truth and God, Which is the Only Source of Truth. You found the way that God chose for you, and you made the choice to follow it as God wants you to. God's Holy Spirit has held you up, God's Thoughts have lit the darkness of your mind, and God's Love has called to you unceasingly since time began.

9. You wished that God's Extension could be cut off from God, you wanted God to change Itself and be what you wanted God to be, and you believed that these insane desires were the truth. Now, you

can be glad that this is all undone, and that you no longer think that illusions are true. The Memory of God lights your entire mind; a moment more, and your Whole Mind will rise again. A moment more, and you who are One with God will be safely Home, Where God wants you to be.

10. Now, your need for practice is almost over, because in this final section you will come to understand that you only need to call on God and all temptation to believe that you are separate from God will disappear. Instead of words, you only need to feel God's Love. Instead of prayers, you only need to call on God. Instead of judging, you only need to be Still and let all things be healed. Accept the way that God's plan will end as you received the way that it began. Now it is complete. This year brings you to Eternity.

11. One further use for words still remains. From time to time, a theme of special relevance will be interspersed between your daily lessons, which should be followed by periods of wordless, deep experience afterward. Review these special thoughts each day, until the next one is given to you. Read them slowly and think about them for a little while before one of the blessed Holy Instants of the day.

Mentor's Notes

To clarify the instructions for the remaining lessons: Each morning, read and contemplate the question and answer that precedes the section that contains that day's lesson. Then, read the lesson. After this, simply quiet your mind and take a listening attitude as you wait for God to reveal Itself. In the evening, read the lesson only, before you sink into quiet communion with God. The duration of these longer meditations will vary, depending on how long it takes for you to feel that you have opened yourself to God. Also, once an hour, repeat the day's lesson, and give it a moment's thought. Of course, you should call on God throughout the day when you feel tempted to give up your Peace.

This type of meditation where you simply open your mind to God is essential if you seriously desire Peace. You should try to sit through any discomfort, but if it increases or doesn't pass, then don't force yourself. Do not expect anything *dramatic* to come from these meditations. God is very natural to you, so you will experience God in subtle forms. For example, during the meditation itself, you may not feel anything in particular, but you can be sure that if you find yourself spontaneously taking a deep breath and relaxing deeper, that you have connected to God. You may not feel immediate Peace, but you will find, as you practice this way, that God's Peace, shifts in understanding, deep insights, answers to your questions, and an overall sense of well-being will come to you throughout the day, often when you are not looking for them.

1. What is forgiveness?

1. In your forgiving, you are recognizing that what seems to happen in the world has not really occurred. You are not pardoning sin, thereby making it real to you; you are recognizing that there is no such thing as sin. Therefore, you are forgiving yourself your perception of separation from God. The personal mind's perception of sin, wherever you see it, is only a false idea about yourself, and your forgiving recognizes its falseness, and therefore lets it go. Now, the Will of God is free to take Its place in your mind.

2. An unforgiving thought is a judgment of the personal mind that you do not raise to doubt. You close your mind, and you refuse to release it. Unforgiving thoughts protect the personal mind's projections, and tighten their hold on you by hiding and obscuring their source. Then, you are less likely to doubt them, and they are kept further away from your True Reasoning Mind. Nothing can come between a fixed projection of the personal mind and its chosen goal for you of separation from God.

3. An unforgiving thought frantically pursues its goal of separation from God, twisting and overturning anything that it perceives as interfering with its chosen path. Its purpose is to distort, and its means is distortion as well. It sets about furiously attempting to smash Reality, and it is unconcerned with anything that appears to contradict its point of view.

4. But when you are forgiving, you are Still and Quiet, and you do nothing. You do not try to attack Reality, nor try to twist appearances that the personal mind likes into 'reality'. You merely perceive without judgment. When you do not want to forgive yourself, you must judge to justify your failure to forgive. But when you want to forgive yourself, you must learn to welcome Truth exactly as It is.

5. Do nothing, then, and let the Holy Spirit, your Guide, your Savior, and your Protector, show you how to forgive. Be strong in hope, and certain of your success. The Holy Spirit has already forgiven you, because that is the function that God gives to the Holy Spirit. Now, you must share the Holy Spirit's function and forgive

yourself, whose Innocence the Holy Spirit sees, and whom the Holy Spirit honors as One with God, as you must.

Mentor's Notes

An 'unforgiving thought' is any thought that makes separation from God seem real to you. It can be a 'negative' or a 'positive' thought that validates the personal self and the world as reality. All thoughts of the personal mind are unforgiving thoughts.

In paragraph 4 it says that if you don't want to forgive, you must judge to justify your failure to forgive. It is through judgment (good/bad, right/wrong, useful/not useful) that you give meaning to people and situations and make them real to you, so, if you choose to not forgive, you must judge to justify your not forgiving. For example, 'He's wrong and I'm right, so I can't overlook this' or 'She's pretty, so I can't see past her body' or 'I was unfairly treated, so I can't let this go'.

Lesson 221

'Peace to my mind; I will still my thoughts.'

1. *'God, I come to You today to seek for the Peace that You alone can give to me. I come in silence, and I wait and listen for Your Voice in the Quiet Center of my Being, and in the deep recesses of my mind. Dear God, speak to me today. I come to hear Your Voice in silence, in certainty, and in Love, sure that You will hear my call and answer me.'*

2. Now, you wait in quiet. God is here, because you wait with the Christ in you. Your Christ Mind is sure that God will speak to you, and that you will hear God. Accept Christ's confidence, because It is your Mind. You wait with these intentions: to hear God's Answer to your call, to still your thoughts and find God's Peace, and to hear God tell you What you are and reveal Itself to you who are One with God.

Lesson 222

'God is with me; I live and move in God.'

1. God is with me. God is the Source of my Life, the Life within me, the air that I breathe, the food by which I am sustained, and the water that renews and cleanses me. God is my Home, Where I live and move; the Spirit that directs my actions, offers me Its Thoughts, and guarantees my safety from all pain. God covers me with kindness and care, and holds in Love my Christ Mind, on Which God shines, and Which shines on God. How still I am when I know the Truth of What I speak today!

2. *'God, I have no words except Your Name on my lips and in my mind, as I come quietly into Your Presence now, and ask to rest with You in Peace for a while.'*

Mentor's Notes

The references to air, food, water, and home in this lesson are figurative, not literal.

Lesson 223

'God is my only Life.'

1. I was mistaken when I thought that I lived apart from God, a separate entity in isolation, unattached, and housed in a body. Now, I know that my Life is God's Life; I have no other home, and I do not exist apart from God. All of God's Thoughts are a part of me, and my only Real Thoughts are God's Thoughts.

2. *'Dear God, I choose to see my Christ Mind instead of my mistakes, because I am One with You and Innocent. I want to look on my Innocence, because guilt proclaims that I am not One with You. I no longer want to deny You, because I am lonely in the world that I perceive, and I long for Heaven, Where I am at Home. Today, I will return. My Name is Yours, and I acknowledge that I am One with You.'*

Lesson 224

'God is my Source, and God loves me.'

1. My True Identity is so Secure, Innocent, Glorious, and wholly Good that Heaven looks to It to give Heaven Light, and It extends to all that I perceive as well. It is the Gift that God gives to me, and the One that I extend, too. My True Identity is the Only Gift that can be given and received. This is Reality, and only This. This is the end of illusions; This is the Truth.

2. *'My Identity, dear God, is still known to You. I have forgotten It, and I do not know where I am going, who I am, or what it is that I do. Remind me now, dear God, because I am weary of the world that I perceive. Reveal What You want me to perceive instead.'*

Lesson 225

'God is my Source, and I love God.'

1. *'God, I return to You Your Love for me, because giving and receiving are the same, and you have given all of Your Love to me. I return Your Love to You, because I want It fully in my awareness and blazing in my mind. I want to be held within Its Kindly Light, Safe and Beloved. Fear is behind me, and only Peace is ahead of me. How Still is the way that I am Lovingly led along to You!'*

2. Find that Stillness now within your Christ Mind; the way is open. Now, you can follow it in Peace, in Oneness with the Christ in you. You have reached within for Christ, and It will never leave you. You are One, and it is this Oneness that you perceive as you accomplish these final steps that end a journey that never really began.

Lesson 226

'My Home waits for me; I will hurry There.'

1. If I choose, I can depart from the world entirely. It is not death, but changing my mind about the purpose of the world, that makes this possible. If I believe that the world has value as I now perceive it, it will remain valuable to me. But if I see no value in it as I now perceive it, nothing that I want to keep, or search for as a goal, then it will depart from me. I have been trying to make illusions replace the Truth in my mind.

2. *'God, my Home is waiting for my return. Your Arms are open, and I hear Your Voice. I have no need to linger in a place of futile desires and shattered dreams, when Heaven is so easily mine.'*

Lesson 227

'This is my Holy Instant of release.'

1. *'Dear God, I am free today, because my will is Yours. I thought that I made another will, but nothing that I thought apart from You exists. I am Free, because I was mistaken, and I have not affected my own Reality with my illusions. Now, I give them up and lay them down before Truth, so that they can be removed forever from my mind. This is my Holy Instant of release. God, I know my will is One with Yours.'*

2. Today, you make your Happy return to Heaven, Which you have never really left. Today, you lay down your illusions and go Home again, released from your belief in sin, and dressed only in Holiness. Your Real Mind is restored to you at last.

Lesson 228

'God does not condemn me, and neither do I.'

1. God knows my Holiness; I will not deny God's Knowledge and believe in what God's Knowledge makes impossible. I will not accept as true what God proclaims is false. I will take God's Word for What I am, since God is my Source and knows my True Condition.

2. *'God, I have been mistaken in myself, because I have failed to realize that You are my Source. I have not left you to enter into a body and die. My Holiness is a Part of me, as I am a Part of You. My mistakes about myself are only illusions. I let them go today, and I stand ready to receive Your Word alone for What I really am.'*

Lesson 229

'Love created me, and Love is What I am.'

1. I seek my own Identity, and I find It in these words: 'Love created me, and Love is What I am.' Now, I don't need to seek any more; Love has prevailed. It has waited in Stillness for my homecoming, so I will no longer turn away from my Holy Christ Mind. Now, What I perceive attests to the Truth of the Identity that I sought to lose, but Which God has kept safe for me.

2.*'God, I thank You for What I am, and for keeping my Identity untouched and Innocent in the midst of all of the thoughts of separation from You that I foolishly made up. I thank You for saving me from them. Amen.'*

Lesson 230

'Now, I seek and find the Peace of God.'

1. I was created in Peace, and I remain in Peace. I do not have the power to change my True Self. God is Merciful, because when God extended Itself to me, God gave me Peace Forever. Now, I ask only to be What I am. This cannot be denied to me, because It is Forever True.

2. *'God, I seek the Peace that You extended to me in my creation. What You gave then must be here now, because my creation was not in time and is beyond change. The Peace in Which I extend from Your Mind is shining There unchanged. I am as You created me, and I only need to call on You to find the Peace that You extend to me. It is Your Will that extends Peace to me.'*

2. What is salvation?

1. Your salvation is a promise made by God that you will remember God. This promise can only be kept. It guarantees that time will end, and that all thoughts that you have in time will end as well. God's Word is given to your mind, which thinks that it has thoughts that are separate from God, and It will replace these thought of conflict with the Thought of Peace.

2. The Thought of Peace was given to you the instant that you thought of conflict. There was no need for a Thought of Peace before, because Peace does not have an opposite; It merely *is*. But your mind is split and needs healing, so the Thought that has the Power to heal this split is a part of your mind, which still is One, though you do not recognize This. You think that you do not know yourself; you think that your Identity is lost.

3. Your salvation is *un-doing* in the sense that to be saved you *do nothing* to support the illusory world of malice. You let illusions go; by your not supporting them, they quietly fade from your mind. What they hid is now revealed to you: Your Christ Mind, on Which is written God's Word, with the gifts of your forgiving laid before It, and your Memory of God just beyond.

4. Come daily to this Holy Place, and spend a while with Christ. Here, you share your final illusion. It is an illusion in which there is no sorrow, because it holds a hint of all of the Glory that God gives to you in Christ. Your Christ Mind will be renewed in your awareness, and your Real Perception will be with you. And the darkness of denying God will be gone from your mind as your entire mind will join in God's Light.

5. From Here, you will extend salvation in your perception, because it is Here that you will receive your salvation. Your rejoicing will call out to your entire mind that you have returned to Freedom, that time is almost over, and that you have only an instant more to wait until you wholly remember God. Illusions will be done, Eternity will shine away the world that you perceive, and only Heaven will exist for you.

Lesson 231

'God, I will only to remember You.'

1. *'There is nothing to seek for but Your Love, dear God. Maybe I think I seek for something else; something that I have called by many names. But Your Love is all that I have ever really sought. There is nothing else that I could ever want to find. I will to remember You, because I desire only the Truth about myself.'*

2. This is your will, and you share it with your Christ Mind. Heaven is in your remembering God. This is What you seek, and only This is what you can truly find.

Lesson 232

'Dear God, be in my mind throughout the day.'

1. *'Be in my mind when I awake, dear God, and shine on me throughout the day. Every minute will be time that I spend with You. I will not forget to be grateful every hour that You are with me, and that You will always be here to answer my call to You. As evening comes, all my thoughts will still be of You, and of Your Love. I will sleep sure of my Safety, certain of Your Care, and Happily aware that I am One with You.'*

2. This is how every day should be. Today, practice the end of fear. Have faith in God; trust all things to God. Let God reveal All Things to you, and do not be dismayed, because you are One with God.

Lesson 233

'I give my life to God to guide today.'

1. *'God, I give You all of my thoughts to guide today. I do not want any of the personal mind's thoughts. In place of them, give me Your Own. I let You guide all of my acts as well, so that I will do Your Will instead of seeking for goals that I cannot attain, and wasting time on futile imagining. Today, I come to You; I will step back and follow only You. You be the Guide, and I will be the follower, and I will not question the Wisdom of the Infinite, nor Your Tender Love, Which I cannot understand, but Which is your Perfect Gift to me.'*

2. Today, you have only One Guide to lead you. As you walk with God, you will give this day to God without reservation. This is God's Day, so it is a day of countless Gifts and Mercies to you.

Lesson 234

'God, today I am aware again that I am One with You.'

1. Today, you will anticipate the time when your illusion of separation from God and guilt are gone from your mind, and you are wholly aware again of the Holy Peace that you have never left. Only a tiny instant has elapsed in Eternity; so brief an interval that there is no lapse in Its Continuity; no break in Thoughts that are Forever One. Nothing has ever happened to disturb the Peace of God and of God's Extension. You will accept this as wholly true today.

2. *'I thank you, God, that I cannot lose my Memory of You and of Your Love. I recognize my Safety, and I thank You for all of the Gifts that you have bestowed on me, for all of the Loving Help that I have received from You, for Your Eternal Patience, and for the awareness that I am saved.'*

Lesson 235

'God, in Its Mercy, wills that I be saved.'

1. I only need to look on all things that seem to hurt me and say to myself, with perfect certainty, 'God wills that I be saved from this', and they will disappear. I only need to keep in mind that God wills only my Happiness to find that Happiness has come to me. And I only need to remember that God's Love surrounds my entire mind, and keeps my Innocence Forever Perfect, to be sure that I am saved from my illusions, and Safe Forever in God. I am the One that God loves, and I am saved, because God, in Its Mercy, wills it so.

2. *'God, Your Holiness is mine. Your Love extends to me, so my Innocence is Forever Part of You. There is no guilt or sin in me, because there is none in You.'*

Lesson 236

'I alone rule my mind.'

1. I have a mind that I must rule. At times, it does not seem that I rule it at all; it seems to triumph over me, and to tell me what to think, what to do, and what to feel. But it serves whatever purpose I perceive in it. My mind can only serve, and today I give its service to the Holy Spirit to use as It sees fit. This is how I direct my mind, which I alone can rule. This is how I set my mind free to do the Will of God.

2. *'God, today my mind is open to Your Thoughts, and closed to any other thoughts. I rule my mind, and I offer it to You. Accept my gift, because it is Yours to me.'*

Lesson 237

'Now I am as God created me.'

1. Today, I accept the Truth about myself. I arise in Glory, and throughout the day I allow God's Light within me to extend in my mind where I perceive a world. I extend in my perception glad tidings of my salvation, which I hear as God speaks to me. I perceive as my Christ Mind perceives, aware that this ends my bitter illusion of death; aware that this is God's Call to me.

2. *'Today, I perceive and I listen to the Holy Spirit through my Christ Mind. God, I come to You through my True Self, the Christ in me, Which is One with You. Amen.'*

Lesson 238

'My salvation from illusions rests on my decision.'

1. *'Dear God, Your Trust in me is so Great that I must be worthy of It. I am One with You, and You know me as I am. You placed the salvation of What is One with you in my hands, and let it rest on my decision. I must be Beloved of You indeed! I must always be Holy as well, since You are certain that What is Eternally Part of You is safe with me, because It is my True Self.'*

2. Pause again today, and think of how much God loves you. How dear you are to God, because you are the Extension of God's Love. In you, God's Love is made Complete.

Lesson 239

'God's Glory is my own.'

1. Do not let the Truth about you be hidden by false humility, but be thankful instead for God's Gifts to you. There is no trace of sin or guilt in you, who share God's Glory. God loves you Forever, with Perfect Constancy, knowing that you are One with God.

2. *'I thank you, God, for Your Light, Which is Eternally in me. I honor It, because You share It with me. I am One with You in Your Light, and at Peace with myself in Your Extension.'*

Lesson 240

'Fear is not justified in any form.'

1. Any form of fear that you experience is self-deception, because it proves that you see yourself as you can never be, therefore you perceive a world that is impossible. Not one thing that you perceive in the world is true, no matter the form that appears to you. It only witnesses to your own illusion of yourself. Do not be deceived today; you are One with God. There is no fear in you, because you are Part of Love Itself.

2. *'How foolish are my fears! God, You will not allow me to suffer. Give me Your faith today, so that I will recognize my Christ Mind, Which is One with You, and set It free. I forgive myself in Your Name, so that I can recognize my Holiness, and feel the Love for my True Self that is Your Love as well.'*

3. What is the world?

1. The world is a false perception of your mind. It was born of your mistaken perception of separation from God, and it has not left its source. It will remain no longer in your awareness than your cherishing the idea that you are separate from God remains. When you have truly forgiven this idea, you will see the world in another Light; one Which leads to Truth, Where the world will disappear, along with all of the errors that you perceived in it. Its source will be gone, so its effects will be gone as well.

2. The world is meant to be your attack on God. It symbolizes fear, which is your perception of the absence of Love, so the world was meant to be a place where God could not enter, and where you who are One with God could be apart from God. This is where perception was born, because Knowledge can not make such insane thoughts. But eyes deceive, and ears hear falsely. Now mistakes seem possible to you, because Certainty is gone from your mind.

3. Your mechanisms for perceiving illusions go out from you to find the separation from God to which they are meant to witness. Making separation from God real to you is their aim and purpose. They see in the illusion of the world a solid base of 'truth', but everything that they report is illusion that is kept apart from Truth.

4. You made perception to lead you away from Truth, but it can be redirected. What you hear can become the Call of God, and all that you perceive can be given a new purpose by the Holy Spirit, Which God appointed to save your entire mind. Follow the Holy Spirit's Light, and perceive the world as the Holy Spirit perceives it. Hear only the Holy Spirit in all that speaks to you. Let the Holy Spirit give you Peace and Certainty, Which you have thrown away, but Which Heaven preserves for you in the Holy Spirit.

5. Do not rest until your changed perception extends to all of your mind where you perceive a world. Do not be satisfied until your forgiving is complete. Do not attempt to change your function: You must save your entire mind. You made the world that you perceive, and you must perceive it through your Christ Mind, so

that what was made to die can be restored to Everlasting Life.

Mentor's Notes

The 'you' that made the world is the split mind, or the dreamer-of-the-dream. The personal 'you' is a part of the split mind's illusions, though it, too, makes its own illusions. After you accept that you are responsible for your own projections as a personal self, then you are ready to accept that you are the dreamer-of-the-dream. The split mind is the level of your mind called the 'decision maker', because this is the level at which you can choose the Truth that you are or the illusions that you made.

Lesson 241

'Salvation is here, in this Holy Instant.'

1. What Joy for you today! It is a time of special celebration, because today you experience the Instant when you release your mind from the dark world. Today is the day when sorrows pass away and pain is gone, and the Glory of your salvation extends to all that you perceive. This is the time of hope for your entire mind; let your entire mind be united as you forgive all that you perceive. You forgive yourself today.

2. *'I have forgiven myself by forgiving what my mind perceives, and now I come at last to You again, dear God. I, who am One with You, return to Heaven and my Home. How glad I am that my Sanity is restored to me, and to remember that my entire mind is One.'*

Lesson 242

'Today is my gift to God.'

1. I will not be lead by the personal mind today. I do not understand the world that I perceive through it, so to be lead by the personal mind is foolish. But the Holy Spirit knows all that is best for me, and the Holy Spirit makes only the choices that lead me to God. I give this day to the Holy Spirit, because I do not want to delay my arrival Home, and it is the Holy Spirit that knows the way to God.

2. *'I give today to You, dear God. I come to You with a wholly open mind, and I do not ask for anything that I think I may want in my identification with a personal mind. Give me What you want me to receive. You know What I really want, and You will give me everything that I need to help me to find my way to You.'*

Lesson 243

'Today, I will not judge anything that occurs.'

1. I will be honest with myself today. I will not think that I already know what is beyond my present understanding. I will not think that I understand the whole from the bits that I perceive, and which are all that I can see. Today, I recognize this, so I am relieved of judgments that I cannot make accurately. This is how I free myself and my mind where I perceive a world, so that my entire mind can be at Peace, as God created it.

2. *'God, today I leave your Extension free to be Itself. I honor all of Its Parts, in Which I am included. My entire mind is One, because each part contains my Memory of You, and Truth must shine in my entire mind as One.'*

Lesson 244

'I am not in danger anywhere in the world.'

1. *'Dear God, I am safe wherever I perceive myself, because You are here with me. I only need to call on You, and I will remember Your Safety and Your Love, Which are One. I cannot fear or doubt or think that I can suffer, be in danger, or experience unhappiness when I belong to You. I am Beloved and Loving in the Safety of Your Embrace.'*

2. Here I am in Truth. No storms can come into the Hallowed Haven of my Home. I am Secure and unafraid, because nothing can threaten God, and I am One with God.

Lesson 245

'God, Your Peace is with me; I am Safe.'

1. *'Your Peace surrounds me, dear God. Wherever I perceive myself, Your Peace is with me. It sheds Its Light on all that I perceive, and I extend It to replace my perceptions of desolation, loneliness, and fear. I extend Your Peace to my perceptions of those who seem to suffer pain, or grieve for loss, or who appear to be without hope and Happiness. Let them come to me, dear God, and I will bring Your Peace with me. I want to save my entire mind, as is Your Will, and recognize my True Self.'*

2. And so you go in Peace. To all that you perceive, you extend the messages that you have received, so that you come to hear the Holy Spirit. The Holy Spirit speaks to you as you relate Its Word, and you recognize the Holy Spirit's Love, because you share in the Word that It has given to you.

Lesson 246

'For me to love God is for me to love God's Extension.'

1. If I have hatred in my mind, then I cannot find the way to God. If I try to hurt myself or anything that I perceive, then I cannot know God or my True Self. If I fail to recognize my True Self, Which is God's Extension, then I do not believe that I can be aware of God, or that I can conceive of all of the Love that God has for me, and all of the Love that I return to God.

2. *'Dear God, I accept the way that You have chosen for me to reach You. In this I will succeed, because it is Your Will, and I want to recognize that What You will is all that I will as well. So I choose to love Your Extension. Amen.'*

Mentor's Note

You are not One with God as a personal self, but as God's Extension, Which is your Whole Mind. Your entire mind – you and the part of your mind where you perceive a world – is your Whole

Mind, or God's Extension (also, Christ Mind). However, you are not aware that you are God's Extension when you see yourself as a personal self in a world of diverse, separate people and things. Your Real Perception extends your awareness of yourself as One with God to the part of your mind where you perceive a world, and brings your entire mind back together in Oneness, so you can remember God, Which is One.

Lesson 247

'I would still be blind without forgiveness.'

1. My belief in separation from God is an attack on myself. If I believe in it anywhere, I suffer. But my forgiving is the means by which the Perception of my Christ Mind comes to me. Today, I accept What Christ's Perception shows me is the simple Truth, and I am healed completely. The Loveliness and Innocence that I perceive reflects my own. I am forgiven as I forgive all that I perceive.

2. *'God, this is how I perceive today: My entire mind is One with You. You created my Whole Mind, and You extend It as Part of You, and as my True Self. Today, I honor You through all that I perceive, so I hope to recognize my True Self.'*

Lesson 248

'What can suffer is not part of me.'

1. I have disowned the Truth; now I will be faithful in disowning illusions. What can suffer is not part of me. What grieves or is in pain is only an illusion of myself in my mind. What can die was never living in Reality, and it only mocks the Truth about me. Now, I disown self-concepts, deceits, and lies about What is One with God. Now, I am ready to accept again my Oneness with God.

2. *'God, my Timeless Love for You has returned to my awareness, and I love my True Self, Which is One with You. I am as You created me. Now, I remember your Love, and my own. Now, I understand that they are One.'*

Lesson 249

'My forgiving ends all of my suffering and loss.'

1. Your forgiving perceives that suffering is over, loss is impossible, anger makes no sense, attack is gone, and insanity has ended. In forgiveness, you cannot conceive of suffering, nor sustain a sense of loss. You perceive Joy, Abundance, Charity, and Endless Extension. Your Perception is so like Heaven that It quickly transforms into the Light that It reflects, and your journey ends in the Light from Which it came.

2. *'God, I return my mind to You. I have betrayed it, held it in a vise of bitterness, and frightened it with thoughts of violence and death. Now, I want to rest again in You, as You created Me.'*

Lesson 250

'I will not see myself as limited.'

1. I will behold Christ today, and witness to my Mind's Glory. I will not obscure Its Holy Light, see Its Strength diminished and reduced to frailty, or attack Its Wholeness by perceiving lacks in It.

2. *'My Christ Mind is One with You, dear God, and today I will behold Its Gentleness instead of the illusions that I made. Christ is What I am, and as I see Christ, I see myself. Today, I want to perceive Truly, so that this day I will at last identify with Christ.'*

4. What is sin?

1. Your belief in sin is insane. It is the means by which you try to make illusions take the place of Truth. This is insane, because you perceive illusions where the Truth is. Your wanting to perceive sin made a body with eyes to perceive it, because in your Innocence, there is nothing for you to perceive. In your Innocence, you have no need of sights, sounds, or touch; there is nothing for you to see, hear, or reach toward. You have no need of sense at all, because *to sense* is *to not know*. Truth is Knowledge, and nothing else.

2. The body is an instrument that you made to deceive yourself. Its purpose is to strive for separation from God, but you can change the goal toward which it strives. What it can seek for now is the Goal that your mind has taken to replace the goal of self-deception. Truth can be its Goal as easily as lies. Its senses, then, will seek for witnesses to Truth.

3. The idea of 'sin' is the home of all of your illusions, which only stand for what you have imagined, and issue from thoughts that are untrue. They are the 'proof' that what is not real is reality. Sin 'proves' that you are evil, that Timelessness has an end, that Eternal Life must die, and that God has lost Part of Itself. Now what can be corrupted takes God's Place, God's Will is overcome by death, Love is slain by hate, and Peace is to be no more.

4. Your insane illusions are frightening, and sin seems to terrify you, but what you perceive as sin is only a childish game. You who are One with God may play that you have become a body, prey to evil and guilt, and with only a little 'life' that ends in death, but God always shines on you, and God loves you with an Everlasting Love, Which your pretenses cannot change at all.

5. How long will you, who are One with God, play the game of sin? Put aside these sharp-edged children's toys. How soon do you want to be Home? Today? There is no sin; God's Oneness is unchanged. Do you still want to hold back your return to Heaven? For how long?

Mentor's Notes

Remember from the Text how this course juxtaposes the ideas of 'error' and 'sin': An *error* can be corrected; a *sin* cannot. *Sin* is your belief that separation from God is real, so it cannot be undone, and is deserving of punishment from God. Whenever you believe that the world that you perceive is real, you believe in sin, you feel guilty, and you fear punishment.

In paragraph 2 it says that the body's senses can seek for witnesses to Truth. In actuality, the body does not see, hear, or feel; what it *seems* to see, hear, or feel is what the mind directs it to see, hear, or feel. So, it's not really that the *body's* senses witness to a new goal; you change your mind by choosing to see, hear, and feel differently. The body is only a symbol for these actions.

Lesson 251

'I need only the Truth.'

1. I have sought for many things, and I've only found despair. Now, I seek for only One Thing, because in that One is All that I need, and only What I need. All that I sought for before I did not need, and did not even want. I did not recognize my only need. Now, I see that I need only the Truth. In Truth, all of my needs are satisfied, my cravings end, all of my hopes are fulfilled, and my illusions are gone. In Truth, I have Everything that I could need and Everything that I could want. Now, at last, I find myself at Peace.

2. *'For Your Peace, dear God, I thank You. What I denied myself, You have restored to my awareness, and only That is What I really want.'*

Lesson 252

'Christ is my Identity.'

1. My True Self is Holy beyond all of the thoughts of Holiness of Which I can now conceive. Its Perfect Purity is far more Brilliant than any light that I have ever perceived with the body. Its Love is Limitless; It holds All Things within It, in the Calm of Quiet Certainty. Its Strength does not come from the impulses that move the world that I perceive, but from the Boundless Love of God. My True Self is far beyond the world, but One with me and with God.

2. *'God, You know my True Identity; reveal It to me, as I am One with You, so that I will become aware again of the Truth in You, and know that Heaven is restored to me.'*

Lesson 253

'My True Self rules everything.'

1. It is impossible for anything to come to me that I have not asked for. Even in the world that I perceive, I rule my destiny. What happens is what I desire; what does not occur is what I do not want to happen. I must accept this, because this is how I go past the world to my Extension of God, Which is my True Will, in Heaven, Where my Holy Self abides in extension of God.

2. *'God, You are the Self that You created One with You through extension of Yourself. Like You, Your Extension extends You. My True Self, Which rules everything, is Your Will in Perfect Union with my will, which can only be One with Your Will, so that You may extend Yourself.'*

Mentor's Notes

The prayer in Lesson 253 highlights how God is your True Self and your True Self is God. In God there is only God. This is the meaning of Oneness. In God, there are no concepts like *God's Extension*; this concept is only necessary in your perception that you are separate from God. It answers your question, which only exists in your perception of separation, 'What am I?' You are One with God; you are God's Extension.

Think of your *extending* God this way: Think of God as an ocean, extending infinitely in all directions. In the ocean is only the ocean; the ocean is one. The ocean does not have 'parts', but draw an imaginary circle on the ocean that is meant to separate part of the ocean from the ocean. Despite the imaginary circle, the ocean *extends* into the part-of-the-ocean, and the part-of-the-ocean continues to be the ocean's *extension* (this would be true no matter where you drew the imaginary circle). It also continues to extend the ocean, because it is still the ocean. So it is with you and God. Despite an imaginary separation, in Truth, God continues to extend Itself to you, and you continue to be God's Extension, and to extend God.

The reason that this course does not say, 'You are God' but instead says, 'You are *One with* God' (Christ or God's Extension) is because, in your perception that you are in a world, the highest awareness that you can reach is 'I am One with God', which is just short of *being* God. When all that you perceive reflects God, then you will lay perception aside, and God will take the 'last step', meaning, you will simply *be* God again.

Lesson 254

'I quiet all but God's Voice in me.'

1. *'Dear God, today I want to hear only Your Voice. I come to You in deepest silence to hear Your Voice, and to receive Your Word. This is my only prayer: I ask You for the Truth. Truth is Your Will, Which I share with You today.'*

2. Today, I will not let any thoughts of the personal mind direct my actions. When those thoughts occur, I will quietly step back and look at them, and then let them go. I do not want the pain that they bring with them, so I do not choose to keep them. They will be silent, and in the Stillness of my mind, Hallowed by God's Love, God will speak to me, and tell me of my Will in Oneness with God, because I have chosen to remember God.

Lesson 255

'I choose to spend today in Perfect Peace.'

1. It does not seem to me that I can choose to have only Peace today, but God assures me that I am like God. Today, I will have faith in That Which says I am One with It, and I will let the Peace that I choose to be mine bear witness to the Truth of what God says. What is One with God can not have concerns, and must remain forever in the Peace of Heaven. In God's Name, I give today to finding What God wills for me, accepting It as mine, and extending It to my entire mind.

2. *'And so, dear God, I want to pass this day with You. I who am One with You have not forgotten You. The Peace that You give to me is still in my mind, and it is in Your Peace that I choose to spend today.'*

Lesson 256

'God is the only Goal that I have today.'

1. The way to God is through your forgiving your perception of a world apart from God. There is no other way. If you did not cherish the idea of being separate from God, then you would have no need to find the way to Where you are in Truth. You would not be uncertain of where you are, or of who you are. You would not doubt your Holiness. In your perception that you are in a world, you only have illusions, but you can have illusions of forgiving the 'sin' in you that is impossible, and it is forgiving illusions that you can choose today. God is your Goal; your forgiving is the means by which your mind returns to God at last.

2. *'And so, dear God, I want to come to You in Your appointed way. I have no goal but to hear Your Voice, and to find the way that Your Sacred Word points out to me.'*

Lesson 257

'I will remember what my purpose is.'

1. When I forget my Goal, I am confused, unsure of what I am, and, therefore, conflicted in my actions. I cannot serve contradicting goals, or function without deep distress and great depression when my goals conflict. So today, I am determined to remember What I want, so that my thoughts and actions will be meaningfully unified, and I will achieve only what God wants me to do today.

2. *'God, my forgiving is Your chosen means for my salvation. I will not forget today that Your Will is my will, so my purpose must be Yours as well, if I want the Peace that You will for me.'*

Lesson 258

'I will remember that my Goal is God.'

1. All that you need to do is to train your mind to overlook all little, senseless goals, and to remember that your Goal is God. The Memory of God is in your mind, obscured only by meaningless goals that offer you nothing, because they do not exist. Do not continue to hide God's Grace in denial while you seek for the toys and trinkets of the world. God is your only Goal; your only Love. Your only goal is to remember God.

2. *'God, my only goal is to follow the way that leads to You. I want only to remember You, because I seek my own Identity.'*

Lesson 259

'I will remember that there is no sin.'

1. Your belief that your separation from God is real, and is therefore a 'sin', is the only thought that makes your Goal of God seem unattainable to you. This is what blinds you to the Obvious, and makes the strange and distorted seem more real to you. Only your belief that you have sinned causes you to attack, is the source of your guilt, and demands your punishment and suffering. Only your belief in sin is the source of your fear, which obscures your Oneness with God, and makes Love seem to you like fear and attack.

2. *'Dear God, I will not be insane today. I will not be afraid of Love, or hide from It in Its opposite, because Love has no opposite. You are the Source of Everything- that-is, and Everything-that-is, is with You.'*

Mentor's Notes

Lesson 259 says that your belief in sin makes Love seem like fear and attack to you. This is because your belief in sin is your belief that separation from God is your reality. Love is Oneness, so it seems to 'attack' what you think is your reality. In your identification with a personal self, Love *is* a threat, because It undoes your identification with a personal self.

Lesson 260

'I will remember that God created me.'

1. *'God, I did not make myself, although in my insanity I thought that I did. But, as Your Thought, I have not left my Source; I remain a Part of You. God, I call on You today, and I will remember that You created me. I will remember my Identity, and let my Innocence rise again in the Perception of my Christ Mind, through Which I will look on everything and myself today.'*

2. Now, I remember my Source, and in It I find my True Identity. I am Holy indeed, because my Source cannot know sin, and, being One with my Source, I am like my Source.

5. What is the body?

1. Bodies are fences that, in your split mind, you believe that you have built to separate parts of your Self from other parts of your Self. In your identification with a personal self, you think that you live within one of these fences, to die as it decays and crumbles. Within this fence, you think that you are 'safe' from Love, and you identify with where you think your safety lies. This is how you make certain that you remain 'in' a body, and keep Love outside of you.

2. Bodies do not last, and in your split mind, you see this as double safety, because this impermanence is 'proof' that its fences do the task that it assigns to them. If the Oneness of your Mind remained intact, then who would attack, and who would be attacked? Who would be the predator, and who would be the prey? Who would be the murderer, and who would be the victim? If bodies did not die, then your split mind would not have 'proof' that it destroyed Part of God.

3. Bodies are illusions, and, like other illusions, they sometimes picture happiness, but can quite suddenly revert to fear, which is the source of all illusions. Only Love creates Truth, and Truth can never fear. Bodies are made to be fearful, and they serve the purpose for which they were made. But you can change the purpose that the body obeys by changing what you think that it is for.

4. The body can be the means by which you return to Sanity. Though it was made to fence you off into a hell that you cannot escape, you can exchange this purpose for the Goal of Heaven. Through the body, you can extend your mind to encompass all that you perceive in Oneness. Now, the body is Holy; now, it serves to heal the mind that it was meant to kill.

5. You identify with what you think makes you safe. Whatever it is, you will believe that it is one with you. Your Safety lies in Truth, not in lies. Love is your Safety; fear does not exist. Identify with Love, and you are Safe; identify with Love, and you are Home; identify with Love, and you find your True Self.

Mentor's Notes

Paragraph 1 states that the body makes you feel 'safe' from Love. Refer to the Mentor's Notes for lesson 259 for an explanation of this.

How can you be both the split mind that imagines all personal selves, and yet seem to be one of those personal selves? In Truth, of course, both ideas are absurd and impossible; you are One with God. But, when you dream at night in the world, every figure in your dream is in your mind, but you identify with only one of those figures. Mid-dream, you may even change which dream-figure with which you identify. This can serve as an example of what is occurring in your illusion that you are in a world. All personal selves, even the one that you seem to be identifying with, are in your one split mind. Each one seems to have its own mind, but when each one goes within to Truth, it is going within to the same Christ Mind. Personal minds are separate and diverse, but the Christ Mind is universal. This is why your journey is inward.

This is not something that you will understand looking out at the world, or when you feel immersed in the world. You will come to understand this as you experience the Holy Instant more and more. Only from Reality can you understand that illusion is illusion.

Paragraph 4 says that you can use the body to extend your mind to all that you perceive, and that the body can help you heal the mind. What this means is that, as the body moves about the world, you will be presented with perceptions that push your buttons. Those perceptions represent false beliefs to which you still cling, so they present you with opportunities to forgive, or heal, your mind back to Oneness, by overlooking the appearance, and remembering that God is all that is really here in your mind.

Lesson 261

'God is my Refuge and Security.'

1. I identify with what I think is my refuge and security. I see myself where I perceive my strength, and I think that I live within the citadel where I am safe and cannot be attacked. Today, I will not seek for security in danger, nor attempt to find my Peace in murderous attack. I live in God. I find my Refuge and my Strength in God. My Identity is in God; Everlasting Peace is in God. Only in God will I remember What I really am.

2. *'God, I will not seek in idols. I want to go Home to You today. I choose to be as You created me, and to find the Part of You that You created as my Self.'*

Lesson 262

'I will not perceive differences today.'

1. *'God, You are One, and it is This that I will look on today. You have One Extension, and I have no need to look on thousands of forms to replace It. I do not need to give thousands of names to what is in a Mind that is One, because What is One with You bears Your Name. I will not make a part of my mind a stranger to its Creator, or to myself. My mind is One, and You are its Source. It is Eternally United in Your Love; Eternally One with You.'*

2. You, whose entire mind is one, want to recognize today the Truth about yourself. Go Home, and rest in Oneness. Peace is There, and there is nowhere else for you to seek for and to find Peace.

Lesson 263

'Through my Real Perception, I see all things as Pure.'

1. *'Dear God, Your Mind extends All-that-is, Your Spirit is in All-that-is, and Your Love gives Life to All- that- is. I do not want to perceive my mind, which is One with You, as though it can be sinful. I do not want to perceive dark and frightening images. The choice of insanity is not fit to be my choice when You offer me all of the Loveliness of Your Extension: Its Purity, Its Joy, and Its Eternal Quiet Home in You.'*

2. While you remain outside of Heaven, look on all that you perceive through the Real Perception of your Christ Mind. Look past all appearances to Purity, so that you can pass them by in Innocence, and walk with a united mind to God's House.

Lesson 264

'I am surrounded by the Love of God.'

1. *'Dear God, You stand before me, behind me, beside me, and in my place; You are everywhere that I go. You are in all of the things that I look upon, in the sounds that I hear, and in every hand that seems to reach for me. Time disappears in You, and 'place' becomes a meaningless belief, because What surrounds me and keeps me safe is Love Itself. The only Source is Your Love, and only What shares Its Holiness and is Its Extension exists. God, Your Extension is like You. I come to You in Your Own Name today, to be at Peace within Your Everlasting Love.'*

2. Join with your Christ Mind today in this prayer, which states your salvation. You must join in what will save your entire mind.

Lesson 265

'The Gentleness of God's Extension is all that I perceive.'

1. I have misunderstood the world, because I have laid what I thought were my sins on it, and I saw them looking back at me. How fierce they seemed! How deceived I was to think that what I feared was in the world instead of only in my mind. Today, I perceive the world with the Gentleness of God's Extension. There is no fear in this Perception. I will not let any appearance of my 'sins' obscure the Light of Heaven shining in my Perception. What is reflected, then, will be God's Mind. The images that I perceive are my thoughts, and my mind is One with God's Mind, so I can perceive the Gentleness of God's Extension.

2. *'God, in Quiet I perceive the world, which then reflects Your Thoughts, and mine. When I remember that they are the same, I will see the Gentleness of Your Extension.'*

Lesson 266

'You are my Holy Self.'

1. *'Dear God, You have me perceive all seeming other 'selves' as my saviors, and the bearers of Your Holy Voice to me. I perceive You reflected in them, and my Christ Mind looks back at me from my True Self. I will not forget Your Holy Name, or that You are my Source, or that my name is Yours.'*

2. Today, you enter into Paradise, calling on God's Name, and on your own; acknowledging your True Self in your perception, and uniting your entire mind in the Holy Love of God. How many saviors God wants you to perceive! You cannot lose the way to God when God has you fill the world that you perceive with those who point the way to God, and God gives you the Perception with Which to look on them.

Lesson 267

'My heart beats in the Peace of God.'

1. I am surrounded by all of the Life that God extends in Its Love. It calls to me with every heartbeat, in every breath, in every action, and in every thought. Peace fills my heart, and floods the body with the purpose of forgiving. Now, my mind is healed, and all that I need to save my entire mind is given to me. Each heartbeat brings me Peace; each breath infuses me with Strength. I am a messenger of God, directed by God's Holy Spirit, sustained by God's Love, and held Forever Quiet and at Peace in God's Loving Arms. Every heartbeat calls God's Name, and every call is answered by God's Holy Spirit, assuring me that I am at Home in God.

2. *'I will listen to Your Answer, God, not to the answer of the personal mind. God, my heart is beating in the Peace that the Heart of Love created. It is There, and only There, that I can be at Home.'*

Lesson 268

'I will perceive Reality exactly as It is.'

1. *'I will not be Your critic today, dear God, by judging against You. I will not attempt to change Your Extension, and distort it into sickly forms. I am willing to withdraw my wishes from Its Oneness, and so to let It be as You created It. This is how I will recognize myself as You created me. I was created in Love, and I will remain in Love Forever. Nothing can frighten me when I let Truth be exactly as It is.'*

2. I will not let my perception be blasphemous today, nor listen to lying tongues. Only Reality is free of pain, only Reality is free of loss, and only Reality is wholly Safe. And it is only Reality that I seek today.

Lesson 269

'I perceive Christ today.'

1.*'Dear God, I ask Your blessing on my perceptions today. It is the means that You have chosen to show me my mistakes, and then to look beyond them. You have given me a new Perception to find through the Holy Spirit, and through Its lessons I will surpass perception and return to Truth. I ask for the one illusion of forgiving that transcends all of those illusions that I made. Today, I choose to forgive the world by seeing Christ everywhere, and by learning that What I perceive belongs to me. Your Holy Extension is All-that-is.'*

2. Today, your perception is blessed indeed! You share One Perception with your Christ Mind as you look on Christ everywhere and see your True Self. You and all that you perceive are One, because your entire mind is Christ, your True Identity.

Lesson 270

'I will not use the body's eyes today.'

1.*'God, the Perception of my Christ Mind is Your Gift to me, and It has the Power to translate all that the body's eyes see into a forgiving perception. How Glorious and Gracious is this perception! There is so much more to perceive than what the body's eyes see. My forgiving perception signifies that I acknowledge You as my Source, and allows my illusions to be brought to Truth to be undone. I wait expectantly for the one instant more of time which ends time forever, as my Memory of You returns. Now, my will is One with Yours, my function is Your Own, and every thought except Yours is gone from my mind.'*

2. The quiet of today will bless you, and, through it, Peace will extend to your entire mind. Christ is your eyes today. With your Real Perception, you will extend healing to your entire mind through Christ, the Extension of God, Which is Whole and One.

6. What is the Christ?

1. Christ is God's Extension. Christ is your True Self: your entire mind united as One, and with God. It is the Thought that is still in Its Source, God's Mind. Christ has not left Its Holy Home, nor lost the Innocence in Which It was created. It abides Forever unchanged in the Mind of God.

2. Christ is the Link that keeps you One with God, and that guarantees that your perception of separation from God is only an illusion of despair, because your hope of salvation abides forever in your Christ Mind. Your Christ Mind is the part of you in Which God's Answer lies, Where all decisions are already made, and Where all of your illusions are over. Christ is untouched by anything that the body's eyes perceive, because, though Christ is the Means for your salvation, like God, It does not know sin.

3. Christ is at Home in God, and is the Home of the Holy Spirit, and Christ remains at Peace in the Heaven of your Holy Mind. Christ is the only Part of you that has any Reality. The rest is an illusion, but you will give this illusion to your Christ Mind so that it can fade before Christ's Glory, and at last reveal to you your Holy Self.

4. The Holy Spirit reaches from the Christ in you to your illusions, and translates them into Truth. The Holy Spirit will exchange them for the final illusion of forgiving that God has appointed as the end of illusions. When your forgiving rests on all that you perceive, and Peace has been restored to your entire mind, there will be nothing to keep separate, because all that you will perceive is Christ.

5. You will not see Christ for long, because It is the symbol that the time for learning is over, and your Goal of Atonement has been reached. Therefore, seek to perceive only Christ. As you behold Christ's Glory, you will know that you have no more need of learning, perception, time, or anything except your Holy Self, the Christ, Which is One with God.

Mentor's Notes

It is essential for you to realize that Christ is in *you*, not in the personal self. At its most grandiose, the personal mind would have no problem with you thinking that you are Christ, as long as you still perceive yourself as a personal self. But, in actual fact, you cannot know that you are Christ unless you also perceive Christ everywhere. Your mind always perceives itself, but the difference in perception between the personal mind and your Christ Mind is striking, and revealing of the nature of both. The personal mind sees itself as isolated among other personal selves outside of it; in your identification with it, you live in separation. You are still perceiving your own mind, but you project part of it away, so that there seems to be 'you' and a world outside of you. But your Christ Mind perceives Itself everywhere, and in your identification with It, you live in Oneness, and you willingly acknowledge that your mind is not only what you think of as 'you', but all that your mind perceives as well.

Lesson 271

'I will use Christ's Perception today.'

1. Every day, every hour, every instant I am choosing what I want to perceive, the sounds that I want to hear, and the witnesses to what I want to be the truth for me. Today, I choose to perceive what my Christ Mind wants me to perceive, to listen to the Holy Spirit, and to seek for witnesses to Truth. In my Christ Mind's Perception, my perception of the world and God's Extension meet, and as they come together, all perception disappears. Christ's Kindly Light redeems my mind from death, because It perceives Life by remembering God, and unifying God and God's Extension.

2. *'Dear God, my Christ Mind's Perception is the Way to You. What It perceives invites my Memory of You to be restored to me. This is What I choose to perceive today.'*

Lesson 272

'Illusions cannot satisfy Christ.'

1. *'Dear God, the Truth belongs to me. My Home is in Heaven, by Your Will and mine. Illusions cannot content me, or bring me Happiness. Only my Memory of You can satisfy me, because I am One with You. I will accept no less than What you have given to me. I am surrounded by Your Love, Forever Still, Gentle, and Safe. I must be as You created me.'*

2. Today, you will pass by illusions, and if you are tempted to stay and linger in them, you will turn aside and ask yourself if you who are One with God can be content with illusions when you can choose Heaven as easily as hell, and Love as easily as fear.

Lesson 273

'The Stillness of the Peace of God is mine.'

1. Perhaps you are now ready for a day of undisturbed tranquility. If this is not yet feasible, you will be more than satisfied to learn how to achieve such a day. If you give way to a disturbance, you can learn how to dismiss it and return to Peace. You only need to tell your mind with certainty, 'The Stillness of the Peace of God is mine', then nothing will intrude on the Peace that God has given to you.

2. *'Dear God, Your Peace is mine. I have no need to fear that anything can rob me of What You want me to keep. I cannot lose Your Gifts to me, so the Peace that You give to me in Oneness with You is still with me, in Quietness, and in my own Eternal Love for You.'*

Lesson 274

'Today belongs to Love. I will not fear.'

1. *'God, today I will let Your Extension be as You created It, and give What is One with You the Love and honor due to Its Innocence. Through this, I will be redeemed. Through this, Truth will enter my mind where illusions were, Light will replace darkness, and I will know that I am One with You.'*

2. A special blessing from God comes to you today. Give this day to God, and you will not experience fear, because you will be giving the day to Love.

Lesson 275

'God's healing Voice protects all things today.'

1. Listen to the Holy Spirit, Which speaks a Timeless lesson. Though it is no truer today than any other day, today has been chosen as the time when you will learn and understand it. Join your Christ Mind in hearing it, because the Holy Spirit tells you of what you cannot understand when you think that you are separated off in a personal mind. It is in this joining that all things are protected, and in this joining that you find the healing Voice of God.

2. *'God, Your healing Voice protects all things today, so I leave all things to You. I do not need to be anxious over anything, because Your Voice will tell me what to do, where to go, to whom to speak, what to say, what thoughts to think, and what words to give. The Safety that I bring with me is given to me. God, Your Voice protects all things through me.'*

Lesson 276

'The Word of God is given to me to speak.'

1. What is the Word of God? 'You are One with me, and as Pure and Holy as Myself.' This is how God is your Source, and you are God's Extension; this is how God extends God to you. This is the Word that you did not create with God, because in It God extends God to you. Accept God as your Source, and all is given to you; deny that God created you by extending Its Love to you, and you deny your True Self, and end up unsure of who you are, your source, and for what purpose you exist. You only need to acknowledge that God extends Itself to you to remember God, and recall your True Self.

2. *'God, Your Word is mine, and it is This that I want to extend to all that I perceive, because I must cherish it as part of my mind, as I am loved, blessed, and saved by You.'*

Mentor's Notes

Lesson 276 reiterates a point made in the Text: God creates you, and you are co-creator with God, but you do not create God. God (Creator) extends God to you (Creation), and you also extend God (co-Creator), but you are not the originating source of God. Again, this is only a concept needed in your perception of separation from God, because in God there is only Oneness, and no delineation of parts. Continuing with the ocean metaphor from the Mentor's Notes for Lesson 253, the ocean extends into the imaginary circle, and the part-of-the-ocean in the circle, being the ocean, extends the ocean, but the part-of-the-ocean is not the source of the ocean.

Lesson 277

'I will not limit What is One with You with laws that I made.'

1. *'In my Oneness with You, dear God, I am Limitless. I will not imagine that I have bound myself with laws that I made to rule a body. I am not subject to any laws that I made to make the body more secure, I am not changed by what is changeable, I am not a slave to the laws of time. I am as You created me, because I know no law but the Law of Love.'*

2. Do not worship idols, or believe in any law that idolatry makes to hide your Limitlessness in God. You are only bound by your beliefs, but What you are is far beyond your faith in limitedness. You are Limitless, because you are One with God, and you cannot be limited, unless God is a lie, and God wills to deceive Itself.

Lesson 278

'If I am limited, so is God.'

1. If I accept that I am limited to a body, in a world in which everything dies, then God is limited with me. And I do believe this when I maintain that I must obey the laws of the world, that the frailties and 'sins' that I perceive are real, and that I cannot escape them. If I am limited in any way, I do not know God, my True Self, or Reality. Truth is Limitless, and what is limited is not a part of Truth.

2. *'God, I ask only for the Truth. I have had many foolish thoughts about myself and my origin, and I have brought an illusion of fear into my mind. Today, I will not make illusions. I choose the way to You, instead of insanity and fear, because Truth is Safe, and only Love is Certain.'*

Lesson 279

'The Limitlessness of Reality is my own.'

1. The end of my illusions is promised, because I am not abandoned by God's Love. Only in my illusions do I seem to be in time and limited, and I wait for freedom in the future, not certain if it exists at all. But in Reality, I have no illusions, only Truth. Limitlessness is already mine, and I have no need to wait in limitations that are not here, when God is offering me Limitlessness now.

2. *'God, I will accept Your Promises today, and I give my faith to Them. You love What is One with You, and You will not withhold the Gifts that You give to me.'*

Lesson 280

'I cannot limit God's Extension.'

1. What God created Limitless *is* Limitless. I can invent limits for myself, but only in illusions, not in Truth. As a Thought of God, I have not left God's Mind, I am Limitless, and I am Forever Pure. I cannot lay limits on God's Extension when God wills that I be Limitless Love, like God.

2. *'God, today I honor Your Extension in me, because this is the only way to You. I put no limits on What You love and created Limitless. The honor that I give to Your Extension is Yours, and What is Yours belongs to me.'*

7. What is the Holy Spirit?

1. The Holy Spirit is the mediator between your illusions and the Truth in you. Since the Holy Spirit bridges the gap between your Reality and your illusions, Its Perception leads you to Knowledge of God, through the Grace that God gives to It to give to you when you call on Truth. Across the Bridge that is the Holy Spirit, your illusions are carried to Truth to be dispelled before the Light of Knowledge. There, you lay aside sights and sounds forever, and, where you perceived them before, your forgiving them ends all perception in Tranquility.

2. The goal of the Holy Spirit's teaching is this ending of your illusions. First, the sights and sounds that you perceive must be translated from witnesses to fear to witnesses to Love. When you have wholly accomplished this, your learning will have achieved the only goal that it had in truth. As the Holy Spirit perceives the purpose of learning, learning is your means to go beyond learning, which is then replaced by Eternal Truth.

3. If you only knew how much God yearns to have you recognize your Innocence, you would not let the Holy Spirit appeal to you in vain, nor would you turn your perception away from the Holy Spirit, Which is God's Replacement for the fearful images and illusions that you made. The Holy Spirit understands the means that you made to attain your separation from God, which is forever unattainable. If you offer these means to the Holy Spirit, It will use them to restore your mind to Where it is truly at Home.

4. From Knowledge, Where the Holy Spirit is with God, the Holy Spirit calls to you to forgive your illusions, and to be restored to Sanity and Peace of mind. If you do not forgive your illusions, they will remain to terrify you, and your Memory of God's Love will not come to your mind to signal that your illusions are over.

5. Accept God's Gift; It is the Call of Love to Love to be Itself. The Holy Spirit is the Gift from God by which Heaven is restored to you. Do not refuse to take up your function of completing God, when all that God wills is that you be Complete.

Lesson 281

'Only the personal mind's thoughts can hurt me.'

1. *'God, I am Perfect in Oneness with You. When I think that I have been hurt in any way, it is because I have forgotten What I am; I have forgotten that I am as You created me. Your Thoughts can only bring me happiness. Whenever I am sad, hurt, or ill, I have forgotten What You think, and I have put the personal mind's little, meaningless ideas where Your Thoughts belong, and where They are in Truth. Only the personal mind's thoughts can hurt me; the Thoughts that I think with You can only Bless. The Thoughts that I think with You are All that is True.'*

2. I will not hurt myself today, because I am far beyond all pain. God holds me safely in Heaven, and is watching over me. I will not attack What God loves, because What God loves is mine to love as well.

Lesson 282

'I will not be afraid of Love today.'

1. If I fully realize this today, I will reach the salvation of my entire mind. This is my decision not to be insane, and to accept myself as God created me. This is my decision to not deny God in illusions of death while Truth remains Forever living within me in the Joy of Love. This is my choice to recognize my True Self, Which God created One with God, and Which is my One Identity.

2. *'God, Your Name is Love, and so is mine. This is the Truth, and Truth cannot be changed by giving It another name. The name of fear is simply a mistake. I will not be afraid of Truth today.'*

Lesson 283

'My True Identity is in You, God.'

1. *'God, I made an image of myself and called it Your creation, but Your Creation is as It always is, because It is unchangeable. I will not worship idols, because I am That Which God loves. My Holiness is the Light of Heaven and the Love of God. What is beloved of You is Secure, the Light of Heaven is Infinite, and my Identity is in You, Who created Everything that is.'*

2. Now, you know that your Identity is only Christ, God is your Source, and Everything that God created is One with you. So, offer blessing to all things that you perceive, Lovingly uniting your mind, which your forgiving makes you aware is One.

Lesson 284

'I can choose to change all thoughts that hurt me.'

1. There is no loss when I perceive Truly. Pain is impossible, grief has no cause at all, and suffering of any kind is only an illusion. This is the truth, which I will first say, then repeat many times. Then, I will partly accept it as true, with many reservations. But I will consider it seriously, more and more. Finally, I will accept it as truth. I can choose to change all thoughts that hurt me. I will go beyond these words today, past all reservations, and arrive at full acceptance of the truth in them.

2. *'God, What you give cannot hurt, so grief and pain must be impossible. I will trust You today, and accept Joy as Your Gift, and as Truth.'*

Lesson 285

'My Holiness shines Bright and Clear today.'

1. Today, I wake with Joy, expecting only Happy Things of God to come to me. I will ask Them to come, and I will realize that my invitation will be answered by the Thoughts to Which I send my invitation. I will ask only for Joyous Things the instant that I accept my Holiness, because pain has no use to me, suffering has no purpose to fulfill, and grief and loss cannot affect me if insanity departs from me today, and I accept my Holiness instead.

2. *'God, my Holiness is Yours. I rejoice in It, and, through my forgiving, I am restored to Sanity. I am still as You created me. My Holiness is Part of me, and Part of You, and nothing can alter Holiness.'*

Lesson 286

'I am centered in the Quiet of Heaven today.'

1. *'Dear God, how Still today is! How Quietly do all things fall into place! Today is the day that You have chosen for me to understand the lesson that I need do nothing. Every choice is already made in You; every conflict has been resolved in You. Everything that I seek has already been given to me; Your Peace is mine. I am centered in Quiet, and my mind is at Rest. Your Love is Heaven, and Your Love is mine.'*

2. Today's Stillness will give you hope that you have found the way, and that you have traveled long to a Wholly Certain Goal. Today, you will not doubt the End that God has promised you. Trust in God, and in your True Self, Which is still One with God.

Lesson 287

'Only You are my Goal, dear God.'

1. I can only go to Heaven. There is no substitute for Happiness. The only gift that I can want is the Peace of God. There is no treasure that I could find that can compare with my Identity. I would rather live in Love than in fear.

2. *'You are my Goal, dear God. You are all that I can desire to have. The only path that I can desire to walk is to You. Only my Memory of You can signal to me the end of my illusions and futile substitutes for Truth. You are my only Goal; I want to be as You created me. This is the only way that I can expect to recognize my True Self and be at One with my Identity.'*

Lesson 288

'I will forget the personal past today.'

1. *'This is the thought that leads the way to You, dear God, and brings me to my Goal. I cannot come to You without my entire mind, because to know my Source, I must first recognize that you created my mind as One. The part of my mind where I perceive a world belongs to You. The sins that I perceive there are in a personal past, and I am saved, because the past is not here. I will not cherish it, or I will lose the way as I walk to You. I can perceive my salvation instead, so I will not attack what can save me. I will honor What bears Your Name, and therefore remember that It is my own.'*

2. Forgive yourself today. You will know that you have forgiven yourself if the Light of Holiness is in your perception. The part of your mind where you perceive a world cannot be less Holy than your Christ Mind, and the Christ in you cannot be Holier than it.

Lesson 289

'The past is not here; it cannot touch me.'

1. Only if the past is over in my mind can I use my Real Perception, because otherwise I perceive nothing; I perceive what is not here. I will not be perceiving What my forgiving offers to me. My Real Perception is What is present, and is What a personal past is meant to hide from me. There is no past. I can only forgive an illusion of the past, and, when it is forgiven, it is gone.

2. *'God, I will not look on a past that is not here. You have offered me Your Own Replacement in a Perception that the past cannot touch. This is the end of my guilt, and It readies me for Your last step. I will not demand that You wait longer for What is One with You to find the Loveliness that You plan to be the end of all of my illusions and pain.'*

Mentor's Notes

Lesson 289 states that you can only forgive the past. If you are truly present, then you are in the Holy Instant, in Which there are no illusions to forgive. All that you perceive with a personal mind is in the past, in two senses: First, your perception of separation from God was undone by God's All-encompassing Nature the moment that the idea entered your mind. So it is over; it is 'past'. Second, the personal mind cannot exist in the Holy Instant, so it cannot be in the present. It always perceives through what it thinks is its story, which was made in a past that never happened. That is why all that it perceives is an illusion, and why all that you have to forgive is the past.

Lesson 290

'My present Happiness is all that I perceive.'

1. I perceive my present Happiness, unless I am choosing to perceive what is not here. I am beginning to perceive Truly at last, and I want the Real Perception of my Christ Mind today. What I perceive without God's Own Correction for the perception that I made is frightening and painful. But I will not allow my mind, for an instant longer, to be deceived by a belief that the illusions that I made are real. Today, I seek my present Happiness, and I perceive only What I seek.

2. *'With this resolve, I come to You, God, and ask for Your Strength to hold me up while I seek to do Your Will. You cannot fail to hear me, God, because What I ask for, You have already given to me. I am sure that I will see my Happiness today.'*

8. What is your Real Perception?

1. Your Real Perception sees symbols, just as the personal mind's perception does, but what it sees stands for the opposite of what you made. The personal mind perceives through fear, and brings witnesses to terror to your mind. But your Real Perception can only bless through forgiveness, so that terror is impossible, and you do not see witnesses to fear.

2. Your Real Perception has a counterpart for every unhappy perception of the personal mind; a sure correction for the perception of fear and conflict. Your Real Perception looks through the Quiet eyes of a mind at Peace. With It, you do not hear cries of pain or sorrow, because you forgive all that you perceive. You perceive only Gentleness, because only happy sights and sounds can reach a mind that has forgiven itself.

3. When your mind is thus, you have no need for thoughts of death, attack, and murder. You can only perceive yourself surrounded by Safety, Love, and Joy. You see nothing to choose to condemn, or to judge against. Your Real Perception arises from a mind that is at Peace within itself, so no danger lurks in anything that it perceives, because it is Kind, and can only perceive Kindness.

4. Your Real Perception sees symbols that your illusion of sin and guilt is over, and that you are no longer denying God. In your growing awareness of God, you perceive the sure reflection of God's Love, and the certain promise that you are redeemed. Your Real Perception signals the end of time, because your Real Perception makes time purposeless.

5. The Holy Spirit has no need for time when time has served the Holy Spirit's purpose. Then, the Holy Spirit waits one instant more for God to take the final step, time disappears, and perception goes with it, leaving Truth to be Itself in your mind. That instant is your goal, because it contains your Memory of God. And as you perceive through forgiveness, it is God that calls to you, and comes to take you Home, reminding you of your Identity, Which your forgiving restores to your awareness.

Lesson 291

'This is a day of Stillness and Peace.'

1. Christ uses Its Real Perception through me today, and through It I perceive all things forgiven and at Peace, and this Perception extends throughout my entire mind. I accept this Perception for my entire mind, both what I think of as 'me' and the part of my mind where I perceive a world. What Loveliness I perceive today! What Holiness I see surrounding me! This Holiness extends everywhere; It is the Holiness of God.

2. *'God, today my mind is quiet, so that I can receive the Thoughts that You offer to me. I accept What comes from You, instead of from the personal mind. It does not know the way to You, but You are Wholly Certain. God, guide me along the quiet path that leads to You. My forgiving will be complete, and my Memory of You will return.'*

Lesson 292

'A Happy outcome to all things is certain.'

1. God's Promises have no exceptions, and God guarantees that only Joy can be the final outcome for everything. It is up to you when you reach this; when you stop allowing an alien will to appear to oppose God's Will. While you think that this will is real, you will not find the Happiness that God has appointed as the outcome to all problems, trials, and every situation that you perceive. But this Outcome is certain, because God's Will is done, in your perception that you are in a world, and in Heaven. You will seek and find as directed by God's Will, Which guarantees that your will is done.

2. *'Thank You, God, for Your Guarantee of only Happy outcomes. Help me to not interfere and delay the Happy endings that You have promised me for every problem that I perceive; for every trial that I think I must meet.'*

Lesson 293

'All fear is past, and only Love is here.'

1. All fear is past, because its source is gone, and all its thoughts are gone with it. Love is the only present state, because Its Source is Eternally here. I cannot perceive the present as bright, clear, safe, and welcoming with all of my past mistakes oppressing it and showing me distorted forms of fear. But in the present, Love is obvious, and Its Effects are apparent. All that I perceive shines in a reflection of Its Holy Light, and I forgive the world at last.

2. *'God, your Holy Perception will not escape me today, nor will my ears be deaf to the Holy sounds of gratitude that I can hear underneath the sounds of fear. My Real Perception in the present is safe from all seeming past mistakes. I will see only with my Real Perception today.'*

Lesson 294

'The body is a wholly neutral thing.'

1. I am One with God, and I cannot be something else as well. God did not create the mortal and corruptible. I have no use for what must die. But, when I see that the body is neutral, it does not die, because it is not invested with thoughts of fear, nor made to be a mockery of Love. Its neutrality protects it while it has a use, and, afterward, when it has no purpose, I will merely lay it aside. It will not be sick, old, or hurt; it will be functionless, and I will cast it away. I will not see the body as more than this today: Of service and fit to serve me for a while, then to be released for my own good.

2. *'The body, dear God, cannot be One with You. What you did not create is not sinful or sinless; neither good nor bad. I will use this illusion, then, to help Your plan to release me from all of the illusions that I have made.'*

Lesson 295

'The Holy Spirit looks through me today.'

1. Christ asks to be my eyes today, and so redeem all that I perceive. It asks this gift of me, so that It can offer me Peace of mind, and take away all terror and pain. And, as they are removed from me, my illusions are gone. As I am saved, the part of my mind where I perceive a world must be saved as well. My entire mind must be redeemed as One. Fear appears in many different forms, but Love is One.

2. *'God, Christ has asked a gift of me; one that I give so that a Gift can be given to me. Help me to use the eyes of Christ today, and allow the Holy Spirit's Love to bless all things upon which I happen to look, so that the Holy Spirit's forgiving Love may rest on me.'*

Lesson 296

'The Holy Spirit speaks through me today.'

1.*'The Holy Spirit needs my voice today, dear God, so that I can extend Your Voice through my entire mind. I am resolved to let You speak through me, because I want to use only Your words, and to have only Your Thoughts, because only Yours are True. I want to save the part of my mind where I perceive a world, which I made. Having damned it, I want to set it free, so that I can escape from limitations, and hear the Word that Your Holy Voice speaks to me today.'*

2. I will teach today only what I want to learn, so that I do not contradict my learning goal, I reach it easily, and I quickly accomplished it. The Holy Spirit comes gladly to rescue me from hell when I allow Its teachings to persuade me to seek and find the easy path to God.

Lesson 297

'My forgiving is the only gift that I give.'

1. My forgiving is the only gift that I give, because it is the only gift that I want. Everything that I give, I give to myself. This is salvation's simple formula. I want to be saved, so I want to make forgiving the world the way in which I live in my perception that I am in a world from which I need to be saved. I will be saved as I accept correction of my perception that I am separate from God.

2. *'God, Your ways are certain, their Final Outcome is sure, and every step in my salvation is already set and accomplished by Your Grace. I thank You for Your Eternal Gifts, and for my Identity in You.'*

Lesson 298

'I love You, God, and I love Christ in me.'

1. My gratitude permits me to accept my Love without fear, and this is how I am restored to my Reality at last. All that intruded on my Holy Perception will be removed by my forgiving. I draw near the end of senseless journeys, mad careers, and artificial values. I accept instead What God establishes as mine, sure that in That alone I am saved; sure that I go through fear to meet my Love.

2. *'God, I come to You today, because I want to follow only Your way. You are beside me; Your way is certain. I am grateful for Your Holy Gifts of Certain Sanctuary and escape from everything that obscures my Love for You and the Christ in me.'*

Lesson 299

'Eternal Holiness abides in me.'

1. My Holiness is far beyond my ability to understand, or know, in my belief that I am separate from God. Yet, God, my Source, Which created my Holiness, acknowledges my Holiness as Its Own. Our Will, united, understands this, and knows that it is so.

2. *'God, I did not make my Holiness, so it is not within my ability to destroy It with 'sin', and I cannot make It suffer from attack. Illusions can obscure my Holiness, but they cannot dim Its Radiance, nor put out Its Light. It stands Forever Perfect and untouched. All things are healed in Its Reality . I can know my Holiness, because Holiness Itself created me, and I can know my Source, because It is Your Will that I know You.'*

Lesson 300

'The world that I perceive endures for only an instant.'

1. This is a thought that you can use to say that death and sorrow are inevitable, because your joys in the world are gone before you even grasp them. But this is also an idea that releases you from false perception, which is no more than a passing cloud on an eternally serene sky. It is unclouded Serenity that you seek today.

2. *'I seek Your perception today, God. I have lost my way for a while, but I have listened to Your Holy Spirit, and learned exactly what to do to be restored to Heaven and my True Identity. I am grateful that the world that I perceive lasts for only an instant; I want to go beyond that tiny instant to Eternity.'*

9. What is the Second Coming of Christ?

1. The Second Coming of Christ, which is as sure as God, is merely the correction of your mistakes, and the return of Sanity to your mind. It restores to you What you never lost, and re-establishes What is Forever True in your mind. It is your invitation to God's Word to take the place of your illusions, and your willingness to forgive all things, without exception or reservation.

2. The all-encompassing nature of Christ's Second Coming embraces all that you perceive, and holds you safe within it. There is no end to the release that Christ's Second Coming brings to you, because God's Extension is Limitless. Your forgiving lights the way for Christ, because it shines on everything as one. This is how you recognize the Oneness of your mind at last.

3. Christ's Second Coming ends the Holy Spirit's lessons for you, making way for the Last Judgment, in which your learning ends in one last summary that extends beyond itself, reaching up to God. It is the time when your entire mind is given to Christ, to be returned to Spirit in the name of God's Extension and Will.

4. Christ's Second Coming is the one event in time which time itself cannot affect. All that you ever made, or imagined for the future, is wholly released from your mind in it. Christ is restored as the One Identity of your entire mind, and God smiles upon you, God's Extension and Joy.

5. Pray that the Second Coming of Christ is soon, but do not rest there. It needs your eyes, ears, hands, feet, and voice. Most of all, it needs your willingness. Rejoice that you can do God's Will, and join together in Its Holy Light. God's Holy Extension is One in you, and you can reach God's Love through It.

Mentor's Note

From *The Message of A Course in Miracles: A translation of the Text in Plain Language*:

The 'Second Coming of Christ' simply means the end of your

perception of separation from God, and the healing of your mind. (MACIM-4.4.10)

The Second Coming of Christ is not the return of Reality, but merely your awareness that It is always here. (MACIM-9.4.11)

Lesson 301

'God will wipe away all of my tears.'

1. *'God, only if I judge do I weep, suffer pain, feel abandoned, or feel unneeded in my perception that I am in a world. The world can be my home when I do not judge it, because then it reflects only what You will. Today, I will perceive the world as free of my condemnation, through Happy eyes that my forgiving has released from all distortion. I will see the world as Yours instead of as the personal mind's, and I will forget all of the tears that I have shed, because their source will be gone. God, I will not judge Your Perception of the world today.'*

2. God's Perception of the world is Happy. When you look on It, you can only add your Joy to It, and bless It as a cause of further Joy to you. You wept, because you did not understand, but you have learned that the world that you perceived was false, and you can look on the world as God's today.

Lesson 302

'Where I perceived darkness, I look on God's Light.'

1. *'God, my mind is opening to You at last. Your Holy world awaits me as my Real Perception is finally restored to me. I thought that I suffered, but I had forgotten myself as You created me. Now, I see that the darkness of denying You was of my own making, and that Your Light is here for me to look upon. The Perception of my Christ Mind changes darkness into Light, because fear disappears when Love comes. I will forgive the world that the personal mind perceives today, so that I may see Your Holiness, and understand that It only reflects my own.'*

2. Your Love walks beside you as you go to God, and It shows you the way. God cannot fail. God is the End that you seek, and also the Means by Which you go to God.

Lesson 303

'The Holy Christ is born in my awareness today.'

1. Watch with me today, Holy Thoughts of God; surround me, and be still with me while Christ is born into my awareness. The sounds of the world will be quiet, and the world that I am used to perceiving will disappear. I will welcome Christ into my mind, where It is at home. Christ will hear the sounds that It understands, and It will perceive God's Love. Christ is no longer a stranger in my mind, because Christ is born again in me today.

2. *'Your Extension is welcome in me, dear God. It has come to save me from the 'evil' self that I made. Christ is the Self that You give to me; Christ is What I am in Truth. Christ is the Extension of You that You love as Everything. Christ is my True Self, as You created me. It is not Christ that can be crucified; safe in Your Arms, I receive Christ back into my awareness.'*

Lesson 304

'I will not let the personal mind's world obscure my awareness of Christ.'

1. I can obscure my Real Perception only if I intrude the personal mind's world upon it. I can only see as Christ if I use Christ's Perception. Perception is a mirror, not a fact. What I look upon is my state of mind, reflected outward. I want to bless all that I perceive by looking at it through the Perception of my Christ Mind. I will to perceive the certain signs that I have forgiven myself all of my 'sins'.

2. *'God, You lead me from darkness to Light; from a perception of sin to a perception of Holiness. I will forgive, and receive salvation for my entire mind. This is Your gift, dear God, given to me to offer to my Christ Mind, so that I remember You, and myself as You created me.'*

Lesson 305

'There is a Peace that my Christ Mind bestows on me.'

1. When you use the Perception of your Christ Mind, you find a Peace so Deep and Quiet, so Whole and Changeless, that the world that you perceive has no counterpart to It. All opposites are undone before this Peace. The world of the personal mind departs from you in silence as Peace envelops your mind, and gently carries it to Truth, so that it is no longer the home of fear. Love heals your perception of the world by giving it Christ's Peace.

2. *'God, the Peace of Christ is mine, because It is Your Will that I be saved from my illusions. Help me to accept only Your Gift today, and to not judge It. It comes to save me from my erroneous judgment on myself.'*

Lesson 306

'The Gift of Christ is all that I seek today.'

1. The Perception of my Christ Mind is all that I want to use today, because It offers me a day in which my perception is so like Heaven that a Timeless Memory returns to me. Today, I forget the world that I made, and I go past all fear, to be restored to Love, Holiness, and Peace. Today, I am redeemed and born again into a Perception of Mercy, Loving Kindness, and the Peace of God.

2. *'And so, dear God, I return to You, remembering that I never went away from You, and remembering Your Holy Gifts to me. I come in gratitude, and with an open mind, to ask for only What You give. I cannot offer enough for Christ, but in Your Love, the Gift of Christ is mine.'*

Lesson 307

'Conflicting wishes are not my will.'

1. *'God, only Your Will is mine; there is no other will for me to have. I will not try to make another will, because this is senseless and will only cause me pain. Your Will alone can bring me Happiness, and only Your Will exists. I want only What You give, so I must accept Your Will for me and enter into Peace, Where conflict is impossible, I am One with You in Being and in Will, and nothing contradicts the Holy Truth that I am as You created me.'*

2. With this prayer, I silently enter into a State Where conflict cannot come, because I join my Holy Will with God's Will, recognizing that They are the same.

Lesson 308

'This Instant is the only time that there is.'

1. I have conceived of time in a way that defeats my Goal of Peace. To reach past time to Timelessness, I must change my perception of what time is for. Time's purpose, then, cannot be to keep the past and the future the same. The only interval in which I can be saved from time is *now*, because in *this Instant*, my forgiving sets me free. The birth of Christ into my awareness can only happen now, without past or future. Christ comes into my awareness now to bless all that my mind perceives, restoring my mind to Timelessness and Love. Love is ever-present; It is here and now.

2. *'Thank You for this Instant, dear God. It is* now *that I am redeemed. This is the Instant Which You have appointed for the release of my entire mind.'*

Lesson 309

'I will not fear to look within today.'

1. Within me is Eternal Innocence, because It is God's Will that It be there Forever. I, who am One with God, and whose Will is as Limitless as God's Will, cannot will a change in this. For me to deny God's Will is for me to deny my will. When I look within, I find my Will as God created It and as It is. I fear to look within, because I think that I made real another will that is not true, but it has no real effects. Within me is the Holiness of God; within me is my Memory of God.

2. *'The step I take today, God, is my sure release from my pointless illusions of sin. The center of my Mind, as You created It, is Serene and Undefiled; It is Where I find my True Identity.'*

Lesson 310

'I spend today without fear, and in Love.'

1. *'I want to spend today with You, dear God, as You have chosen for me to spend all of my days, and What I will experience is not of time at all. The Joy that comes to me will not be limited to days or hours, because It will come from Heaven to What is One with You. Today will be Your sweet reminder to me to remember You, Your Gracious Call to me, the sign that Your Grace has come to me, and that it is Your Will that I be set free.'*

2. You will spend today with Christ, and your entire mind will join in gratitude and Joy to God, Which has given salvation to you, and Which sets you free. You will be restored to Peace and Holiness. There is no room in you for fear today, because you have welcomed Love into your awareness.

10. What is the Last Judgment?

1. The Second Coming of Christ in your mind gives you this gift: God's Holy Spirit proclaiming to you that illusion is illusion, and that the Truth has never changed. This is the judgment in which perception will end. At first, you will perceive that this is true in a corrected projection from your mind, then, with a silent blessing from this Holy Perception, all perception will disappear as its purpose will be done.

2. The Final Judgment on the world that you made contains no condemnation, because It forgives your perception of separation from God as an illusion, not as a sin. Without a cause, and now without a function in your Christ Mind's Perception, the world will merely slip away from your mind. It began as nothing, and it will end as nothing. And all the figures in your illusion of the world will disappear as well, because bodies will be useless when you know yourself as Limitless again.

3. You have believed that God's Last Judgment will condemn you and your world to hell, but accept this Holy Truth: God's Judgment is the Gift of Correction that God bestows on your errors, freeing you from them, and from all of the effects that they seemed to have on you. For you to fear God's Saving Grace is for you to fear your complete release from suffering and your return to Peace, Security, Happiness, and your own Identity.

4. God's Final Judgment is as Merciful as every step in God's plan to bless you and call you to return to the Eternal Peace that you share with God. Do not be afraid of Love, because It alone can heal all of your sorrow, wipe away all of your tears, and gently lead you away from your illusion of pain. Do not be afraid of this. Your salvation asks you to welcome it, and your entire mind waits for your glad acceptance to set it free.

5. This is God's Final Judgment: 'You are still One with Me, Forever Innocent, Loving, Loved, as Limitless as I, completely Changeless, and Eternally Pure. Therefore, remember and return to Me. I am your Source, and you are One with me.'

Lesson 311

'I judge all things as I want them to be.'

1. You made judgment to be a weapon against the Truth. You have used it to separate everything from everything else, and then to make of everything what the personal mind wants it to be. You cannot understand what you judge with a personal mind, because a personal mind cannot see Wholeness, so it judges incorrectly. Do not use judgment with the personal mind today, but give judgment to the Holy Spirit, Which has a different use for it. The Holy Spirit will relieve you of the agony of all of the judgments that you made against yourself with a personal mind, and will re-establish your Peace of mind by giving you God's Judgment on you.

2. *'God, I wait with an open mind today, to hear Your Judgment of me, whom You love. I do not know my True Self, so I cannot judge It, so I will let Your Love decide What You created must be.'*

Lesson 312

'I perceive all things as I want them to be.'

1. Perception follows judgment. You judge, then you perceive what you want to perceive. Perception can only offer you what you want. It is impossible for you to overlook what you want to perceive, or for you to fail to perceive what you have chosen to perceive. How surely, then, does your Real Perception come to you when you take the Holy Spirit's purpose as the goal for your perception. Then, you will perceive what your Christ Mind wants you to perceive, and you will share Christ's Love for what you perceive.

2. *'My only purpose today is to perceive the world without all of the judgments that I made on it with a personal mind. God, this is Your Will for me today, so it is my goal as well.'*

Lesson 313

'I will let a new Perception come to me.'

1. *'Dear God, there is a Perception that looks on all things as sinless, so that fear is gone from my mind, and where it was, I invite Love to be. Love will come wherever I ask. This Perception is Your Gift. The Perception of my Christ Mind forgives the world that I made. It forgives all seeming 'sin', because It cannot perceive sin. Now, I let Christ's Perception come to me, so that I may undo my illusion of 'sin', and look within at my Innocence, Which You keep completely undefiled in my True Self, with Which I want to identify.'*

2. Today, perceive all things through the Perception of your Christ Mind. How Beautiful, Holy, and Loving everything is! Join your Christ Mind today, and save your entire mind, because in your Christ Mind's Perception, all that you perceive is as Holy as the Light within you.

Lesson 314

'I seek a future that is different from the past.'

1. In your new Perception, your future will be different from the personal self's past; it will be an extension of the present instead. The personal self's past will not cast its shadow on the future, so that fear will have no idols or images, and, having no form, it will have no effects. Death will not claim the future for you now, because Life is your goal, and all the means that you need to know Life will be provided. You will not grieve or suffer when you free the present and extend its Security and Peace into a quiet future filled with Joy.

2. *'Dear God, I was mistaken in the past, and I choose to use the present to be free of it. I leave the future in Your Hands, and I leave behind my past mistakes, sure that You will keep Your present Promises, and guide my future in Their Holy Light.'*

Lesson 315

'All of the gifts that others give belong to me.'

1. Every day, a thousand treasures come to me with every passing moment. I am blessed with gifts throughout the day, in value far beyond what I can conceive. A person smiles to another, and I am blessed; someone speaks words of gratitude or mercy, and my mind receives these gifts. Everyone becomes my savior as I extend God to them, and they point out the way to me, giving me the certainty that What I perceive is mine.

2. *'I thank You, God, for the many gifts that come to me today, and everyday, from all that I perceive, which is limitless in its gifts to me. I offer my gratitude to others, so that they may lead me to remember You.'*

Lesson 316

'All of the gifts that I give to others are my own.'

1. As every gift that others give are mine, so every gift I give belongs to me. With each one, I allow a past mistake to go, and I leave no shadow on my Holy mind, which God loves. God's Grace is given to me in every gift anyone has received throughout time. My treasure house is full, and God's Thoughts watch that no gifts are lost, only added. I will go to my treasure house and enter where I am truly welcome and at home, among the gifts that God gives to me.

2. *'God, I accept Your Gifts today. I do not recognize Them, but I trust that You will provide me the means by which I can perceive Them and their Worth, and cherish Them as all that I want.'*

Mentor's Notes

These lessons are saying that you can look on all expressions of Love, whether from others to you, from you to others, or from others to others as a reminder of the Love within you.

Lesson 317

'I follow the way that God appoints for me.'

1. I have a special place to fill; a role for me alone. My salvation waits until I take this part as what I choose to do. Until I make this choice, I am limited to time and a human destiny, but when I willingly and happily go the way that God appoints for me, then I will recognize that salvation is already here for my entire mind.

2. *'Dear God, Your way is what I choose today. I choose to go where it leads me, and to do as it needs me to do. Your way is Certain, and its End is Secure. My Memory of You waits for me There, and all my sorrows end in Your Embrace, Which You promise to me, who mistakenly thought that I had wandered from Your Sure Protection.'*

Lesson 318

'The Means and End of my salvation are One in me.'

1. I am One with God, so in me, all parts of Heaven's plan to save my entire mind from illusions are reconciled. Nothing can conflict in this plan, because all of its parts have only One Purpose and One Goal. No part stands alone, or is of more or less importance than the rest. I am the means by which my entire mind is saved, because the aim of my salvation is to find the Innocence that God placed in me. What I seek is What God created. I am the Goal of all of my searching. I am One with God; I am God's Eternal Love. I am the Means and End of my salvation.

2. *'Today, God, I take the role that You offer to me in Your request that I accept the Atonement for myself. This is how What is reconciled in You becomes just as certainly reconciled in me.'*

Lesson 319

'I am here to save my entire mind.'

1. This is a thought from which all arrogance is removed, and only truth remains, because arrogance is what opposes truth. Where there is no arrogance in my mind, the Truth will come immediately to fill up the space that is empty of the personal mind's lies. Only the personal mind is limited, therefore it must seek for goals that are limited and limiting. The personal mind thinks that what one part of my mind gains, the other must lose, but it is the Will of God that I learn that what is in one part of my mind is in my entire mind.

2. *'God, Your Will is Total, and the Goal that stems from It shares Its Totality. The only goal that You can give to me is to save my entire mind from my illusions. This is all that the Will of my True Self can share with You.'*

Lesson 320

'God gives all Power to me.'

1. What is One with God is Limitless. There are no limits on Its Strength, Its Peace, Its Joy, nor any attributes that God gives to It through God's extension of God to It. What I will with God must be done. My Holy Will cannot be denied, because God shines in my mind and gives it all Strength and Love, in my perception that I am in a world, and in Heaven. I am That to Which All is given by God. I am That in Which the Power of God's Will abides.

2. *'Dear God, Your Will can do all things* in *me, then extend to all that I perceive* through *me. There is no limit on Your Will, so all Power has been given to me in my Oneness with You.'*

11. What is Creation?

1. Creation is the sum of all of God's Thoughts, Infinite and Limitless. Only Love creates, and It creates only like Itself. There is no time in which All that Love creates is not here, nor is it possible for Creation to suffer loss. Eternally, God's Thoughts are exactly as They are, unchanged through your perception that you are in time, and after time is gone from your mind.

2. God's Thought's have all of the Power of God, because God wants to add to Love through extension, so God's Creation extends God. What God wills to be Forever One is not changed by your perception of time. It is One now, throughout your perception of time, and when your perception of time is over.

3. Creation is the opposite of all of your illusions, because It is the Truth. Creation is the Holy Christ in you, because in Creation, God's Will is complete in every aspect, making every Part container of the Whole. Creation's Oneness is guaranteed to be Forever untouched, Forever held in God's Holy Will, beyond all possibility of harm, separation, imperfection, or any stain on Its Innocence.

4. The Christ in you, and the Christ that you extend in your perception, is Creation. Your mind seems to be separated into many 'selves' and things, and unaware of its Eternal Oneness in God. But behind all of your doubts and fears, you are still certain of God, because Love remains with Its Thoughts, and Its Sureness is yours. Your Memory of God is in your Holy Mind, Which knows of your Oneness with God. Let your function be only to let this Memory return to you, to let God's Will be done in your perception that you are in a world, to let yourself be restored to Sanity, and to let yourself be only as God created you.

5. God calls to you; as you hear God, you forgive Creation in the Name of Its Source, Holiness Itself, the Holiness in Which Creation shares. God's Holiness is still Part of you.

Mentor's Notes

Again, there would be no need for the concept of *Creator* and

Creation if not for your perception of separation from God. In God, All is One, and God is not delineated into parts.

The central teaching of this course is that, because God and the world that you perceive are both in your mind, you can choose to perceive God in the world. This is what is meant by 'God's Thoughts'. You perceive a tree, a body, a street, and a car. Though they are meant by the personal mind to block God from your awareness, you can choose to see them as a reminder of God by seeing beyond them. This is what is meant in paragraph 1 by God's 'Thoughts'. God did not make the tree, body, street, or car, but your thinking of God beyond them seems like a different thought of God each time. So the 'sum' of these 'Thoughts' is Infinite, because you can choose to see God everywhere, and, in fact, you must do so to remember that only God is in your mind. This is how you become aware of God's Extension, or Creation, in your perception that you are in a world that is meant to be separate from God. When your entire mind is returned to an awareness of God, your entire mind is returned to Creation.

Lesson 321

'God, my Freedom is only in You.'

1. *'I did not understand what would make me free, what my freedom is, or where to find it. God, I searched in vain until I heard Your Holy Spirit directing me. I will no longer choose the personal mind to guide me, because it does not make or understand the way to my Freedom. But I trust You, Who endow me with my Freedom in Oneness with You, so that You will not be lost to me. Your Holy Spirit directs me, and the way to You is open and clear to me at last. Dear God, my Freedom is only in You, and it is my will that I return to you.'*

2. Today, you answer for your entire mind. How glad you will be to find your Freedom through the certain way that God establishes for you. How certain is the salvation of your entire mind when you learn that your Freedom can be found only in God.

Lesson 322

'I can give up only what was never real.'

1. I seem to 'sacrifice' my illusions, and nothing else. As my illusions fall away, I will find the Gifts that I tried to hide with my illusions waiting for me with a Happy welcome, and in readiness to give to me God's Timeless Messages. My every illusion only served to conceal the Self that is One with God within me.

2. *'God, to You all sacrifice is inconceivable, so I can only sacrifice in illusions. As You created me, I give up nothing that You give to me. What You did not give has no reality, so the only loss that I can anticipate is the loss of fear, which results in the return of Love to my mind.'*

Lesson 323

'I gladly 'sacrifice' fear.'

1. *'This is the only 'sacrifice' that You ask of me, God: That I give up all suffering, all sense of loss and sadness, all anxiety and doubt, so that Love can come pouring into my awareness, to heal me of pain, and to give me Your Own Eternal Joy. This is the 'sacrifice' that You ask of me, and that I gladly make. This is the only 'cost' of restoring my Memory of You, for the salvation of my entire mind.'*

2. As I 'pay' the 'debt' that I owe to Truth, a debt that is only my letting go of self-deceptions and of images that I worshipped mistakenly, Truth will return to me in Wholeness and in Joy. I will no longer be deceived. Love will return to my awareness, and I will be at Peace again, and because fear will be gone, only Love will remain in my mind.

Lesson 324

'I only follow You, God; I do not want to lead.'

1. *'God, You are the One Who gives me a plan for my salvation. You have set the way I am to go, the role I am to take, and every step on my appointed path. I cannot lose the way, though I can choose to wander off for a while. But, Your Holy Spirit will always call me back and guide me to You again. I will bring my entire mind with me as I follow the way to You, as You direct me and want me to go.'*

2. I will follow the One That knows the way. I do not need to hesitate, and I can only stray for an instant from God's Guiding Hand. I walk with the Christ in me, because I follow God, and it is God that makes the Ending sure, and guarantees my safe return Home.

Lesson 325

'What I think that I perceive reflects ideas in my mind.'

1. This is the key to my salvation: What I perceive reflects a process in my mind, which starts with my idea of what I want. From there, my mind makes up an image of what I desire, judge valuable, and therefore seek to find. I then project these images outward, look at them as real, and guard them as my own. An insane world comes from my insane wishes; a condemned world comes from my judgment; and a gentle, merciful world, which offers me a kindly home where I can rest as I journey to God, comes from my forgiving thoughts.

2. *'Dear God, Your Ideas reflect the Truth, but mine apart from Yours are only illusions. I want to perceive only What Yours reflect, because only Yours establish Truth.'*

Lesson 326

'I am Forever God's Effect.'

1. *'God, I was created in Your Mind, a Holy Thought that has never left Its Home. I am Forever Your Effect, as You are Forever my Cause. I remain as You created me, and I abide Where You established me. All of Your Attributes abide in me, because it is Your Will that What is One with You be like Its Cause, so that Cause and Effect are One. I want to know that I am an Effect of God, and that I have the Power to create like You. As it is in Heaven, so be it while I perceive myself in a world. I follow Your plan in the world, and I know that, in the end, You will gather Your Effect into the Tranquil Heaven of Your Love, Where the world will vanish, and all seemingly separate Thoughts will unite in Your Glory.'*

2. Today, watch the world disappear from your awareness: transformed at first, then, forgiven, fading entirely into God's Holy Will.

Lesson 327

'I only need to call on You, God, and You will answer me.'

1. God does not ask me to accept my salvation on the basis of an unsupported faith. God has promised that It will hear my call, and that It will answer me. I will learn from experience that this is true, then I will certainly have faith in God. This is faith that will endure, and that will take me far on the road that leads to God. This is how I will be sure that God has not abandoned me and still loves me, but is only waiting for my call to give me the help that I need to reach It.

2. *'God, I thank You that Your Promises will never fail me if I test Them. Therefore, I will try Them before judging Them. Your Word is One with You. You give me the Means by Which conviction will come to me, and I will gain certainty of Your Love at last.'*

Lesson 328

'I choose to follow to become the Leader.'

1. What seems to be following is the way that I become the Leader that I follow, because, in my perception that I am in a world, my thinking is upside down until I listen to the Holy Spirit. In the world, it seems that I gain my independence by perceiving the rest of my mind as separate and outside of me, but all I find is sickness, suffering, loss, and death. This is not what God wills for me, and there is no will but God's Will. When I join with God's Will, I will find my own, and since my will is God's Will, it is to God that I must go to recognize my Will.

2. *'God, there is only Your Will. I am glad that nothing that I imagine can truly contradict What You want me to be. It is Your Will that I be Wholly Safe and Eternally at Peace. Happily, I share Your Will, dear God.'*

Lesson 329

'God, I have already chosen What You will.'

1. *'God, I thought that I wandered from Your Will, defied It, broke Its Laws, and made a will that was more powerful than Yours. But, What I am in Truth is Your Will, extended and extending, and this will never change. Just as You are One, I am One with You. This is what I choose in Creation, Where my Will is Forever One with Yours. I choose this for Eternity, and It cannot change and be opposed to Itself. God, my will is Yours, and I am Safe, Serene, and Eternally Joyful, because It is Your Will that I be so.'*

2. Today, you will accept your One Mind and your Source. You have no will apart from God, and your Mind is One because It is God's Will Throughout. Through your Will joined with God's, you will recognize that your Mind is One. Through It, you will find your way to God at last.

Lesson 330

'I will not hurt myself again today.'

1. Today, accept forgiving as your only function. Do not attack your mind with images of pain. Do not teach it that it is powerless, because God holds out Its Power and Love, and asks you to take What is already yours. When you are willing to accept God's Gifts, you will be restored to Spirit, and you will extend Its Freedom and Its Joy, Which is God's Will. The Self that God created cannot sin, therefore It cannot suffer. Choose this Self today as your Identity, and escape forever from all the things that your illusion of fear offered to you.

2. *'God, I am One with You, so I cannot be hurt. If I think that I suffer, it is because I fail to know the Identity that I share with You. I return to It today, to be free forever from my mistakes, and to be saved from what I thought that I was.'*

12. What is the personal self?

1. The personal self is an idol; a symbol of limitation and separation, born in a body, doomed to suffer, and to end its 'life' in death. It is the 'will' that thinks that God's Will is its enemy, and it takes a form that denies God's Will. The personal self is the 'proof' that True Strength is weakness, Love is frightening, Life is really death, and that only what opposes God is true.

2. The personal mind is insane. In fear, it thinks that it stands beyond the Everywhere, apart from All, and separate from the Infinite. In its insanity, it thinks that it is a 'victor' over God. In its terrible isolation, it perceives that it has destroyed God's Will. Its illusion is full of punishment, and it trembles at the figures in its illusion, whom it considers enemies seeking to murder it before it can ensure its own safety by attacking them.

3. The Christ in you is not a personal self. It does not know of insanity or the 'death of God', because It lives in God. It does not know of sorrow or suffering, because It lives in Eternal Joy. It does not know of fear and punishment, of sin and guilt, of hatred and attack, because It is surrounded by Everlasting Peace. The Christ in you is Forever free of conflict, undisturbed, and lives in the Deepest Silence and Tranquility.

4. For you to know Reality is for you to not perceive the personal self and its thoughts, its actions, it dreams, its hopes, its plans for its own salvation, or the cost that your belief in it entails. The price of your faith in the personal self is suffering so immense that your crucifixion is offered to it daily in preparation for your inevitable death.

5. But one act of forgiving by you can change this dark illusion in your mind into Light; your perception of illusions into a Reflection of Life. Then, Peace will be restored Forever to your Holy mind, which is One with God, is God's Home, God's Joy, God's Love, and God's Completion.

Mentor's Notes

You have two thought systems in your mind: your Christ Mind – the thought system that reflects your Oneness with God; the personal mind – the thought system that is the opposite to God in every way. These thought systems are diametrically opposed to each other and cannot be reconciled; neither can be made like the other. So, to know again your Oneness with God, you must let go of the thought system of the personal mind. It can never be made to be like your Christ Mind.

Of course, initially, you probably are not aware that, in your identification with a personal self, you think that you killed God. This is not a conscious thought, nor is it one that the personal mind wants you to see. But it is there in your mind in your simple belief that the world is real, and the 'proof' that it is there is in your mind is in your suffering the consequences of this belief.

To the personal mind, God is death, so it perceives God's Attributes (True Strength, Love, Life) as threatening to it.

Lesson 331

'God, I have no conflict, because my will is Yours.'

1.*'How foolish of me, dear God, to believe that I can cause myself to suffer. I cannot make a plan for my damnation and be left without a certain way for my relief. You love me, God, and You will never leave me desolate, to die in a world of pain and cruelty. How could I think that Love has left Itself? The only Will is Love's Will. Fear is an illusion, and it has no will that can conflict with Yours. Conflict is the result of my denial of You, and Peace is the result of my awareness of You. Death is an illusion; Life is Eternal Truth. There is nothing to oppose Your Will. I have no conflict, because my will is Yours.'*

2. Forgiving shows me that God's Will is One, and that I share It. I will perceive only the Holiness that forgiving shows me today, so that I may find the Peace of God. Amen.

Lesson 332

'Fear limits my mind; forgiving sets it free.'

1. The personal mind makes illusions, but Truth undoes them by shining them away. Truth never attacks; It simply *is*. In the Presence of Truth, my mind is recalled from illusions, and I remember What is Real. My forgiving asks Truth to enter my mind, and to take Its Rightful Place. If I do not forgive, I limit my mind, and I believe that it is ineffectual. But, through forgiving, God's Light shines through my dark illusions, offers me hope, and gives me the Means to realize that my mind is Limitless.

2. *'I will not limit my mind again today; fear holds it prisoner. But Your Love, dear God, gives me the Means to set it free. I want to release it now, and as I extend Freedom in my perception, It is given to me. I will not remain limited while You offer me Limitlessness.'*

Lesson 333

'My forgiving ends my illusion of conflict.'

1. I must resolve conflict if I want to escape from it. I cannot evade it, set it aside, deny it, disguise it, see it somewhere else, called it by another name, or hide it by deceit of any kind. I must see it exactly as I think that it is, where I think that it is, in the form that I think it is real, and with the purpose that I've given to it. Only then will I have lifted its defenses so that the Truth can undo it.

2. *'God, my forgiving is the Light that You use to shine away all of my conflict and doubt, and to light the way for my return to You. Only this Light can end my illusions of evil, and save my entire mind. This alone will never fail, being Your Gift to me.'*

Lesson 334

'Today, I claim the Gifts that my forgiving brings to me.'

1. I will not wait another day to find the Treasures that God offers to me. My illusions are pointless and gone the moment that they are made out of thoughts that rest on my erroneous perceptions. I will not accept such meager gifts again today. The Holy Spirit is offering the Peace of God to me, and I hear, and choose to follow, the Holy Spirit. I go to find the Treasures that God gives to me.

2. *'God, I seek for only the Eternal, because I cannot be content with less than This. Only What You offer to my bewildered and frightened mind can be my Solace and give me Certainty and Peace. Today, I will extend Innocence to all that I perceive. This is Your Will for me, because this is how I will perceive my Innocence.'*

Lesson 335

'I choose to perceive Innocence.'

1. Forgiving is a choice. I never perceive What *is*, because That is far beyond perception. What I do perceive is what I want to perceive, because it stands for what I want to be the truth. This is to what I respond, however much I seem impelled by what seems outside of me. I choose to perceive what I want to perceive, and this is all that I do perceive. When I choose to perceive Innocence, it means that I want to look on my own Innocence, and I will perceive It, having chosen It.

2. *'Only perceiving Innocence will restore to me my Memory of You, dear God. The Holiness that I perceive in the part of my mind that seems outside of me reminds me that my mind is One in Holiness. In it, I find my True Self, and in my True Self, I find my Memory of You.'*

Lesson 336

'My forgiving reminds me that my mind is One.'

1. My forgiving is the means that God has given to me to end perception. Knowledge of God is restored to me after my perception first changes, and then gives way entirely to What remains Forever past perception's highest reach. At best, sights and sounds can serve to remind me of What lies beyond them all, but my forgiving sweeps away all distortions in my mind, and opens it to Truth. The Light of Truth shines into my mind, and calls me to look within, to find What I futilely sought outside. Here, and only here, my Peace of mind is restored, because my mind is where God dwells.

2. *'In Quiet, my forgiving sweeps away my illusion of separation and sin. God, I look within and find that Your Promise of my Innocence is kept, Your Word is unchanged within my mind, and Your Love is still at the center of my Being.'*

Lesson 337

'My Innocence protects me from all harm.'

1. My Innocence ensures me Perfect Peace, Eternal Safety, Everlasting Love, Freedom Forever from all loss, and complete deliverance from suffering. Only Happiness is my True State, because God gives me only Happiness. To know that all of This is mine, I only have to accept correction of my perception that I am separate from God. God has already done all that needs to be done. I must learn that I need do nothing but accept my True Self, my Innocence, Which is already mine; to feel God's Love protecting me from harm, to understand that God loves Its Extension, and that I am the Extension of God that God loves.

2. *'God, You Who created me Innocent are not mistaken about What I am. I* was *mistaken when I thought that I 'sinned' against You, but I accept correction for this misperception. God, my illusions end now. Amen.'*

Lesson 338

'I am affected only by my thoughts.'

1. I only need this thought to save my entire mind, because in it I am released from fear. I have learned that no one frightens me, and nothing can endanger me. I have no enemies, and I am safe from all things that seem external to me. My thoughts can frighten me, but since they are *my* thoughts, I have the power to change them, and exchange each fearful thought for a happy thought of Love. I have crucified myself, but God has planned that I will be redeemed.

2. *'Your plan alone is sure, dear God. All other plans that I perceive will fail. I will have thoughts that frighten me until I learn that You have given me the only Thought that leads me to my salvation. The personal mind's plans will fail, since they lead me nowhere, but the Thought that You give to me promises to lead me Home, because It holds the Promise that You made to me.'*

Lesson 339

'I will receive whatever I request.'

1. You may not desire pain, but you can confuse pain with pleasure. You don't want to avoid your Happiness, but you can think that True Joy is painful, threatening, and dangerous to you. You receive whatever you request, but you can be confused about what you want, and the state that you want to attain. So, what you request may not be what you meant to receive when you requested it. You have asked for what will frighten you and bring you suffering. Resolve today to ask for only What you really want, so that you can spend the day without fear, without confusing pain with Joy, or fear with Love.

2. *'God, today is Yours. It is a day in which I will do nothing with the personal mind, but I will hear Your Holy Spirit in everything that I do. I will request only What You offer to me, and accept only Thoughts that You share with me.'*

Mentor's Notes

The first paragraph in Lesson 339 is referring to all the seeking that you do in the world. You want Love, Peace, Joy, and Wholeness, and you think that you are asking for Them in your perception that you are in a world, but you are confused about where to find Them. By seeking in the world, where They are not and can never be, you actually ask for fear and suffering, which then are the result of your seeking in the world. For example, you may want a new car, thinking that it will make you happy. But, when you receive it, you find that the happiness that the car brought you was shallow and fleeting, and you are left with emptiness again. Now, you have to seek elsewhere for happiness, and you will do this again and again and again until you stop seeking outside of yourself. Only within can you find Lasting Happiness, because Lasting Happiness comes only from God.

Lesson 340

'I can be free of suffering today.'

1. *'Dear God, I thank You for today, and for the Freedom that I am certain that it will bring. Today is Holy, because today Christ is redeemed in my mind. My suffering is done, because I will hear Your Holy Spirit directing me to find Christ's Perception by forgiving and being Free Forever from all suffering. Thank You for today, dear God. My purpose in my perception that I am in a world is to achieve what today holds in Joy and Limitlessness for What is One with You in me, by releasing the world that I made, and being entirely released from it.'*

2. Be glad today! There is no room for anything but Joy and gratitude today. God has redeemed you, and your entire mind is saved as One. No perception of fear will remain in your mind, and God will gather your entire mind to Itself. You will be aware again of Heaven, Which is in the Center of Love.

13. What is a miracle?

1. A miracle corrects your perception. It does not create, and it does not change anything Real. It occurs when you look on devastation and you recognize that what you see is an illusion. A miracle undoes error in your mind, but it does not go beyond perception or forgiving. It stays within the limits of time, but paves the way for Timelessness and Love to return to your awareness. In the gentle remedy that is a miracle, fear slips away from you.

2. A miracle is a gift of God's Grace, because your mind gives and receives a miracle as One. So it demonstrates the Law of Truth that the world that you perceive does not obey, because the world cannot understand the miracle. A miracle turns your perception right-side-up, so it ends the strange distortions that your mind manifested. It opens your perception to Truth, so that you see that your forgiving is justified.

3. Your forgiving is the home of miracles. The Perception of your Christ Mind delivers miracles to all that you look upon in Mercy and Love. Your perception is corrected in the Perception of your Christ Mind, so that what you made to curse yourself will now bless you. Your every act of forgiving offers to your entire mind the silent miracle of Love, and each act is offered to God in you in the Light of Perfect Purity and Endless Joy.

4. At first, you will take the miracle on faith, because your asking for it implies that you are not ready yet to conceive of What you cannot perceive and understand. And through your faith, you will perceive witnesses that show you that What your faith rests on is really here. So the miracle will justify your faith in it, and show you that it rests on a Perception more real to you than what you perceived before; a Perception redeemed from what you thought was really here.

5. Miracles fall like drops of healing rain from Heaven on your dry and dusty mind, where you imagined a world where you came to starve and thirst and die. Now, you have water, and your mind is green with life everywhere, showing you that what has Life can never die, because Life is Immortal.

Lesson 341

'I can attack only my own Innocence, but it is only This Which keeps me Safe.'

1. *'Dear God, What is One with you is Holy. I am That Which you smile on in Love and Tenderness so Deep and Still that All-that-is smiles back at You, and shares Your Holiness. How Pure, how Safe, and how Holy I am abiding in Your Smile, with all of Your Love bestowed on my entire mind, in Oneness with You, in Complete extension of You, and in Innocence so Perfect that You know me as Your Extension and Completion.'*

2. Do not, then, attack your Innocence, because It contains the Word of God in you. In Its kind reflection, you are saved from your illusions.

Lesson 342

'I forgive all things, and this is how forgiveness is given to me.'

1. *'I thank You, dear God, for Your plan to save me from the hell that I made. It is not real, and You have given me the means to prove its unreality to myself. My forgiving is the means, and I have reached the point beyond which lies the end of my illusions. I stand before Heaven, wondering if I should enter and be at Home. I will not wait any longer today. I will forgive all things, and let Your Extension be as It is. I will remember that I am One with You, and I will forget illusions in the blazing Light of Truth as my Memory of You returns to my awareness.'*

2. Forgive your Christ Mind the illusions that you have held against It, because It is here now to take you Home. Your entire mind goes with you as you go to God.

Lesson 343

'I am not asked to make a sacrifice to have God's Mercy and Peace.'

1. *'The end of my suffering cannot be my loss; Your Gift of Everything can only be my gain. God, You only give; You never take away. You extended Yourself to me in my creation, so sacrifice is impossible for me, because it is impossible for You. I, too, must extend You, so that All Reality is given to me Eternally. As You created me, I am. What is One with You cannot sacrifice, because I must be Complete, since my Function is to complete You. I am Complete, because I am One with You. I cannot lose, because I can only extend You, and Everything is mine Eternally.'*

2. God's Mercy and Peace are free; your salvation has no cost. It is a gift that you must give freely to receive it. It is this that you learn today.

Lesson 344

'Today, I learn the Law of Love: What I extend is my Gift to me.'

1. *'This is Your Law, dear God, not a law of the personal mind. I have not understood what giving means, and I sought to save what I want for myself alone as a personal self. And as I look on the 'treasure' that I thought that I had, I find an empty place where nothing ever was, is, or will ever be. I cannot extend an illusion, so illusions offer me nothing. But when I forgive, everything that I perceive offers me a Gift beyond the worth of anything in the world. Let all that I forgive fill my mind with Heaven's Treasures, Which alone are Real. This is how the Law of Love is fulfilled, and how Christ returns to my awareness, and I return to You.'*

2. You, and all that your mind perceives, are united as you go to God, and God is united with your entire mind. The end of your illusion of sin is close, as is the redemption of you who are One with God.

Lesson 345

'I extend only miracles today, because I want them returned to me.'

1. *'God, miracles reflect Your Gifts to me. Every one that I extend returns to me, reminding me that the Law of Love is everywhere. Even in my perception that I am in a world, It takes a form that I can recognize and see working. The miracles that extend from me return to me in a form that I need to help me with a problem that I perceive. Dear God, in Heaven it is different, because There I have no needs, but in the world, the miracle is closer to Your Gifts than anything else that I can give. Today, I give this gift alone, which, born of my truly forgiving, lights the way that I must travel to remember You.'*

2. Peace to your seeking today! The Light has come into your awareness to offer miracles to your tired perception. It will find Rest today, because you will offer it what you have received.

Lesson 346

'Today, God's Peace envelops me, and I will forget everything, except God's Love.'

1. *'Dear God, today I awake with miracles correcting my perception of everything. This is how I share Eternity with You today, because I will step aside from time. I do not want the things of time, so I will not look on them. What I want today transcends all laws of time, and the things that I perceive in time. I want to forget everything, except Your Love. I want to live in You, and to know only Your Law of Love. I want to find the Peace that you created for me, and to forget all of the foolish illusions that I made, as I perceive Your Glory, and my own.'*

2. And when the evening comes today, I will remember only the Peace of God, because I will learn today that God's Peace is mine, when I forget everything but God's Love.

Lesson 347

'Anger comes from the judgment of the personal mind, and its judgment is the weapon that I use against myself when I want to keep the miracle away from me.'

1. *'God, I want what goes against my Will, and I do not want What is my Will. Correct my mind, dear God, because it is sick. You have offered me freedom from my sickness, and I choose to claim Your gift today. So, I will give all judgment to Your Holy Spirit, WhichYou have given to me to judge for me. The Holy Spirit perceives what I perceive, but It knows the Truth. The Holy Spirit looks on my pain, and It understands that it is not real, and, in Its understanding, my pain is healed. The Holy Spirit gives me the miracles that my illusions hide from my awareness. I will let the Holy Spirit judge for me today. I do not know my Will, but the Holy Spirit is sure that It is Yours. The Holy Spirit will speak for me, and call Your miracles to come to me.'*

2. I will listen today. I will be very still, and I will hear God's Gentle Holy Spirit assuring me that It has judged me as What God loves.

Lesson 348

'I have no cause for anger or for fear, because You surround me, God. In every need that I perceive, Your Grace is enough.'

1. *'God, I remember that You are here; I am not alone. I am surrounded by Everlasting Love. I only have cause for the Perfect Peace and Joy that I share with You. I have no need for anger or for fear; surrounding me is Perfect Safety. I cannot be afraid when Your Eternal Promise goes with me. I am surrounded by Perfect Innocence. I cannot fear, because you have extended Your Holiness to me in my creation.'*

2. God's Grace is enough in anything that God wants me to do. This is all that I choose to be my will and God's Will.

Lesson 349

'Today, I let the Perception of my Christ Mind look on all things for me, and instead of judging them, I extend to them a miracle of Love.'

1. *'God, this is how I will liberate my mind from the world that I perceive, and perceive instead the Freedom that I seek. This is how I obey the Law of Love, by extending What I want as my own. I will receive What I choose to give. Dear God, Your Gifts are mine, and Each One that I accept gives me a miracle to extend. Giving as I receive, I learn that Your healing miracles belong to me.'*

2. God knows my needs, and God gives me the Grace to meet them all. So, I trust in God to send to me miracles to bless my perception, and to heal my mind as I return to God.

Lesson 350

'Miracles reflect God's Eternal Love. When I extend them, I remember God, and through my Memory of God, I save my entire mind.'

1. *'What I perceive when I forgive my illusions becomes a part of my perception of myself. My Christ Mind incorporates all things within Itself, as You created It. My remembering You, dear God, depends on my forgiving what I made. What I am in Truth is unaffected by my illusory thoughts, but what I perceive is the direct result of my thoughts. Therefore, dear God, I turn to You. Only my Memory of You will set me free from my illusions, and only my forgiving allows my Memory of You to return to my awareness, and to gratefully extend It to be all that I perceive.'*

2. As I gather miracles from God, I will indeed be grateful. As I remember God, my Christ Mind will be restored to me in the Reality of Love.

14. What am I?

1. *'I am One with God, Complete and healed and Whole, shining in the Reflection of God's Love. In me, God's Extension of God is sanctified and guaranteed Eternal Life. In me, Love is Perfect, fear is impossible, and Joy has no opposite. I am the Holy Home of God; I am the Heaven Where God's Love resides. I am God's Holy Innocence, because in my Purity lies God's Purity.'*

2. Your use for words is almost over, now. In these final days of this one year that you have joined with Christ in you to give to God, you find a single purpose with Christ. What Christ is, you are as well. The Truth of What you are cannot be described in words, but you can realize your function in your perception that you are in a world, and you can use words to teach and learn the Truth, if you exemplify them.

3. With Christ in you, you are your own Savior. Accept your part in saving your entire mind, which is redeemed through your forgiving through your Christ Mind. What you extend in your perception is given to you. Perceive all things as One with you; perceive Kindness and Goodness. You are not seeking your Function in Heaven; Knowledge will return to you when you have done your part in your perception that you are in a world. Be concerned only with welcoming the Truth.

4. It is through you that the Perception of your Christ Mind redeems your entire mind from every thought of sin's reality. It is within you that you hear God's Holy Spirit proclaim that there is no sin. Join your mind with Christ to bless all that you perceive, and through this Oneness, you will call to your entire mind to share your Peace and consummate your Joy.

5. You are God's Holy Messenger, and extending God's Word to everyone and everything that you perceive, you learn that It is written within you. This is how you change your mind about the goal that you serve in your perception that you are in a world. Extend glad tiding to your entire mind, which seemed to suffer, and it is redeemed, and as you perceive Heaven before you, you will enter into and disappear within God.

Lesson 351

'The Innocence that I perceive is my Guide to Peace; the sin that I perceive is my guide to pain. Which I choose to perceive, I will perceive.'

1. *'The part of my mind that I perceive as a world is Your Extension, dear God. If I perceive sin in it, I proclaim myself a sinner, alone and friendless in a fearful world, not One with You. But this perception is a choice that I make, so that I can relinquish it. I can choose to see Innocence, Your Holy Extension, instead. With this choice, I see my Innocence, my Everlasting Comforter, beside me, and that my way is secure and clear. Choose, then, for me, dear God, through Your Holy Spirit. The Holy Spirit alone judges for me in Your Name.'*

Lesson 352

'Judgment and Love are opposites. From one comes all of the sorrows that I perceive, and from the Other comes the Peace of God.'

1. *'Forgiving means perceiving Innocence, and not judging with the personal mind. Through my forgiving, I come to You, dear God. Judging with the personal mind shuts my mind to You, but Your Love is reflected in the world by my forgiving it, which reminds me that You have given me the way to find Your Peace again. I am redeemed when I choose to forgive. You have not left me without Comfort; I have within me both my Memory of You and Your Holy Spirit, Which leads me to my Memory of You. God, I want to hear Your Holy Spirit and find Your Peace today, because I love my own Identity, and I find It in my Memory of You.'*

Lesson 353

'The body's eyes, tongue, hands and feet have one purpose today: to serve my Christ Mind, and bless my perception with miracles.'

1. *'Dear God, I give all that I seem to have to my Christ Mind today, to use in any way that best serves the purpose that I share with It. Nothing is mine alone, because I have joined in purpose with Christ. My learning is almost at its end, but, for a while, I work with Christ to serve Its purpose. Then, I will blend into my Identity, and recognize that Christ* is *my Self.'*

Lesson 354

'With my Christ Mind, I stand in Peace and certainty of purpose. God is in Christ, as Christ is in me.'

1. *'My Christ Mind establishes me as One with You, dear God; beyond the reach of time, and under only Your Law. My only Self is the Christ in me; my only Purpose is Christ's Purpose. Christ is One with You, so I am One with You. My Christ Mind is Your Extension, God, as I am the extension of Christ in me.'*

Lesson 355

'There is no end to the Peace, Joy, and miracles that I will extend when I accept God's Word. I accept It today.'

1. *'I have no reason to wait, dear God, for the Joy that You promise to me. You will keep Your Word, Which You have given to me in my perception that I am in exile from You. I know that my Treasure waits for me, and I only have to be willing to find It. It is very close; I do not need to wait for another instant to be at Peace Forever. I choose You, God, and my Identity in You. I want to be my True Self, and know You as my Source and my Love.'*

Lesson 356

'Sickness is only another name for sin; healing is another name for God. The miracle is my answer from God.'

1. *'God, You have promised that You will never fail to answer my call. It does not matter where I perceive myself, what seems to be my problem, or what I believe I am. I am One with You, and You will answer me. A miracle reflects Your Love, so it answers me. Your Name replaces my every thought of sin, and in Innocence I cannot suffer pain. Your Name answers me, because when I call on Your Name, I call on my own.'*

Lesson 357

'Truth answers my every call to God. It responds first with miracles for me to perceive, then It returns me to full awareness of the Truth in me.'

1. *'My forgiving, which reflects Truth, shows me how to offer miracles, therefore, how to escape from the limitations in which I think that I live. God, first you point out Your Holy Extension in my perception, then I perceive It is in me. Your Holy Spirit instructs me to patiently hear Your Word, then to extend What I receive. As I look on your Holy Extension today, God, I hear Your Holy Spirit instructing me to find the way to You, as You appointed the way to be:*

"Perceive Innocence, and you will be healed"'

Lesson 358

'My every call to God is heard and answered. I can be sure of this: God's Answer is the only one that I want.'

1. *'Holy Spirit, You Who remember What I really am, remember What I really want. You speak for God, so You speak for Me. What you give to me comes from God. God, Your Holy Spirit is Your Voice and mine as well, and all that I want is What You offer to me, in just the form that You choose that It be mine. I acknowledge that I do not know You, and I will quiet the voice of the personal mind, so that I can remember. I will remember Your Love and Care, and I will keep Your Promises to me in my awareness always. I will remember that the personal self is nothing, but my True Self is All.'*

Lesson 359

'God's answer is some form of Peace. All of my pain is healed, and all of my misery is replaced with Joy. All limitations fall away, and I understand that what I thought was sin was only a mistake.'

1. *'Dear God, today I forgive the world and let Your Extension be. I have misunderstood everything, but I have not made my Holy Self into a sinner. You created me Innocent, and I am so Forever. I rejoice to learn that I have made mistakes that have no real effects. Sin is impossible, and this is the solid fact on which my forgiving rests. Help me to forgive, dear God, because I want to be redeemed. Help me to forgive, because I want to be at Peace.'*

Lesson 360

'Peace to me, the Christ. Peace to all that I perceive, which is One with me in Christ. I bless my entire mind with Peace through Christ.'

1. *'God, it is Your Peace that I want to extend, receiving It from You. I am One with You, forever just as You created me, because Your Love remains Forever Still and undisturbed within me. I want to reach It in silence and certainty, because only Here can I find certainty. Peace to me, and to all that I perceive. My mind was created in Holiness, and it remains in Holiness. My Whole Mind is like You, God, in Perfect Sinlessness. With this thought, I gladly say, 'amen'.'*

Final Lessons

Introduction

1. Your final lessons will be as free of words as possible. You will use them at the beginning of your practicing, and only to remind you that you are going beyond them. Turn to the Holy Spirit, Which leads the way and makes your efforts certain. Leave these lessons to the Holy Spirit, just as you give the Holy Spirit your life in the world from now on. You do not want to return to your belief in sin, which made you perceive an ugly, unsafe, attacking, destroying, dangerous, treacherous world as your reality, which was beyond your trust, or your hope for escape from pain.

2. The Holy Spirit is the only way for you to find the Peace that God has given to you. It is the Holy Spirit's way that you must travel in the end, because God has already ended your illusions. In your illusion that you are in time, the end of your illusions seem far off, but, in truth, their end is already here in the Holy Spirit, Which Graciously guides you in the way to the end of them. Follow in the way to end your illusions that Truth points out to you, and bring with you your entire mind.

3. Dedicate your mind to this purpose, and direct all of your thoughts to serve the function of your salvation. God has given you the goal of forgiving the world in your perception, and you want God's ending to your illusions, not the personal mind's ending, because you will perceive that all that you forgive is your own mind, and you will recognize that it is Part of God. And this is how your Memory of God will return to you, completely and Complete.

4. In your perception that you are in a world, it is your function to remember God, just as in Reality your Function is to be God's Completion. So, do not forget that you share your goal with your entire mind, because it is by extending your Memory of God to all that you perceive that you remember God, and you find the way to

God, and the Heaven of God's Peace. Do not forget that your forgiving all that you perceive offers you this. This is the way, the truth, and the life that shows you the way. In your Real Perception is your salvation, offered to you through your forgiving and your extending It in your awareness.

5. You will end this year with the gift that God promises to you. You are forgiven now, and you are saved from the 'wrath of God' that you found was an illusion. You are restored to Sanity, in Which you understand that anger and attack are insane, and vengeance is only a foolish fantasy. You are saved from wrath, because you have learned that you were mistaken, and nothing more. God is not angry with you because you didn't understand the Truth.

6. Go in honesty to God, and say that you did not understand, and ask God to help you to learn Its lessons through the Voice of God's Teacher, the Holy Spirit. God will not hurt you who are One with God. God will rush to answer you with, 'You are One with Me, and you are All that I have.' You can be certain that this is God's answer, because these are God's Own Words to you. You can never have more than this, because in these Words is All that there is, throughout time and Eternity.

Mentor's Notes

Paragraph 2 points out that God has already ended your illusions. The moment that the idea of not-God arose in God's Mind it was undone, because God is All-encompassing and cannot have an opposite. But, in that moment is *time*, the opposite of Eternity. Only in time it seems as though you separated from God in a far distant past, and that you will return to an awareness of God in an indefinite future. But in Eternity, that moment is over. In time, the symbol of God's undoing of not-God is your awareness of the Holy Spirit. Your awareness of the Holy Spirit is your awareness that you are not separate from God, and that time is an illusion.

Lessons 361-365

'Holy Spirit, I give You this Holy Instant; You are in charge of It. I want to follow You, because I am certain that Your direction will bring me Peace.'

1. If I need words to help me, the Holy Spirit will give them to me; if I need a thought, the Holy Spirit will give me that also; and if I need to be still, tranquil, and have an open mind, these are the gifts that I will receive of the Holy Spirit. The Holy Spirit is in charge of my request, and It will hear me and answer me, because the Holy Spirit speaks for God, and for the Christ in me.

Epilogue

1. This course is a beginning, not an ending. The Holy Spirit is with you; you are not alone. You cannot call on the Holy Spirit in vain. Whatever seems to trouble you, you can be sure that the Holy Spirit has the answer to undo it, and will gladly give it to you, if you simply turn to the Holy Spirit and ask for it. The Holy Spirit will not withhold any answers that you need for anything. It knows the way to solve all seeming problems, and to resolve all of your doubts. The Holy Spirit's Certainty is yours; you only need to ask for It from the Holy Spirit.

2. You can be as certain that you will make it Home as you are certain of the sun's path in your perception of a world. In fact, you can be more certain, because it is not possible to change the course of one whom God has called to God. Obey your Will, and follow the Holy Spirit, Which you have accepted as your Voice, to speak to you of What you really want and really need. The Holy Spirit is the Voice for God and for you, so It speaks to you of your freedom from illusions, and of Truth.

3. There are no more specific lessons assigned for you, because you no longer need them. From now on, hear only the Holy Spirit when you withdraw from the world to seek Reality. The Holy Spirit will direct your efforts, and will tell you exactly what to do, how to direct your mind, and when to go within to the Holy Spirit in silence to ask for Its sure direction and certain Word. The Holy Spirit's Word is God's Word; It is the Word that you have chosen to be your own.

4. The Christ in you places you in the Hands of Its Holy Spirit for you to follow It faithfully. The Holy Spirit will guide you through every difficulty that you perceive, and all of the pain that you think is real. The Holy Spirit will not give you pleasures that will pass away, because It gives you only the Eternal and the Good. Let the Holy Spirit prepare you further. It has spoken to you daily of God, your True Self, and of the Oneness of your entire mind, and It will

continue to do so. Now, you walk with the Holy Spirit, as certain as It is of Where you go and of how you should proceed, and as confident in your safe arrival at your Goal of God.

5. The End that you seek is certain, and the means to reach It as well. To this say 'Amen.' You will be told exactly what God wills for you every time that you have a choice to make. The Holy Spirit will speak for God and for your True Self, making sure that the hell that you made will not claim you, and that every step that you take will bring you closer to Heaven. And so you walk with the Holy Spirit from now on, and you will turn to It for guidance, Peace, and sure direction. Joy attends you on your way, because you go Home, Where there is a door which God has held open to welcome you.

6. Trust your way to the Holy Spirit, and say, 'Amen.' In Peace, you will continue on the Holy Spirit's way, and trust all things to the Holy Spirit. In confidence, you can wait for the Holy Spirit's answers, as you ask for Its Will in everything that you do. The Holy Spirit loves you as God's Extension, as you want to love yourself. The Holy Spirit will teach you how to perceive God's Extension through Its eyes, and love yourself as It does. You do not walk alone; God's Thoughts hover all around you. God's Love surrounds you, and of this you can be sure: God will never leave you without Comfort.

Mentor's Notes

For a year now, this Workbook has provided you with a structure for centering your mind in God throughout the day. Use these four habits that your practice using this Workbook has instilled in you to maintain your center in God as you go forward:

1. *Formally commune with God daily.* Set aside a minimum of a half-hour at least once every day to clear your mind and open it to God. The best time is when you feel most motivated to meditate, and you can be assured that you will not be interrupted. If you do nothing else, this habit alone will transform your experience. But,

you will find, this habit will lead to the other habits, because it will motivate you to stay centered in God throughout the day.

2. *Practice the Holy Instant throughout the day.* As soon as you can after you awaken, several times throughout the day, and just before you go to sleep, take a moment to go within and remember that you are One with God. Do not just *think* of God, but allow yourself to *experience* God's Presence within you. You can do this anytime, in any place, with your eyes open, or with them closed. This can take a few seconds, or a few minutes, if you have the time. You may find that a phrase, perhaps from this course, will help you to center yourself at these times.

3. *Extend God's Love to keep God's Love in your awareness.* Remember, what isn't Love is a call for Love, therefore every situation, no matter what it is, can remind you of God's Love. So every situation is an opportunity for you to extend God's Love in your awareness. If you are not centered and you find yourself in a situation that threatens your Peace of mind, whether you judge it as 'good' or 'bad', use the situation to remind yourself of the Truth: You are One with God.

4. *Share your life with the Holy Spirit.* The Holy Spirit is your Constant Companion in your perception that you are in a world that is separate from God. It is your Guide and Teacher as you awaken from this illusion. Talk to the Holy Spirit throughout the day; bring It all of your perceptions, questions, and problems, whether they are about the world or your spiritual awakening. Share everything with the Holy Spirit. The Holy Spirit will always answer you, and, in time, you will become certain of the Holy Spirit's Constant Presence, and you will know that you have nothing to fear, because you always have your Answer and Protection with you.

Volume 3 of the

Plain Language A Course in Miracles:

The Way of *A Course in Miracles*

A translation of the Manual for Teachers in plain language, with mentor's notes

Contents

Translator's Introduction

What is a 'teacher of God'?

As defined in the Manual for Teachers of *A Course in Miracles,* anyone who has a conscious experience of God, through direct Revelation or through a miracle, is a 'teacher of God'. You are always simultaneously teacher and student; what you teach you learn. So only by teaching from God within you can you learn that you are One with God.

You do not have to be a student of *A Course in Miracles* to fit the description of a teacher of God, but, as a student of the *Course,* you are potentially a teacher of God, because the *Course* aims at opening you to experiencing God directly.

The Way of A Course in Miracles is a translation of the Manual for Teachers of *A Course in Miracles* into plain, everyday language. It is the third and final book of the *Plain Language A Course in Miracles,* and it is a companion to *The Message of A Course in Miracles: A translation of the Text in plain language* and *Practicing A Course in Miracles: A translation of the Workbook in plain language.* But you do not need to read it last; in fact, its question-and-answer style is geared toward the new student.

Like the other books in *PLACIM, WACIM* is interpreted through the *Course's* central message and the translator's experiences of Oneness with God. Included in this book are Mentor's Notes from the translator.

WACIM is based on the first edition Manual for Teachers of *A Course in Miracles,* which is in the public domain.

Introduction

1. The roles of teaching and learning are separated in the personal mind's thinking. This separation is characteristic of the personal mind, because it teaches you that your mind is split between 'you' and 'the world', so you seem to teach others, not yourself. In the personal mind's world, the act of teaching is regarded as a special activity; one which you engage in for only a small portion of your time. This course teaches you, however, that you learn what you teach, so you are simultaneously the teacher and the student, and teaching yourself is a process in which you are engaged constantly. You are teaching yourself what you believe that you are every moment, even when you are sleeping.

2. When you teach, you are demonstrating to yourself what you believe is real and true. You have two thought systems in your mind – your Christ Mind, which is your Real Thought System, and the personal mind, which is the erroneous thought system that you made – and, all the time, you are demonstrating to yourself which you believe is true. From your demonstration, others may choose to learn, but you will definitely learn. The question is not whether or not you will teach, because you have no choice in this. The question is what do you want to teach? Your answer is based on what you want to learn, and the purpose of this course is to provide you with the means to make a choice. You cannot give to someone else, but only to yourself, and you learn this by consciously teaching, then observing what *you* learn. You demonstrate what you teach yourself by the beliefs to which you see witnesses to attest. Teaching can be a method for converting yourself to another belief system. You do not do this by words alone. Every situation is an opportunity for you to extend in your awareness what you believe that you are by perceiving what you believe reflected back to you. No more than this, but never less.

3. The lesson plan that you find yourself in, then, is determined

exclusively by what you think that you are, and what you believe the relationship of what you perceive is to you. In a formal teaching situation, you may feel that these questions are totally unrelated to what you think that you are teaching. But, for any situation, it is possible only for you to use the content of your mind on behalf of what you are really teaching yourself, and, therefore, what you are really learning. In this case, what you say as you seem to teach others is irrelevant. Your words may or may not coincide with what you are really teaching yourself. It is the thought system from which you are teaching that teaches you, and this teaching reinforces what you believe about yourself. The fundamental purpose of your teaching yourself is to diminish your self-doubt. This does not mean that the self that you are trying to protect is real, but it does mean that the self that you think is real is what you will teach yourself.

4. This is inevitable, and there is no escape from this for you. It cannot be otherwise. When you follow the lesson plan of the personal mind, which you *will* follow until you change your mind, you teach yourself to convince yourself that you are what you are not. This is the purpose of your perceiving yourself in a world. What else could the personal mind's lesson plan be? Into this hopeless and seemingly closed learning situation, which teaches you only despair and death, God sends you as a teacher of God. As you teach God's lessons of Joy and Hope, your learning Them will become complete.

5. Unless you become a teacher of God, you will have little hope of salvation from your illusion that you are separate from God, because the world of sin will seem forever real to you. When you are self-deceiving, you must deceive, because you must teach deception. What else is hell? This is a manual for you as a teacher of God. You are not yet Perfect, or you would not still perceive yourself in a world. But, it is your mission to become Perfect again in your awareness, so you must teach Perfection over and over, in many, many ways, until you have learned It. When you have put the body aside, your Real Thoughts will remain a Source of Strength and Truth Forever. Who are you that you are a teacher of God? How are

you chosen by God? What do you do as a teacher of God? How can you work out the salvation of your entire mind by working out your seemingly individual salvation? This manual attempts to answer these questions.

Mentor's Notes

This course uses the terms *teaching, giving,* and *extending* interchangeably. What you teach, you learn; what you give, you receive; what you extend in your perception, you keep in your awareness. You are simultaneously teacher and student; giver and receiver; the cause of your perception, and its effect.

Just as you teach only yourself, others will learn from you what they are teaching themselves. For example, you may be coming from the Holy Spirit, but if another is coming from the personal mind, they will perceive the personal mind in you, not the Holy Spirit. Likewise, you may be coming from the personal mind, but another will perceive the Holy Spirit in you if they choose to learn from the Holy Spirit. Everyone, at every moment, is teaching themselves. This is why it makes no sense to take what others say to you personally; they are teaching themselves what they believe that they are, and you will hear in them what you believe that you are. This reflects the Law of Mind that mind can only perceive itself. Awakening to God is wholly an inward journey.

Paragraph 3 points out that, in formal teaching situations, your words and your thought system may not coincide. For example, in many situations you will find yourself speaking to others about issues in the world; issues that you have come to learn are not real. But, in your mind, you will know that only God is Real. You will be centered in your Christ Mind, though the words that you say, because of their content, may seem to come from the personal mind. But because of the Content of your mind, not of your words, you will learn that you are Christ. The words will then be irrelevant. You teach yourself what you believe that you are, not from what you say or do, but from the thought system that you choose.

1. How am I a teacher of God?

1. You become a teacher of God when you choose to be one. Your only qualification is this: somehow, somewhere, you deliberately made the choice to see your True Self reflected back at you from someone or something in your mind where you perceive a world. Once you have done this, your road is established, and your direction is sure. God's Light will have entered the darkness of your mind. It may be only a single instance of Light, but that is enough. You will have entered into an agreement with God, even if you do not yet believe in God. You will have become your own Savior; you will have become a teacher of God.

2. It does not matter where you perceive yourself in the world; it does not matter if you are religious or not. You will have answered God's Call to remember God, Which is everywhere in your mind, so behind everything that you perceive, without exception. It goes on all the time, and It calls to you to teach God to redeem your entire mind. Though the Call is in your entire mind, it might seem to you that you perceive few in the world who answer It, but it is only a matter of time before you will perceive *your* answer everywhere. This could be a long way off, and this is why the 'plan of the teachers' was established. Your function is to save time. You begin by perceiving a single Light, but you cannot limit the Light at the center of God's Call to you. Each time that you perceive God's Light in the part of your mind where you perceive a world you save an immeasurable amount of time as you judge time in your perception that you are in a world. But, to the Call Itself, time has no meaning.

3. The world that you perceive contains many and varied courses for teachers of God, and their teaching aids vary as well. But the content of their lesson plans is always the same: 'You are Innocent, and in your Innocence lies your salvation.' This can be taught by actions or thoughts; with or without words; in any language, or in no language; in any place, time, or manner. It does not matter who you are before you answer the Call, because you become a Savior by answering the Call. You will have perceived your True Self in the

part of your mind that you thought was outside of you, therefore, you will have saved your entire mind. The part of your mind where you perceive a world will be reborn with you.

4. This is a manual for a specific lesson plan; a specific form of the universal content. There are many thousands of forms for this, but their outcome is all the same. And they all merely save time. Time winds on wearily, and your mind is very tired from it. The world that you perceive is old and worn and without hope. There has never been any question about your remembering God, because nothing can change God's Will. But time, with its illusions of change and death, wears you down. However, time has an ending, and this is what you, as a teacher of God, are appointed to bring about. Time is in your hands. This was your choice, and it was given to you.

Mentor's Notes

Paragraph 2 mentions that you will not see many who answer God's Call, but that your perception of others will change as you change *your* mind. Remember, Christ is not outside of you, so do not look for others to manifest Christ. You will see Christ as you extend Christ in your awareness from Christ within you.

Time is the great illusion on which all other illusions rest. Only in time does it seem as though you separated from God in a distant past, and that you will wholly remember God at an indefinite future time. In Eternity, none of this has happened at all. That is why this course emphasizes the Holy Instant, in Which you step out of time for a moment and remember Eternity. When you return to time after a Holy Instant, it no longer has the same hold over you. Letting God back into your conscious awareness is how you 'save time' as a teacher of God.

2. Who are my pupils?

1. Certain pupils will show up for you in the world that you perceive as soon as you have answered God's Call. They are at a level of understanding that is ideal for you to teach and learn the

universal lesson plan through your relationship with them. Your meeting them is certain; it is only a matter of time. Once you have chosen to fulfill your role as a teacher of God, they are ready to fulfill their role for you. You choose the time when you are ready to learn, but not who will show up. When you are ready to learn, the opportunities to teach will be provided for you.

2. In order for you to understand God's teaching-learning plan for your salvation, you must grasp the concept of time that this course sets forth. The Atonement corrects illusions, not Truth, so it corrects what has never happened. Also, the plan of correction was established by God and completed simultaneously, because God's Will is completely apart from time. So is all Reality, Which is of God. The instant that the idea of separation from God arose in your mind it was undone by God. In time, this seems to have happened long ago; in Reality, it has not happened at all.

3. The world of time is the world of illusion. What happened and was undone before time seems to be happening now. Its undoing, which is already complete, appears to be a choice that you have yet to make. The undoing that you learned and understood and have passed by seems to be a new thought, a fresh idea, a different approach. But, because you have Free Will, you can accept what has already happened at any time that you choose, and only then will you realize that the undoing is always here. As this course emphasizes, you are not free to choose the lesson plan, or even in which form you will learn it, but you are free to decide *when* you want to learn it. And, as you accept it, you will have already learned it.

4. Time, then, really goes backward to before time and memory. Time is really an instant of separation-correction that you relive again and again and again, and it seems to be now. So, it seems as though you find a part of your mind with which to reconnect in the present with a 'pupil'. Each pupil will arrive at the right place and time for you to learn a lesson in forgiveness. It is inevitable that your mind will re-connect as One, because you made the choice to undo your perception of separation from God in the instant before time

that you now seem to be reliving. In time, it only *seems* that God's Will takes time to work out, but nothing can delay the Power of Eternity.

5. When you, as a teacher of God, come together with anyone in your perception that you are in a world, a teaching-learning situation begins. If you choose to learn Truth, the personal mind will not be the teacher who does the teaching. The Holy Spirit will be the Teacher whenever you choose to use a relationship with another to learn Truth. Then, the relationship will be Holy because of its purpose, because God has promised to send the Holy Spirit into any relationship that you choose to be Holy. In a teaching-learning relationship that you give to Truth, you will learn that giving and receiving are the same. The demarcations that you drew between you and the part of your mind that you perceive as another to define yourself as a personal self will fade and grow dim and disappear. With those who seem to be learning the same lesson plan with you, you will share One Interest and One Goal, so you will each be teachers of God, because you will each have made the one decision that called your Teacher to you: You chose to see your True Self in another who seemed outside of you.

Mentor's Notes

Paragraph 1 is pointing out that, once you have chosen to become a teacher of God, you can recognize that those who show up in your life are there to present you with opportunities to forgive your illusion of separation from God, and to remember your Oneness with God.

God, being All, must contain even the *idea* of Its Own opposite. But, being All, God cannot have an opposite. So, the moment that the idea of not-God occurred in God's Mind it was undone. Only in time does it seem like part of God's Mind is split between God and not-God. This part of God's Mind that seems split within itself, and split off from God, is the one mind that is the source of the world and all personal minds. So, all seemingly individual and separate minds in the world are just different versions of the one split mind. Their great number and diversity are the illusions that seem to deny this. But, in fact, all personal minds are simply not-God, and their different forms do not change this. And the Christ Mind, Which is the other part of the split mind, is everywhere, and is the same everywhere, without exception. This is why you can choose to see Christ instead of not-God.

The 'you' that seems to have made the choice for separation from God is the split mind, not the personal mind. All personal selves, including the one with which you identify, are figures in the split mind's illusion of separation from God. You will first come to accept that you are the one split mind, then you will be able to undo your illusion of separation from God.

3. What are the levels of teaching?

1. As a teacher of God, you do not have a set teaching level. Every teaching-learning situation in which you find yourself involves a seemingly different relationship at the beginning, although the ultimate goal is always the same: to make the relationship Holy in your perception, so that you can look on the Innocence within yourself. You can learn from everyone, because you can teach yourself in every relationship. However, from a practical point of view, you cannot meet everyone in the world that you perceive, so the plan for you involves very specific relationships in which you will practice forgiveness. There are no accidents in your salvation. You will meet those with whom you have the potential for a Holy relationship when you are ready to meet them.

2. The simplest level of teaching may appear to you to be quite superficial. It consists of what might seem to you to be very casual encounters: a 'chance' meeting with a stranger on an elevator; a child running into you 'by accident'; your finding yourself walking in the same direction with someone you hardly know. These are not chance encounters; each has the potential to be a teaching-learning situation for you. Maybe you will smile at the stranger on the elevator;

perhaps you will not scold the child for running into you; maybe the acquaintance with which you walk along will become a friend. Even at the level of the most casual encounter, it is possible for you to choose to see your True Self instead of the personal mind's projections, if only for a moment. That moment is enough for salvation to come to your mind.

3. It may be difficult for you to understand that the concept that there are levels of teaching yourself the universal course is as meaningless in Reality as is time. Actually, the illusion of one permits the illusion of the other. In time, you seem to begin to change your mind about what is real with a single decision, then you learn more and more about your new direction as you teach it. You may even think that the illusion of levels of teaching is different from the illusion of time. Perhaps the best way to state that these levels cannot exist is that any teaching-learning situation in which you find yourself is a part of God's plan to correct your perception that you are separate from God, and they cannot have levels, because they reflect God's Will, Which is One. Your salvation is always right here. You may seem to teach at different levels, but the result is always the same.

4. Every teaching-learning situation in which you find yourself is maximal in the sense that everyone involved will learn the most that they can from the other at the time. Only in this sense can you think in terms of levels of teaching. Using the term in this way, the second level of teaching is a relationship that is more sustained before you and the other appear to separate. These relationships are also not accidental, nor is the end of the relationship an end of your learning. You will each have learned the most that you could at the time, but you will always have more opportunities to learn of your Holiness, which is the goal of all relationships for you. God is not mistaken in you.

5. The third level of teaching-learning, then, is lifelong relationships. In these situations, you and the other are presented with unlimited opportunities for learning. You will have few of these

relationships, because you and the other must have the perfect teaching-learning balance. You and the other may or may not recognize this, and you may even be hostile to each other for life. But, if you decide to learn it, the perfect lesson in forgiving is before each of you, and if you decide to learn it, you will become the Savior of your entire mind. As a teacher of God, you cannot fail to find the Help that you need.

Mentor's Notes

From the Holy Spirit's point of view, every relationship has one purpose only: Your forgiving your perception of separation from God. It does not matter how seemingly casual or intense the relationship appears; the goal is always the same, therefore, there are no levels of teaching-learning.

Remember, in your relationships with others you are always encountering what you believe about yourself, so you will either perceive a projection of a personal self, or you will choose to overlook the personal and perceive the Presence of Christ. Your relationships in the world are simply opportunities for you to heal your mind of its perception that it is split between 'you' and a world that seems outside of you, and that it is split off from God.

Relationships are not 'pre-ordained' in the sense that their form matters. Since all relationships have the same purpose, and the purpose is to forgive the form that is appearing, their form is irrelevant. Everyone who shows up in your life is there for you to forgive your perception of separation from God, and to remember your Oneness with God.

Of course, you are going to learn in any relationship only what you are ready to learn. Those who show up merely represent to you ideas that you are ready to release or that you are not ready to release, and the relationship will be Holy or perpetuate your sense of separation accordingly.

4. What are the characteristics of a teacher of God?

1. On the surface, as a teacher of God, you do not appear to be any different from any other personal self. You have a unique body and personal past, and your experiences and personality are distinct. And, in the beginning of your functioning as a teacher of God, you will not yet have acquired the deeper characteristics that will establish you as one. As a teacher of God, you have a special role in the plan of the Atonement, and you will develop special characteristics from God as you fulfill it. This specialness is only temporary, of course. In time, it is only a means to lead you out of time. These special characteristics, which develop in the awareness that you attain through the Holy relationship, toward which all of your teaching-learning is geared, will become your attributes as you advance in your learning. In this respect, all who seem to be teachers of God are alike.

2. Any differentiation that you perceive is only temporary, but, in time, it can be said that as an advanced teacher of God you will have the following characteristics:

a. Trust in the Holy Spirit

1. Trust in the Holy Spirit is the foundation on which will rest your ability to fulfill your function as a teacher of God. What you perceive is the result of what you learn. In fact, perceiving is learning, because cause and effect are never separate. As a teacher of God, you will have trust in what you perceive, because you will have learned that your perception is not governed by laws that the split mind made up. Your perception will be governed by a Power that is *in* you, but that is not *of* you, and it is this Power that keeps all things safe. And it is through this Power that, as a teacher of God, you will forgive the world that you perceive.

2. When you have once experienced this Power, it will be impossible for you to trust the personal self's 'strength' again. You will not attempt to fly with the tiny wings of a sparrow when the mighty power of an eagle has been given to you. You will not place your

faith in the shabby offerings of the personal mind when God's Gifts are laid before you. This is what will induce you to make the shift:

1. Your development of trust in the Holy Spirit

1. First, you will go through a 'period of undoing', which dislodges you from your current value system. This does not need to be painful, but you may experience it as such. It may seem to you that some things are being taken away, but what is really happening is that you are recognizing their lack of value. You can only perceive the lack of value of what you once valued when you perceive it in another Light. At this stage, you will not yet be at a point where you will make this shift entirely internally, so there may be what seem like external changes that take place. These are always helpful, and when you have learned this much, you will go on to the second stage.

2. Next, you must go through a 'period of sorting out'. You may find this somewhat difficult, because, having learned that changes can be helpful to your spiritual awareness, you must now decide all things on the basis of whether or not they help or hinder your spiritual awareness. You may find that many, if not most, of the things that you valued before will only hinder your ability to transfer forgiveness to new situations as they arise. Because you valued what was really without value, you may not generalize forgiving because of fear that you will experience loss and sacrifice. It will take great learning for you to understand that all things, situations, and encounters with others can be helpful, if you perceive them correctly. It is only the extent to which they are helpful that you should accord them any degree of 'reality'. In fact, the word 'value' can apply only to this.

3. The third stage that you must go through as a teacher of God can be called the 'period of relinquishment'. If you interpret this as giving up what you think is truly valuable, you will experience enormous conflict. In any case, you will probably not entirely escape from a distressing sense of sacrifice. However, there is no point in

your sorting out the Valuable from the valueless unless you take the next obvious step of letting go of the valueless. Therefore, you are likely to interpret the period where the last stage and this one overlap as one where you are being called upon to give up your own best interests on behalf of Truth. You will not yet have realized how wholly impossible this demand would be if it could be made, and you will learn this only as you actually give up what lacks value. By doing this, you will learn that, where you anticipated grief, you find a happy lightheartedness instead; where you thought that you were being asked to sacrifice, you find a gift bestowed on you.

4. Now comes a 'period of settling down'. This is a quiet time in which you will rest a while in relative peace, and you will consolidate your learning. Now, you will begin to see the transfer value of all that you have learned so far, and its potential may stagger you. You will begin to see your whole way out of illusions: 'Give up what you do not value, and keep What you do value.' The obvious is so simple and easy to do! You will need this period of respite, though you will not yet have come as far as you think. But, when you are ready to go on, you will go on with an awareness that God is with you. For now, you will rest awhile, and you will solidify this awareness. You will not go on from here feeling alone.

5. The next stage is indeed a 'period of unsettling'. Now, you must understand that you did not really know what was Valuable and what was valueless. All that you really will have learned so far is that you want the Valuable, and that you don't want the valueless. The personal mind's sorting out did not teach you the difference. Your belief in sacrifice, which is so central to the personal mind's thought system, had made it impossible for you to judge. You thought that you learned to be willing to follow only the Holy Spirit; now you see that you did not understand that your willingness meant completely releasing your identification with a personal self. Now, to attain Complete Peace, you must learn to lay aside the personal mind and forgive in every circumstance. This may take you a long, long time, but each step that you take in this direction will be

heavily reinforced by your awareness of the Holy Spirit, or it would be very hard for you indeed!

6. Finally, you will experience a 'period of achievement'. It is here that you will consolidate all of your learning. Now, your insights into Truth, which were vague before, will become solid, and you will be able to count on them in 'crisis', as well as in your more tranquil times. In fact, your Tranquility will be their result; the outcome of your honest learning, consistency of thought, and full transfer of forgiveness to everything. This is the stage of Real Peace, because it reflects Heaven, and your way to Heaven will be open and easy. In fact, it will be here. Your Peace of mind will already be complete, so that you will have no where to go, and nothing to seek.

Mentor's Notes

The 'special' characteristics from God that you attain as a teacher of God are potential in you until you choose to experience Oneness. They are 'special' only in the sense that you will not manifest them until you experience Oneness.

The stages that you will go through as you develop trust in the Holy Spirit will be hard for you to recognize when you are in them. In time, as you reach the later stages, you will probably be able to look back and recognize them in retrospect. Part of your confusion will be that, to some degree, the whole process is one of 'undoing', 'sorting out', 'relinquishing', and feeling 'unsettled'. You will also seem to have many quiet episodes where you rest and assimilate all that you have learned so far. Also, each stage seems to be a micro version of the whole process. For example, as you enter the 'period of unsettling' you find yourself undoing, then sorting out, then relinquishing, etc.

It does not really matter which stage you are in. You do not have to know, because it is actually the Holy Spirit that will take you through the process. Your whole part is setting it in motion by inviting the Holy Spirit into your awareness, then maintaining your center in the Holy Spirit. The Holy Spirit does the rest. The personal mind may try to interfere and make you go through the process faster, or try to convince you that you are further along than you are, or tell you that you 'should' be further along, but these are only distractions. After all, in practice, if you could be further along than you are, you would be. You can learn only what is right in front of you to learn.

The external changes mentioned in the 'period of undoing' are changes that align your life in the world with your new goal of God. These can be minor or major, depending on how authentic and simple your life is when you make the shift in goal. The more 'lies' that you have been living, the more you will find being undone. For example, if you are a homosexual who has been repressing their sexuality, then you will find that you must come out to continue on this path. If you have been in a job that you detest, you will find yourself quitting or being fired. If you have been living beyond your means, you will find yourself filing for bankruptcy, foreclosure, etc. If you have been in a marriage that does not reflect your true values (for example, married the first person who asked because you were afraid of being alone; married to please others, etc.), you may find yourself getting a divorce. The reason for this is that these lies are obstacles to you turning inward to God. What motivated you as a personal self to live an inauthentic life is a belief that you are not worthy of a life that is true to your nature. This sense of unworthiness makes you fear looking inward, therefore, you will not be able to continue on an inward path to God if you do not first correct these errors.

Also, an authentic life takes less effort, less attention, and is simpler. It requires a lot of effort and energy to maintain a lie, and all of this distracts you from God.

This may seem to contradict the idea that your personal life in a world is an illusion, but remember that God meets you where you are at the moment. At first, the personal self and its life will still be very real to you, and your thoughts and beliefs about them will be obstacles to God if they are based in unworthiness and fear. So, your first steps are going to be to bring your personal life into alignment with an awareness of God's Love for you, and this will manifest as positive changes in your life in the world. As it says above, at this stage, you are not yet at a point where the only changes necessary are internal.

What you are 'sorting out' in the 'period of sorting out' are the two thought systems in your mind: Your Christ Mind, Which is your Real thought system, and the personal mind, which is the erroneous thought system that you made. You are sorting out Truth and illusion, so that you will be able to make a choice between them. Until you do so, they will be confused in your mind: Truth will seem like illusion, and illusion will seem like Truth, and the choice between them will not be clear to you.

This stage takes years, in which you will vacillate daily between the personal mind and the Holy Spirit. First, you will learn how to discern the Holy Spirit from the cacophony of voices and myriad experiences of the personal mind. But, even as the Holy Spirit becomes clearer to you, you will not yet wholly trust the Holy Spirit. Learning to trust the Holy Spirit is what this process is for, and you will have only just begun. You have already made the choice for the Holy Spirit or you wouldn't even be in this process, yet, at this stage, the disruption to your life and thought system that is the result of your choice will make you want to undo your choice. But you will not be able to, because you will have let God into your conscious awareness, and you will no longer be able to wholly deny God.

Your desire to undo your choice will result in a high degree of conflict during this stage. Your fear of God will be enormous, because you will not yet have done any comprehensive work undoing your belief that you are guilty for separating from God. So, you may feel that you have chosen loss and sacrifice and your doom by choosing God. You may find yourself angry at the choice that you have made; you might blame God or yourself or both. But you will not be ready to look at your guilt and fear, so you will try hard, both consciously and unconsciously, to convince yourself that illusions are true and that Truth is the illusion. You may try to keep your distance from God by closing yourself off from experiencing miracles by keeping your spiritual study only at the intellectual level.

Often, you will feel that nothing is happening, that you are not making any progress toward God, and that you are lost, but, actually, the Holy Spirit will be with you and guiding you, though you will not always perceive this just yet.

The 'period of relinquishment' is also in a way a 'period of undoing', but it is much more internal than the first period of undoing. At this stage, you will have sorted out Truth from illusion enough to be more aware of how valuable Truth is to you, though you may not yet wholly feel that illusions have no value. But your willingness to follow the Holy Spirit will outweigh your attachment to illusions, and you will find that, in practice, giving up beliefs that have no value is no sacrifice at all. You are likely to experience some external changes as you make this shift, but, unlike in the 'period of undoing', you will have much greater trust in the Holy Spirit, so much less fear and sense of sacrifice. In fact, what you are 'relinquishing' in this stage is your desire for the personal mind to be in charge. After the initial phase of this stage, where you will learn that giving up nothing is not loss, the whole process of learning to trust the Holy Spirit will get easier and easier for you.

It says above that in the 'period of settling' you will not yet have come as far as you think. This is because it is a period of True Peace, but not of Complete Peace. In fact, you will come to realize that, so far, all that you have done is *prepare* for the real undoing of your identification with a personal self. But, you cannot undo your misidentification without an identity with which to replace it. This is why you are learning to trust the Holy Spirit, Which is your True Self. Only when you have a solid awareness of the Holy Spirit within you will you be able to look at the guilt and fear of the personal mind, not believe in them, and let the personal self go. Without an awareness of the Holy Spirit within you, you would think that guilt and fear are justified.

The Peace of this stage will never leave you, but it is only the beginning of Real Peace for you, and you will still have some real work to do to totally relinquish the personal self and know only God. The stage where you do this is the 'period of unsettling'. This is the stage where your journey becomes wholly inward. It is where you will complete sorting out the thought systems in your mind, and you will accept that you cannot reconcile them. The personal mind cannot be 'fixed' or 'spiritualized'; you must release it to be totally at Peace. You won't do this by fighting it, which only makes it real to you, but by recognizing that it has no value. You won't have to make this happen; merely by observing how it works next to how your Christ Mind works, you will see that it has no value, and you will automatically let it go. You will be bringing illusion to Truth, and watching illusion be undone.

This stage is 'unsettling' because you will be looking into the center of the personal mind, which is disturbing. But you will have been prepared to do so, and it will not harm you. Also during this stage, you will confront your attachment to the personal self, and you will fully accept that your perceiving separation from God is your choice, not something that is done to you.

The 'period of achievement' is your ultimate goal in your perception that you are in a world. It is the stage where you attain your Real Perception as you perceive through your Christ Mind. When this stage is complete, you will have nothing more to learn, the world and perception will fall away from your mind, and your mind will extend only God again.

How long does this whole process of learning to trust and identify with the Holy Spirit take? It is not so much a question of time, but of willingness, and, of course, the more you trust, the more willing you will be. However, in very general terms, it can be said that it takes a minimum of 20 years to reach the 'period of unsettling', where you will do the real work of letting go of the personal self. (This does not mean that you have to be a student of this course for 20 years before you attain this stage. The process of undoing your identification with a personal self is the same, no matter on which path you seem to be. For example, you may have invited the Holy Spirit into your awareness, and gone through one or two of the initial stages, before you became a student of this course). If you find that this seems long, do not be discouraged. You are doing your part by being present to the Holy Spirit right where you are now, and there is real Peace for you to experience right now in the Holy Instant. You cannot force this process, but your trust and willingness will speed it along. Lean into the process, and allow the Holy Spirit to carry you.

b. Honesty

1. All of the traits of a teacher of God rest on trust in the Holy Spirit. Once you have achieved this trust, the other traits will automatically follow. Only in trusting the Holy Spirit can you be honest, because then you will see the value of honesty. The term 'honesty' here does not apply only to what you say; it actually means 'consistency'. Nothing that you say or do will contradict what you think; no thought or word will oppose another. This is being truly honest: At no level are you in conflict with yourself, so it is impossible for you to be in conflict with anyone or anything in your mind where you perceive a world.

2. The Peace of mind that you will experience as an advanced teacher of God will be due largely to your perfect honesty. It is only the wish to deceive yourself that makes you conflicted, and self-deception is dishonesty. As a teacher of God, you will never feel challenged, because feeling challenged means that you doubt, and the trust in the Holy Spirit on which you will rest as a teacher of God will make doubt impossible for you. Therefore, you will be at Peace, because in all things you will be honest, and you will never be doing what is only for you as an isolated personal self. You will make the choice for Peace for your entire mind: for all that you perceive; for the changing, and the Unchanging beyond appearances; for the

Christ in you, and for God. How could you not succeed? You will choose Peace in perfect honesty; sure of your choice, and of yourself.

c. Tolerance

1. As a teacher of God, you will not make judgments with a personal mind. To judge with a personal mind is to be dishonest, because to do so is to assume a position that you do not have, and to deceive yourself. It means that you are deceived in what you are. Judging with a personal mind means that you lack trust in the Holy Spirit, and trust in the Holy Spirit is the bedrock of your whole thought system as a teacher of God. If you lose this, all of your real learning goes with it. Without the personal mind's judgment, you will not choose between illusions; you will perceive your entire mind as One, and you will not perceive differences to judge. The personal mind's judgment destroys your hope, and shatters your trust in the Holy Spirit. You cannot use the personal mind's judgment and hope to learn of the Holy Spirit.

Mentor's Notes

The personal mind judges to define the personal self apart from the rest of the world, and to make the world real to you. If you saw that the world is not real, you would have no reason to judge it. In fact, judging is the whole way that the personal mind thinks. It is constantly evaluating: good/bad, right/wrong, valuable/valueless, etc.

As a teacher of God who identifies with the Holy Spirit, you will accept the world as it is because you won't have a need to make one illusion more meaningful than another. You will recognize that the personal self is not you, so you will have no need to define it or to defend it, and you will recognize that the world is not real, so you will have no need to judge it.

d. Gentleness

1. As a teacher of God, it will be impossible for you to harm or

be harmed, because harm is the outcome of the judgment of the personal mind. It is the dishonest act that follows from a dishonest thought. It is a verdict of guilt on another, and therefore, first on yourself. It is the end of your Peace, and the denial of what you have learned through the Holy Spirit. It demonstrates that God's lesson plan is absent from your thoughts, and that you have replaced it with insanity. As a teacher of God, you must learn, fairly early in your training, that harmfulness completely wipes out your function from your awareness. It will make you confused, fearful, angry, and suspicious of God and others. It will make it impossible for you to learn from the Holy Spirit. You can only hear the Holy Spirit when you realize that harm achieves nothing, and that you cannot gain anything from it.

2. Therefore, as a teacher of God, you will be wholly gentle. You will need the Strength of True Gentleness, because in This the function of salvation will become easy for you. Your salvation is impossible when you want to do harm, but when harm has no meaning for you, your salvation is only natural. This is the only choice that is meaningful when you are sane. You will not choose hell when you clearly perceive the way to Heaven. You will not choose the weakness that comes from harm in place of the Unfailing, All-encompassing, Limitless Strength of True Gentleness. Your Strength as a teacher of God will lie in your Gentleness, because you will understand that evil thoughts do not come from the Christ in you, or from your Source, so you will join your thoughts with God. Your will, which has always been God's Will, will be free to be itself.

Mentor's Notes

Remember, it does not matter if you perceive harm in your mind or as coming from another; if you perceive it, it is in your mind, and if it is real to you, it will disturb your Peace. And, if you believe that harm is real, then you believe that you have truly separated from God, so you will first have harmed yourself with this belief before you perceived harm. So, the personal mind's thought system, being erroneous, is harm, and the thought system of your Christ Mind is Gentleness.

As a teacher of God, you will recognize that all that you perceive, whether within yourself or what seems outside of you, is a part of you, so you will have no motive to do harm.

e. Joy

1. The experience of Joy is the inevitable result of you being aware of the Gentleness within you. When you are aware of your Gentleness, it will be impossible for you to fear, because you will be incapable of perceiving anything that could interfere with your Joy. The open hands of Gentleness are always filled with Joy. In your Gentleness, you will have no pain, and you will not suffer, so of course you will be Joyous. You will be sure that you are loved and safe. Joy attends Gentleness as surely as grief attends attack. As God's teacher, you will trust in God, and you will be sure that the Holy Spirit will go before you to make sure that no harm can come to you. You will hold God's Gifts and follow in God's way, because the Holy Spirit will direct you in all things. Joy will be the gift that you extend in gratitude, as the Christ in you will extend gratitude to you. God's need of you is just at great as your need of God. How Joyous for you to share the purpose of salvation with the Christ in you!

f. Defenselessness

1. As God's teacher, you will learn how to be simple. You will have no illusions that you need to defend against the Truth. You will not try to make yourself; your Joy will come from your understanding that God created you, and that What God created cannot need defense. You will not become an advanced teacher of God until you fully understand that defenses are foolish guardians of your illusions. The more distorted your illusions, the fiercer and more powerful your defenses of them seem to be. But, when you finally decide to look past them, you will find that nothing is there. Slowly,

at first, you will let yourself be undeceived, but you will learn faster as your trust increases. Danger is not what comes to you when you lay down your defenses; what comes to you then is Safety, Peace, and Joy. What comes to you is God.

g. Generosity

1. The term 'generosity' has special meaning for you as a teacher of God. It does not mean here what the personal mind thinks that it means. In fact, you must learn its True meaning, and very carefully. Like all of the other attributes of a teacher of God, this one ultimately rests on your trust in the Holy Spirit, because without this trust you cannot be generous in the True sense of the word. To the personal mind, 'generosity' means 'to give away' in the sense that you lose what you give; as a teacher of God, the word means 'to give away' in order to keep. This concept has been emphasized throughout the Text and Workbook of this course, but it is perhaps more alien to the personal mind's thought system than many of the other ideas in this lesson plan. Its strangeness lies in how obviously it reverses the personal mind's thinking. In the clearest way possible, and at the simplest level, 'generosity' will mean the exact opposite to you as a teacher of God than it does to you as a personal self.

2. As a teacher of God, you will be generous out of the interests of your True Self. As a teacher of God, you won't want anything that you could not give away, because you will realize that it would be valueless to you by definition. What would you want it for? You could only lose, therefore you will not seek for what you could only keep, because then that would guarantee loss for you, and you will no longer want to suffer. But you will want to keep for yourself all Things that are of God, therefore, that are for you. These are the Things that belong to you. These are the Things that you can give away with True Generosity, and you will then protect Them in your awareness Forever.

Mentor's Notes

The 'things' that you can only keep are material forms and limited ideas. If you give these away, you lose them. For example, if you give a car away, you no longer have that car. If you have an idea that is limited to form – say, an invention – if you give it away, you 'lose' it. Another example of a limited idea is a fantasy, or ambition, for yourself in the future, which you cannot give away at all, because it is only for you as a personal self. You lose by being attached to these things, because your desire for them is based on your erroneous identification with a personal self.

The 'Things that are of God' are Thoughts and Ideas of God that you can extend in your awareness: Love, Peace, Joy, Wholeness. By extending these Ideas to the part of your mind where you perceive a world, you increase Them in your awareness.

h. Patience

1. When you are certain of the outcome, you have no problem waiting, and without anxiety. Patience will be natural to you as a teacher of God, because all that you will perceive is a Certain Outcome, at a time that you may not know, but that you will not doubt. You will know that the time will be as right as the Answer, and that this is true for everything now and in the future. You will see that the past as well had no mistakes, only what served your entire mind well. Maybe you didn't understand this at the time of certain occurrences, but, as a teacher of God, you will be willing to reconsider your past interpretations if they are a source of pain anywhere in your mind. Patience is natural to you when you trust the Holy Spirit. When you are sure of the ultimate interpretation of all things in time, no outcome that you think already happened, or that seems yet to come, will cause you fear.

i. Faithfulness

1. The extent of your faith in the Holy Spirit is the measure of your advancement in this lesson plan. Do you still select some

aspects of your life in the world for your learning of God while you keep others apart? If yes, then you have limited your advance, and your trust in the Holy Spirit is not yet firmly established. Your faith in the Holy Spirit is your trust in the Holy Spirit to set all things right; not some, but all. Generally, your faith will begin by resting on just some 'problems', which you will carefully limit for a time, because for you to give up all problems to one Answer is for you to entirely reverse the thinking of the personal mind. This alone deserves to be called 'faithfulness'. But each degree of faith, no matter how small, is worth your achieving. As it is noted in the Text, *readiness* is not *mastery*.

2. True faithfulness does not deviate. Being consistent, it is wholly honest; being unswerving, it is full of trust; being based in fearlessness, it is gentle; being certain of God, it is Joyous; and being confident that only God is Real, it is tolerant. Faithfulness, then, combines in itself the other attributes of a teacher of God. It implies your acceptance of the Holy Spirit and of God's Definition of you as God's Extension. In the Truest sense of the word, it is only to God that you look in faithfulness, seeking until you find God, and, having found God, resting in Quiet Certainty on God, to Which alone all of your faithfulness is due.

j. Open-mindedness

1. You will understand the centrality of open-mindedness, perhaps the last of the attributes that you will acquire as a teacher of God, when you recognize its relationship to your total forgiveness of all of your illusions. Open-mindedness will come to you when you lay aside the judgment of the personal mind. As the personal mind's judgment shuts your mind to the Holy Spirit, so your open-mindedness invites the Holy Spirit into your awareness. As condemnation makes you judge 'evil' as real, so your open-mindedness permits the Holy Spirit to judge all that you perceive on God's behalf. As your judgment of guilt sends you to hell, so your open-mindedness extends Christ in your awareness. Only with an open

mind can you be at Peace, because only then will you see a reason for Peace.

2. How will you forgive with an open-mind? You will let go of all of the beliefs that prevented you from forgiving. You will abandon your perception of a world for Truth, and you will let your perception be restored for you in newness and Joy so Glorious that you could never conceive of such a change in your identification with a personal mind. You will perceive nothing as you did formerly. What seemed dull and lifeless before will sparkle with God's Love, and, above all, you will perceive all things as welcoming rather than as a threat. No denial will remain in your mind to hide Christ from your awareness. You will have achieved the final goal of this lesson plan: total forgiveness, which paves the way for What is far beyond what you can learn. This lesson plan makes no effort to exceed its legitimate goal. Your totally forgiving all illusions is its only aim, at which all of your learning ultimately converges. This is enough.

3. You may notice that this list of characteristics for you as a teacher of God does not include things that belong to you in your Oneness with God. Terms like *Love, Innocence, Perfection, Knowledge,* and *Eternal Truth* would be inappropriate in this context. What God gives to you is so far beyond this lesson plan that the concept of *learning* disappears in Its Presence. But, while Its Presence is obscure to you, your focus properly belongs on *learning* this lesson plan. It is your function as a teacher of God to extend what you learn to the part of your mind where you perceive a world. Properly speaking, it is *unlearning* that you extend, because that is true learning in your perception that you are in a world. The Holy Spirit gives to you, as a teacher of God, Glad Tidings of complete forgiveness to extend in your perception. You are blessed indeed, because you bring salvation to your entire mind!

Mentor's Notes

What is meant here by an 'open-mind', then, is that your mind is free of all illusions, so it is wholly open for God to return fully to your awareness.

5. How is healing accomplished?

1. For healing to occur, you must understand what you use the illusion of sickness for. Otherwise, healing will be impossible for you.

a. The purpose that you perceive for sickness

1. Healing is accomplished the moment that you no longer see any value in pain. You choose suffering because you believe that it gives you something of value. You think it is a small price to pay for something of greater worth. Sickness is a decision that you make; it is your choice for weakness, in your mistaken conviction that weakness is strength. When this occurs, you see True Strength as a threat and health as a danger. Sickness is the method that your split mind conceived in insanity to replace God with a personal self. So, in your identification with a personal self, you see God as outside of you, fierce and Powerful, eager to keep all power to Itself, and you believe that you can conquer God only through your death.

2. In this insane belief, you think that healing stands for your defeat and God's triumph over you. Healing represents God's total opposition to the personal self in a direct form that you are forced to recognize. It stands for All that you want to hide from yourself to protect your personal 'life'. Because, if you are healed, then you are responsible for your thoughts, and you believe that God will kill you to prove to you how weak and pitiful you are. You feel that if you choose death yourself, then your weakness becomes your strength. Through death, you give yourself what you think that God wants to give to you, so you think that you have entirely taken God's Power for your own.

Mentor's Notes

You can read the 'sickness' and 'healing' in this section as referring to the error of your identification with a personal self and its correction, as well as to physical illness and healing. There is no difference. Physical sickness is a manifestation of your misidentification with a personal self, and a healed body is a result of healing your mind of this misidentification.

What paragraph 2 means is that, in your identification with a personal self, you believe that God wants to kill you, so you mean to kill yourself first to take God's Power away from God. Remember from the Text that all forms of illness represent death, because they emphasize the body, and remind you that, in your identification with a body, you will die. The belief that God wants to kill you is inherent in the personal mind, which is the opposite of God in every way. The personal mind cannot be changed, but you can, and must, let it go altogether to be released from all of the effects of believing that it is you. As long as you identify with a personal self in any way, you will experience the effects of this belief, like guilt, fear, sickness, and death.

b. Your shift in perception

1. Healing occurs in direct proportion to your recognition that sickness is without value. Faced with sickness, you only need to say, 'There is no gain to me in this' and you will be healed. But, to mean these words, you must first recognize certain facts. First, obviously, decisions are made in your mind, not in a body. Sickness is a faulty solution to your perceived problem of being powerless in the face of God's Power. It is a decision, so it is your mind, not a body, which makes it. Your resistance to recognizing this is enormous, because the existence of the world that you perceive outside of you depends on you believing that the body is the decision-maker. Terms like 'instincts' and 'reflexes' represent your attempts to endow the body with non-mental motivators, but they actually describe your problem of misidentifying with a body; they do not correct your problem.

2. The basis for healing, then, is your accepting that sickness is a decision of your mind, which then uses a body for its purposes. This

is true for healing in all forms. Decide that this is so, and you will heal. If you decide against recovery, you will not heal. So the 'physician' is always your mind, and the outcome is what you decide that it will be. You may see others as attending to the body, but they are only giving form to your choice. You choose to perceive them to give tangible form to your desire, and this is all that they do. You don't actually need them, because you could rise up without their aid and say, 'I have no use for this'. Any form of sickness will be cured at once if you mean these words.

3. The only thing that you need for this shift in perception to occur is to simply recognize that sickness is of the mind, and that it has nothing to do with a body. But this recognition will 'cost' you the whole world that you perceive, because it will never again appear to you to rule your mind. With this recognition, responsibility is placed, not on the world, but with you, who mistakenly perceive the world as real. You perceive what you choose to perceive; nothing more, and nothing less. The world that you perceive does nothing to you; you only thought that it did. And you have done nothing to the world, because you were only mistaken about what it is. This is your release from guilt and sickness, because they are the same. But, for you to accept this release, you must accept the insignificance of the body.

4. With this awareness, pain will be gone from you forever. But, also with this idea, all of your confusion about your source will go. This necessarily follows, because if you place cause and effect in their true sequence in one respect, your learning will generalize and transform your perception. The transfer value of one true idea has no end or limit. The final outcome of this lesson is your remembering God. Guilt, sickness, pain, disaster, and suffering will then no longer have meaning for you. Without a purpose, they will be gone from your mind, and so will all of their seeming effects. Cause and effect always reflect creation, and if you see them in their proper order, without distortion and fear, they re-establish Heaven in your awareness.

Mentor's Notes

Guilt and fear is the first place that the personal mind goes to when you read that sickness is a decision of your mind. Guilt, of course, is not correction; it further perpetuates your fear of God. Guilt and sickness go hand-in-hand. The appropriate response is for you to go to the other thought system in your mind, Which is represented by the Holy Spirit. You do not have to ask the Holy Spirit for healing, because healing is always here, and it is your choice, but you can ask the Holy Spirit to help you to recognize and undo your fear of healing.

Paragraph 2 makes it clear that, even when it looks as though others may be responsible for your healing because of their treatment of the body, it is really always only your decision to heal that results in healing. Until you let go of the personal mind completely, sickness may seem to come and go in various forms.

What paragraph 4 is referring to is that your denial that you are the source of sickness that you experience is the same as your denial that God is your Source. In your perception that you are separate from God, you must do a double dissociation: God, with Which you are One, seems to be a separate Being, and the personal mind, which you made, seems to have power over you. This split is necessary, because to be not-God you have to seem to be some*thing* other than God (personal self), and some*where* (world) other than God. But you wouldn't be convinced of this if you knew that you made it, so you have to seem to be made by what you made, and powerless over it. So when you accept that you are the cause of what you perceive and experience, then you will heal your mind back to a state where you can accept that God is your Source.

c. Your function in healing others as a teacher of God

1. As a teacher of God in your perception that you are in a world, what can you do for what seems like another, who, like you, must change their mind in order to be healed? You certainly cannot change their mind for them. You only need to rejoice with those who

choose to change their minds, because then they are a teacher of God with you. But, you have a specific function when you perceive those who have chosen sickness, but who seem to think that sickness has chosen them. They are not open-minded, and they believe that the body tells them what to do, and they obey it. They do not know that this concept is insane; if they suspected so, they would be open to healing. But they don't suspect anything; to them it seems that separation from God is real.

2. In the midst of your perception of others who choose sickness, your function is to represent another choice. Your simple presence is a reminder. In your thoughts, you question what seems to be appearing. As God's messenger and teacher, you are a symbol of salvation. In Christ's Name, you forgive the thoughts of sickness that you perceive in another. With God's Word in your mind, you stand for the Alternative to sickness. You come in benediction, not to heal the sick, but to remember the Remedy that is already here. You do not heal with your hands, or with your voice; you merely extend What you have. Very gently, you turn away from the appearance of death, and you behold Christ; you do not choose to perceive sickness in place of Life.

3. You never have to consider the form of sickness that appears to you. If you do, you are forgetting that all forms have the same purpose, so they are not different. Perceive the Holy Spirit in place of the deceiving appearance of suffering, and remind yourself that you did not make yourself, and that your entire mind must remain as God created it. Recognize that illusions do not have real effects. Extend in your perception the Truth within you, so that you do not reinforce illusions in your mind. This is how you bring your illusions to Truth, instead of trying to bring Truth into your illusions. So sickness is dispelled in your perception, not by your will over another, but by the One Will that *is*. This is your function as a teacher of God: to not see any will that is separate from yours, nor your will as separate from God's Will.

Mentor's Notes

If you perceive it, it is in your mind, so it does not matter if you perceive sickness as real in yourself or in others; the perception is in your mind. So your purpose is not to heal what you perceive as 'others', but to heal your own mind of the perception that separation from God, therefore sickness, is real.

6. Is healing certain?

1. Healing is always certain. You cannot bring illusions to Truth and expect to keep the illusions, because Truth demonstrates to you that illusions are illusions and have no value. When you bring illusions to Truth, you see the Correction of your belief that sickness is real, in yourself or in what seems like another in your mind where you perceive a world, and you recognize It for What It is. Having accepted the Atonement for yourself, you accept It for your entire mind. But what if someone in the world uses sickness as a way of 'life', and believes that healing is the way to death? If this is so, a sudden healing might result in intense depression for them, and a sense of loss so deep that they may choose to destroy themselves. They may feel that they have nothing to hope for, and ask for death. In this case, for their protection, healing must wait.

2. Healing always stands aside when it is perceived as a threat, but the instant that it is welcome, it is here. Where healing is extended, it is received; time has no meaning before the Gifts of God. The Text refers to the 'Storehouse of Treasures' that God lays by for your entire mind. Not one Treasure is lost; your Storehouse only increases. As a teacher of God, you do not need to be disappointed if you extend healing and it does not appear as though another has received it. It is not up to you to decide when your gifts will be accepted in the world. Be certain that you have received healing, and trust that it will be accepted in the world when it is recognized there as a blessing, and not thought of as a curse.

3. It is not your function as a teacher of God to evaluate the outcome of your gifts; it is only your function to give them. Once you

have done so, you have also extended the outcome, because that is part of the gift. You are not really giving if you are concerned with the seeming results of your giving. Then, you are limiting giving, so you have not really given a gift. Trust is an essential part of your giving; in fact, it is the part of extension that makes it possible. It is the part that guarantees that as the one extending the gift, you will only gain. If you give a gift and remain with it to be sure that it is used as you deem appropriate, you are imprisoning yourself, not giving.

4. It is your relinquishing all concern about what you give that makes it truly given, and it is your trust in the Holy Spirit that makes true giving possible for you. The Holy Spirit is in what seems to be 'you' and in the part of your mind where you perceive a world, so how can a gift of healing that you extend be lost, ineffectual, or wasted? God's Treasure House can never be empty; It would not be full if even one gift was missing. However, its fullness is guaranteed by God. You can have no concern, then, about what becomes of what you extend. You give from God to God, so who is there in this Holy exchange that can receive less than Everything?

Mentor's Notes

You can see in this answer how the two thought systems in your mind work. When you give, or extend, from the Holy Spirit, you receive What you give immediately. Giving and receiving are simultaneous and inward, so you have no concern with what is appearing. But the personal mind, which wants to reinforce in your mind the reality of the world, emphasizes what appears in the world. If you give and someone does not appear to receive, then you believe that what you have given is lost. What is the world that you should care what happens there? It is nothing and nowhere. It is an error in perception.

Remember, forgiving, or healing, means overlooking illusions and remembering Truth. You experience the Truth within you. If you are attached to an outcome in the world, then you are looking for

Truth in illusions.

7. Should I repeat a healing?

1. This question answers itself: If healing has occurred, what is there to heal again? And since healing is certain, no matter what is appearing, then there is nothing to repeat. As a teacher of God, for you to be concerned about the results of healing is for you to limit healing. Any concern about the outcome of healing indicates that it is your mind that needs to be healed. So this is what you must facilitate, by regarding yourself as the one who needs to be healed. You have made a mistake, and you must be willing to change your mind. You lacked the trust in the Holy Spirit that makes your offer of healing truly offered, so you have not received the benefits of your gift.

2. Whenever you try to be a channel for healing, you succeed. If you doubt this, you do not need to repeat your previous effort. That was already maximal, because the Holy Spirit accepted it as so, and used it. Now, you have only one course to follow: You must remind yourself that you have given the seeming problem to One that cannot fail, and you must recognize that your own uncertainty is not Love, but fear, and therefore, hate. Now, you are trying to offer hate where you extended Love. This is impossible, because, having extended Love, you received Love.

3. As a teacher of God, you must trust in this. This is what is meant by the statement that, as a miracle worker, your one responsibility is to accept the Atonement, or correction of your perception of separation from God, for yourself. As a teacher of God, you are a miracle worker, because you extend the Gifts of God that you receive. To extend Them, you must first accept Them for yourself; you do not need to do any more than this, nor is there any more that you can do. By accepting healing, you extend it in your entire mind. If you doubt this, remember What extends healing and What receives it. This is how your doubt is corrected. You think that you can withdraw the Gifts of God, but this is a mistake, and hardly one

for you to keep. Recognize it for what it is, and let it be corrected for you.

4. One of the most difficult temptations for you to overcome is to doubt a healing because of the appearance of continuing symptoms. This is a mistake in the form of a lack of trust in the Holy Spirit, and it is an attack on yourself. Usually, it seems to you to be the opposite; it does not appear reasonable to you that continued concern is an attack, because it appears as 'love'. But Love without trust is impossible, and doubt and trust cannot coexist. Hate must be the opposite of Love, whatever form it takes. Do not doubt the gift, and it will be impossible for you to doubt the result. This is the certainty that gives you the power of a miracle worker, because you will have put your faith in God.

5. The real basis for your doubt about the outcome of any problem that you have given to the Holy Spirit to resolve is always Self-doubt. Doubt implies that you have put your trust in an illusion of yourself, because you can only doubt the personal self. The personal self's doubts can take many forms: fear of weakness and vulnerability; fear of failure; shame associated with a sense of inadequacy; guilty embarrassment stemming from false humility. The form of the mistake is not important; what is important is that you recognize the mistake *as* a mistake.

6. The mistake is always some form of concern for the personal self to the exclusion of the rest of your mind. It is your failure to recognize that what you perceive is a part of your True Self, and this represents your confusion in identity. Conflict about what you are enters your mind, and you become deceived about yourself. And you are deceived about yourself, because you have denied your Source. If you are offering only healing, you cannot doubt, because doubt is the result of conflicting wishes. When you are sure of What you want, doubt will be impossible for you.

Mentor's Notes

This answer makes it clear that, since healing is certain, there is really nothing to heal. Since God's Gifts are given from God to God, then there is nothing for you to do. Healing, then, occurs when you recognize this.

When you are faced with an appearance of illness, then, in yourself or in 'another', all that you need to do is acknowledge that only God is Real. Anything else is an attack on yourself, because it means that you believe something else is real.

Paragraph 4 points out that continued concern when a healing has been offered, but does not seem to be received, is an attack in the form of 'love'. In your perception that you are a personal self in a world with other personal selves, concern for others is deemed appropriate and 'good', but this concern stems from the error that you are a personal self in a body in a world with other personal selves. When you rest in God, you know that all is well, and you are not affected by appearances.

8. How can I avoid the perception that some forms of sickness are more difficult to heal than others?

1. The belief that some forms of error are harder to correct than others is the basis of the personal mind's perception. It is the source of the diversity and contrast that it perceives, and of the competition for its attention that it perceives between everything in the world. It is the idea that one illusion can be less of an illusion than another; that different forms actually make illusions different from each other. But what the body's eyes look on is only conflict; do not look to them to understand that all illusions are all the same.

2. The illusions that you perceive are always illusions of differences; how could it be otherwise in a mind that is really One? By definition, an illusion is something that you know to be unreal, but that you attempt to make real and important out of your intense desire that it be true. Illusions are your attempts to distort reality; to make lies into truth. In your desire to be separate from God, you find Truth to be unacceptable, you revolt against It, and you have an illusion of 'victory' over It. You find Wholeness a burden, so you

retreat into feverish illusions of separation, where your mind is split into 'you' and 'other' minds, all with different interests of your own, and each only able to gratify your needs at the expense of others.

3. It is in the sorting out and categorizing activities of the personal mind that your errors in perception occur, so it is here that you must make correction. The personal mind classifies what the body's eyes see according to its preconceived values, judging where every little thing it senses fits into its categories. There is no basis for judgment that could be faultier than this. Unconsciously, it asks for experiences that will fit into its categories, then, having the experience, it concludes that its categories must be true. Its judgment of differences rests on this, because it is on this that its judgments of the world depend. You cannot depend on this confused and senseless 'reasoning' for anything.

4. It is not harder for you to heal some forms of sickness than for you to heal others, because all sickness is an illusion. It is not harder for you to dispel an hallucination that seems 'larger' than one that seems 'smaller'. It is not easier for you to recognize that a voice is unreal because it is softer than a loud one, nor to dismiss a whispered demand to kill than a shouted demand to kill. The number of pitchforks you see the devil carrying will not affect its credibility in your perception. Your mind categorizes these differences as real, so they are real to you, but when you recognize that they are all illusions, they will disappear from your mind. This is how healing occurs. The properties of illusions that seem to make them different are really irrelevant, because their properties are as illusory as they are.

5. The body's eyes will always see differences, but when you let your mind heal, you will no longer acknowledge that differences are real. You will perceive some people as 'sicker' than others, and the body's eyes will report changed appearances, but your healed mind will put them all in the same category: They are unreal. This is the Holy Spirit's gift: The understanding that only two categories – Love and the call for Love – are meaningful for you in sorting out the

messages that you receive from what appears to be a world outside of you. And of these two, only Love is Real. Just as Reality is One throughout, with no size or shape or time or place, because differences cannot exist within It, so too are all illusions, illusion. The one answer to sickness of any kind is healing; the One Answer to all illusions is Truth.

Mentor's Notes

'Sickness' and 'healing' in this answer refer not just to physical sickness and healing, but to your perception of separation from God and its correction.

Paragraph 2 mentions your 'desire to be separate from God'. Inevitably, the question arises, 'How can I, who am One with God, have a desire that is counter to God?' The answer is, 'You cannot', which is the central lesson of this course. God, being All, must contain even the *idea* of Its own opposite, but, being All, God cannot have an opposite. So the idea of not-God is over the instant that it arises; it is impossible. However, since God is Eternal, *time* is the opposite of God, and only in time it seems as though you separated from God in a distant past, and you will again be One with God in an indefinite future. So, only in time, which is already over, can not-God seem to be real, and, like God, it wants to perpetuate itself. Your desire to be separate from God, then, exists only in the idea of not-God, which manifests as a world of personal selves, all seeking independence from God. In your perception that you are a personal self, then, this desire is the source of your guilt and fear of God, but these have no real basis, because the desire itself is not real.

Paragraph 3 points out that sorting and categorizing is the way that the personal mind thinks, and it is here that you must make correction. This does not mean that you have to 'fix' or change the personal mind, which is not-God and cannot be made God-like, but that you make correction by letting go of the personal mind.

The circular reasoning of the personal mind mentioned in paragraph 3 is typical of the way that it projects. It decides what it wants to experience, perceives a justification for the experience, then decides the experience is real because it has interpreted events to justify the experience it has chosen. In this process, of course, it is denying that it is only having the experience that it invited. For example, let's say a person is invested in being a 'victim'. They then perceive whatever occurs through a lens that justifies their feelings of victimhood, and they reason that, because they have interpreted events to justify their feeling like a victim, they *are* a victim. Your Christ Mind, on the other hand, always experiences only Christ, willingly acknowledging that This is What It has invited and wants to experience.

Even though only Love is Real, the call for Love is an opportunity for you to remember Love.

9. Are changes required in my life situation when I become a teacher of God?

1. Changes are required in your *mind;* this may or may not involve changes in what seems like your external situation. Remember, 'accident' or 'chance' does not play a part in God's plan for your salvation from illusions. It is most likely that changes in attitude are the first step in your training as a teacher of God, but there is no set pattern, since this training is highly individualized. You may be called upon to change your life situation almost immediately, but that would be unusual. You are more likely to be given a slowly evolving training program in which as many of your previously attained erroneous beliefs will be corrected. In particular, you must properly perceive your relationship with the part of your mind where you perceive a world, and let all dark corners of unforgiveness be cleared from your mind. Otherwise, you will hold onto the personal mind's thought system.

2. As you advance in your training, you will learn one lesson with increasing thoroughness: To not make decisions with a personal mind, but to ask the Holy Spirit to guide you. This will become easier and easier as you learn to give up the personal mind's

judgment. Giving up the personal mind's judgment, which is obviously necessary for you to hear the Holy Spirit, is usually a slow process, not because it is difficult, but because you are likely to perceive it as personally insulting. The personal mind's lesson plan is directed toward achieving a goal that directly opposes the lesson plan of this course. The personal mind trains you to rely on personal judgment as the criterion for 'maturity' and 'strength'; this course trains you to relinquish personal judgment as the necessary condition of your salvation.

Mentor's Notes

To 'properly perceive your relationship with the part of your mind where you perceive a world' means that you recognize that the world is in your mind; you are not in the world. As long as you believe that anything that you perceive is separate from you, you will not be able to accept the world as an illusion and forgive it. You will continue to perceive yourself as split between God and not-God, and you will perceive each as equally real.

10. How do I relinquish judgment?

1. In your identification with a personal self, you totally misunderstand judgment, just like the other devices by which the personal mind maintains the world of separation. You confuse it with 'wisdom', and you substitute it for Truth. As the personal mind uses the term, you see yourself as capable of 'good' or 'bad' judgment, and your education has been aimed at strengthening the former and minimizing the latter in you. But you are rather confused about what these categories mean. In your perception that you are in a world, what is considered 'good' judgment by one person is considered 'bad' judgment by another. Further, what you classify as 'good' judgment in one situation you may judge as 'bad' in another. Nor can you really learn any consistent criteria for determining what these categories are. At any time, you and others will disagree, and you will be inconsistent in what you believe. Neither 'good' nor 'bad'

judgment means anything in this context.

2. It is necessary for you, as a teacher of God, to realize, not that you *should not* judge with a personal mind, but that you *cannot* judge with a personal mind. When you give up the personal mind's judgment, you are only giving up what you never had. You have an illusion of giving up what was really an illusion, and you actually become more honest. When you recognize that personal judgment was always impossible, you will no longer attempt it. This will not be a sacrifice, because you will put yourself in a position where the Holy Spirit's judgment can then come into your mind. This judgment will be neither 'good' nor 'bad', because it is the only judgment that there is: 'You are Innocent, and sin does not exist'.

3. The aim of this lesson plan, unlike the personal mind's goal for your learning, is your recognizing that the personal mind's judgment is impossible. This is not an opinion, but a fact. In order to judge anything correctly in your perception that you are in a world, you would have to be fully aware of an inconceivably wide range of things, past, present, and to come. You would have to recognize in advance all of the effects of your judgment on everyone and everything involved in any way, and you would have to be certain that there was no distortion in your perception, so that your judgment would be wholly fair. Are you in a position to do this when you identify with a limited personal self? Only in the personal mind's grandiose fantasies could you say 'yes'.

4. Remember how many times in your identification with a personal self that you thought that you knew all of the 'facts' you needed for judgment only to find out how wrong you were. This is a universal experience for all personal selves. Do you want to know how many times you only thought that you were right and never realized that you were wrong? Do not choose such an arbitrary thought system for making decisions. You won't find Wisdom in the personal mind's judgment, but in your relinquishment of the personal mind's judgment, so make only one more judgment: There is Something in you with Perfect judgment. It knows all of the facts,

past, present, and to come. It knows the effects of Its judgment on everyone and everything involved in your perception that you are in a world, and It is wholly fair, because there is no distortion in Its perception.

5. So lay down the personal mind's judgment without regret, and with a sigh of gratitude. You will free yourself of a burden so great that you staggered and nearly fell beneath it. It was all an illusion; nothing more. Now, as a teacher of God, you can rise up unburdened, and walk on lightly. But relief from burden is not the only benefit to you in giving up the personal mind's judgment. You will find yourself without concerns, which you gave away with the personal mind's judgment. You will give yourself to the Holy Spirit, the judgment of Which you have now chosen to trust. You will no longer make mistakes, because your Guide is Certain. Where you once would have judged, you will now bless; where you once would have wept, you will now laugh.

6. It is not difficult for you to relinquish the personal mind's judgment, but it is difficult for you to hold onto it. As a teacher of God, you will lay it down happily the moment that you recognize What it costs you, and you acknowledge its outcome: all of the ugliness and pain that you perceive; all of your loneliness and sense of loss; your sense of passing time and growing hopelessness; your sickening despair and fear of death. You will know that these things do not need to be. Not one is true. You will give up their cause, and they, which were only the effects of your mistaken choice, will fall from you. Teacher of God, this step will bring you Peace; is it difficult for you to want only This?

Mentor's Notes

Judgment in this answer refers to both *evaluating* (right/wrong, good/bad, valuable/invaluable, etc.) and to *deciding* (yes or no) on the best course of action.

Paragraph 1 points out that the personal mind has no consistent criteria for judgment, therefore, judgment is impossible through it.

What it calls 'judgment' is really conclusions and decisions based on shifting and arbitrary criteria.

Notice how the personal mind's judgments always center on the world, where the Holy Spirit's judgment simply affirms the Truth in you. In God, Where all is One, there is nothing to judge. Only in a world of perception, separation, and diversity do you need to make decisions, so you need judgment. The personal mind uses judgment to perpetuate your sense of separation from God, and from all that you perceive. It is its chief tool for making separation from God real to you. But the Holy Spirit uses judgment only to lead you back to full awareness of God. Which thought system's judgment you choose depends on whether you want to continue perceiving yourself as separate from God, or if you want to be aware again that you are One with God.

When you first put aside the personal mind's judgment, it seems like you are putting aside your own best interests to make room for what seems like an alien will: the Holy Spirit. But remember, the Holy Spirit is your True Self. The reason that the Holy Spirit's judgment seems alien to you is that you don't have to make it up; it is your natural judgment. In your identification with a personal self, everything, including judgment, requires effort, because you have to make it up, so, at first, your Natural Thought System seems foreign to you. But you will get used to effortlessness!

As it says in question 9, you find putting aside personal judgment personally insulting. You are so used to *making* and *doing* that being told that you don't need to do anything may make you feel lost, and even 'useless'. But these feelings are indications that you are listening to the personal mind. Your Natural State is just *being*. In time, as you put aside the personal mind's judgment (which is how you put aside the personal mind, since *judging* is how it thinks) you will learn how to just *be* within while the body goes about its business.

11. How is Peace possible for me while I perceive myself in a world?

1. This is a question that you must ask, because it certainly seems impossible for you to be at Peace while you perceive yourself in a world. But the Holy Spirit promises you other things that seem impossible, too: that there is no death, and that your Christ Mind will be resurrected in your awareness. The world that you perceive cannot be what God Loves, but the Holy Spirit assures you that God has a Loving Perception of the world. The Holy Spirit has promised you that it is possible for you to be at Peace while you perceive yourself in a world, and only what God promises is possible. But it is true that you must look at the world in a different way from the way that you have perceived it with a personal mind if you are to accept God's Promises. That the world is not of God is a fact, and you cannot change this. But you can, and must, change how you perceive it.

2. Again, you must address the issue of *judgment*. Ask yourself whether the personal mind's judgment or the Holy Spirit's judgment on the world is more likely to be true? They each say different things about the world; things that are so opposed that they cannot be reconciled. God offers you salvation through the Holy Spirit's judgment on the world; the personal mind wants to condemn you through its judgment on the world. God says there is no death; the personal mind sees death as the inevitable end of Life. The Holy Spirit assures you that God has a Loving Perception of the world; the personal mind says it is unlovable. It must be that only one can be right.

3. The Text explains that the Holy Spirit is the Answer to any problems that you have made. These problems are not real, but that is meaningless to you when you believe in them. Of course you believe in what you have made, because you made it by believing in it. Into this strange and paradoxical situation, which is without real meaning, is devoid of sense, and out of which no way seems possible for you, God has sent Its Judgment to answer the personal mind's

judgment. Gently, God's Judgment substitutes for the personal mind's judgment, and through this substitution, the un-understandable is made understandable to you. How is it possible for you to be at Peace in your perception that you are in a world? In the personal mind's judgment, it is not possible, but in God's Judgment, all that is reflected back to you from your perception of the world is Peace.

4. Peace is impossible for you when you look on conflict and think that it is real. Peace is inevitable for you when you extend Peace in your awareness. See how easily you can escape the personal mind's judgment of the world! It is not the world that makes Peace seem impossible to you; it is the way that you perceive the world with a personal mind that makes Peace seem impossible to you. God's Judgment on your distorted perception of the world redeems your perception of the world, and makes the world seem fit to welcome Peace. And Peace descends on it in Joyous answer. Peace belongs in your perception when you allow a Thought of God to enter your mind. Only a Thought of God turns hell into Heaven merely by being What It is. Your perception bows before Its Gracious Presence, and It leans down in answer, to raise up your perception again. Now your question is no longer, 'How is Peace possible for me while I perceive myself in a world?', but is instead, 'Is it not impossible for Peace to be absent from my awareness?'

Mentor's Notes

God's Judgment on the world is that it is nothing. As you learned in the early lessons in the Workbook, since the world has no meaning of its own, you can choose how you perceive it. It is never something in the world that bothers you; it is your perception, or interpretation, of the person, thing, or situation that bothers you. You always have the choice to perceive with the Holy Spirit instead.

12. How many teachers of God are needed to save the world?

1. The answer to this question is 'one': you, as a wholly perfect

teacher whose learning is complete. When you are this One that is sanctified and redeemed, you will be the Self that is One with God; you will be Christ. You, who have always been Spirit, will no longer see yourself as a body, or even in a body. You will know that you are Limitless, and, being aware that you are Limitless, your thoughts will be joined with God's Thoughts Forever. Your perception of yourself will be based on God's Judgment, not on the judgment of a personal mind, so you will share God's Will and extend It in your awareness to all that you perceive. You will know that your mind is Forever One, because you are as God created you. You will have accepted Christ as your Self, and been saved.

2. And so you will become aware that you are One with God. This is about a change of *mind;* nothing external will change, but everything in your mind will reflect only God's Love. You will no longer fear God, because you will no longer see a cause for punishment. You may perceive *many* of God's teachers in your perception that you are in a world, because that is what it seems that the world needs. But God's teachers are joined in one purpose that they share with God, so they are not separate from each other. It does not matter that they appear in many forms, because they know that Mind is One. God will work through you all as One, because that is What you are.

3. In your perception that you are in a world, you have an illusion of many teachers, because in separation the Reality of Oneness cannot be manifested. So, it seems that only very few hear the Holy Spirit at all, and even they cannot communicate God's Messages directly through the Holy Spirit, Which gave Them. They are mediums that communicate the Holy Spirit's message to you when you are not ready to recognize that you are Spirit. You can see a body and hear a voice that you understand and listen to, without the fear that you would experience hearing Truth directly. Truth can only come into your awareness when you welcome It without fear. So, for a while, you need to perceive God's teachers in bodies when you are not yet ready to recognize their Oneness.

4. What will make you a teacher of God will be your recognition

of the proper use of the body. As you advance, you will become more and more certain that the body's only function is for you to let the Holy Spirit speak through it to teach you that you are the Holy Spirit. You will hear messages that are not of the world, and you will understand them because of their Source within you. From this, you will recognize what the body's purpose really is. This lesson will be enough for you to let Oneness return to your mind. As a teacher of God, you will seem to share the illusion of separation, but because of what you use the body for, you will not believe the illusion, despite appearances.

5. The central lesson about the body is this: What you use it for, it will be for you. Use it for separation or attack, and you will see it as sinful, therefore as weak, and, being weak, as something that suffers and dies. But, use it to bring the Holy Spirit into your perception of the world, and the body will be Holy in your perception. Being Holy, it will not become sick or die. When it is no longer useful to you, you will lay it aside; that's all. You will make this decision with your mind, just as your mind is responsible for all of the body's conditions. But you will not make this decision as a personal self, because that would give the body a purpose that is not Holy. The Holy Spirit will tell you when you are done with the body, just as it tells you what your function is. You will not suffer, either, in continuing to perceive a world, or in letting it go. Either way, sickness will be impossible for you.

6. Oneness and sickness cannot co-exist in your mind. As a teacher of God, you will choose to look on illusions for a while. This will be a conscious choice, because you will have learned that all choices are made consciously, with your full awareness of their consequences. In your illusions you have believed otherwise, but you will no longer put your faith in illusions once you recognize them for what they are. As a teacher of God, your real function is to be aware that illusions are illusions. You will watch personal selves come and go, shift and change, suffer and die, but you will not be deceived by what you see. You will recognize that to perceive a

personal self as sick and separate is no more real than to perceive it as healthy and beautiful. Oneness alone is not an illusion, and This is What you will acknowledge is behind all appearances, and is certainly yours.

Mentor's Notes

Does the salvation of the whole world depend on you alone? No, because the 'one' mentioned in the first paragraph is not 'you alone' - a personal self – but 'you everywhere' – the split mind that projects the world, and that, healed and Whole, is Christ.

In your perception that you are in a world, you are going to meet the whole range of personal selves, from those who seem completely in denial of God, to those, like you, who are teachers of God. But these are all just ideas in your mind given form. Those in denial help you to remember God, because their seeming lack reminds you of What is missing, and those who, like you, remember God, reinforce God in your mind. Remember, others do not teach you what you are, but you project the personal mind or the Holy Spirit onto them to teach yourself what you are. It does not matter what they seem to be teaching themselves.

The world is in your mind; you are not in the world, so you only have to correct *your* perception of the world for it to be 'saved' in your perception. Remember, Jesus manifested Christ Consciousness, not because he manifested certain attitudes or behaviors, but because He perceived Christ, or Oneness with God, everywhere. Christ is an awareness of God, not a type of person.

Paragraph 2 states that all teachers of God know that Mind is One. As a teacher of God, in time you will recognize that there are not *many minds* that are split between God and not-God (personal mind), but that there is really *only one split mind* that takes many forms. You cannot become aware of Christ through the personal mind, but only from the awareness that you are the one split mind, because Christ is not in only what the personal mind teaches is 'you'; Christ is everywhere. You will come to the awareness that there is only one split mind, and that it is in you, when you have recognized that your personal projections are causing your perception of the world, and you begin to generalize your awareness of the personal mind's projections by recognizing that their content is the same thing over and over again – separation from God - despite their seeming differences.

13. What is the real sacrifice?

1. Although in Truth the idea of 'sacrifice' is completely meaningless, in your perception that you are in a world, you think it has meaning. Like everything in the world, it is a temporary idea, and it will ultimately fade into the nothingness from which it came when you no longer have a use for it. But now, learning What you really seem to sacrifice is your lesson. Like all lessons, it is an illusion, because in Reality you have nothing to learn. Yet, you must first correct this illusion by learning What you really seem to sacrifice, then the idea of sacrifice will disappear altogether. The version of sacrifice that you must let be displaced by another version before your Real Thought System can take hold in your mind is that it is a sacrifice for you to give up the world. This can only be an illusion, because the world itself is an illusion.

2. It will require great learning on your part to accept the fact that the world that you perceive has nothing to give to you. Then you will know that giving up nothing is not a sacrifice, and that you cannot have less by giving up nothing. All ideas of sacrifice in your perception that you are in a world involve the body. Think about what the personal mind calls sacrifice: Giving up power, fame, money, physical pleasure. These could only have meaning to a body. But a body cannot evaluate, and by seeking after these things, you associate yourself with a body, obscuring and losing sight of your Real Identity.

3. Once you have become confused about your identity it becomes impossible for you to understand that all of the 'pleasures' of the world are nothing. But the real sacrifice is what this entails:

You condemn yourself to seek without finding, to be forever dissatisfied and discontented, and to not know What you really want to find. You can only escape this self-condemnation through the Holy Spirit within you, because self-condemnation is a decision that you make about your identity, and you will not doubt what you believe you are. You can doubt anything but this.

4. As God's teacher, you will have no regrets about giving up the 'pleasures' of the world. You will see that it is no sacrifice to give up pain, just as an adult does not resent giving up children's toys. Having perceived Christ, you will not look back with longing on a slaughterhouse. Having escaped the world and all of its ills, you will not look back on it with condemnation, but you will rejoice that you are free of all of the sacrifice that valuing the world demanded of you. To value the world, you sacrificed your Peace and Freedom. To value the world, you sacrificed your hope of Heaven and your Memory of God's Love. You have to be insane to choose nothing as a substitute for Everything.

5. What is the real sacrifice? It is the cost of your believing in illusions; it is the price that you pay for denying the Truth. Every 'pleasure' of the world demands payment of you, but you don't see that its 'pleasures' are pain, or you wouldn't seek for them. The idea that giving up the world is a sacrifice makes you blind to the real sacrifice, and you do not see what you are asking for. So you seek for pleasure in a thousand ways, in a thousand places, each time believing that you have found it, but finding yourself disappointed in the end. 'Seek, but do not find' is the personal mind's stern decree, and pursuing its goals, you cannot do otherwise.

6. You may believe that this course requires you to sacrifice all that you hold dear. In one sense this is true, because you *do* hold dear things that crucify you, and it is this course's aim to set you free from crucifying yourself. But don't be mistaken about what you *really* sacrifice. Sacrifice always means giving up what you want, and what, teacher of God, do you really want? You have answered God's Call; do you want to sacrifice that Call? It seems that you perceive

few in the world that hear It, but it is up to you to extend God in your awareness. Only your voice can echo God's Voice for you to hear It. If you want to sacrifice the Truth, you will perceive hell, and if you perceive hell, you will remain aware of hell.

7. Do not forget that sacrifice is total; there are no half-sacrifices. You cannot partially give up Heaven; you cannot be a little bit in hell. The Holy Spirit makes no exceptions; it is this that makes the Holy Spirit Holy and beyond your perception of a world. It is the Holy Spirit's Holiness within you that points to God, and that makes you safe. You deny your Holiness when you attack anyone or anything, because here you split-off your mind from God. This split is impossible in Reality, but you believe in it, because you have set up a situation that is impossible, and in which the impossible can seem to happen. This seeming-to-happen, then, is your 'sacrifice' of Truth.

8. Do not forget What you really sacrifice, and remember what each decision costs you. Decide for God, and you have Everything at no cost; decide against God, and you choose nothing at the expense of your awareness that you have Everything. Remember that what you want to teach is what you want to learn. This is what you should concern yourself with, because the Atonement, which is the correction of your perception that you are separate from God, is for you. Your learning this is how you claim the Atonement, and your learning this extends the Atonement in your awareness. You will not find Atonement in the world, but learn this course and the Atonement is yours. God gives Its Holy Spirit to you, because God needs you to be a teacher of God. There is no other way to save you.

14. How will the world end?

1. The world has no beginning, so it has no ending. It will end in an illusion as it began, but its ending will be merciful. The illusion of your forgiving, which will be complete, exclude nothing of the world, and will be limitless in Gentleness, will cover the world, undoing all of your thoughts of evil or of sin, and ending your guilt

forever. This is how the world that your guilt made will end, because it will have no purpose, so it will be gone from your mind. The origin of your illusions is your belief that they have a purpose, serve a need, or gratify a want, but when you understand that they have no purpose, you will no longer perceive them. This is how all illusions end: they are brought to Truth, and Truth cannot see them. Truth merely overlooks what has no meaning.

2. But, until your forgiving is complete, your perception that you are in a world does have a purpose for you. It is where your forgiving begins, and where it grows to encompass everything in your perception. Your forgiving is nourished in the world, because it is needed in your perception of a world. Here, where sin was made, and guilt seemed real, Christ will be reborn in your awareness. Here, Christ is home, because it is where your awareness of Christ is needed. Christ brings the end of the world for you, calling to you to turn to Christ and learn the Truth. The world will end when all things in it have been correctly judged by Christ; the world will end with the benediction of Holiness on it. When you no longer have a single thought that sin is real, the world will be over for you. It will not be destroyed, or attacked, or even touched; it will merely cease to seem to be.

3. 'When not one thought that sin is real remains' may seem to be a long-range goal indeed, but time stands still when it serves the goal of a teacher of God. No belief that sin is real will remain the instant that you accept the Atonement for yourself. It is not easier for you to forgive one illusion of sin than for you to forgive altogether the belief that sin is real. The illusion that some forms of sin are harder for you to forgive than others is an obstacle that you must leave behind. One form of the belief that sin is real that you forgive perfectly will make your salvation complete. You cannot understand this in your belief that the world is real, but it is the final lesson in which Oneness is restored to your awareness. It goes against the thinking of the personal mind, but so does Heaven.

4. The world will end for you when you have let the personal

mind's thought system be completely reversed. Until then, bits and pieces of its thinking will still seem sensible to you. The final lesson, which will end the world for you, cannot be grasped by you when you are not yet ready to leave the world and go beyond its tiny reach. Your function as a teacher of God in this final lesson is to merely learn how to approach the final lesson; how to go in its direction. You only need to trust that, if the Holy Spirit tells you that you can learn it, you can learn it. You do not need to judge it as either hard or easy. The Holy Spirit will point to it, and you can trust that the Holy Spirit will show you how to learn it.

5. The world will end in Joy for you, because the world is your perception that sorrow is real. When Joy has returned to your awareness, the purpose of the world will be done for you. The world will end in Peace for you, because the world is your perception that conflict is real. When Peace has come to your awareness again, the world will have no purpose for you. The world will end in Laughter for you, because the world is your perception that sadness is real. When you see justification for Laughter, you will no longer see justification to weep. Only your completely forgiving the world will bring all of this to bless your perception of the world. In blessing, the world will depart from your awareness; it will not end as it began. As a teacher of God, your function is to transform your perception of hell into Heaven, because what you will teach yourself are lessons that reflect Heaven. Now, in true humility, realize that all that God wants you to do, you can do. Do not be arrogant and say that you cannot learn God's lesson plan. God says otherwise. God's Will is done; it cannot be otherwise, and be thankful that this is so.

Mentor's Notes

In essence, your forgiving your illusion that you are separate from God will occur in one instant, then the world will be gone from your mind Forever. Forgiving is total, or it is not at all. Until that final instant, then, you are preparing for it by practicing forgiving over and over again. Each time that you do so, you experience the

Freedom that forgiving offers to you, which motivates you to accept that 'final lesson' in forgiving which will undo completely your perception of a world as real, and restore you to the awareness that you are One with God. But as long as anything in the world remains true for you, you have not really forgiven at all.

15. Will I be judged in the end?

1. Indeed, yes! You cannot escape God's Final Judgment, because you cannot run forever from the Truth. But God's Final Judgment will come into your awareness only when you no longer associate It with fear. One day, you will welcome It with your entire mind, and on that day, It will be given to you. You will perceive your Innocence everywhere, and you will free your mind from the world as you receive God's Final Judgment. This is the Judgment in Which your salvation lies; this is the Judgment that will set your entire mind Free. Time will pause as Eternity comes into your awareness again, and Silence will lie across all that you perceive, so that you will hear with your entire mind this judgment on you:

> 'You are Holy, Eternal, Limitless, Whole, and at Peace Forever in God. There is no world, and there is no sorrow.'

2. Teacher of God, is this your judgment on yourself? Do you believe that this is wholly true? No; not yet. But this is your goal; this is why you still perceive yourself in a world. It is your function to prepare yourself to hear this Judgment, and to recognize that It is True. One Instant of complete belief in it, and you will go beyond belief to Certainty. One Holy Instant out of time can end time for you. Do not judge yourself with a personal mind, because then you delay your awareness of God's Final Judgment on you. Teacher of God, what is your judgment on the part of your mind that you perceive as a world? Have you learned yet to put aside the personal mind's judgment, and to hear the True Voice of Judgment in yourself? Or do you still attempt to give this role to a personal self?

Learn to be quiet, because you will hear God's Voice in stillness, and God's Judgment comes to you when you put the personal mind aside and listen quietly and wait for God.

3. You, who are sometimes sad and sometimes angry; who sometimes feel that what is justly due to you is not given to you; who feel that your best efforts meet with a lack of appreciation, and even contempt, give up these foolish thoughts! They are too small and meaningless to occupy your holy mind an instant longer. God's Judgment waits to set you Free. The world cannot hold out to you anything that you would rather have, regardless of your judgment on its gifts. You will be judged, and judged in Fairness and in Honesty. There is no deceit in God; God's Promises are sure. You only have to remember this. God's Promises guarantee that you will accept only God's Judgment in the end. It is your function to make that end be soon. It is your function to hold God's Judgment in the center of your mind, and to extend It in your awareness to keep It safe in your mind.

16. As a teacher of God, how should I spend my day?

1. This question is meaningless to an advanced teacher of God, because, as such, you will know that there is no structure, since the form of your lessons in forgiving will change each day. And you will be certain that they do not change at random. Understanding that this is true, you will rest content. As a teacher of God, you will be told what to do every day, and those who best serve your lesson in forgiving for the day will find you so that you can learn it with them. Anyone that you need you will find, and with everyone that you meet, you will have a learning goal that you can learn that day. As an advanced teacher of God, then, this question is not necessary, because you will keep in constant contact with the Answer. Your way is set, and the path on which you walk stretches surely and smoothly before you.

2. But if you have not yet reached certainty, then you are not ready for a lack of structure. There are some general rules that you

need to learn to give the day to God, and you must use them the best way for you. Routine for routine's sake is dangerous for you, because it can become an idol in itself that threatens the very goal for which it was set up. Broadly speaking, then, it is well for you to start the day centered in God, but it is always possible to begin again if you begin the day in error. However, in terms of saving time, there are some obvious advantages in starting the day centered in God.

3. In the beginning, it is wise for you to think in terms of saving time. This is not the ultimate criterion, but at the outset, it is probably the simplest for you to observe. Saving time is emphasized early, but, although it remains important throughout your learning process, it will be emphasized less and less. At the start, time that you devote to starting the day right does indeed save time. How much time should you spend in starting your day right? This depends on where you are in your process as a teacher of God. Since you are learning within the framework of this course, you cannot call yourself a 'teacher of God' until you have completed the Workbook. After you have completed its structured practice periods, your individual needs will become your chief consideration.

4. This course is always practical. It may be that you are not in a situation that fosters quiet soon after you wake up. If this is so, simply remember that you want to spend time with God as soon as possible, and then do so. Duration is not the major concern here. You can easily sit still for an hour with your eyes closed and accomplish nothing; you can just as easily give God an instant and join wholly with God for that instant. The one generalization is this: As soon as possible after awaking, take your quiet time, continuing for a minute or two after you begin to get uncomfortable. You may find that the discomfort will diminish and drop away; if not, this is the time for you to stop.

5. You should follow the same procedure at night. If it is not feasible for you to have your quiet time just before you go to sleep, then your quiet time should be fairly early in the evening. It is not wise for you to lie down for this time; it is better that you sit up in a

position that you prefer. After completing the Workbook, you should have an idea of what is comfortable for you. If possible, however, just before going to sleep is a desirable time for you to devote to God. This sets your mind into a pattern of rest, and orients you away from fear. If it is more expedient for you to spend this time earlier, then spend a brief moment thinking of God with your eyes closed just before you go to sleep.

6. There is one thought in particular that you should remember throughout the day. It is a thought of Pure Joy, of Peace, and of Limitlessness. You think that you have made a place of safety for yourself in a personal self. You think that you have made a 'power' that can save you from all of your fearful illusions. It is not so. Your safety does not lie in a personal self. When you give it up, you are only giving up an illusion of a protecting illusion. And giving it up is all that you fear. How foolish for you to be afraid of nothing at all! The personal mind's defenses do not work, but you are not in danger. You do not need them. Recognize this, and they will disappear. Only then will you accept your Real Protection.

7. Time will slip by simply and easily when you accept your Real Protection. All that you did before to feel safe will no longer interest you, because you *are* safe, and you will know it. You will know that you have a Guide with you that cannot fail you. You will not have to make a distinction between the problems that you perceive, because the Holy Spirit, to Which you turn with all of them, recognizes that there is no order of difficulty in resolving them. You will know that you are as safe in this moment as you were before you accepted illusions into your mind, and as you will be when you let go of them. There will be no difference in your state of being at different times or in different places, because they are all the same to God. You will find your safety in recognizing this, and you will have no need for more than this.

8. But you will be tempted to believe that you are separate from God along the way, so you will need to remind yourself of your Protection throughout the day. How can you do this, especially

when your mind is occupied with external things? You can only try, and your success will depend on your conviction that you will succeed. You must be sure that you know that your Protection does not come from a personal mind, but will be given to you anytime, in any place, and in any situation in which you call on It. There will be times when your certainty will waver, and, when this occurs, you will return to placing your trust in the personal self. Do not forget that this is magical thinking, and magic is a sorry substitute for True Assistance. It is not good enough for you as God's teacher, because it is not good enough for What is One with God.

9. Your avoiding magic will be your avoiding the temptation to believe that you are separate from God. All temptation is only your attempt to substitute another will for God's Will. These attempts may indeed seem frightening to you, but they are only pathetic. They have no real effects; nothing good or bad, rewarding or demanding sacrifice, healing or destructive, calming or fearful. When you recognize that all magic is merely nothing, you will have reached the most advanced state as a teacher of God. All lessons before this will lead you to this, and bring it nearer to your awareness. Magic of any kind, in all of its forms, simply does nothing. You can escape from it precisely because it is powerless. What has no effects cannot terrify you.

10. *There is no substitute for God's Will.* Simply, it is to this fact that you devote your day as a teacher of God. Every substitute that you accept as real can only deceive you, but you are safe from deception if you decide to be so. Maybe you will need to remember, 'God is with me; I cannot be deceived.' Maybe you will prefer other words, or only one word, or none at all. But you must abandon every temptation to accept magic as true through your recognition, not that magical thinking is fearful, sinful, or dangerous, but merely that it is meaningless. Magical thinking is rooted in the idea that sacrifice and separation from God are real; when you give it up, you give up only what you never had, and for this 'sacrifice', Heaven will be restored to your awareness.

11. Isn't this an exchange that you want to make? As a teacher of God, you must teach yourself that this exchange can be made, because it is your function to learn it. The only risk possible for you throughout the day is for you to put your trust in magic, because it is only this that leads you to pain. 'There is only God's will.' As a teacher of God, you will know that this is so, and you will have learned that everything but this is magical thinking. All of your belief in magic is maintained by only this simple-minded illusion: It works. All through your training, every day, every hour, and even every second of every minute, you must learn to recognize every form of magic that your mind holds, and its lack of meaning. When you have withdrawn your fear from it, it will go from your mind. This is how you will be made aware of Heaven again, and how Its Light will shine on your untroubled mind.

Mentor's Notes

'Magical thinking' is another way of referring to the personal mind's thoughts. The Holy Spirit's Thoughts are 'miraculous'.

17. As a teacher of God, how do I deal with magical thinking?

1. This is a crucial question for you as a teacher of God. If you mishandle this, you will attack yourself, which will reinforce your fear, and will make magic seem quite real to you. Dealing with the personal mind's magical thinking, whether it seems to come from 'you' or you perceive it as though it is coming from 'another', is a major lesson for you to master as a teacher of God. Your first responsibility in this is to not attack the magical thoughts. If a magical thought arouses anger in you in any form, you can be sure that you are strengthening your belief in sin, and you are condemning yourself. You can be sure, too, that you are asking for depression, pain, fear, and disaster to come to you. Remember, then, that this is not what you want to teach yourself, because this is not what you want to learn.

2. However, you will probably be tempted to respond to the

personal mind's magical thinking in a way that reinforces it. This temptation is not always obvious; in fact, you may conceal it beneath a wish to 'help' another. It is this double wish to reinforce magical thinking and to be of help that makes the help of little value, and will lead to an outcome that you do not want. Nor should you forget that the outcome will come to you as both teacher and student. This course has emphasized many times that you can only give to yourself. And this shows up when you seem to give help to those who seem outside of you. This is where you find that what you seem to give to 'another' is given to you, because you can only extend in your awareness what you have chosen for yourself. And in this gift is your judgment on your entire mind.

3. It is easier for you to correct errors where they are most obvious to you, and you can recognize an error by its results. A lesson that you teach yourself from Truth can only release you, but attack has entered your mind when you have a separate goal for 'yourself' and for what you perceive as outside of you, and this is indeed the case if the result is anything but Joy for you. But if, as a teacher of God, you have a single aim for everything, you turn your conflict into a call for help. You can easily respond to this, then, with one Answer, and this Answer will enter your mind without fail. From there, It will shine outward in your perception, uniting your mind in Oneness.

4. Perhaps it will help you to remember that you are never angry at a fact; it is always an interpretation of yours that gives rise to negative emotions in you, regardless of their seeming justification by what seems like facts. It does not matter, either, how intensely your anger is aroused. You may feel a slight irritation that is so mild that you hardly recognize it; you may feel intense rage, accompanied by thoughts of violence that you fantasize about or act out. All of these reactions are the same. They obscure the Truth, and this is never a matter of degree. Either Truth is apparent to you, or It is not; you cannot partially recognize Truth. When you are unaware of Truth, you perceive illusions.

5. Anger in response to magical thinking is a basic cause of your fear. Consider what this reaction means, and you will see its centrality in the personal mind's thought system. A magical thought acknowledges separation from God as reality. It states, in the clearest possible form, that you have a will that can oppose God's Will, and that you believe that you can succeed at opposing God. That this can hardly be a fact is obvious, but your belief in this is the birthplace of your guilt. You seem to take God's place for yourself, and now you have an 'enemy' in God. You believe that you must stand alone with only the protection of a personal mind, and shield yourself from a fury that can never be abated, and from vengeance that will never be satisfied.

6. The end of this unbalanced conflict is inevitable: Your death. So how can you believe in your defenses? Magical thinking comes to help again: Forget the conflict. Accept it as a fact, and then forget it. Do not remember the impossible odds against you; do not remember the Immensity of the 'enemy', and do not think of your own frailty in comparison. Accept your sense of separation from God, but do not remember where it came from. Believe that you have won the conflict, but do not retain the slightest memory of What your great 'opponent' really is. Instead, project your own forgetting onto God, so that it seems as though God has forgotten, too.

7. Your reacting to magical thinking as though it is real, then, can only reawaken your sleeping guilt, which you have hidden, but you have not undone. Every time that you react to magical thinking as though it is real you say to your frightened mind, 'You have taken God's place. Do not think that God has forgotten.' Here, your fear of God is made apparent, because in this thought, your guilt raises insanity to take God's place. Now you have no hope, except to kill God, and you think that this is your salvation. An angry God pursues you, and you must kill or be killed. You have no choice beyond this, because what you did cannot be undone. Your guilt can never be removed, so you must meet with death.

8. Into this hopeless thinking God sends you as God's teacher, to bring the Light of hope from God to your mind. There is a way in which your escape from magical thinking is possible, because you can teach this way and so learn it, but it requires your patience and your willingness. With them, the lesson's manifest simplicity will stand out like an intense white light against a black horizon. Since anger comes from an interpretation and not a fact, it is never justified. Once you even dimly grasp this, the way will be open for you. Then it will be possible for you to take the last step; you will allow your interpretation to be changed. Magical thinking does not need to lead you to condemn yourself, because it does not really have the power to make you guilty. You can overlook it, and forget it in the truest sense.

9. Insanity only seems terrible; in Truth, it has no power. Like the magical thinking that serves it, it neither attacks nor protects you. When you look on and recognize the personal mind's thought system, you look on nothing, and what is nothing hardly justifies your anger. Remember, then, that your anger means that you perceive illusion as real, and that your anger witnesses to your belief that illusion is fact. Escape then seems impossible to you, until you recognize that you are responding only to your own interpretation, which you have projected onto what seems outside of you. Let your grim interpretations be taken from you. There is no death; what you interpret so grimly does not exist. Your fear of God does not have a cause, but God's Love is the Cause of Everything beyond fear, therefore, Everything Real and Always True.

Mentor's Notes

It does not matter whether you perceive a magical thought as coming from within you or as coming from someone outside of you. If you perceive it, it is in your mind, and if you react to it with anger, you believe that it is real. Reacting to magical thinking in a way that makes it real to you is an attack on yourself, because this means that you are reinforcing the unreal as real in your mind. Anger does not undo magical thinking; recognizing that it is not real undoes it.

Paragraph 2 mentions reinforcing magical thinking in a guise of helpfulness. For example, you have a friend who is upset because of a problem that they have seen on the news. They think that the solution being attempted will not work, and that they have a better idea. As a student of this course, you've read that the world isn't real, and you think that you know that all solutions in illusion are illusions, but you are irritated because your friend still thinks that the world is real, and that real solutions can be found in it. Your irritation, however, indicates that you also think that the world is real, because otherwise you would overlook both the seeming problem and your friend's attitude toward it. You may have read in this course that the world is not real, but you have not yet had a shift that makes you truly aware that it is not real. Rather than recognizing that your irritation indicates that it is you who needs correction by going to the Holy Spirit within you, you decide to 'help' your friend by telling them that what they are seeing is not real. This will not undo your guilt and fear, because it is not your friend's mistaken beliefs that are irritating you; it is your guilt and fear over your own mistaken beliefs that are irritating you. While on the surface it seems like your intention is to help your friend, you are really reinforcing your guilt and fear by not addressing them where they are. The outcome for you may be a feeling of smugness and superiority for 'knowing' what is real, but not the Peace that you would feel if you really knew What is Real and let go of the unreal. (And, probably, the outcome is an argument with your friend about what is real!)

Paragraph 8 says that magical thinking does not have the power to make you guilty. As it says in the Text, the personal mind always speaks first, but this does not mean that you have to listen to it. Let it have its say, let its thoughts go, and choose to come from the Holy Spirit instead.

18. How do I correct erroneous thinking?

1. You will not correct your erroneous thinking in a way that lasts, which is the only true correction, until you have stopped confusing interpretation with Fact, or illusion with Truth. If you argue about magical thoughts, attack them, try to establish them as erroneous, or demonstrate that they are false, you are witnessing to their reality. Then it is inevitable that you will be depressed, because you will have 'proved' to yourself that you are attempting, by following this course, to escape from what is actually real. Of course, this is impossible, because Reality is Changeless, and magical thinking is an *illusion* that you undo, otherwise your salvation would only be the age-old illusion of salvation in another form. And it is not in the form alone that your new method of salvation is different from the illusions that the personal mind has offered you in the past; it has a new content.

2. As a teacher of God, your major lesson is to learn how to react to magical thinking entirely without anger. Only in this way will you proclaim to yourself the Truth about yourself. Through you, then, the Holy Spirit will be able to speak to you of your Reality in Oneness with God. Then, you will be able to extend your Innocence, the one Unchanged, Unchangeable Condition of All that God created, in your perception. Then, you will hear the Holy Spirit speak through you, and you will use the Real Perception of your Christ Mind. Then, you will be free to teach your entire mind the Truth of What you are, so that the Truth will be returned to you. Through the Holy Spirit in you, and through your Real Perception, you will overlook and forgive guilt completely.

3. Your anger screeches, 'Guilt is real!', and then Reality is blotted out as this insane belief replaces the Holy Spirit in your mind. Then, the body's eyes seem to 'see', and its ears seem to 'hear' for you. Its little space and tiny breath become your measure of 'reality', and Truth seems small and meaningless to you. Your correction is this answer:

'You only mistakenly think that your interpretations are truth. But a mistake is not a sin, and Reality is unchanged by your mistake. God is Truth Forever, and only God's Law prevails over your entire mind. God's Love is the only thing that there is. Fear is an illusion, because you are like God.'

4. In order to heal, then, it is essential for you to let your mistakes be corrected. If you sense even the faintest hint of irritation in yourself as your respond to anyone or anything in your perception that you are in a world, instantly realize that you have made an interpretation that is not true. Then, turn within to the Holy Spirit, and let It judge what your response should be. This is how you will be healed. Your only responsibility as a teacher of God is to accept the Atonement for yourself. Atonement means correction, or the undoing of your errors. When this is accomplished, you will be a miracle worker. You will have forgiven yourself your perception that you are a sinner, and you will no longer condemn yourself, so you will no longer condemn anything that you perceive. There will be nothing that your forgiving yourself will fail to heal.

Mentor's Notes

The way that the personal mind thinks is to *interpret* according to its goal for you of separation from God, and since its goal is impossible, its interpretations are always meaningless. When you fight against the personal mind's interpretations, you are making another erroneous interpretation, which is that its interpretation is fact. Correction, then, is simply dismissing the personal mind's thoughts about everything, and turning to the other thought system in your mind, the Holy Spirit.

The 'age-old illusion of salvation' referred to in paragraph 1 is any form of 'salvation' that reinforces in your mind separation from God as reality. These forms of salvation usually require that you make payment, sacrifice, or submit to punishment, because you are a 'sinner'.

19. What is True Justice?

1. True Justice is the Divine Correction of the injustice of perceiving yourself as separate from God. This injustice is the basis for all of the personal mind's judgments. True Justice corrects the mistaken interpretations to which the personal mind's injustice gives rise by canceling them out. Neither True Justice nor injustice exists in Heaven, because, in Heaven, error is impossible, so correction is meaningless. But, in your perception that you are in a world, your forgiving rests on True Justice, since your perception that illusions are real is an unjust attack on yourself. True Justice is the Holy Spirit's judgment on the world that you perceive. Only in the Holy Spirit's judgment is True Justice possible, because, in your identification with a personal self, you are incapable of making only just interpretations, and of laying all injustice aside. If you could judge your entire mind fairly you would not need salvation, because then the thought that you are separate from God and from all that you perceive would be forever inconceivable to you.

2. True Justice, like Its opposite, is an interpretation. However, It is the one interpretation that leads you to Truth. This is possible, because, while it is not Truth Itself, True Justice does not include anything that opposes Truth. There is no conflict between True Justice and Truth; True Justice is just the first small step in the direction of Truth. Your path will become quite different as you go along. Nor can you foresee at the outset the Grandeur and Magnificence that you will perceive. Yet, even this Splendor that reaches inconceivable heights as you proceed will fall short of All that awaits you when your journey and time end. But you must start somewhere, and True Justice is the beginning.

3. All of your concepts for personal selves, whether the one with which you identify or 'others', and all of your fears for the future or concern for a personal past, stem from the personal mind's injustice. This injustice is the lens that you hold before the body's eyes to distort perception, and to bring back to your mind, which made the lens and holds it very dear, witnesses for a distorted world. With the

personal mind, you build up, selectively and arbitrarily, every concept that you have for the world in this way. You perceive and justify 'sins' through a process of careful selection, in which you lose all thoughts of Wholeness. Your forgiving has no place in this scheme, because every seeming sin seems to be forever true.

4. Your salvation is God's Justice. It restores to your awareness the Wholeness of your mind, which you perceive as broken off and separate fragments. It is through God's Justice that you overcome your fear of death, because separate fragments must decay and die, but Wholeness is Immortal. It remains Forever like God, being One with God. God's Judgment is God's Justice. Onto God's Judgment, Which is wholly lacking in condemnation, and is an evaluation of you that is based entirely on Love, you have projected the personal mind's injustice, thinking that God has the warped lens through which it looks. You think that this lens belongs to God, not to the personal mind, so you are afraid of God, and you do not see that you hate and fear your True Self as your enemy.

5. Open yourself to God's Justice, and do not confuse God's Mercy with the personal mind's insanity. You can perceive whatever you choose to perceive. Remember this, because in this lies either Heaven or hell for you, as you elect. God's Justice points to Heaven for you, because It is entirely impartial. It accepts all of the evidence that is brought before It, omitting nothing, and accessing nothing as separate and apart. It judges only from the Standpoint of Oneness. Here, all attack and condemnation are meaningless, and they cannot be defended. Here, you lay aside the personal mind's perception, your mind is still, and God's Light returns to your mind again. Your Real Perception is restored to you, and What you thought that you had lost, you find you always had. The Peace of God descends on all that you perceive, and you perceive Truly.

Mentor's Notes

Very simply, injustice is perceiving yourself as separate from God, and all of the perceptions that result from this misperception.

True Justice, then, is acknowledging your Oneness with God, and all of the Perceptions that result from this correction of your mind.

Paragraph 4 says that your mind in Wholeness is Immortal, but that, when you perceive it as fragmented and separated – as a world of separate selves in bodies - you must perceive that its fragments decay and die. This is because your mind in Wholeness is Life, so perceiving it as fragmented and separated, you perceive Life's opposite.

20. What is the Peace of God?

1. It has been said that there is a Peace that is not of this world. How do you recognize It, experience It, and keep It in your awareness? These questions are considered separately here, because each reflects a different step along the way.

2. First, you recognize the Peace of God by just one thing: In every way, It is totally unlike any experience that you have had in your identification with a personal self. It does not remind you of anything that you have experienced as a personal self; It seems like an entirely new experience for you. There is a contrast between It and all of your personal past experiences, but it is not a contrast of true differences. The personal past slips away from your mind, and in its place is Everlasting Quiet. Even the contrast goes, and Quiet extends Infinitely in your mind.

3. Second, you experience the Peace of God by meeting Its conditions. God's Peace cannot come into your mind when you are holding onto the personal mind's anger, because its anger denies that Peace exists. If you see anger as justified in any form, you proclaim to yourself that Peace is meaningless, and then you must believe that It does not exist. You cannot experience Peace in this condition, so your forgiving the personal mind's perceptions is the necessary condition for your experiencing the Peace of God. Actually, when you forgive the personal mind you *must* experience Peace, because the personal mind's attacks lead you to conflict, and God's Peace is the opposite of conflict. When you initially experience God's Peace,

the contrast between It and conflict are obvious, but then conflict will be wholly meaningless to you. You will perceive that conflict is nonexistent; it is not real.

4. Third, you keep the Peace of God in your awareness by not holding onto the personal mind's anger in any form, because this will drop a heavy veil between you and Peace, and the belief that Peace is not real will certainly return to you as you accept again that conflict is reality. To be at Peace again you will have to put aside conflict, although you may not always recognize that you have picked it up again. But you will learn to recognize this when you are unhappy, and you will remember, maybe only very faintly, that you were happy without conflict, so you will realize that you must've picked it up again as your defense. This is the moment to stop and ask yourself if you want the personal mind's conflict, or if God's Peace is the better choice for you. Which gives you more? A tranquil mind is not a little gift. Would you rather live or die?

5. Living is Joy; death is sadness. You see in death escape from the pain that you made, but you do not see that you made death, and it is only an illusion of an end to pain. Death cannot be your escape, because it is meant to be the opposite of Life, and Life is not your problem. Life has no opposite, because It is God. Life and death seem to you to be opposites, because you have decided that death ends Life. But forgive your perception of a world as reality and you will understand that Everything that God created cannot have an end, and nothing that God did not create is real. In this one sentence, this course is explained. In this one sentence, your practicing is given one direction. In this one sentence, the Holy Spirit's whole lesson plan is explained exactly as it is.

6. What is the Peace of God? No more than this: Your simple understanding that God's Will has no opposite. No thought that contradicts God's Will can be true. A conflict between God's Will and your will can only seem to be real; in Truth, there is no conflict, because God's Will *is* your Will. God's Mighty Will is God's Gift to you. God does not seek to keep Its Will apart from you, so why

should you seek to keep your tiny, frail illusions apart from God? God's Will is One, and It is All that there is. It is yours. The Reality that is beyond the sun and stars, and beyond all of the thoughts of which you conceive in separation from God, belongs to you. God's Peace is the condition for God's Will. Attain God's Peace, and you will remember God.

Mentor's Notes

Paragraph 2 says that the Peace of God will seem to be an entirely new experience for you. This is true from the point of view of your identification with a personal self, but you will find that God's Peace is not wholly unfamiliar. A Part of you will recognize It.

The personal mind's anger, or attack, does not always take a form that you can easily recognize. Really, any thought that reinforces the personal self as your reality, no matter how benign it seems, is the personal mind's anger, because it is an attack on the Truth, Which is that you are One with God, not a personal self.

In this answer, you can see clearly the differing experiences of the two thought systems in your mind: Your experience of the personal mind is conflict; your experience of the Holy Spirit is Peace. When you hold onto conflict, you cannot experience Peace, and Peace undoes conflict entirely. When you experience the contrast between Truth and illusion, you find that there is no contrast, because only Truth is Real. Illusion simply fades away in the Presence of Truth.

In paragraph 3 you see that, if you do not forgive, you are choosing the personal mind, so you are attacking yourself, and you must experience conflict. Since you can only forgive illusions, you can only forgive from the Holy Spirit in your mind.

21. Do words have a role in healing?

1. Strictly speaking, words do not have a role in healing. What precipitates your healing is your asking for it. What you truly ask for, you will receive. But true prayer is your desiring from deep within yourself; it is not words. Sometimes, the words that you use in

prayer contradict your true prayer, sometimes they agree with your true prayer. It does not matter, because God does not understand words, since they were made by your split mind to maintain your illusion of separation from God. As a beginner, you may use words to help your concentration, or to facilitate the exclusion, or control, of unrelated thoughts, but don't forget that words are only symbols of symbols, so they are twice removed from Reality.

2. As symbols, words refer to something very specific. Even when the words are abstract, you tend to picture something concrete. Unless you do picture something concrete, the words will have little or no practical meaning for you, and will not help your healing process. Your true prayer does not ask for anything concrete; rather, it requests an experience, and the specific thing that you picture is what you expect will bring you the experience. The words you use, then, are symbols of the things for which you are asking, but the things themselves are symbols for the experience that you hope for.

3. Your prayer for things in the world will bring you experiences of the world. If your true prayer is for an experience of the world, then this is what will show up, because this is what you will accept. It is impossible for your true prayer to remain unanswered in your perception. If you ask for the impossible, for what does not exist, for illusions, then this is what you will receive. Your power of choice offers you what you choose. In this lies Heaven or hell for you. In your perception that you are separate from God, this is the only power left to you. It is enough, and your words do not matter. The only symbol that has any real meaning for you is the Holy Spirit, because It is the Symbol of God, and It, too, is enough.

4. As a teacher of God, are you to avoid using words? No! You are not yet ready to experience God only in silence, and you still learn by using words. However, you must learn to use words in a new way. Gradually, you must learn how to let the Holy Spirit choose your words by ceasing to let the personal mind decide for you what to say. This process reflects Lesson 155 in the Workbook, 'I step back

and let the Holy Spirit lead the way.' As a teacher of God, you will accept the words that come from the Holy Spirit within you, and you will say them as you receive them. You will not let the personal mind control the direction of your words; you will listen for them, hear them, then speak them.

5. What may be a major hindrance for you in this practice is your fear about the validity of what you hear to speak. In fact, what you hear may be quite startling to you. It may also seem quite irrelevant to the problem as you perceive it, and it may, in fact, embarrass you. But all of these personal judgments have no value. They come from a shabby self-perception that you will be leaving behind. Do not use the personal mind to judge the words that come to you from the Holy Spirit, but offer them in confidence. They are far wiser than the personal mind's words. As God's Teacher, you have the Holy Spirit behind your symbols, and God gives to your words the Power of the Holy Spirit, Which raises them from meaningless symbols to the Call of Heaven Itself.

Mentor's Notes

Paragraph 2 says that when you pray for a thing, you are really seeking the experience that you think that the thing will bring to you. For example, you may truly desire a new car in the expectation that having a new car will bring you happiness. Paragraph 3 says that your prayer for things of the world will bring you experiences of the world, because this is what you are willing to receive, and that you cannot fail to receive what you really want. So, if you really want a new car, you will find a situation manifesting where you can get one, but you will find your happiness is the short lived happiness of the world, not the Lasting Happiness of God.

So your true praying can be for God or for not-God. Your true desire for God will result in your experiencing God's Limitless Love, Peace, and Joy, and your true desire for the world will result in you experiencing the pain and loss of perceiving yourself as separate from God. You, then, are wholly responsible for your experience.

God is always right here, but God can only come into your awareness through your desire to be aware of God. Your true prayer to God, then, is simply your opening yourself to God.

Continuing to use the example of the car, apart from you really needing a new car, if you recognize that your desire for a new car is really only to feel Happy, then you recognize that the lack you are feeling is God, not a new car. Then, rather than going through the expense and effort of buying a new car, which will not bring you the Happiness that you truly seek, you can simply quiet your mind and invite God into your awareness.

You learn to listen to, to hear, and to say what the Holy Spirit gives to you to learn that you are the Holy Spirit. Otherwise, your only experience is following the personal mind. 'What you teach you learn' is not so much about the words you say as it is about the thought system from which you teach. Another way to say this is, 'The thought system from which you teach is the thought system that you learn that you are.'

22. Are my healing and my Atonement related?

1. Your healing and your Atonement are identical. Some miracles are not harder than others for you, because there are no degrees in your Atonement, which is the correction of your perception that you are separate from God. Your Atonement is the one concept in your perception that you are in a world that is possible of completion, because it is the source of your wholly unified perception. *Partial Atonement* is a meaningless idea, just as it is not possible to have special areas of hell in Heaven. Accept correction of your perception that you are separate from God, and you are healed. Your Atonement is God's Will, and, if you accept God's Will, what is there to make sickness possible for you? Accept God's Will, and every miracle is accomplished for you. For you to forgive is for you to heal. As a teacher of God, you must accept your Atonement as your only function. Then, there will be nothing that you cannot heal, and no miracle will be withheld from you.

2. Your progress as a teacher of God will be slow or rapid, depending on whether you recognize that your Atonement encompasses your entire mind, or if you exclude some problems that you perceive from Atonement. You may be suddenly completely aware of how to perfectly apply correction to all situations, but this is not likely. You are more likely to accept the function that God has given to you long before you learn all that this acceptance holds out for you. But the end is certain, and, anywhere along the way, you may reach the necessary realization that correction is possible in every situation. If your way seems long, be content, because you have accepted the direction that you want to take. Nothing more has been asked of you, and, having done what was required of you, God will not withhold the rest from you.

3. If you are to make progress as a teacher of God, you must understand that your forgiving is your healing. The idea that a body can be sick is a central concept in the personal mind's thought system. This thought seems to make the body independent, to separate it from the mind, and keeps the idea of attack from being undone. If the body could be sick, then your Atonement would be impossible. A body that can order your mind to do what it wants would take the place of God, and prove to you that your salvation is impossible. What would there be left for you to heal, then? The body would be the lord of your mind, so your mind could only be returned to the Holy Spirit if the body was killed. Would you want a body at this price?

4. Certainly, it does not appear as though sickness is a decision of your mind, and you probably don't believe that you want to be sick. Maybe you can accept this idea in theory, but you rarely, and inconsistently, apply it to all specific forms of sickness, in your perception of yourself and of others. But this is not the level at which you call for healing. You must overlook the personal mind and the body, and see only Christ, Which corrects all mistakes, and heals all of your perception. Healing is the result of your recognizing that it is your mind that needs healing. This recognition must be applied to your

entire mind; in this recognition, all of your illusions will be undone.

5. When you fail to heal, it is because you have forgotten What you are. When you perceive sickness in another, it becomes your own if you identify with their personal self and you think that their body is real. When you do this, you refuse to accept the Atonement for yourself, so you can hardly extend Christ in your awareness. In fact, you will not recognize that Christ is What is really here, because God did not create bodies, so you are seeing what is not real. Mistakes do not correct mistakes, and distorted perception does not heal your mind. When this happens, step back; you have been mistaken. Do not let the personal mind lead the way, because, following it, you have lost your way. Turn quickly to the Holy Spirit, and let yourself be healed.

6. The offer of Atonement is for your entire mind; it is equally applicable in every circumstance. It is the power to heal all manifestations of sickness. If you don't believe this, you are being unfair to God, therefore, unfaithful to God. A sick person perceives themselves as separate from God; do not perceive them as separate from you. It is your task to heal your perception of separation that makes their sickness seem real to you. It is your function to recognize, whether they do or not, that what the other believes about themselves is not the Truth. It is your forgiving that demonstrates this. Healing is very simple: You extend Atonement and you receive It. Having received It, you must accept It. It is in the receiving, then, that your healing lies. All else follows from this.

7. The personal mind cannot limit God's Power. It cannot say what can be healed, and what must be beyond your forgiving through God's Power. This would be insane. It is not up to the personal mind to limit God, because it is not up to it to judge you who are One with God. Both of these are equally meaningless. But, you will not understand this until you recognize that these are the same mistake. Then, you will receive the Atonement, because you will withdraw the personal mind's judgment from What God created One with God. You will no longer stand apart from God,

determining with a personal mind to which perceptions you should extend healing, and to which perceptions you should withhold it. You will say with God, 'My entire mind is One with God, created Perfect, Forever.'

Mentor's Notes

Again, this answer emphasizes that it does not matter where you perceive sickness is real. If you perceive it, it is in your mind, so it is your mind that must be healed. Correcting, or healing, your perception that separation from God is real, in every form, is your Atonement.

23. Does Jesus have a special place in my healing?

1. You may not be willing to receive God's Gifts directly through your Christ Mind, and, even as an advanced teacher of God, you will sometimes give in to the temptation to believe that the world is real. It would not be fair for your extension of healing to your entire mind to be limited because of this. The Bible says, 'Ask in the Name of Jesus Christ'. This is not for you to appeal to magic. A name does not heal, and an invocation does not call forth special powers. What does it mean for you to call on Jesus Christ? What does calling on His Name confer to you? Is appealing to Him a part of your healing?

2. One Who has perfectly accepted the Atonement for Himself has healed His perception of a world. Temptation may recur to you, but not to Jesus, Who now wholly represents your Christ Mind. He overcame death, because He accepted Life. He recognizes Himself as One with God, so perceives all things as part of Himself. There is no limit on His Power, because It is the Power of God. So Jesus' Name has become the Name of God, because He no longer sees Himself as apart from God.

3. This means for you that in remembering Jesus, you remember God. Your whole relationship to God lies in Him. The Christ in Jesus is the Christ in you, and His completed learning guarantees your own success. He is still available to help you. Remember His

promises, and ask yourself honestly if it is likely that He will fail to keep them. God cannot fail What is One with God, and One Who is One with God must be like God. Jesus has transcended the body, so has transcended limitation. The Greatest Teacher is available for you to follow Him.

4. The Name of Jesus Christ is only a symbol, but It is a symbol of Love that is not of the world. It is a symbol that you can use to replace the many names of the idols to which you prayed in your identification with a personal self. It is the shining symbol of God's Word, so close to That for Which It stands that there is no space between Them the moment that the Name of Jesus enters your mind. Your remembering the Name of Jesus Christ is your giving thanks for all of the Gifts that God gives to you. Gratitude to God is the way in which you remember God, because Love is not far behind a grateful heart and a thankful mind. God enters your mind easily, then, because these are the conditions for your coming Home.

5. Jesus has led the way for you; be grateful to Him. He asks for your Love, but only so that you may experience Love. In your identification with a personal self, you do not love yourself, but in Jesus' perception your Loveliness is so Complete and Flawless that He sees God. In His perception, you are a Symbol of God in your perception that you are in a world. He looks hopefully to you, because He sees no limit or stain to mar your Beautiful Perfection. In Jesus, Christ's Perception shines in Perfect Constancy. Jesus is with you; learn the lesson of your salvation through His learning. You do not need to start again when He has made the journey for you.

6. From your perception that you are in a world you cannot grasp Heaven or What God is, but you have Witnesses, and it is to Them that you are wise to appeal. There are Those who have gone past learning, and they do not want to teach the limitations that you have laid on Them. As a true and dedicated teacher of God, you must extend your teaching, but what you teach is limited by what you want to learn. Turn to One Who has laid all limits aside, and Who has gone past all learning. He will take you with Him, for He

brought with Him his entire mind. As part of His mind, you were with Him then, as you are now.

7. This course has come to you from Jesus, because you needed it in a language that you can love and understand. There are other Teachers as well, Who speak in other symbols. God gives Help in the form of Saviors Who can symbolize God. The lesson plan must come in many forms, though with one content, because symbols must suit the need. Jesus has come to answer your need, and in Him you can find God's Answer. Teach with Jesus, because He is always with you.

Mentor's Notes

Paragraph 1 reassures you that Christ within you is untouched by your occasionally giving into temptation and believing in the world. Your healing is guaranteed because of this. You have Jesus, whose story transcends this temptation completely, as proof that Christ is unchanged by illusions. Jesus represents the Perfection of your Christ Mind, Which cannot be altered in any way. Jesus also stands as a model for you to follow; Jesus is, again, the 'proof' that transcending your illusions is possible.

Jesus is Christ because Jesus perceives only Christ, not because of anything He did or any behavior or attitudes he adopted. As Christ, He sees only the Christ in you.

Those Witnesses, 'who have gone past learning' mentioned in paragraph 6 refers to those, like Jesus, whose stories in the part of your mind where you perceive a world reveal Christ Consciousness. You need to un-learn separation from God, so re-learn that you are One with God. After you have attained this awareness, you will have no more need of learning.

The 'language' mentioned in paragraph 7 means the terminology of Christianity. As is stated here, and elsewhere in this course, the lesson plan is universal, though it comes in many forms, languages, and symbols. In essence, any spiritual teaching that you study with the Holy Spirit will teach what this course has to teach.

Some students find the concept of the 'Holy Spirit' too abstract and are more comfortable calling on Jesus, a more concrete form to which they can relate. They are One and the Same. The Holy Spirit is the teaching aspect of your Christ Mind; the Name and image of Jesus are symbols of your Christ Mind. Though the symbol of Jesus is available to you if It resonates with you, you are not required to call on Jesus, or any other symbol in personal form, to use this course.

24. Is there such a thing as reincarnation?

1. Reincarnation is impossible. There is no past and no future, and, whether you believe it happens once or many times, the idea of birth into a body has no meaning. The concept of reincarnation, then, is not true. Your only question should be, 'Is this concept helpful to me?', and that depends, of course, on how you use it. If you use it to strengthen your recognition that Life is Eternal, it is helpful. Are there other ways for you to look at it that are useful? Like many other beliefs, you can bitterly misuse it. At the very least, you may be preoccupied with a nonexistent past life; at worst, you may be induced to inertia in the present. In between, many other kinds of folly are possible for you.

2. Whatever you believe, reincarnation is never the problem for you to deal with *now*. Even if a past life could be responsible for some difficulty that you are experiencing now, your task would still be to escape from your belief in that cause *now*. If you believe that you are laying out the groundwork for a future life, you can still work out your salvation only *now*. You may find some comfort in the concept of reincarnation, and if this is so, then the concept's value is self-evident. It is certain that you can find your way to salvation whether or not you believe in reincarnation. So, the idea is not essential to this lesson plan. There is always some risk of you perceiving the present in terms of the past; there is always some good in any belief that strengthens your awareness that Life and the body are not the same.

3. For the purposes of learning this course, it is not helpful for

you to take a definite stand on reincarnation with others. You should be as helpful to those who believe in it as you are to those who do not. If you were required to take a stand, it would merely limit how useful you are to the Holy Spirit, as well as your own decision-making. This course is not concerned with making concepts unacceptable, whatever your formal beliefs. The personal mind is enough for you to deal with; it would not be wise to add sectarian controversies to your burden. Nor is there any advantage to you prematurely accepting this course merely because it advocates a belief that you have long held.

4. It cannot be too strongly emphasized that this course aims at a complete reversal of your thought system. When you finally accomplish this, issues like the validity of reincarnation will be meaningless to you. Until then, they are only controversial, and, as a teacher of God, it is wise for you to step away from them. You have much to teach and to learn apart from them. You should both teach and learn that theoretical concepts only waste your time, draining time away from its appointed purpose of your salvation. If some aspects of a belief are helpful, the Holy Spirit will tell you about it and how to use it. You don't need to know more than this.

5. This does not mean that you should not believe in reincarnation yourself or discuss it with others that do. If you do believe in it, it would be a mistake for you to renounce it before the Holy Spirit advises you to do so. And even this is unlikely to happen. It is more likely that the Holy Spirit will advise you if you are misusing the belief in some way that is detrimental to your advancement. Reinterpretation would then be necessary. All that you must recognize is that birth into a body is not the beginning, and that death is not an ending. But even as a beginner, this much is not required of you. You only need to acknowledge that what you think you know is not necessarily all that there is to know. With this, your journey to God begins.

6. The emphasis of this course is always the same: It is at *this moment* that your complete salvation is offered to you, and it is at *this*

moment that you can accept it. This is still your only responsibility. You can equate your Atonement with total escape from the past, and a total lack of interest in the future. Heaven is here; there is nowhere else. Heaven is now; there is no other time. Any teaching that does not lead to this awareness is not your concern as a teacher of God. All beliefs will point to this awareness, if you properly interpret them. In this sense, you can say that the truth in any belief lies in its usefulness. You should honor all beliefs that lead to your progress to God. This is the only criterion that this course requires of them; no more than this is necessary.

Mentor's Notes

You can only understand that illusion is illusion from the perspective of Truth. Concepts that perpetuate individuality-as-reality, like reincarnation, will fall away naturally the more you experience the Holy Instant and know that God is All-that-is, and that there is no time, no world, no personal identity.

Paragraph 3 is merely stating that you can best serve the Holy Spirit by keeping your mind open and by not deciding ahead of time what you should or should not say to others. The goal is for you to learn to teach from the Holy Spirit to learn that you are the Holy Spirit, not for you to advocate for or against certain beliefs. In practice, you will find yourself saying to others what they need to hear, not necessarily what you personally want to say to them.

Remember, there is only One Mind and One Spirit; there are no individual spirits, or 'souls'. Even the split mind is only one, though in the not-God part of it, it seems to take many forms. What seems like a 'past life experience' is merely an individual mind tapping into the split mind's story for the world. This is why many individuals can claim to have had past-life experiences of the same famous figures from 'history'.

25. Are 'psychic powers' useful?

1. The answer to this question is much like the answer to the

preceding question. There are, of course, no 'unnatural' powers, and it is magical thinking if you make up powers that do not exist. But, you may also have abilities of which you are not aware. As your awareness of your Limitless Mind increases, you may develop abilities that startle you, but nothing that you do in your perception that you are in a world can compare even slightly with the glorious surprise of remembering What you are. Let all of your learning and efforts be directed toward this one great surprise, and you will not want to be delayed by the little surprises that come to you along the way.

2. Certainly, there are many so-called 'psychic' powers that are clearly in line with this course. Your mind is not limited to the small range that you recognize in your identification with a personal self. If it was, there would be no point in teaching you salvation, because then it would be impossible. The limits that you put on your mind are the chief barriers to your experiencing the Holy Spirit directly. The Holy Spirit is always here, and Its Voice is always available to you, if you only listen. You place limits on your mind out of fear, because without them, all of the separation that you perceive would fall away at the sound of the Holy Spirit's Voice. When you transcend the limits of the personal mind, you only become more natural. You are not doing anything special, and there is no magic involved.

3. Any seemingly-new abilities that you gather on the way to wholly remembering God can be very helpful to you. If you give them to the Holy Spirit, and you use them under the Holy Spirit's direction, they will be valuable teaching aids. The question of how they arise is irrelevant; what is important is how you use them. If you use them as ends in themselves, no matter how you do this, you will delay your progress. Their value also does not lie in 'proving' anything, whether that be achievements from a perceived past personal life, unusual attunement with what cannot be perceived by the body, or 'special favors' from God. God does not give special favors; What God gives is Everywhere, Always. Your 'demonstrating' abilities as 'special favors from God' would only turn them

into magic tricks.

4. An ability used for Truth cannot deceive. The Holy Spirit is incapable of deception, so It can only use your abilities for Truth. When you use an ability for magic, it is useless to the Holy Spirit, and when the Holy Spirit uses it, you cannot use it for magic. However, 'unusual' abilities have a particular appeal to the personal mind, and you may find them tempting. These abilities are strengths that the Holy Spirit wants and needs, but the personal mind sees in them an opportunity to glorify itself. It is a tragedy to use strengths for weakness, but what you don't give to the Holy Spirit you must give to weakness. What you withhold from Love you give to fear, and the consequence for you will be fear.

5. Even when you no longer value material things of the world, you may still be deceived by 'psychic' powers. As you withdraw your investment in the world's material gifts, the personal mind will be seriously threatened. You may still value it enough to let it rally under this new temptation, and strengthen itself by guile. You may not see through the personal mind's defenses here, even though they are not very subtle. But, if you wish to be deceived, you will be deceived. Then, you will no longer be able to use the ability dependably. It is almost certain that, unless you change your mind about the ability's purpose, you will bolster its undependability with increasing self-deception.

6. Any ability that you develop has the potential to be used for your good. There is no exception to this. The more unusual and unexpected the ability, the greater its potential usefulness. For your salvation, the Holy Spirit has need of all of your abilities, because What the personal mind wants to destroy, the Holy Spirit wants to restore to your awareness. You can use 'psychic' abilities to call on 'the devil', which only means to strengthen the personal mind, but they can also be a great channel of hope and healing in the Holy Spirit's service. If you develop 'psychic powers', it merely means that you have let some of the limitations that you placed on your mind be lifted. Then, it would only be to further limit yourself if you

use your mind's increased freedom to validate limitation. The Holy Spirit needs your gifts, and if you offer them to the Holy Spirit only, you will have the gratitude of Christ within you, and Christ's Holy Perception will not be far behind.

Mentor's Notes

There is a tendency to lump together all 'supernatural' experiences under the heading 'spiritual'. But only your experiences of miracles or direct Revelation of God are of Spirit; all the rest is simply your tapping into the one split-mind. For example, if you have a premonition of something that then occurs in your perception of a world you are simply having an awareness that arises from the one split mind to the personal mind; it is not from the Holy Spirit, though you can give the ability and the situation to the Holy Spirit to use on behalf of your spiritual awakening. If nothing else, the premonition would teach you that your mind is not limited to a personal mind.

26. Can I reach God directly?

1. You can indeed reach God directly, because there is no distance between you who are One with God and God. God is in your mind, and God is the Center of your Being, and your Memory of God will arise across the threshold of your awareness when you let all of your barriers to Truth be removed. How likely is this? This is your role as a teacher of God: You gain the necessary awareness of God when you join your mind with the part of it where you perceive a world. This is what sets you apart from the personal mind, and it is this that enables you to save your entire mind. Alone, as a personal self, you are nothing, but in your joining your entire mind as One is the Power of God.

2. In your perception that you are in a world, there are stories of Those who have reached God directly, and Who retained no trace of worldly limits, so remembered Their True Identity perfectly. You can call these the Teachers of God's teachers, because, though They are

not physically in the world, you can call upon their image. They will appear to you when and if it is helpful for Them to do so. If their appearing would frighten you, you can still receive Their ideas. You cannot call on Them in vain; they are aware of you. They know all needs, and They overlook all mistakes. The time will come when you understand this; meanwhile, they give you all of Their gifts when you look to Them for help, and you ask for help in Their Name only.

3. Sometimes, you may have a brief experience of direct Union with God, but in your perception that you are in a world, it is almost impossible that this awareness endure. You can perhaps attain it after much devotion and dedication, and then maintain it for much of the time that you continue to perceive a world, but this is so rare that you should not consider it a realistic goal. If it happens, so be it. If it does not happen, so be it as well. All worldly states are illusory, so if you sustained an awareness of God, you would not long maintain an illusion that you are in a body. Those Who have laid down the body extend their helpfulness to you who have not yet done so. They need you, in your perception of limitation and denial of God, to extend your growing awareness of God to your entire mind.

4. So do not despair because you still perceive yourself as limited to a personal self. In your perception that you are in a world, it is your function to escape from this, and you must learn how right where you are now. You must first understand what you need to escape, because your salvation is not theoretical. Behold your problem, ask the Holy Spirit for its solution, then accept the solution when it comes. Its coming will not be delayed for long. All of the help that you can accept will be provided to you, and not one need that you have will go unmet. Do not, then, be concerned with goals for which you are not yet ready. God accepts and welcomes you where you are. What more could you want, when this is all that you need?

Mentor's Notes

The 'you' mentioned in Paragraph 1 that is set apart from the personal mind is the 'decision-maker' – the part of your mind that is split between what it is – God – and what it made - the personal mind. Only after you recognize that the personal mind's thought system is not you, but is a choice, can you make a decision for God.

Even in the part of the split mind that is supposed to be not-God the awareness of God breaks through in stories of personal selves who have overcome the split to remember that only God is Real. Those stories and images are available to you as Guides and Models, as was expressed in question 23 about Jesus.

Paragraph 4 makes it clear that your remembering your Oneness with God is a process, and that you cannot force this process. Let the Holy Spirit lead you.

27. What is death?

1. The concept of death is the central illusion from which all of your other illusions stem. It is madness for you to think of Life as being born, aging and losing vitality, then dying. This has been addressed in this course before, but here you will consider it more carefully. The one fixed, unchangeable belief of the personal mind is that reality is a world where all things are born only to die. The personal mind regards this process as 'natural'; something that does not need to be questioned, but accepted as the 'law of life'. The cyclical, the changing, the unsure, the undependable, the unsteady, the waxing and waning – this is what the personal mind calls the 'Will of God'. You should ask if a harmless Creator could will this!

2. If this perception were Reality, it would be impossible for you to think of God as Loving. You would be justified in fearing a god that decrees that all things must pass away, ending in dust, disappointment, and despair. God would seem to hold your little life by a thread, and to be ready to break it off without regret or care at any moment. And even if God waited to do so, the ending for you would still be certain. If you love such a god, you do not know of Love,

because you deny that Life is Real. Death, then, would be the symbol of life for you. Your reality would be a battleground where conflict reigns as opposites make endless war, because where there is death, Peace is impossible.

3. The concept of death is the symbol or your fear of God. The idea blots out God's Love, holding It away from your awareness like a shield held up to block the sun. The grimness of this symbol is enough to show you that it cannot co-exist with God. It is an image in which you who are One with God are 'laid to rest' in the arms of devastation, where worms wait to greet you, and to last a little while on your destruction before they are doomed to be destroyed themselves. In this idea, all things seem to 'live' because of death. Devouring is 'nature's law of life', God seems to be insane, and fear alone seems to be reality.

4. The curious belief that there is something that goes on apart from the body which dies also does not proclaim that God is Love, nor re-establish grounds for you to trust God. If death is real for anything, then there is no Life, but if Life is Real, then there is no death. There is no compromise possible in this. God is either Love or fear. The personal mind attempts a thousand compromises, and it will attempt a thousand more. As a teacher of God, you cannot find any of them acceptable, because none of them would be acceptable to God. God did not make death, because God did not make fear. Both are equally meaningless to God.

5. Your belief that death is real is firmly rooted in your belief that you are a body. If God created bodies, then death would be real, but God would not be Loving. There is no point at which the contrast between your Real Perception and the world of illusions becomes more sharply evident. God is Love, so if death were real it would be the death of God, because death is the opposite of Love. As God's Creation, you would be justified in being afraid of God, because God would not be your Creator, but your destroyer and avenger. God's Thoughts would be terrible, and God's Image would be frightening. To look on God's Creation would be to die.

6. The Bible says, 'And the last to be overcome will be death'. Of course! Without the idea of death, there is no world for you to perceive. All illusions end for you with the illusion of death. Your salvation is the end of your belief in illusions, and in the idea of death all illusions are born. But what is born of the idea of death is not Life, and What is from God cannot die. The inconsistencies, the compromises, and the rituals that the personal mind fosters in its vain attempts to cling to death and still think that Love is Real are mindless magic, ineffectual, and meaningless. God *is*, and All-that-is is in God, and must be Eternal. See here clearly that otherwise God has an opposite, and fear would be as real as Love.

7. Teacher of God, your one assignment could be stated like this: Accept no compromise in which death plays a part. Do not believe in cruelty, or let attack conceal the Truth from you. You have misperceived yourself as what can die, and you have made yourself an illusion to yourself. Now it is your task to bring the illusion to the Truth in you. Be steadfast only in this: Do not be deceived into thinking that any changing form is Reality. Truth does not waver, or sink into death and dissolution. What is the end of your belief that death is real? Only this: the realization that you are Innocent now and Forever. Only this, and do not forget that it is not less than this.

Mentor's Notes

It is true that the personal mind's world is all the things mentioned in paragraph 1; what isn't true is that it is reality. The goal is not for you to try to make the world like God, but for you to let go of the world and know God again. To do this, you must first recognize the world as the illusion that it is, and how it contrasts with Truth.

Paragraph 4 brings up a very commonly accepted concept in the world: The body dies, but a 'soul' or 'spirit' goes on apart from it. This implies that there are two realities: God and the world, and that you are split between Spirit and body. To die, then, would be to 'leave' or 'cross over' from one reality to another. But the body, and the world in which it seems to be, is never real. What seems capable of 'dying' has no reality, so death is an empty concept. There is only One Reality, and that is God.

When it says in paragraph 7 to accept no compromise in which death plays a part it means not just the idea of death itself, but its symbols: the body and the world. If they are real to you, death is real to you.

If death is real to you, then you must believe that you are a 'sinner'. Alternately, the personal mind will tell you, unconsciously, that death is the way for you to take God's Power, and that death is God's means of punishing you for the 'sin' of separating from God. So your awareness of your Innocence is the end of your belief in sin and death, because it is your awareness that you are One with God, Eternal and Infinite.

28. What is the resurrection?

1. Very simply, the resurrection is your overcoming of your belief that death is real. It is your reawakening to God, and the rebirth in your awareness that you are One with God. It is your change of mind about the world, and your acceptance of the Holy Spirit's interpretation of the world's purpose. It is your acceptance of the Atonement for yourself. It is the end of your illusions of misery, and your glad awareness of the Holy Spirit's final illusion of forgiving. It is your recognition of God's Gifts to you. It is the illusion in which the body functions perfectly as a communication device. It is the lesson in which your learning ends, because it is consummated, and you surpass your need for learning. It is your invitation to God to take Its final step. It is your relinquishment of all other purposes, interests, wishes, or concerns. It is your single desire for God, in your acknowledgement that you are One with God.

2. The resurrection is your denial that death is real, and your assertion that Life is Real. So, the personal mind's thinking will be completely reversed as you recognize that Life is your salvation, and that pain and misery of any kind are hell. You will no longer fear

Love, but will gladly welcome It. Idols will disappear, and your Memory of God will extend unimpeded throughout your mind where you perceive a world. You will perceive Christ everywhere, and you will hold nothing in darkness, apart from the Light of your forgiving. There will be no sorrow to perceive, because you will perceive the Joy of Heaven everywhere.

3. The resurrection is where this lesson plan ends. From then on, you will no longer need guidance. Your perception will be wholly corrected, and all of your mistakes will be undone. Attack will be meaningless to you, and Peace will have come to you. You will have achieved the goal of this lesson plan. Your thoughts will turn to Heaven, and away from hell. All of your desires will be answered, because you will be aware of your Completion. The last illusion, total forgiveness, will spread across the part of your mind where you perceive a world, replacing all attack. The whole reversal of the personal mind's thought system will be accomplished. Nothing will be left in your mind to contradict God's Will. There will be nothing in your mind to oppose Truth, and Truth will come wholly into your awareness at last. How quickly It will come when you ask for It to enter and envelop your entire mind!

4. All of Life within you will be tranquil with a stir of deep anticipation, because the time of Everlasting Things will have come. You will know that there is no death. You who are One with God will be Free, and, in your Freedom, fear will end for you. No hidden places will remain in your mind to shelter sick illusions, dreams of fear, and misperceptions of reality. You will perceive all in God's Light, and, in This Light, their purpose will be transformed, and you will understand them. And you who are One with God will rise up from the dust and look on your Perfect Innocence. The song of Heaven will sound throughout your entire mind as it is lifted up and brought to Truth.

5. There will be no distinctions; all differences will disappear as Love looks on Itself. You will no longer have a need for perception, because there will be nothing more for it to accomplish. You will see

Christ's Innocence and Love behind all forms and purposes. You will know that you are Holy, because your Christ Mind's Holiness will have set you Free. You will accept Christ's Holiness as yours, which It is. As God created you, you are Forever, and you will wish for nothing but God's Will to be your own. You will no longer have illusions of another will, because you will have found Oneness.

6. This is what awaits you, but you are not yet prepared to welcome all of this with Joy. As long as you perceive evil illusions as real anywhere, the thought of hell is real to you. Your goal as God's teacher is to wholly waken your mind by seeing Christ in place of illusions. You will replace the thought that you murdered God with blessing; you will lay the judgment of the personal mind aside, and give judgment to the Holy Spirit, Where it belongs. And, in the Holy Spirit's final judgment, you will find the Truth of your Oneness with God restored to your awareness. You will be redeemed, because you will have heard God's Word and understood Its Meaning. You will be Free, because you will have let the Holy Spirit proclaim the Truth in you, and all that you sought before to crucify will be resurrected with you as you prepare your entire mind to be One with God again.

29. As for the rest…

1. This manual is not meant to answer all of the questions that one may have as a teacher or as a student. In fact, it covers only a few of the more obvious questions in the form of a brief summary of some of the major concepts in the Text and Workbook. It is a supplement, not a substitute, to these. While it is called a 'Manual for Teachers', you must remember that only the illusion of time seems to divide you into 'student' and 'teacher'. Differences are only temporary by definition. When others seem interested in this course, it may be helpful for them to read this Manual first, or to start with the Workbook, or at the more abstract level of the Text.

2. Which is the best way for them? Who would profit more from prayers only? Maybe some are only ready to accept a smile from you. You have certainly come far enough as a teacher of God to

realize that you should not attempt to answer these questions with the personal mind. This lesson plan is highly individualized, and all aspects are under the Holy Spirit's particular care and guidance. Ask, and the Holy Spirit will answer. The responsibility for answering belongs only to the Holy Spirit, and the Holy Spirit alone is fit to assume it. To do so is Its function; to refer questions to the Holy Spirit is yours. You are not yet ready to be responsible for decisions about which you understand so little in your identification with a personal self. Be glad that you have a Teacher with you that cannot make a mistake. The Holy Spirit's answers are always correct; you cannot say that about the personal mind.

3. There is another very important advantage to you in referring all decisions to the Holy Spirit. Maybe you have not thought of this aspect, but its centrality to your Peace is obvious. When you follow the Holy Spirit's guidance, you are absolved of the guilt that comes from following the personal mind. This is the essence of the Atonement, and the core of this lesson plan. Your illusion that, in your identification with a personal self, you have taken functions that do not belong to you, is the basis of all of your fear. The whole world that you perceive reflects this illusion, and makes fear seem inevitable to you. So, to return a function to the Mind in you to Which it belongs is your escape from fear. It is this that lets your Memory of Love return to you. Do not, then, think that following the Holy Spirit's guidance is necessary because you are inadequate; it is necessary as the way out of hell for you.

4. Here, again, is the paradox often referred to in this course: For you to say, 'I can of the personal self do nothing' is for you to gain all Power. But it is only a seeming paradox, because, as you are One with God, you have all Power, and the image of yourself as a personal self has none. The Holy Spirit knows the Truth about you; the image that you made does not. Yet, despite its obvious and complete ignorance about you, this image assumes it knows all things, because you have projected that belief onto it. This is what you teach in your belief that you are not-God, and this is what you

have taught yourself with the world that you made to uphold this belief. But, the Holy Spirit is the Teacher that knows the Truth in you, and the Holy Spirit has not forgotten It. The Holy Spirit's decisions benefit your entire mind, because It is wholly without attack. The Holy Spirit is, therefore, incapable of arousing guilt in you.

5. When, in your identification with a personal self, you assume a power that you do not have, you deceive yourself, but when you accept the Power that is given to you by God, you acknowledge that you are One with God, and you accept God's Gifts. God's Gifts are Limitless. When you ask the Holy Spirit to decide for you, you are simply accepting What is yours. This does not mean, however, that you cannot make a decision without consulting the Holy Spirit. This would not be practical, and this course is concerned with what is practical. If you have made it a habit to ask for help, when and where you can, you can be confident that the Holy Spirit's Wisdom will be here when you need It. Prepare for this every morning, remember God throughout the day, ask the Holy Spirit for Its help when it is feasible to do so, and then thank the Holy Spirit for Its guidance at night. Then your confidence will be well founded.

6. Do not forget that the Holy Spirit does not depend on your words. It understands your deepest desires, and answers them. This does not mean, however, that while attack still remains attractive to you, the Holy Spirit will respond with evil. The Holy Spirit translates your deepest desires into Its language, and It understands that your attacks are calls for help, so It responds with help. God would be cruel if It let your ideas replace Its Own. It would not be Loving for God to let Part of Itself harm Itself, or to choose Its Own destruction. You might ask for injury, but God will protect you.

7. Remember, you are One with God, so you are God's Completion and Love. Your seeming weakness in the personal self is God's Strength. Do not read this last line hastily or incorrectly. God's Strength is in you; what you perceive as your weakness is an illusion. God has given you the means to prove that this is so: Ask

all things of the Holy Spirit, and all things will be given to you, not in the future, but immediately. God does not wait, because waiting implies time, and God is Timeless. Forget your foolish images, your sense of frailty, your fear of harm, your illusions of danger and selected 'wrongs'. God knows you as One with God, and so you are. In confidence, Christ in you places you in God's Hands, and gives thanks that this is so.

8. And now, in all that you do, you are blessed. God turns to you to save your entire mind. Teacher of God, God thanks you, and the world is stilled in the Grace that you bring from God. You are God's Love, and it is given to you to be the means through which God's Voice is extended through your entire mind, to erase all things of time, to end perception, and to undo all things that change. Through you, a new Perception is ushered into your mind, unseen and unheard in the world, but truly here. You are Holy, and in your Light, your Perception of the world reflects the Holiness of your Christ Mind. Your Christ Mind thanks you for your efforts on behalf of God, which are on Its behalf, so on behalf of your entire mind.

AMEN

Mentor's Notes

As is stated in paragraph 3, if the source of your guilt and fear of God is your belief that you have truly separated yourself from God, then calling on God within you, the Holy Spirit, is the way that you correct this mistaken perception, and undo guilt and fear.

About the Author

Liz Cronkhite has been a student of *A Course in Miracles* since 1984, and has mentored other students of the Course since 2006. She published *The Message of A Course in Miracles: A translation of the Text in plain language* through O-books in 2010. You can learn more about her and what she offers at www.acimmentor.com.

BOOKS

O is a symbol of the world, of oneness and unity. In different cultures it also means the "eye," symbolizing knowledge and insight. We aim to publish books that are accessible, constructive and that challenge accepted opinion, both that of academia and the "moral majority."

Our books are available in all good English language bookstores worldwide. If you don't see the book on the shelves ask the bookstore to order it for you, quoting the ISBN number and title. Alternatively you can order online (all major online retail sites carry our titles) or contact the distributor in the relevant country, listed on the copyright page.

See our website **www.o-books.net** for a full list of over 500 titles, growing by 100 a year.

And tune in to myspiritradio.com for our book review radio show, hosted by June-Elleni Laine, where you can listen to the authors discussing their books.